MAVERICK DAUGHTER
She Rode the Waves of Life and Triumphed

Gloria Hamilten

Integration International
Publishing

BOOKS BY GLORIA HAMILTEN

Wake Up and Live: 5 Steps to Revolutionise Your Life and Powerfully Live Your Purpose

How to Succeed in all Areas of Your Life

Want a Better Mother-Daughter Relationship? A Short Course to a Deeper, Loving Connection

Fast and Furious Against ADHD: The Natural Way (with Alpha Murgev)

ADHD Super Simple Meals: 5 Day Meal Plan and Shopping List (with Alpha Murgev)

Administrative Office:
Integrational International Publishing
PO Box 3188, Norman Park, 4170, Australia

Copyright © 2016 by Gloria Hamilten

All rights reserved. No part of this publication may be reproduced, distributed, or transmitted in any form or by any means, including photocopying, recording, or other electronic or mechanical methods, without the prior written permission of the publisher, except in the case of brief quotations embodied in critical reviews and certain other noncommercial uses permitted by copyright law. For permission requests, write to the publisher, addressed "Attention: Permissions Coordinator," at the address below:

Publisher:
Integration International Publishing
PO Box 3188, Norman Park
Queensland, 4170 Australia

www.GloriaHamilten.com
MaverickDaughter@gmail.com

Design and layout: Alpha Schulte
Cover Design: Alpha Schulte

Ordering Information:
Quantity sales. Special discounts are available on quantity purchases by corporations, associations, and others. For details, contact the publisher at the address above.

Printed in the United States of America

Publisher's Cataloging-in-Publication data
Hamilten, Gloria
Maverick Daughter: She Rode the Waves of Life and Triumphed/Gloria Hamilten

ISBN-13: 978-0-9806827-3-1
ISBN-10: 980682738
1. The main category of the book – Fiction, Personal History. 2. Personal Development. 3. Self-help. 4. Philosophy. 5. Psychology
First Edition

This is a work of fiction.

Names, characters, places and incidents, any and all, are products of the author's imagination or are used fictitiously.

Any resemblance to actual events or locales or persons, living or dead, is entirely coincidental.

DEDICATION

To my extraordinary, wonderful
Daughter, Alpha.

Without her unconditional love
And lifelong support,
This tale would not have been told.

I love you very much.

ACKNOWLEDGMENT

Apart from my daughter, I'd like to thank Professor Brian Merrett whose encouragement was invaluable.

When I was neglectful and indecisive about completing and publishing this story, out of the blue an email would come from him enquiring how the 'Opus' was progressing.

I thank him also for his editing advice and especially in his professional knowledge of historical and geographical accuracy.

To you both, my deepest gratitude.

THE INDIVIDUAL

WE ARE EACH GIVEN OUR OWN
UNIVERSE TO DESIGN AS WE CHOOSE.

AND WE CREATE EVERYTHING
THAT OCCURS WITHIN IT.

OUR OUTER WORLD IS NOTHING MORE
THAN A REFLECTION OF OUR INNER WORLD,

BECAUSE THE UNIVERSE CHANGES
BASED UPON WHO OR WHAT
IS OBSERVING IT.

Anonymous

PREFACE

This is the story of two women. One was born after the end of World War I, the other (her daughter) just prior to the end of World War II. They are linked by the men in their lives, the betrayals, abuse, triumphs and love.

Their journey spans half the globe from the tip of the northern hemisphere to the extreme of the southern hemisphere.

As people, we each have an innate resource that enables us to enhance and enrich our lives. What is this resource that allows us to have heaven on Earth, hell on Earth and anything in between? It's our imagination and how we use it. When we voluntarily use it, we create our life by how we choose to react to circumstances.

Each of these two women used this powerful tool, imagination, to create her life in different ways with vastly different results.

You will be intrigued as you experience the personal and political events that unfolded in the mother's life preceding World War II, the impact of bombing and familial separation at the end of that war, and clandestine migration of the family from cities in Europe to their ultimate destination at the other end of the world, Australia.

You may see parallels in your own life, in the lives of members of your family or in the lives of people you know.

Both mother and daughter rebelled in their own way, and the effects this had on each of their lives could not have been more different. We all choose our path and it is our right to do so.

Perhaps we can learn from their story and create a better world.

These women honour us by sharing their lives.

BACKGROUND

Hannelore was an ambitious 17 year old girl who came from a respectable, but lower working-class family in Vienna, Austria. Her full name, Hannelore, was only used when her mother, Maria Schmid, was angry with her and imminent punishment by a violent slap across the face or elsewhere on the body was a certainty. Otherwise, she was called Hanna.

Her mother was a single-parent and living was tough. Her husband, Alois Pachatz, had disappeared when Hanna was a baby. Her father's sudden and permanent departure was a blessing in disguise because his excessive drinking created a volatile domestic environment.

Hanna was born in 1920, two years after the end of the Great War. In this troubled time, her mother barely made ends meet. Food was scarce; money was tight and not spent on unnecessary items. Because of her mother's domineering behaviour, she had learnt to keep her thoughts to herself and respond in ways that would least antagonise her maternal parent.

Hanna successively attended kindergarten and primary school in her working-class area, Vienna's 21st District, Hirschstetten, Wurmbrand but, as an adult, the vocational school she attended five nights a week, the Handelsakademie situated at Hammerling Platz, in the 8th District was where she quickly observed how middle-class girls dressed, spoke and behaved in ways significantly different from those in her own social environment.

Keen to rise over her background, Hanna thought, 'With bookkeeping I'll work in an office, there I'll meet a better class of man. I can then climb higher on the social ladder. I know it won't be easy but, I'm attractive, I'll manage it. I know I can. I can do anything I put my mind to.'

She started University in 1939, aged 19 but did not continue as Austria's War Laws were in place then. These laws meant that it was compulsory for Hanna to join the Reichsarbeitsdienst für

Frauen, Reich Labour Service for Women, because of her age. She didn't want that; it would have upset her plans.

Her first employment was as an apprentice bookkeeper at a well-respected bookkeeping firm, Grünbaum und Familie, Grünbaum and Family. When Hanna started with Grünbaum's she was obliged to hand over her total earnings to her mother. Because she had quickly realised the need to buy clothes suitable for her professional life, Hanna withheld from her mother details of her real salary. She also realised that she needed to dress-up not only for her office but also to attract a possible husband.

It was while going to night school that she met a young man called Hermann. He was studying business to take over his family's food distribution consortium. As soon as he saw Hanna, he was infatuated. He came from a good, middle class family who owned a wholesale and retail food emporium in a better part of Vienna, Austria's capital. It had been in the family for generations, consequently, they were well-established and well-connected. Hermann and his parents lived in an apartment in one of Vienna's better districts, the 2nd District. The family also owned a vacant city apartment which would become Hermann's when he married. In addition, they owned a house in the country not far from capital. The only other sibling was Hermann's sister, Adele, who was married and lived elsewhere in Vienna.

Hermann was quite a catch being 1.9 metres tall, well built, confident, and gregarious. His light brown, short unkempt hair gave him a cheeky air, and he was kind and gentle. Soon, Hanna and Hermann dated regularly.

After three months, unbeknown to her mother, Hermann took Hanna to meet his parents. By this time, Hanna had not only bettered herself professionally but also in her social behaviour.

In December 1937, when Hanna was 17, they married. Even though they had only known each other a short time, no one thought it strange that they should marry so soon. People married sooner because of the political uncertainty of the future. The marriage took place four months before the Anschluss in March 1938, which saw the Austrian-born German dictator, Adolf Hitler, forcibly absorb Austria into Germany.

Hanna's marriage to Hermann was happy, not exciting but pleasant. Hermann's immaturity shown by playing practical jokes annoyed Hanna at times but as he often went away on mandatory army manoeuvres, these bouts of immaturity were tolerable. Once married, they occupied the beautiful apartment on the Danube Canal.

Hanna's mother died in an accident shortly after Hanna and Hermann married. She fell out the window of her third floor apartment to the courtyard below. Something inside Hanna died then as well. She knew she was now more than ever alone in the world. Although she was adored by her new family, there was a void.

She knew being accepted was, of course, conditional on her being married to their son. Hanna realised, she was the only one she could depend on and would need to keep even more silent about what she thought and how she felt. Hanna skillfully developed a public face and a private world.

She charmed everyone, and her ability to flirt without offending was endearing. She always knew the right thing to say to the right people. Hanna was as accomplished as the best actress.

When she moved into the apartment on the Danube Canal with her husband, she had it refurbished to her taste. Hermann was delighted. He was actually in awe of her. Although he came from the 'better family', it was she who had both poise and dignity and who brought elegance into their marriage.

Hermann had been out of Vienna for two months. He had been suddenly called away and the reasons for his departure were shrouded in secrecy. During this time, she had only heard twice from him. Each letter simply dealt with generalisations, which didn't make any sense. He hadn't told her where he was going, what he would be doing or the duration of his absence, but Hanna didn't mind. 'Life is a lot less complicated without a man permanently at home she philosophised.' On Hanna's part, there had seldom been any passion in the marriage. But they were content, and Hanna conceded inwardly that this was more important than passion.

And so, life went on uneventfully for the two months that Hermann was away.

PART 1

Vienna to Townsville
1938 - 1951

CHAPTER 1
VIENNA
1938...

'Ah, good, it's not raining,' Hanna thought as she peeked through the silk curtains. 'I'll still take an umbrella as it is quite overcast.' It had started out a day like any other. Not even the air gave any indication of imminent change. The only immediacy that Hanna could relate to was what had become her routine from Monday to Friday; rise at 6.00 AM, get ready, and walk to work. She enjoyed the fresh morning air and the exercise.

On this day however, she had an uneasy feeling that things would not stay the same. 'Goodness, it's all that hysteria in the paper,' she reproached herself.

As Hanna walked from one room to the next, she had the confirming sense of security and contentment that she always felt in her apartment. It had the traditional parquet floors of middle class residences, kept spotlessly clean by Gina, her new cleaning lady. The pale cream and lace and permanently-drawn ruffled curtains were framed by heavy self-patterned, deep royal blue velvet side-drops secured by tasseled ties. The valances above the windows matched the gold of the chandelier-like light fittings. The window panes were large.

And the furniture? Well, how do you describe Chippendale? Ornate and elegant. From either side of the entrance hall, the rooms looked out onto the Danube Canal. It was a corner apartment, spacious, and light with high ceilings. Hanna fitted into this classiness, perhaps more so than the family she had married into.

It was not a typical March day. The weather was chilly, but not threatening enough for an overcoat. Even her clothes were a testimony to the elegance and outward serenity of her life. Hanna's spring coat, from one of the best tailors, was cream linen. Her the autumn coat, was a beautifully tailored light-weight *pied de poule*; her winter coat, fox fur; and for summer, a white self-patterned pure silk creation.

You would have thought she had been born into this world of wealth and elegance. She had managed to obscure her roots. The new apartment was where she now belonged. Her maturity and poise belied her youthfulness - almost 18 years.

'The cream linen coat will be just right for today,' she decided. Hanna caught sight of her tall, slender silhouette as she passed the long mirror, her light brown hair softly accentuating her blue eyes and fair skin. 'Umm,' she murmured in approval, and opened the wardrobe, and took out the dark verdant suit and cream crêpe blouse. A touch of demure pale pink lipstick completed her toilet and she was ready. Her sensuous Arpège perfume always captured all in its path. It was as though everyone became engulfed in her web as she moved.

One final look around and Hanna closed the door behind her, walked down the one flight of stairs through the secured courtyard and out the exterior heavy wooden and iron gates onto the street.

Without noticing those around her, she turned left, and walked a distance along the Danube Canal before turning into the main street. She had walked for about 10 minute, past newspaper vendors, shoeshine stands with impatient customers waiting to have their shoes polished, past Tabak kiosks selling local and international newspapers and journals, bus and train tickets, stamps and lottery lures.

Although Vienna was a cosmopolitan city, each of its Districts functioned as an independent suburb within the capital, just like the Arrondisements in Paris or like the German Gau. There was the familiarity of the same street cleaners, chimney sweeps, council workers, food stall operators, and the same faces commuting at the same time.

Many of these families had lived here for generations, with apartments and businesses being handed down. Leases were for life as long as someone was linked to the family, accordingly, residents knew they had a place to live and a place to work.

'I do love it here,' flashed through Hanna's mind. Momentarily she almost felt guilty for not missing her husband during his absences. 'Such stupid thoughts,' she reprimanded herself, 'Hermann's surely having fun wherever he is.' Hanna had learned to justify any thought and any deed.

She walked briskly, stopping only for traffic lights, and even these seemed to be in her favour this morning. She had walked four blocks before she noticed advertising billboards proclaiming their headlines to passersby. Some of these billboards were fixed on buildings others were swaying, carried by people in labourer's clothing.

'Die Freiheit für Wien! Freedom for Vienna!' they screamed. The only telltale image was the Swastika and the bold, gigantic, square letters, simple yet effective. 'Die Freiheit für Wien! Freedom for Vienna!'
As soon as Hanna saw the words on the placards, she gasped as though struck by a sudden pain. 'Oh, no, it can't really be happening,' escaped involuntarily.

Suddenly, she saw myriad billboards, see-sawing up to her and away. She started to feel dizzy. She couldn't believe what she was seeing and reading. It was only then that she noticed the throng of people that had gathered around her, enveloping her and pushing her along in their frenzy. She knew she had to get out of their path or be dragged along, or trampled. Collecting her wits, she mustered her energy and pushed her way to the curb.

It was then that Hanna became truly aware of her surroundings. People in business suits were buying the morning newspapers from the Tabak kiosk and from paper boys who had been called in. Some people read the headline on the front page showing disbelief, others displayed no emotion, while others responded with jubilation.

As if operating on auto-pilot, Hanna bought a paper. 'Hier, gnädige Frau. Here Madam,' grinned the toothless vendor as he handed her the paper. 'Danke, thank you,' she replied. She loved being called, 'Madam'.

She tucked the paper under her elegantly-clad arm, not wishing to express any emotion, which she felt certain she would show if she read the newspaper's front page. Hurriedly, she strode along the street trying to avoid the crowds to get to the safety of her office.

As she approached the local square Hanna saw a large crowd had already gathered. There were men and women dressed in overalls, windcheaters and muddied gumboots. The men wore caps on their heads and the women, scarves. Suddenly there was a roar from the crowd. As though rehearsed, upstretched hands with clenched fists aimed at the sky in unison. An orchestrated choir shouted, 'Hail to our hero! Hail to our hero! Hail to our hero.' It pierced the air with its repetition. The outburst was so synchronised, so quick and sharp, that Hanna thought for a moment she had imagined it. Just as suddenly as the roar blasted, it stopped and silence ensued. A solitary figure diminished by the size of the balcony and the height of the Town Hall behind him stood motionless, right hand upstretched and fist clenched.

Hanna stood still. The silence only lasted a moment but to her it seemed an eternity. She did not dare move. To continue walking would be foolish, because it could seem as though she either didn't care about what was happening or was against it. It would have exposed her true feelings. She was not politically-minded and although she came from a working class background, it was exactly that background she left behind. Hanna saw herself now as above all those who were part of this protest, not because she saw herself as a better human being but she felt that, with the hard work she had put into achieving her new life, she was now entitled to more. Furtively she observed her surroundings and noticed that there were other well-dressed people standing motionless with blank stares that divulged nothing.

However, an invisible thread drew in those standing apart from those in working class attire. They silently and obediently allowed themselves to be floated toward the main body of the enthusiastic crowd. Clanging trams came to a halt. Whirring bus engines were turned off because any forward movement was impossible. Cars followed suit. Those who dared blast their horns were menacingly dissuaded by groups of overalled stick-in-hand workers. It was as though everyone was now engulfed in the same invisible, timeless, hypnotic bubble.

While the scene was unfolding, unobtrusive, uniformed men with menacing weapons moved in pairs around the perimeter as though they were herding their flock to a central point. Hanna allowed herself to be herded, aware that her dress didn't blend in with the dominating crowd. She felt herself stoop trying to be less conspicuous as her 1.7 metre, high-heeled frame stood out.

At last a voice from the balcony boomed over the microphone, 'My dearest believers in justice and equality, and patriots for a better future for Vienna, for Austria and for the world, we WILL together as a group (slight pause), WE WILL UNITE WITH THE FORCES OF FREEDOM AGAINST THOSE IN OUR SOCIETY WHO ARE UNFIT TO LIVE AND THOSE WHO ARE FILTHY MONEYMAKERS AND WE WILL….!'

What followed sent shivers through Hanna.

She had to find a way to leave. But when Hanna started to move she immediately felt a nudge from behind. As she slowly turned around with her head bent, she saw a uniformed man glaring at her. With her usual quickness of mind, with her blue eyes she gazed into his as she wiped her brow, and swaying slightly, she said, 'I'm pregnant. I'd like to sit down, officer.' And made as though she were about to faint.
'Out of the way,' the officer yelled as he helped Hanna to a bench. She was about to say, 'Danke, Gott segne Sie, thank you, God bless you, but realised that that wouldn't work in this instance. So she just said, 'Vielen Dank, Herr Offizier, thank you very much, Officer.' Hanna, like many others in Austria, wasn't religious but like many others she was superstitious and she would use the Catholic Church when she needed to. Now, it would have been suicide, so she knew the next best thing was to use flattery and so, 'Herr Offizier' was the way to do it; it expanded his rank.

She waited for a while but just as she was about to leave, her eyes locked with the eyes of the officer. He fixed his gaze on her.

'I'm going to have to sit this spectacle out,' she thought, as she gave the officer a, pain-filled but false smile and slowly lowered herself back onto the bench.

CHAPTER 2
VIENNA

Hanna had no recollection of how she arrived at her office. All she knew was that her life had changed forever, as had the lives of those around her, in Vienna, in Austria, and in Europe, and quite possibly in other parts of the world also. Her beloved Vienna had been gripped by a monstrous clenched claw unable to be pried open.

At the office, she exchanged forced pleasantries with colleagues. It seemed they were also in shock although she knew that from now on no one could be trusted. Some of her colleagues would have personally experienced the rally; others would have heard the radio transmission. All scheduled radio programs had been cancelled.

The Führers, Leader's, visit and his messages dominated all broadcasts. There were propaganda slogans, promises, veiled threats as well as unmistakable threats and bribes, with rewards for followers of the protest, and rewards for denouncing 'traitors' and 'undesirables', described as 'blotches on our culture and its future'. The frankness and blatancy of what was said and implied was alarming.

It wasn't long before Hanna was immersed in her work. She never let emotions get in the way of what had to be done. At a young age she learned from her mother that you only told people what they absolutely needed to know and that the only person you could really trust was yourself. With such a simple philosophy, she was able to quickly get back on task under any circumstance.
Hanna had an appointment at 11.00 AM with a new client and needed to prepare herself. Usually the Chef, the Boss, handled introductory meetings but Hanna, despite her age, had worked herself into a position of high trust and was regarded as much more than a junior employee. Herr Grünbaum had given her only scant information regarding this interview before he left for a business trip outside of Vienna. All she knew was that the potential new client was very important and that he was in heavy industry. He now needed financial advice on the viability of expanding to larger markets.

The company she worked for not only fulfilled accounting services but also offered financial advice, an innovative service for those days. Herr Grünbaum had inherited the firm from his father and developed it from a simple bookkeeping firm to a progressive, benchmark business handling diverse financial matters which he held in partnership with his crippled brother. He was a good boss; honest, kind, and gentle yet with a sharp mind. He believed that to succeed in business you needed the trust of clients and staff loyalty, honesty and integrity were paramount. If staff needed compassion, he was compassionate; if they needed a firm hand to guide them, he offered that also. Hanna was therefore amazed when she heard the elderly mail clerk, Emil Schmidt, complain about Herr Grünbaum's superior attitude toward him. No one ever complained about Herr Grünbaum. 'Vienna doesn't need types like him,' Emil sulked. Hanna was about to ask Emil what he meant by 'types like him', when the Secretary, Ilse, announced that her 11.00 AM appointment had arrived. With head and shoulders bent, Emil scurried out of the room.

She glanced in the mirror for confirmation of her appearance, then left her office. As she approached the meeting room, she was overcome by the scent of a strong, attractive, man's cologne. 'Umm', she thought as she smiled to herself, 'interesting start'. Her smile was firmly in place as she opened the door.

When she entered, two uniformed men rose to their feet, and clicked their heels. She couldn't believe her eyes. For a split second she was speechless; facing her stood her husband Hermann and another man. She was about to say something but the other man took command.

'Good morning, Frau Hollar. My name is Gustav Metternich.' Bowing slightly, he formally and firmly stretched out his hand. Hanna forced herself to a firm grip as their hands connected. Instantly, she was on guard, 'This is not going to be an ordinary business interview,' she thought.
To gain control, she said, 'Hello Hermann. How are you?' Without waiting for a reply, she turned to Metternich and continued. 'I will ring for the Secretary to bring coffee. She had transferred to her

unapproachable persona. An invisible shield protected her from the stares of the men in front of her. Or so she hoped. She certainly didn't feel at ease and her apparent confidence was just bravado. Despite her femininity and outward gentleness, her voice and eyes were powerful tools of curtailment. She knew their effectiveness in setting the ground rules as she wanted them. Still, she sensed this encounter was not going to be an easy one.

'No, thank you,' Metternich replied and the added, 'I wish to begin the meeting at once. There is much to discuss.' His words struck like lightning. The air froze in the room. Unruffled, Hanna replied, 'Certainly. How may I be of assistance?'

'Frau Hollar,' Metternich started, 'I am here today to enlist you, a respected member of this firm, to work for the cause of Austria's liberation and prosperous future to release our country from its current oppressive forces.' He drew a deep breath that sounded like an imminent death sentence was coming. Pompously, Metternich sat down in a chair and continued to deliver a political message almost identical to what she had heard proclaimed at the rally earlier that morning. Metternich paused and then continued with his ideas on taking over Herr Grünbaum's business. 'Nothing will appear to have changed here in the firm. You will continue to carry out your regular duties as well as accommodating my requests. Emil Schmidt, the mail clerk, is a Party Member and will be the intermediary between you and us as needed. Information we need, you can also give to your husband. He has already been briefed.'

Hanna met Metternich's stare. It was only then that she noticed his coal black, impenetrable eyes, devoid of visible pupils. His features were rugged. Because of his cap, not even a hairline was visible to soften his chisel-cut facial features. 'Cruel and heartless,' Hanna thought, 'He would betray his mother to get what he wants.' Gustav Metternich took a breath.
Taking the opportunity presented by Metternich's brief pause, Hanna abruptly stood up from her chair, towered over the still-seated Metternich, and flashed a dismissive glance at her husband who had remained standing, motionless, throughout Metternich's monologue.

Hanna walked briskly to the door, opened it and, with the warmest smile she could muster, said, 'Herr Metternich, the Secretary can schedule another appointment for you as you leave or, you might like to telephone for one.' With this she terminated the meeting. Taken aback, Metternich, who was used to others obeying him, took the cue. Hermann was about to stutter something to Hanna but she cut him off by closing the door in his face.

A stony strength had gradually built itself up in her. Her back stiffened. She turned from the door and stood steadfastly on the spot. Her teeth were clenched as she stared out the window. There was no fear in her after the one-sided exchange; only steely resolve as she took a deep breath. Hanna despised any form of bullying. She had experienced it often enough growing up, and what Metternich proposed and the manner in which it was delivered was, for her, the worst of intimidating tactics.

She suddenly realised how much she loathed her husband for his part in this. He condoned and went along with it. 'He is a gutless coward, a spoilt mummy's boy,' she proclaimed to herself. Hanna checked in the mirror, saw that there was no tension in her face, opened the door and called out charmingly, 'Ilse, could you please bring me a cup of coffee?' She then went back to her desk and sat down. 'What will I tell Herr Grünbaum about the interview? Did he perhaps anticipate this visit? Would his connections have warned him?' She was not one to waste time on speculations and knew she would have her questions answered soon enough.

Luckily, Herr Grünbaum wouldn't be back until Wednesday, giving her a few more days to decide what to do. The immediate issue was to learn who else in the office was in the Nazi Party. She was not going to get drawn into a political intrigue with thugs against a firm whose family had always treated her well.

While she was reflecting on the meeting with Metternich, she hadn't noticed the door to her office open. A slight creak brought her back to the day's business issues. Turning towards the door she saw the mail clerk, Emil Schmidt, saunter in. He was a pitiful man of about 55 who had done little with his life. He had started as a mail clerk with the firm at 15 and there he had stayed. He constantly grumbled when someone like Hanna, who was young, rose quickly in the firm. 'Yes,' she thought, 'I have progressed in the firm because I go to night school five nights a week. I study and I work longer hours.' Slowly closing the door behind him, he approached Hanna with a confident and defiant stance.

With a smirk on his face, he said, 'Looks like we're equals now Hanna, eh? We're going to be working together, eh?' He stared at her as if waiting for her reaction. Although she was stunned at him calling her by her first name, she didn't move. 'Hanna, nice name, eh?' 'Hanna,' he repeated taunting her. 'I'm Emil but then you know that don't you? Emil, just a mail clerk, eh?'

At that moment the door opened and Ilse entered with the coffee. She placed the cup on the desk and asked, 'Will there be anything else, gnädige Frau, Madam?' As she spoke, she shifted her eyes fleetingly from Emil back to Hanna as though warning her.

'Thank you, Ilse,' replied Hanna, 'I need you to take dictation.' With that she indicated to Emil that it was time for him to get out of her office. Brazenly, he laughed and sarcastically quipped, 'Yes, of course, gnädige Frau. I'm always at your service, gnädige Frau,' making a mock-subservient bow as he left.

Ilse looked expressionless at Hanna. Hanna thought quickly. 'Ilse, I need you to take a few notes about this morning's new client.' Timidly, Ilse asked, 'Gnädige Frau, wasn't that Herr Hollar who accompanied the new client?' 'Yes,' replied Hanna, 'When you have typed your notes, please open a file on Herr Metternich and place it in my in-tray as I need to speak with Herr Grünbaum about him when he returns.' With that, Hanna ended the conversation. Ilse left the room.

Hanna was finally alone with her thoughts. She felt a twinge of remorse for having been so cold to Ilse when she saw that she had tried to warn her about Emil but, she also wanted to protect Ilse from whatever might happen in the future.

'The best course of action is to be completely open with Herr Grünbaum. However, it would not be wise to discuss this at the office. Emil's presence is a threat and there is the possibility that the office is already under observation. His place will surely be watched with calls monitored. If I were him,' Hanna thought, 'I would go back home, get my wife and important personal effects and go into hiding or leave Austria.' She had never experienced this situation before, but her visitors that day proved to her that nothing and no one would be safe.

'Good thing I hadn't given in to Hermann when he had asked me if it wasn't time we had a child. This is no time to bring a child into the world. In any case, I'm not ready for a child,' she ruminated. 'I have greater personal aspirations with or without Hermann.' At this point, it seemed it would be without him.

The immediate problem was to find a suitable place for her to meet her Boss. Somewhere, where they could fake an accidental rendezvous, somewhere public. Suddenly she thought, 'Yes, of course, that's it! That will be a perfect place for us to meet.' She made a mental note so that there would be no written evidence to give it away.

CHAPTER 3
VIENNA

Hanna was used to keeping secrets. When she had lived with her mother, she had lead a double life, one according to her mother's expectations, the other when she was away from home. She often indulged in romantic fantasies to make life at home more bearable. 'Ich bin eine Doppelgängerin, I'm a double agent,' she would chuckle to herself.

Her mother was very strict. Standard daily correction methods adopted by her mother included harsh, demoralising verbal outbursts, and threats followed by slaps across the face or elsewhere. She even had different clothes that she would put on after she was out of sight. As long as she appeared to obey the rules, home life was tolerable. Because she went to night classes, she always had an excuse for not being home by the curfew that would otherwise have been imposed.

Hanna realised that she was attractive when young men at night classes frequently sought her company. It was from one of these young men she learned that the best colours to wear were dark colours if you didn't want to be seen at night. She soon discarded her white cardigan and her light-coloured skirt and blouse for darker ones. One of the things Hanna hated most about the clothes she had to wear was that her mother insisted on dressing her in the same frumpy frocks that she wore when they went out together. Hanna was tall and slim with good legs, which she liked to show off.

She had kept in contact with three close friends from school, Helga, Marta and Fritz. Helga had married a train driver, Artur, from Kirchberg-am-Wagram, a village about one-and-a-half hours by train north-west of Vienna. They had moved there after the wedding. Marta came from a 'good' family and had gone on to study fashion design with a famous Viennese couturier. Her ambition was to open her own Atelier near St Stephen's Cathedral in the elegant part of Vienna's City Centre. She was engaged to Gerhardt, who studied engineering. For Hanna, the closest of the three was Fritz who had also graduated in engineering. She knew that Fritz had a crush on her but she didn't find him exciting - he was plump and wore glasses. He was a content teddy bear sort of fellow; Hanna wanted someone who was more exotic, dynamic and handsome.

What kept Hanna and Fritz together, even though he knew that she didn't return his feelings, was their mutual love of music. Fritz sang in a well-known Vienna men's choir and occasionally he and Hanna would attend a symphony concert together.

When it came time to marry, each married someone else. Fritz married a simple, uncomplicated girl he was fond of and who adored him. Hanna married Hermann, who seemed to have the promise of the life she hoped for. Both spouses understood the relationship between Hanna and Fritz and saw in the platonic friendship more a brotherly and sisterly association. They would often meet in Vienna's Stadtpark after work and sit on a bench under one of the massive ancient trees and talk about music, skiing and travelling abroad.

Fritz had choir rehearsals most mornings and evenings. Hanna formulated her plan. She would suggest to Fritz that they meet before rehearsal in the morning for a coffee in the Café of the Hotel Sacher in Vienna's City Centre. She would just tell him enough to get him to co-operate. At 9.00 AM, Herr Grünbaum would come along as though by chance and Hanna could suggest he join them. Fritz would say he had to go to work, and she and Herr Grünbaum could talk alone. If someone was watching, it would seem to be a harmless and accidental social encounter. After all the Hotel Sacher was the perfect place where someone like Herr Grünbaum would have a morning coffee. Later on, even meetings like this would cause suspicion but for now, it should work. 'Yes,' she thought, 'That's a perfect plan.' She knew that Fritz would co-operate.

Hanna phoned Fritz and asked him to meet her that afternoon after work. Knowing her for so long, he could tell from the urgent tone of her voice that something was amiss. 'Is something the matter?' he inquired. 'I'll tell you about it when we meet,' she replied. Just at that moment, Ilse walked in and told her that Herr Grünbaum was on the phone. She hung up on Fritz. 'Thank you, Ilse. Put him through,' she instructed and smiled.

'Herr Grünbaum. How are you?' she began in a formal tone. 'The conversation with the new client?... It was interesting... Pardon? The reception doesn't seem to be very clear. I cannot hear you very well. Yes, I'll give you the details when you return to the office tomorrow morning. Yes, until 9.00 tomorrow morning.' They hung up. She hoped desperately that no one was on another line listening in as her Boss was telling her where they were to meet tomorrow, while she carried on a fictitious conversation with him from her end.

As though he had read her mind Herr Grünbaum proposed the Café at the Hotel Sacher. 'When you wanted to lose yourself, it was best to choose a crowded place,' she smiled feeling pleased with herself. The Hotel Sacher was always crowded, not only was it a favourite with the Viennese, every tourist went there to try its world-famous Sacher Torte.

Hanna rang Fritz back. 'Sorry I had to hang up on you. Meet me at the usual place.' At the other end he asked bewildered, 'Now?' 'No,' she replied, 'after work.' By now Fritz realised she couldn't talk so he added, 'At 6.00 PM?' 'What a wonderful idea,' Hanna confirmed speaking louder now. They hung up.

Hanna had deliberately kept her voice down while making her arrangements with Fritz to avoid being overheard by Emil who should have been busy sorting the morning mail. Ilse would also be occupied. The other staff were related to Herr Grünbaum in one way or another either by birth or marriage. 'Mind you,' she thought, 'that doesn't mean anything in times like these. Perfect opportunity to get rid of unwanted relatives,' she thought matter-of-factly wrinkling her brow.

Leaving the incidents of the morning behind her, Hanna carried on with her work. She didn't want to give Emil anything out of the ordinary to do or he might get suspicious, in any case, he wasn't of use for anything else, the mail was taxing enough for him. By the time he would discover that she wasn't in the office first thing tomorrow morning, it would be too late to have her followed. He would, of course, report her absence but she knew she could handle any interrogation.

She left the office at 5.45 PM and hurried to meet Fritz at 6.00. By this time, it was dark, chilly and windy. Hanna enjoyed the walk. The cool wind blowing in her hair was refreshing and it seemed to cleanse her mind as though the wind wanted to erase the events of the day. Fritz was already waiting. He looked worried. 'What's going on?' he asked. With a note of urgency in her speech Hanna said, 'I can't stay long, Hermann is in Vienna and I must get home.' She then quickly went over the relevant details of Metternich and Hermann's visit to her office.

Hanna didn't allow Fritz the opportunity to discuss the morning's events, or detail the charade she was expecting him to participate in the following morning. He knew better than to even try to say anything. When Hanna was focused on something nothing stood in her way. She told him where he had to be, what he had to do and when he had to leave them. An army general could learn how to strategise by watching Hanna in action. She gave Fritz a peck on the cheek and a loving look that melted his heart. And then, like a whirlwind she was gone.

On the way home she was still thinking about Hermann and Metternich. She had not quite come to grips with Metternich's conversation and Hermann's presence added an element of surrealism to the encounter. She knew that Hermann would be no bother at home; she could freeze him out with a glance. It wouldn't have been the first time she denied him his marital pleasures.

As she approached her apartment block, she observed that only the top apartment had lights on. Her apartment was in darkness. She opened the heavy wooden front security gate, walked across the courtyard, up the flight of stairs, and opened her front door. She was startled by a light on in the living room. It was then she noticed the heavy velvet curtains were drawn explaining why she hadn't seen any light from the street. 'Hallo Hannielein, darling,' Hermann said as he approached her with outstretched arms. She hated when he called her that. He always used Hannielein when he wanted intimacy. She avoided his approach and hung her jacket in the hallway. It was then she became aware of a shadow and sensed they were not alone. She stalled on the pretext of fixing her hair.

Hermann was about to say something when Metternich walked in from another room, 'Well, Frau Hollar, we meet again under less formal circumstances. Your husband very kindly invited me in for an aperitif before we all go out to dinner. I have made a booking at Misha's Restaurant in Grinzing. The booking is for 8.00. My driver will pick us up at 7.15.'

Hanna was inwardly enraged that Hermann allowed Metternich to breach her privacy and it was all she could do to appear calm. Like an actress on a stage she hid that Metternich had just made a grossly ill-mannered faux-pas. Her home was sacred to her and no one came uninvited, no one. Hanna rarely invited home even people she knew well, preferring to meet in a restaurant or Gasthaus if it was for a meal, or a Caféhaus for cake and coffee. Nevertheless, she was aware of the type of person she was dealing with and thought better of showing disdain. She looked charmingly at Hermann and said, 'Darling, I had no idea you'd be home. I've made other arrangements.' Before either could answer, she left the room, went into the bedroom, locked the door and didn't come out until she heard the front door close. Hanna then saw them get into a chauffeur-driven car and drive off. She could not be certain that Metternich hadn't left a spy to check on her movements, however, she didn't relish the thought of being home alone with Hermann when he returned later.

Hanna rang Marta, who apart from Fritz, was the only close friend she had in Vienna. No answer. She waited about 15 minutes and rang again. This time a voice answered, 'Gassinger residence'.

'Is Frau Gassinger at home?' Hanna asked. 'May I ask who is calling, please?' queried the voice. 'Frau Hollar,' replied Hanna.

Marta answered immediately; she had been listening on the extension. 'Hanna, hallo. This is a pleasant surprise. Is everything alright? It's late for you to be calling.'

'Listen,' replied Hanna, 'Can I come over to your place now and stay the night?'

'Hanna, what's wrong?' Marta queried.

'I'll tell you everything when I see you. Is it okay?' Hanna almost pleaded.

'But of course,' replied Marta quickly.

'Okay, see you soon.' Hanna returned the phone to the wall. She had to move fast.

Quickly, she put a change of clothes on a hanger and held it under her coat. She couldn't risk taking an overnight bag in case she was being watched. The other necessities she placed in her roomy handbag. She left a room lamp on. It would look like she intended to return as Hermann knew how pedantic she was about turning off lights. When she walked out of the heavy wooden front gate Hanna looked around but there were just the usual local cars parked in the street. Walking rapidly, she turned left toward the main street to catch a tram to Marta's home. As Hanna sat in the tram she went over the day's events again, and how her life had changed from that of a conservative, 'quiet office girl' to that of a Mata Hari involved in espionage. She almost burst out laughing. It was so ludicrous.

'What on earth is going on?' she wondered for a moment if she imagined it all. The rattling of the tram and the darkness of the night brought her back to grim reality. This was no joking matter. She suddenly felt so alone and vulnerable, tears started.

'Pull yourself together,' Hanna ordered herself, 'Don't be such a coward.' She jolted herself back to being in charge. She went a tram stop further than necessary in case she was followed. As she walked along the street, it didn't seem she was being followed, but it was so dark, it was hard to tell.

Suddenly, she heard a noise beside her. Terrified but alert she quickly turned around. Trying to make out who or what had made that noise was difficult. Then she saw something move. It was a homeless drunk who had collided with a trash can. After that, she took off her stiletto shoes and ran in her hosiery on the uneven cobble stones of the footpath to Marta's apartment.

Although breathless and with aching feet, she ran and ran. 'I mustn't stop,' she panted to encourage herself. Before she turned into Marta's laneway, she looked around again. Quickly she turned into it and then darted into the secluded back entrance that only friends knew. Marta was already waiting for her.

'What in God's name is the matter? What is going on? You look like you've seen a ghost. Come put your clothes in your room. Towels are laid out for you. We'll be alone tonight as Gerhardt is away for a few days.'

'Perfect,' thought Hanna, instantly relieved.

Marta poured some wine. 'Better than coffee for the nerves at this point, I would say,' she philosophised with a grin. Hanna sipped the wine and felt the gradual release of tension caused by the day's events. For the first time that day, Hanna felt herself relaxing and started to feel safe again. For a moment they sat in silence, sipping their wine. Marta let her friend take her time. They had been friends for 20 years, having met on the first day they started kindergarten. Marta knew both sides of Hanna: the cool, calculating, well-balanced, ambitious career woman, and the vulnerable, gentle, sensitive person hiding behind her business-like veneer. Gradually, Hanna let out a sigh and she poured out the day's events.

When she finished, Marta waited a few seconds before responding. She wanted to have Hanna's attention before she said anything.

'We've suspected Hermann for some time but we were not sure so we didn't say anything. When Gerhardt was in North Germany recently on business, he and another colleague went for a walk after a meeting and observed a scuffle in the street as youths intimidated some older folk. A group of men in army uniform watched but did nothing. A pedestrian told them to do something and help the older people but one of the men in uniform told the pedestrian to mind his own business.'

'They deserve everything they're getting,' said another uniformed man.

'Then Gerhardt saw Hermann amongst the group. He was wearing an Austrian army uniform whereas the others were wearing a uniform that Gerhardt didn't recognise. Gerhardt quickly turned away not to be seen. Since then, we've heard of similar incidents from people who know Hermann and saw him in the company of those who were instrumental in physical abuse or who condoned it.' Marta paused.

Hanna sat motionless. It was as though she had been struck dumb. Her mind was incapable of registering what she just heard. The exhaustion of the day, the wine, and now this, were all too much for her. Hanna silently wept. Marta sat beside her friend and held her tight. When Marta released Hanna, she just sat still and said, almost in a whisper. 'I can't believe Hermann has joined up with Hitler's cronies. I know how fanatically Austrian he is but he has never shown any signs of being racist. These thugs are plainly racist, not just to the Jews but to other groups as well. I just can't believe it. Hermann's parents have people from all races and religions working for them and they care about them, as does Hermann.' Hanna repeated, 'And yet, there he was, both times with Metternich,' she added in despair.

'Have you spoken to Hermann about all this?' Marta asked to lighten the situation.

'No,' Hanna replied, 'I was shocked when I saw him with that man at the office. I was even more shocked when Metternich came to our apartment without my invitation. I had to get away from him. I was tired and confused after the day's events.'

'Well,' said Marta, 'Until you have spoken to him, there are too many unanswered questions. You will need to face him alone and talk about this.' 'Marta was making sense,' thought Hanna, 'I am jumping to unfounded conclusions.'

Marta continued, 'Hermann loves you very much, so I doubt he would put you in danger. You need to let him explain. Maybe he had no choice and has to appear to cooperate at this point. Stay the night and have a good rest. You also need to play out your excuse for not going to dinner with them. It will help both you and Hermann. Then tomorrow, meet up with Herr Grünbaum and see what he has to say. You would be surprised how many people here in Vienna and in Austria were prepared for what happened yesterday at the town hall square - the demonstration and the resulting chaos.

The two of them then talked about other things and continued with the wine's help to relax. Marta was excited. She had a new fashion exhibition coming up. She had invited some of the top couturiers in Europe to see her designs and they had all accepted. She also invited Hanna to attend who was happy to accept particularly as Marta had designed her clothes for many years.

The strain of the day started to show its effects and both friends said goodnight.

Hiding in the shadows in the street below, a figure watched as the lights went out.

CHAPTER 4
VIENNA

It was 7.30 when Hanna awoke the next morning. She had set the alarm for a little later than usual, knowing she would need the extra sleep. Marta lived in the City Centre so it would be only a 15 minute walk to the Sacher Hotel where she was to meet Fritz and then Herr Grünbaum at nine.

Gradually Hanna sat up in bed and wondered if Marta had gone to work: she was usually at her Atelier by seven. She wriggled in bed. 'Just a few more minutes to luxuriate,' she thought as she snuggled under the down feathers of the eiderdown, propping herself up on the equally soft, large pillows. She could just make out some light blue sky through the curtains. 'Unusual for an early spring day,' Hanna mused, 'I hope it's a good omen.' One last hug of the eiderdown and she leapt out of bed. As she opened the bedroom door, she heard a noise in the kitchen and smelt the aroma of percolating coffee wafting towards her.

'Morning, sleepyhead,' said a smiling Marta as Hanna came down the stairs, 'I thought I'd have to send Mirabell to wake you.'

Mirabell was Marta's adorable French poodle who loved nothing more than jumping up and frolicking on a soft bed and then snuggling up while providing a loving facial wash and a kiss on your mouth.

'Ugh!' exclaimed Hanna picking Mirabell up and cuddling her, You know I love you but I prefer to wash my face myself,' she told the dog, giving her another big squeeze.

'So, how did you sleep?' inquired Marta.

'Very well,' Hanna replied, giving Marta a hug. 'That bed of yours is so comfortable. I think the wine helped too', she smiled.

'Good, glad to hear it.' Marta added, 'Coffee and juice are on the table as are the pastries. Would you like anything else?' Hanna knew that Marta was just making conversation before getting to the issues of the day, for Marta knew too well that Hanna only ever had a cup of coffee when she first woke up and didn't eat till 9 or 10.

'No, thanks, Marta,' replied Hanna. She was already elsewhere with her thoughts.

'Okay, let's get to it. What are you going to tell Herr Grünbaum?' Hanna replied pensively, 'I'll tell him exactly what took place. I can't see any other alternative. I'll feel terrible repeating some of the things Metternich said and implied, but I don't think we can camouflage the situation. It'll have to be the same when I speak with Hermann. You know I always believe in openness, at least for as long as is necessary, until I get a grip on what is going on and who stands where.'

The two friends then enjoyed their coffee and each other's company as they had often done before each married. They met their respective husbands about the same time; both had married about the same time, and both were planning to soon start a family. 'Luckily,' Hanna thought, 'that is quite a way off. Especially considering how I feel about Hermann at the moment.'

While Hanna and Marta enjoyed this time together, the noise of crowds wafted up to them. They heard a police car heralded by a siren come down the street and stop close by. It was then they heard a loud voice yelling that people should make room for the police and the ambulance. Hanna and Marta looked at each other and then looked out the window. Indeed, there was an ever-increasing crowd of men, women and children gathering around what looked like a man lying on the ground.

The police were putting up barricades to push the crowd away. It was only as the scene cleared that Hanna saw the lifeless body lying at the base the street lamp opposite Marta's apartment. The man wore a Nazi Party uniform and a large pool of dried blood lay on the concrete under his head. A long deep gash was evident on the victim's forehead when the ambulance attendant turned the corpse over, 'So, he was hit from the front,' thought Hanna.

Bewildered and alarmed, the two friends looked at each other. Was it a coincidence that a dead Nazi Party officer lay outside Marta's apartment? How long had he been there? Who was he? Why was he in that part of town? Who could have killed him?

'This is serious,' Marta said keeping her voice low. 'I don't think him being outside my apartment is a coincidence.'

Hanna agreed saying, 'But how could he have followed me? I didn't see anyone, I kept checking. There was only a drunk at the other end of your street and he wasn't in uniform.'

'Diese Idioten! These idiots are smarter than we think, but I don't think he had an opportunity to alert his co-bastards of your whereabouts. Someone killed him before he could go back to make a report.' Marta surmised, 'What's unnerving is that perhaps two people could have followed you; this bastard and his murderer or…, perhaps someone saw him in his uniform standing in the shadow and killed him because this is not a neighbourhood that would welcome anyone from the Party.

Whatever it is, Hanna,' Marta continued sternly, 'You are not to be alone from now on. One of us, Fritz or I, will be with you all the time until we are sure of your safety. I'll take you to the Hotel Sacher, and wait until I see Fritz meet you. You ask Fritz to hang around out of sight until your meeting with Grünbaum is over. Fritz then walks you to your office. His boss won't mind if he comes late to work. He can always say he was with a client.'

'Wait, wait! Enough,' interjected Hanna, now in her command attitude, 'Slow down. You and Fritz aren't going to mess up your lives like that. I won't let you. I haven't done anything wrong. Why should anyone be after me? I admit the whole thing about this dead fellow in the street is odd to say the least, but that's it. Until we have proof that things need to be otherwise, I'm just going to carry on as usual. I'll go to the Hotel Sacher as planned and then I'll see what has to happen next. I will not be bullied and that is that.' Marta knew better than to say anything further.

It was now 8.45. 'I'd better leave,' Hanna said, 'Wish me luck.' 'You'll be fine,' responded Marta encouragingly. They gave each other a hug and hurried downstairs. Skirting around the crowd and the police was easy, everyone was still gawking vicariously at the body.

As the Hotel Sacher came into view, Marta turned the corner towards her design studio and Hanna continued on to the Café. Fritz was sitting at a table and she approached him. 'What's the matter with you? You look terrible,' she said as she saw how disheveled he was.

'I had a rough night,' he said and was going to leave it at that so that they could talk before Herr Grünbaum arrived.

'What do you mean, you had a rough night,' Hanna asked alarmed. Just at that moment, Herr Grünbaum approached. 'Good morning, Herr Grünbaum,' Hanna pulled herself together and greeted politely. 'May I present a friend of mine, Fritz Martinus. Fritz, this is my boss, Herr Grünbaum.'

'Pleased to meet you, sir,' Fritz said as he offered his hand which Herr Grünbaum accepted. 'I must go now, excuse me, Herr Grünbaum,' Fritz said making a slight bow. 'Goodbye, Hanna, see you later'.

'Goodbye, Fritz.'

As Hanna and Herr Grünbaum entered the Hotel Sacher Café, an attendant held the door open and mumbled a formal greeting. Hanna paused as her eyes adjusted to the dim lighting while Herr Grünbaum went ahead to a table behind a heavy curtain so that they couldn't be seen from the street.

Hanna was about to follow him when a now familiar voice spoke from behind her. It belonged to Metternich. As she turned to greet Metternich, she also saw Hermann. 'Ah, there you are Frau Hollar,' said Metternich, 'We missed you at the office. The Secretary said that you were usually in by this time. We can perhaps discuss a few points over a coffee now. Is that suitable?'

Hanna thought quickly, 'It would probably be best to get it over with here in public. Herr Grünbaum will also have a chance to see Metternich and understand why I did not join him.' The only aspect she didn't like was that she hadn't had a chance to speak privately with Hermann. But that could wait because she needed to respond to Metternich. 'Yes that is possible but please, be brief. I must go to the office.'

Hanna took the initiative and walked towards a table in the other direction from where Grünbaum sat. The trio found a vacant booth and Hanna made sure they sat with their backs to Herr Grünbaum. They ordered. Hanna had a Wiener Melange coffee and a plain bread roll. Both men had an espresso coffee.

Metternich started, 'We had a most enjoyable dinner last night. The atmosphere is always so relaxed in Grinzing. I always make a point of visiting a restaurant in that area when I am in Vienna. Such a pity you could not be with us. When people work together, it is always nice to get to know them from all sides. Don't you agree?' he slimed.

Hanna avoided the question and spoke to her husband, 'How long will you be staying home, Hermann?'

'Not sure, Hanna, because details of my next assignment haven't been received, so I'm still officially on duty. You might like to know that my superiors have sent me back to Vienna to help Commandant Metternich acquaint himself with the city. He wants to secure new markets for his import/export business.'
'That is correct,' Metternich interjected, 'I own a company in Germany but as I am…' Hanna interrupted him saying, 'Correct me if I'm wrong, Herr Metternich, but the conversation we had at the office did not give me the impression that that was why you wanted to consult our firm.'

Metternich laughed laconically, 'I see you have given our conversation some thought. Excellent. What are you going to tell your Herr Grünbaum when he asks you about our interview? After all, he will ask you about it.' The stare which followed was more of an interrogation than a question.

Hanna had not expected this turn of events but she knew what to say. 'I will tell him that you were pleased with what transpired but that you would also like to speak with him and that you will make an appointment accordingly.' She waited for the import of her statement to sink in. It was obvious that Metternich wasn't prepared for her response. 'She isn't going to be a pushover,' Metternich thought, 'She'll take more work than I anticipated but she'll do as I say in the end. I'll make sure of that.' Calmly, Hanna continued, 'You mentioned earlier that you had passed by the office to see me. What did you wish to discuss?'

'We have a shipment arriving in Vienna from Munich on Friday. We need a respected firm in Vienna to receive the merchandise; one whose clients often receive goods from Germany; a company the Austrian Border Customs know well. They will then not insist on opening the cargo. If they do ask to see the shipment, we will have a few crates ready for them.'

Hanna was horrified. 'You mean; you want to use the company's name to smuggle secret goods into Austria?'

'Yes,' came the short, icy reply, 'We will do it and you will help us.' 'Thank you for the coffee,' Hanna said with forced civility. Then, without looking at Herman she rose and left the Café. She noticed that Herr Grünbaum had already left. 'Right,' she thought, 'This is it, no more indecisiveness. This thug really means business and will stop at nothing.'

A lesser person might have felt some fear, but Hanna was made of stronger stuff. She was now more resolute than ever to talk to Hermann. 'If he is unwillingly in the clutches of this fellow, we can work around this together. If he is a willing participant, that will change everything. But first things first. I must speak to Herr Grünbaum.'

When Hanna arrived at the office, Ilse had a list of phone calls that had come in and a note about Metternich's visit. She asked Ilse whether Herr Grünbaum was in. 'Yes,' she replied, 'He arrived about 9.15.'

'Good, thanks, Ilse. I'll go to him. Please make sure that we are not disturbed.' Ilse nodded and looked questioningly at Hanna. Hanna noticed this but let it go. Ilse had many times shown her loyalty to the firm and to Herr Grünbaum but these were exceptional times. Hanna entered Grünbaum's office and as she approached his desk she saw the newspaper headline – "German Soldier Murdered".

Ignoring the newspaper, Hanna greeted her boss formally, but cordially, 'Good morning, Herr Grünbaum.' The atmosphere in the room was sombre; the shades were drawn and her boss was frowning.

When he saw it was Hanna, he smiled, 'Good day, Frau Hollar. Please take a seat. Thank you for your presence of mind this morning. It seems you are already aware of circumstances which are very worrying. I have known about this impending possibility for some time but, well, I was hoping that the situation would change. It would seem that the rest of the world can also not believe what is happening, and now, I'm afraid it is too late to avert future events.'

Hanna looked at Herr Grünbaum. A feeling of empathy and compassion rose in her along with a deep feeling of helplessness. To see this kind, generous man so downtrodden was painful.

He continued, 'From this morning's events, I can see that you have been forced into discussions with these people. I saw your husband was there also.' She wanted to say something, but what? She didn't yet know to what extent Hermann was involved.

'Herr Grünbaum,' she started, 'It's not wise to speak here. It is better if we meet away from the office where we can be sure that we won't be seen nor heard.' Hanna continued, 'I have a friend who sings with the Vienna Male Choir. There are rehearsals in the evening every Tuesday and Thursday from 7.00 to 10.00. We can arrange to go there independently. I will get him to meet you in the lane at the back and take you inside through the side entrance and then downstairs, which will be empty. Everyone will be upstairs rehearsing and it will be noisy. I'll meet you there. If anyone were to come down, we would hear them and have a chance to hide.' Herr Grünbaum's face was filled with gratitude, 'Thank you, Frau Hollar. Would tomorrow evening be convenient?' Hanna nodded her agreement.

CHAPTER 5
VIENNA

As Herr Grünbaum opened the office door after their meeting, he said, 'Good, Frau Hollar. I will await a call from Herr Metternich. Please ask Emil to bring me the mail which came during my absence; it doesn't seem to be on my desk.' And with that, Hanna left her boss's office well aware that although the meeting had only taken 10 minutes, while it was long enough to exchange vital information it was brief enough to avert any suspicion from the prying eyes and ears of Emil, the mail clerk.

The day passed without incident. She barely saw Emil. After his initial bravado, he kept his distance. Perhaps he had been made to realise that he was only a little worm in the vermin pit and that any excessive or abrasive behaviour on his part could negatively affect Metternich's operations. Ilse also went about her work with her usual efficiency and lack of emotion.

When everyone had left the office, Hanna telephoned Fritz. When he answered, Hanna carefully avoiding using his name and said, 'We will meet you at the underground side entrance tomorrow evening at 7.00 PM and we can have coffee at Aida's Coffee House before the performance. In his usual acquiescent manner, Fritz just went along with what she asked. 'Yes, of course,' replied Fritz.

Hanna did not ask the question about what Fritz meant by his statement that 'he had had a rough night.' That would have to wait until tomorrow evening.

The day seemed to go quickly. Although Hanna enjoyed her work immensely, she also liked when the day was over and she could go home to her beautiful apartment. But not today. She wasn't looking forward to talking to Hermann about the current situation but philosophically she thought to herself, 'Oh, well, it has to be done.'

Suddenly, she heard a noise at the front of the office. She knew the staff and Herr Grünbaum had already left. 'Could it be Emil? Had he loitered to spy on me?'

Quietly, Hanna opened her desk drawer that housed her pistol and sat with her hand ready on the weapon. She was now glad that she had taken Hermann's advice to keep one with her, although at the time, she thought he was overreacting. She waited. The creaking had stopped, all was silent.

Then she heard footsteps approaching her office. She stiffened and took a firmer grip on the firearm. Previously she would never have become agitated. There had never been a tangible reason to feel unsafe even if she did leave the office late sometimes. However, times had dramatically changed. She was amazed how quickly humans reverted to primitive animal instincts sensing danger and the fight-or-flight reaction hit them.

The door opened. Hanna was ready with the gun.

'Hallo, Hannielein,' It was Hermann, 'I hope I didn't frighten you. The front door was open. I waited for Ilse to come but as she didn't, so I came in. I guess everyone has left for the day,' he continued, trying to make conversation.

Hanna heaved a sigh of relief. 'Oh, Hermann, it's you. I'm so glad it's you. I had no idea who it could be.' She slumped back in her chair, let go of the pistol and closed the drawer. She then went up to him and impulsively hugged him. Hermann's hug was tentative and clumsy and it was obvious that he was nervous because his hug was clumsy.

After a moment, he gently pushed her away and looked at her lovingly. 'Can we please talk,' he pleaded. 'Not here,' he added as he saw that she was about to say something. 'Let's just get out of here and we can then decide where we want to go. We really need to talk.'

Hanna could feel her defences weaken; she so wanted that he hadn't changed. The look in his eyes, and the softening of his face, made her see the Hermann she knew, not the hard, stony-faced military man who had been with Metternich. 'I'll withhold any judgment and give him a chance to explain,' she decided.

'But of course, that'll be nice. We really do need to talk about what's gone on the last couple of days. I'll get my coat,' she replied. 'And now that your 'friend' isn't with you, we can take the opportunity,' she added cheekily. Hanna checked that everyone had left the office and that the back door was locked.

As she was about to pick up her things, Hermann approached her, took her again in his arms, hugged her so firmly that she could barely breathe. 'I love you so much,' Hermann whispered, 'Please trust me. I don't want to lose what we have together yet we must be careful.' With that he gave her a sustained kiss on the lips before releasing her.

Hanna stood still for a moment, looking into Hermann's eyes and said tenderly, 'Come. Let's get out of here.' She picked up her things and they left the office.

The evening was cool as they walked briskly arm-in-arm. The streets were still full of people, which wasn't unusual for Vienna. While Vienna is described as a city of dreams, it is also a city that never sleeps: there was always something to do, or somewhere to relax. Hanna and Hermann loved the pulse of Vienna, you could find whatever you wanted you could find it; music, high culture, philosophy, strip-tease or just a romantic drink for two. They knew the city well and could shake off any unwanted followers if the need now arose.

On this evening, Hanna and Hermann decided that it might not be such a bad idea to be followed because then it would look like they were still close just in case Metternich had started to harbor doubts about the value and usefulness of Hermann, given that Hanna seemed the stronger of the two. They whispered this to each other and suddenly burst out laughing, 'This is all a bit silly, isn't it, Hermann,' Hanna joked. But she could see the serious look on his face and thought better about saying anything more. 'Obviously it's not that simple,' she thought, 'He's been in the thick of things. I'll soon find out what it's all about.'

They walked happily and bounced along the street glad to be together again like old times at the beginning of their relationship. Even the prospect of someone stalking them couldn't dampen their mood. Hanna thought to herself, 'After all it is merely a husband picking up his wife from work and going out to have a bite to eat and a glass of wine. What's wrong with that?' Hanna tried to rationalise away her uneasiness, albeit she could also feel it in Hermann's tense frame, despite his attempt to calm his own fears. Hanna and Hermann passed by roasted Maroni nut vendors, kiosks which only open during the night selling bread rolls with Bratwurst and mustard, while others sold thin, dry roasted potato slices liberally sprinkled with salt. The whirlpool of aromas accentuated by the smell of coffee was so typical of the evening streetscape of this magnificent city.

Tourists were out in full force despite the political situation, looking at the sights by night that they had seen in the daytime. The transition of Vienna from day to night was remarkable. She had not been outside Austria but she was sure no city could surpass the beauty of her beloved Vienna.

Tonight, Hanna's thoughts turned to the multitude of Vienna's underground tunnels filled with bones of long dead and departed Viennese inhabitants from centuries past and other reminders of the city's often turbulent past. 'What's the difference between then and now?' she thought and shuddered. For the time being, she felt safe with Hermann guiding her through the crowd but then, she had always felt safe in Vienna.

'Should we go to the Augustiner Keller?' suggested Hermann. 'We always have a good time there. It'll be busy but not yet so crowded that we can't find a table for two.' When they arrived they found a small table away from large groups. The waiter came immediately, 'What would you like?' he asked them. Hermann replied, 'Two quarter-litre glasses of Gumpoldskirchner wine, please.' He looked at Hanna for confirmation.

'Yes, please,' she affirmed. They exchanged pleasantries while they waited for their order, all the while holding hands across the table and looking into each other's eyes.

The waiter brought the wine. 'Vielen Dank,' said Hermann. 'Bitte sehr, you're welcome,' responded the waiter.

They each lifted their glass, clicked then with a whispered 'prost' and took a sip. Hanna placed her glass on the table and said, 'What is wrong with people that they want to destroy these beautiful moments? Why all this talk of war?' Hermann raised her hands and kissed them. She returned the tender moment with a squeeze of his hands.

'This is going to be a bit long, Hanna, but it is only right that I give you enough to understand what has been happening, and for you to appreciate the danger,' Hermann began. 'I'll start from the beginning and please listen without judging me, until you've heard me out. Also, please always remember that I love you and that I haven't changed.' Hanna had to control her urge to throw her arms around him but instead she gave him a loving smile, squeezed his hands again and said, 'Ja, natürtlich, Liebling; Yes, of course, Darling.'

With a worried expression, Hermann began.

'When I left end of December, I was sent to Berlin. As usual, the assignment was a closely guarded secret. On the train to Berlin initially I was one of six recruits from different parts of Austria on the train. In Frankfurt another four recruits joined us from various parts of Germany including Saarbrücken and Munich.

We each had separate compartments, presumably so that we couldn't interact. However, some of us met in the gangway and started conversations. We had all been instructed to wear only our basic uniform without our position stripes. The other chap from Vienna recognised my uniform and started up a conversation. We didn't see much of the Saarbrücken fellow. The chap from Munich was on the other side of my compartment and joined in our conversations. We had all received the same instructions. Information we each contributed increased the feelings of mystery and intrigue about this commission. When I was alone in my cabin, I kept getting an uneasy feeling, but I was not prepared for what eventuated.'

'I'm already fearful of what I'm going to hear,' Hanna said shaking her head.

'It was late when we arrived in Berlin. A Commandant in the new grey German army uniform picked us up from the station in his chauffeur-driven limousine. He was reserved and uncommunicative. We were taken to an unidentified building outside of Berlin. When inside however, there was no doubt about the political leanings of the occupants. It was a Nazi center of operations. Inwardly I felt terror mounting, but outwardly, like the others, I masked my emotions. We were joined by two more uniformed men from Berlin and two from near the Polish border, making 14 all told.

We were ushered into another room where food and drink was provided, and told to help ourselves and that someone would come shortly.'

'Oh, my goodness,' Hanna interrupted, 'I would have been petrified,' she said putting her hands up as though to hide her face.

Hermann smiled at her and added, 'Yes, I must admit to feeling fearful at the time. We waited four hours. Every noise outside stirred each of us into anticipation and we turned in the direction of the noise. I have noticed that Party leaders often use these delaying tactics to intimidate, to weaken us, by way of showing their power over us.'

Hanna could barely breathe and her eyes widened with anticipation.

Hermann stopped to have a sip of wine, and Hanna did the same.

Then he continued, 'At odd moments, we each tried to make light-hearted comments but because no one was in a frame of mind to carry these further, finally we just waited in silence.

Four hours is an eternity when you don't know what's going on. We heard noises but nothing happened and that added to that the fatigue from the trip.

Eventually, a man appeared and called us to follow him. We walked through a maze of corridors in the bowels of the building. It was a magnificent building and must have belonged to an aristocrat or an affluent business man. The walls were polished mahogany; solid mahogany timber doors were framed by rounded architraves and adorned by highly polished brass door handles. Mirrors were strategically placed so that the host and hostess of days gone by saw everything that was going on in their house.

The walls and doors were so solid that the entire building was totally silent and gave no hint occupancy or emptiness. You would never hear the screams of someone being tortured or killed. Picture frame hooks were still visible where paintings or tapestries had hung. Some had been replaced by pictures of highly-positioned political supporters of the Nazi Party and adorned with the Nazi Party icon and flag.

No one spoke as we followed the Commandant. The floor was so thickly carpeted that even the sound of heavy boots could not be heard as we walked to our unknown intended destination.

Suddenly, the Commandant stopped, turned to face us and raised his right hand in salute and roared, 'Hail to our Hero'. When we all stood still, without saying a word, he turned around and knocked on the door in front of him. Two uniformed men with glazed looks opened the door from inside, saluted and stood motionless, not looking at us by simply staring over our heads.'

'Hermann, this must have been terrible,' said Hanna trying to contain her horror, 'I feel so bad for having behaved the way I did to you. I had no idea.'

What Hermann didn't tell Hanna were the details of what was expected of each of those present at this induction when they were in command of their future troops. The brutal and callous extermination of unwanted races, professions, people of different skin colour, with physical afflictions, and doubtful loyalty. The pain was to be as drawn out as possible from medical experiments while one organ after another was removed or individual organs injected with toxins, to others building Nazi infrastructures under the most extreme weather conditions and inhumane callousness while they starved and lived in subhuman conditions. She would not have been able to handle such information.

'It's alright Hanna, truly, I don't hold it against you. It was so bizarre,' Hermann reassured her and continued, 'We filed into the room being directed to go to the left or right side of the room. There were at least 30 uniformed, armed men. A long, polished table stood on a platform at the other end of the room. Behind the table, with faces rigid as steel, three men sat on high-backed chairs. They wore different uniforms from the others; the one in the middle was obviously of higher rank than the other two because he had red stripes on his cap as well as on his lapels. When the three officers on the stage rose, everyone else in the room snapped to attention; all raised their right hand with clenched fist and roared the salute, snapped their heels together and then stood motionless again. By this stage, we had been on the go without sleep for over 24 hours. We were near collapse.'

Hanna gasped and put her hand over her mouth, 'Oh, Hermann,' and she choked as tears formed.

He took her hand and continued, 'At that moment the man from Saarbrücken collapsed and fell to the floor. He was quickly snatched up by two uniformed men, and roughly dragged out. We never saw him again. I was shocked with the brutality he had been whisked away and after this incident we were very much afraid to show any form of weakness or emotion. It was clear that he had been disposed of. We were each told that we belonged to a squadron, and that we were to do exactly as the squadron leader ordered. There were to be no questions, no hesitation and any break in obedience would be dealt with. We had already witnessed how we would be dealt with.'

Hanna had tears streaming down her cheeks now and she let go of his hand to get a handkerchief. Herrmann continued, 'Once, when I was in Berlin, walking along the street with our group, I saw Gerhardt with another man and I was thankful for both his sake and mine that he didn't show any recognition. Has Marta said anything to you about this?'

'Yes, but only because I went to her the evening you and the German went to Grinzing. I told her what I had experienced during the day, and that was when she told me that Gerhardt had seen you in Berlin, but not before.'

'I see,' Hermann replied and looked embarrassed, lowering his head. With a smile, Hanna quickly took his hand again to reassure him.

Hermann continued, with more of what had happened. When he finished, Hanna took a deep breath, raised her eyebrows, straightened up and said, 'Well, it's obvious that we are both in danger if we don't do as they ask.' It was hard to imagine what they could otherwise do. Only one thing was clear that the life they had previously known was over. They would have to just live each day as it came.

At that moment, gun-shots were heard outside the Augustiner Keller and people were yelling in the streets. Patrons rushed out of the establishment to see what was going on. Newspaper boys were waving a special late edition of "Der Kurier", the Viennese daily newspaper. Indelibly blazed across the front page of the newspaper was the headline, 'Anschluss Österreichs, the Annexation of Austria.'

Hermann grabbed Hanna's hand and said urgently, 'Quickly. Let's go home.' Hanna allowed herself to be led away eager to leave the frenzy of the huge crowds of people rapidly accumulating in the streets. It wasn't easy to navigate through the hysterical crowd but they both knew every side street and alleyway to get back to their apartment.

When they arrived home, they could see fireworks in the City Centre on the other side of the Danube Canal contaminating the beautiful moonlit Viennese sky. For the time being they were safe, even Metternich would be occupied with this evening's events.

'Let's escape across the border,' Hanna suggested, 'We can drive to Switzerland and stay there till it's all settled.'

Hermann took Hanna in his arms, looked at her earnestly and cautioned, 'Liebling, this will not settle, at least not for years. The borders will be guarded by now and people attempting to cross will be shot on sight. I've only mentioned some of the brutality that I saw and not the worst. No, we must stay here and see what game we will need to play.'

Hermann felt it was imperative that they return to their apartment and they intermittently ran and walked until they reached their building. They were panting as they arrived and entered their home. Hermann quickly unlocked the front door and just as quickly locked it again from the inside.

They stood for a moment and looked at each other, enjoying the sudden peace and quiet. They were finally alone. Slowly they moved towards each other as they looked into each other's eyes. Hermann helped her take off her coat and it fell to the floor; she helped him take his off; it too fell to the floor. He took Hanna gently in his arms and they swayed slightly in their embrace as though moving to an inaudible melody that only they could both hear.

After all these months apart their bodies ached for each other's touch and, with the future unknown, their desire to be together was strong.

He picked her up and carried her to their bedroom. She felt herself melt into his arms; she loved it when he carried her; he was strong yet gentle. She felt so feminine when he had her body so close to his. He put her gently on the bed, and carefully undressed her. She moved sensuously as she undressed him. He kissed her tenderly up and down her body and she responded gently by caressing him.

Although their desire was at a feverish intensity, they slowly relished each other's body, enjoying every touch. They were feeling each other as though it was the first time they were intimate. Perhaps it was as they had never been in this situation before, not knowing how long they had together and how long they might even live.
The consummation of their love had never been so beautiful and deep. The connection they had that night was something special. For some time, they lay side by side entwined in each other's arms, before pulling the eiderdown over their naked bodies and falling into a peaceful sleep.

The next morning, they were awakened by repeated knocks on the front door. 'Herr Hollar, Herr Hollar,' a voice shouted. 'Herr Hollar, ein Telegramm für Sie!'

CHAPTER 6
VIENNA
1944

In 1940, Hermann had again been summoned to North Germany, and at least this time Hanna knew where he was. However, there was no indication for how long because war was in full force with many countries, even those not in Europe participating in the conflict. Any news now became unpredictable, and you couldn't believe what you heard as each report had a different interpretation. The only thing you could do was to look after yourself and any loved ones that you had nearby.

Hanna heard that Herr Grünbaum and his family had managed to escape; Grünbaum was one of the lucky ones. Hanna and all other staff had been interrogated about Grünbaum's escape and possible whereabouts but even Emil, the trusted 'Party Puppet' knew nothing.

Herr Grünbaum's firm was closed down as were many others and, as a result, Hanna went to work for her in-laws as their bookkeeper. She still had her apartment and was living there on her own - for how long remained to be seen.

In 1943, after one of Hermann's rare short visits, Hanna discovered she was pregnant. She was quite surprised how well she took it, possibly because the future was unknown.

Vienna was inundated with refugees from the Austria's rural areas and there was no place for them to be housed in the capital's public apartment buildings. All Viennese people living in apartments were being investigated about how many rooms they had and how many occupants these housed. This census was to ascertain how many refugees could be compulsorily billeted. This was something Hanna wanted fiercely to avoid. 'I'm not taking in any peasants to live with me,' she said firmly.

Time moved on. The brutal war intensified as it raged across continental Europe and beyond becoming wilder and fiercer as millions of people faced day-to-day brutality as they struggled for survival. Conditions in Vienna worsened when much of the city was destroyed by bombing raids. Acrid smoke permanently clouded the Vienna skyline, and most food items, especially fresh food were now in short supply.

However, Hanna fared well because of access to the Hollar Food Emporium. To keep trading, they had to let go of staff classified as 'undesirable' by the current regime.

In May 1944, Hanna gave birth to a daughter. She sent Hermann a letter although she wasn't sure how he would take it. His recent letters hadn't been very loving and she had heard that he was having an affair in the north German medieval city of Lübeck. It was not Hanna's style to allow this sort of gossip to get to her. 'That is nonsense, he adores me,' she reassured herself.

The baby, when born, had a mop of dark hair. She was chubby and had all limbs and organs intact. Hanna thought, 'I will give her an exotic name, something Spanish like Carmen,' she thought, but then reconsidered. Spain was still in a mess after its Civil War and not a popular country. 'Maybe I'll choose a neutral name, one that doesn't denote a nationality,' she mused. Also Hanna didn't want a name that foreigners couldn't pronounce, like hers. Few foreigners could say Hannelore, so she changed it permanently to Hanna.

Hanna's so far unnamed daughter had her father's olive skin and brown eyes but she had the dark brown hair from Hanna's Hungarian side. The child was quite different from Hanna who had fair complexion, light brown hair and blue eyes.

'I know', she thought excitedly, 'I'll call her Gilda, it is rather exotic and can't be shortened nor mispronounced it, and even if the name is pronounced with a soft 'g' that would still be alright.'

Hanna often asked her always willing sister-in-law, Adele, to baby-sit. After all, Hanna still had to look after herself. She may have given birth to a child but she was not a nurse-maid. As a professionally-employed woman, Hanna needed time to have her nails manicured, and her massages and hair done. 'I have an image to uphold,' she said emphatically. At a time in war-torn Vienna when its citizens regarded massages, manicures and hair care as extreme luxuries, Hanna considered them personal necessities. 'I am giving employment to people who otherwise would go hungry,' she said to herself proudly. Also, it was easy to get these services at a good price as the numbers of unemployed increased.

After some time, it irritated Hanna that everyone adored Gilda, calling her beautiful, pampering her and paying her excessive attention. Hanna didn't like that at all; she was personally devoted to the idea of being the centre of attention.

When Gilda was three months old, Hanna was called to the Displaced Person's Office and told that she would need to take in boarders. Hanna was horrified. She did all she could from flirting with the civil servant to trying to play on the fact that she had a young baby who screamed a lot.

The official was unmoved saying, 'At least you get a choice. Most people just get told who they must take. So, don't try to be difficult,' the official said unsympathetically.

'What are my choices,' Hanna enquired as sweetly as she could.

'Well, you can either choose a family with six children from a village or a single man from Yugoslavia,' responded the official.

'Oh, good heavens,' thought Hanna in disgust holding back from pulling a face, 'Eight peasants in my elegant home.' 'Could you please tell me about this man from Yugoslavia?' she asked again as sweetly as she could.
'Let me look at his file, um, it doesn't say much,' replied the yawning public servant behind the counter. 'Here, it says he's a doctor, his name is Vladimir Dobinski and he's been living in Graz for a few years studying more medical stuff,' he continued with disinterest. 'Listen, lady, decide now, I haven't got all day. You high and mighty types think we've got time to dilly dally. We're busy. Make up your mind, jetzt, now,' the official bellowed.

As far as Hanna could see, it was an easy, if unpleasant decision to make. The idea of a peasant family with all those children in her exquisite apartment was abhorrent. 'It'll have to be the doctor, although Yugoslavians are a bit backward and hot-tempered. I hope he's trustworthy,' she thought with a shudder. Hanna looked across at the mass of people squeezed into the waiting room and saw a middle-aged-looking man sitting by himself. 'That must be him,' she assumed.

'Hey you,' the civil servant bellowed an order, 'come here'. The doctor got up, and fleetingly glanced at Hanna still standing at the counter. No emotion passed over Hanna's or the doctor's face. The official gave the doctor his papers and told him not to come back again. 'You're stuck at her place, whether you like it or not. And you,' he said turning to Hanna, 'Same thing. If one of you doesn't behave, the other can come back here and report you.' Then he roared with laughter.

Hanna turned haughtily to go and the Jugoslav followed her. As she walked out she caught sight of the family and children and raised her eyebrows in relief. 'If it has to be, this has to be better than that,' she hoped.

The Jugoslav doctor followed her to her apartment. She opened the courtyard door and headed up the stairs, opened the front door and went inside. 'Here is a spare key, but always knock before you come into the apartment. It's still my house and I want to be free to go about as I please when I'm alone and not be surprised by you suddenly coming in. Follow me and I'll show you to your room and around the apartment. My area is out-of-bounds to you.'

Much to Hanna's surprise having Vladimir in the apartment was quite pleasant. He was a gentle man; he was quiet and kept to himself. 'He's more civilised than I expected,' she murmured to herself. After a while, she invited him to have a coffee with her and he would then reciprocate. It was clear that he loved children because he often played with Gilda. Gradually, Vladimir told her about himself.

'I come from a village in Macedonia called Bitola,' Vladimir said. 'My father is a violin teacher and my mother was a school teacher and I have a younger brother who still lives there with his family.' He then continued sadly with bent head, 'I am also married, have a son and a daughter, but things are not going well. My wife is not of the same political views as me and our relationship is now more a convenience for the children. For how long that will last, I don't know.' Vladimir added almost in a whisper, 'I don't know when I will see them again.'

Hanna had listened attentively, and felt a certain pity for him. 'Yes,' she said, 'these are uncertain times. Continue if you would like to.' And so he did. 'I did my general medical studies in Skopje, the capital of my country but I have been living in Graz for the past three years, completing my specialisation in gynaecology and obstetrics. That's really all there is.' he ended. 'Perhaps you would like to tell me about yourself. Where is Gilda's father,' he asked.

'My husband is fighting in North Germany,' responded Hanna, 'He was conscripted and I haven't seen him for some time. Mail is very unpredictable.'

And so, the days went by as pleasantly as they could in Hanna's apartment given the circumstances of the war which continued to rend Europe. She continued to work and Gilda was either cared for by Hermann's mother and sister and now also Vladimir.

Gilda slept most of the time and so was not a great burden. In the evening, Hanna was grateful for Vladimir's company especially when there were air raids, blackouts and frequent power failures. Six months after Gilda was born, Hanna received a letter from Hermann saying that he was coming to Vienna and he wanted to see her. 'That's an odd thing to write,' she thought, 'Of course we will see each other, he lives here.' She started to feel agitated and her hand was shaking as she continued to read the letter, 'I'll be staying with my parents,' he wrote and proposed they meet at a Caféhaus. She had to reread that part again and was taken aback.

Hanna sat down and was suddenly frightened. 'What does that mean? No, it can't be another woman. Not that you idiot,' she rebuked herself. 'As soon as he sees me, I'll have him in the palm of my hand again.' Everything for Hanna was either winning or losing and she always wanted to win.

On the pre-arranged day to meet Hermann, Hanna made sure she looked demure, feminine, yet alluring, splashing on herself what little remained of her trademark Arpège perfume. 'That will remind him of old times, especially that last night we had together.' Pleased with herself, she smiled.

Hanna saw him before he saw her. He still looked dashing and seemed more mature and rugged, which suited him. As he saw her approaching, he walked towards her, smiling, hugged her and kissed her on both cheeks. 'Hallo, Hanna,' he began, 'you do look well. Motherhood becomes you, you've never looked more beautiful.'

That wasn't the welcome Hanna had hoped for. Flustered, Hanna could only manage, 'Danke, Hermann, you also look very well.'

'Please sit down,' he said as he held her chair. 'Shall I call the waiter for coffee,' he asked. 'No, thanks,' replied Hanna, 'what have you come to tell me,' she asked guardedly, shifting in her chair. Hermann began matter-of-factly, 'There is a woman in Lübeck. I love her and I want to marry her. I'll be asking for a divorce while I'm here on leave. You can of course blame the marriage breakup on me, and you can have full custody of Gilda. You can also stay in the apartment till the war is over and I return.'

It was as though a bomb had just fallen on Hanna. She was dazed, speechless. She looked at him unable to comprehend what was happening. Hanna composed herself, glared at him, straightened herself in her chair and said, 'So that's it? You go off to your whore in the North and I'm supposed to look after our child while you can just walk out?'

'Hanna, please,' he said.

'Don't 'Hanna, please me,' she spat at him. 'For months I don't hear from you. I don't get replies to my letters and now you blithely appear and tell me it's over.'

'Hanna, I did write to you and ask about Gilda. The situation with this woman just developed. I don't feel good about it, on the contrary, but it happened. Conditions up there were such that….well…..we didn't know if we'd be alive the next day.'

'And how do you think it has been for me,' said Hanna, 'I have the child to look after, and go to work. What do I do for money? When you come with your whore, I'll lose my job and my home. How will it be then for me and your child?'

She was beside herself. She couldn't believe that she no longer attracted him. When Hanna was angry she couldn't maintain the middle-class role she had learned to play. She reverted to the brutal yelled curses and vulgarities she had learned from her parents in her childhood home.

'I'm stuck with the kid! I never wanted children. You did,' she screamed at Hermann.

'Hanna, I can't take Gilda, Sabine is pregnant'.

'What! You're both whores,' Hanna raged, 'So, that night we made Gilda meant nothing to you?'

'Hanna,' Hermann implored, 'you know that isn't true, but so much has happened since then.' Hermann tried to reason with her but he knew it was impossible. She rose from her chair, glared at him, turned and stormed out. She didn't know what else to do.

Hermann's eyes followed Hanna's back as she quickly faded into the distance. It pained him to see her upset but it had not been the first time that he had seen her when she lashed out. He had seen how vindictive she could be. There was, he thought, a huge difference between Hanna as she was now and the calm, affectionate, homely woman he now planned to marry.

What really pained him the most, was that he might never see Gilda again. He had only had a single, brief meeting with her, then a tiny baby, when he was on leave. He vowed that he would do everything possible to keep in touch with her when the war ended. After Hermann returned to Lübeck Hanna began to take control of herself. With Herrmann gone from her life, as the months passed her thoughts turned to her survival and that of Gilda. From the narrow options open to her she came to the conclusion that Vladimir could be a replacement for Hermann. 'Post-war,' she pondered, 'when life returns to normal, Vladimir's social standing as a doctor would be high and he would become a wealthy member of the Viennese middle class. Gilda and I will be well cared for. I'll make sure that Vladimir wants me and then I'll be a doctor's wife.'

Hanna also vowed to herself, 'From now on, I will live my life as I want it. No one, not even Gilda will I allow to get close to me. No one will hurt me ever again. From my mother I took things because I had to accept them because she was my mother, but now I can choose, and I choose to do what I want. I will even make the most of this blasted war. I will never, ever, ever allow anyone to get the better of me. EVER!'

And so it was. No matter how much she had to suffer as a result of this vow, she maintained her resolution.

When Gilda was eight months old, she developed what was at first diagnosed as a severe cold. Vladimir disagreed saying, 'Hanna you should take Gilda to an eye specialist. I think it is more than a cold. If not checked, it could cause severe nerve damage.'

Hanna made an appointment with one of the best ophthalmologists in Vienna. On the day of the appointment she dressed in her best suit because she knew what an impression clothes made at that level of society. She waited in reception with Gilda and was finally called in. After some tests, the specialist said, 'It is quite clear, Frau Hollar, that your child is already blind in her left eye and the same will happen soon with her right eye.'

Hanna couldn't believe what she heard. 'How could I not have noticed that Gilda was blind in one eye,' she asked herself. She raised her voice at the specialist but tried to control herself, 'But there must be something you can do, you are supposed to be the best in Vienna.'

'I'm sorry, Gnädige Frau, it is too late. There is nothing that can be done. Your child will soon be blind in both eyes.'

So she took Gilda from one specialist to another and each gave the same diagnosis. Hanna was beside herself. She also started to feel guilty that she hadn't taken more notice of Gilda.

In the meantime, Vladimir enquired amongst his medical circle and found someone who the medical profession considered to be a 'fraud' - a doctor who practised alternative methods rejected by the ultra-conservative Viennese medical profession. Hanna was prepared to try anyone and anything to save Gilda's right eye. It was definitely too late for the left eye, but after some weeks of applying herbs and other such odd things, the nerve infection was arrested and the optic nerve for the right eye was no longer in danger.

Hanna had no idea what this man did, but she shed tears of gratitude when that doctor told her that Gilda's eyesight, though impaired, would be saved. He also said, 'Gilda's right eye vision will be exceptionally strong, and because it is in its developmental stage, it will compensate for the left eye.' 'But,' he added, 'because there is no muscle tension in Gilda's left eye she will be will be cross-eyed until she is about 16 years of age. At that time, she will be old enough to have surgery to straighten that eye.'

Hanna didn't care about that; it was too far into the future. For the moment, Gilda's right eye had healed and she could see.

From that moment on Hanna and Vladimir formed a different type of friendship. Partly, because she saw him as the person who was instrumental in saving her daughter's eye sight, and partly because of her plan to increase her upward trajectory into the middle-classes and beyond by replacing Hermann and marrying Vladimir. Nevertheless, she did have a new respect for him and his medical skills.

With the passing of time, Gilda came to consider Vladimir as her father. And over time, Hanna and Vladimir's relationship changed to something deeper and more intimate.

One evening, Vladimir said, 'There is something I have to tell you, Hanna, come and sit beside me. I cannot return to Macedonia. I am an active member of a political movement fighting for the separation of Macedonia from the rest of Jugoslavia. It's called the Internal Macedonian Revolutionary Organisation, IMRO, for short, and since the rise of Josip Broz Tito to power who is opposed to this, my life and anyone else's life in the IMRO is in danger.' Vladimir continued, 'If I were to go back to Macedonia or I am caught by any of Tito's agents, I will be shot as a traitor to Jugoslavia. Once the war is over and things stabilise, it may be different.' He waited for Hanna's reaction. She just looked at him in silent disbelief, waving her hand for him to continue. 'I am in constant contact with IMRO sympathisers and will be warned well in advance should the need to flee arise. I will not put you and Gilda in danger.' Hanna, shocked, remained silent. Vladimir asked her, 'What do you have to say?'

'What can I say', retorted Hanna, 'I have to digest what you have just said. It's not something I expected.' With that Vladimir left the apartment to meet a colleague.

'Well, what else must I endure? What choice do I have,' she asked herself after he left. 'I'll do what's best for me for as long as it suits me. I promised myself that.' But, out of the corner of her eyes, tear drops betrayed her attempt at being tough. She looked over at Gilda, asleep in her cot and thought, 'She is such a good child, never causes me any problems and she is always smiling. Why did that disease have to happen to her eye? It's so ugly. Why did I bring her into the world? That one last stupid night with Hermann.' The tears rolled down her face. Straightening up she said, 'I must stay with him. I have no choice. Where would I go? What would I do?'

She was jolted back to reality by a knock at the door. 'Who is there?' she enquired. No one answered. 'Answer me. Who is there?'

CHAPTER 7
VIENNA TO SALZBURG
1945 – 1946

Hanna saw an envelope slip under the front door followed by footsteps running down the stone outer stairs. The war was finally over but after her last conversation with Vladimir, she was not sure what to expect.

From the time of her birth, Gilda knew Vladimir as her father. Vladimir was a complaisant companion because he must have been used to being hen-pecked. He would always agree to keep the peace whenever he met with Hanna's disapproval or contrary opinion. That didn't always work well for Gilda later on as it meant she had no one to stand up for her when needed.

Vladimir, a Jugoslav, was of a different ethnic origin to Hanna and was much older than Hanna by 17 years. Because Hanna hadn't known her father, a husband and father image now merged via Vladimir into one identity complemented by Hanna's expectations of a higher social standing. In the Vienna Hanna knew, a medical specialist had a higher ranking than a wholesaler/retailer. For Hanna, these things were important.

However, conditions changed quickly due to Dr Vladimir Dobinski's politically involvement. Things in Vienna had gone from bad to worse because of the Russian invasion of the city. One night Vladimir told Hanna, 'I must flee Vienna. It's no longer possible for me to stay. The IMRO partisans are getting too close and it's not clear anymore who is to be trusted.'

'What do you propose to do?' she asked surprised.

'I applied for and have been accepted for a posting in Salzburg as Chief Superintendent of the American Hospital for Refugees. It will give me time and it'll be easier to flee Austria should that become necessary. The Swiss border is close by.'
She looked at him amazed and raised her voice in disbelief, 'Why didn't you tell me you had applied for that position? When were

you going to tell me? What about me, and Gilda, where do we fit into all this? Do we come with you?'

'No, you can't come with me, you'll need to follow and make your own way there. I'll be going in an American army convoy and they will only take wives and children. We'll find a way for you to join me,' he replied.

Hanna looked at him and yelled this time; she couldn't believe what she was hearing, 'Are you insane?' she raged at him, 'All forms of public transport have been blown up or haven't you noticed; there aren't any; there's nothing. All because of your involvement in some stupid cause that hasn't a chance of winning.'

He interrupted her and tried to appease her, 'Hanna, bitte, please, please, listen to me. I've been talking to people who know of American truck drivers who carry goods south and who take passengers for extra money. I'll get you to travel with one of those.'

Hanna looked at her options, woman with no husband, no family, no job, no home, and a baby. She couldn't count on Hermann's family anymore as there was another daughter-in-law on the horizon, and another grandchild, each of which completely severed Hanna from Hermann's family circle.

'Should I stay with him? Or should I ask Fritz or Marta or Helga for help? I could stay with any of them for a while, especially Helga in Kirchberg-am-Wagram, although I've heard the Russians are going through the villages in the north of Austria and coming in from the west of Vienna, ransacking and ravaging everything in their path. No, too risky, even Vienna is becoming too dangerous. I'll be better off with the Americans, they are less barbaric.'

And so, she was forced to prepare to flee her beautiful apartment. Clandestine arrangements were made for her nomadic life to begin. Being so young, Gilda didn't remember any of that and wasn't consciously affected by it, although, as we now know, what happens to a child between the ages 0 to 7 is imprinted on her subconscious mind and in her psyche until removed or replaced by better experiences.

Before Hanna left, she went to see her in-laws and to bid them farewell. 'I am very much against what has happened, Hanna,' her father-in-law said while holding Gilda, 'In my religion, we do not divorce but Hermann is my son and I must support him. The fighting on the front cannot have been easy. You and Gilda are always welcome.' He took a long look at his granddaughter before giving her back to Hanna. Each of the other family members also wished Hanna the best for the future and re-affirmed that she was always welcome.

'Thank you,' Hanna replied emotionally, tears evident in her eyes, 'I'll remember your kind words. I'll leave the key to the apartment in the letter box and I should be out of it within the week.' They all embraced, tears flowed and finally Hanna left to finish packing. They would never see each other again.

Vladimir had already left for Salzburg. He had organised a lift for her to leave Vienna in two days. The American driver would collect her from the apartment because she had Gilda, a pram and luggage. On the day of her departure it was still dark as Hanna went down to the footpath. She felt a great weight on her heart; she felt so alone and she cried like never before, her tears falling on Gilda as she held her in her arms. 'I must be strong. I will survive this. We will survive this, my darling child.'

Suddenly she heard an American voice, 'Come on. Hop on. We've got to get going, Mam.' The truck had arrived. 'We need to be out of the city before daylight.' The driver put the pram and luggage in the back and helped her with Gilda up the high step to the front seat. She was grateful for the warmth inside the cabin.

They travelled south-west to Salzburg as fast as the truck could go given there were farmers with produce on horse-drawn carts on the road, and many detours because large sections of the highway had been destroyed. Gilda was cradled in Hanna's arms and mostly slept or ate. 'She is such a contented child,' Hanna thought looking at her and giving her a light squeeze so as not to wake her.

'Cute kid,' the driver said, 'I have a boy about that age back home. Happened when I was on leave.' He said grinning and winked. Hanna didn't understand what he said and just smiled and nodded. 'She probably can't understand me,' the driver thought, 'At least I'm not talking to myself, not mad yet.' he laughed inwardly. 'By the way, I'm only going to Linz now. You'll have to find another lift to get you to Salzburg. I'll see if any of my buddies are there and where they're going,' he announced.

All Hanna understood was Linz.

This time she could only find a man who had a jeep. 'I can take you to Salzburg but the pram has to stay. It won't fit in the back.' Hanna didn't understand so he took the pram from her, put it on the footpath and made hand movements that left no doubt that he meant 'no' to the pram. And so, she hitched a ride with another American soldier.

The trip from Linz to Salzburg was uneventful. This driver preferred to listen to the radio and not talk, which suited Hanna. He stopped once to buy cigarettes and Hanna took the opportunity to buy snacks for herself but fed the baby with food she had prepared before leaving Vienna.

Finally, Hanna and Gilda arrived at the hospital. The truck driver had been a decent fellow and drove her out into the countryside of Salzburg where the hospital was situated.

'Ah, Liebling, darling,' said Vladimir as he helped her from the jeep, 'I have been so worried about you.' He kissed Hanna on the cheek and picked Gilda up to give her a big hug. 'You must be exhausted,' he said while holding Gilda, 'Let me show you to our quarters. You might like to rest or freshen up and then join us,' he suggested.
'I would like to freshen up,' agreed Hanna, 'and I'll see how Gilda feels after I have given her a bath. She may want to sleep.'

'There is a cot and also a pram in case you want to come and join us. We are on the balcony having drinks. Or I can stay here with you,' Vladimir added quickly.

Hanna replied dramatically, 'No, I think a glass of wine will be just perfect after the last horrific days, you cannot imagine what I have been through.'

Vladimir went back to the balcony while Hanna freshened up and fed Gilda. Hanna always planned ahead with her thinking. 'I must look my best. After all, Vladimir is the Superintendent of the hospital and we have an image to uphold. I will take the pram so that I do not need to hold Gilda.'

It became apparent to Hanna that afternoon drinks on the balcony were a daily routine. She was the only woman in their circle. The other men were either single or their wives were back home. Hanna enjoyed being the only woman, she was quite a coquette and thrived on the adulation of others, especially men. There was always a lot of laughter as the various drinks were consumed and it was clear that, although the war was over, the motto was, 'Live, love and be merry, for tomorrow you could be dead.'
'This is one of the most modern centres for medical treatment I've seen,' Vladimir informed Hanna, 'I am most impressed. I could not have asked for a better posting under the circumstances.'

One morning Hanna said to her 'husband', 'Vladimir, I have been wondering, would it be possible for me to have some sort of work here? Perhaps I could be placed in a nursing ward to learn the basics of nursing?'

He looked at her surprised and asked, 'Why?'
'You know how I always plan for the future. It is clear that we do not know how long we will be here, nor do we know where we will be going should we have to leave, given your political involvement.'

'Yes,' replied Vladimir, still not sure what she was getting at.
'If you could organise that I have some sort of occupation in the wards, I could see first-hand what a nurse does. Why should I hang around and do nothing all day when I could be learning something?'

'Well, I don't know,' replied Vladimir.

'Oh, come on, you are the Boss, the Superintendent of the hospital, you can organise that for me if you want to... or... don't you want to?' She looked accusingly at him.

Vladimir could see that he was cornered. 'Yes, I am in charge but I must also consult with my team.'

'Well, darling, I suggest you consult with your team as a matter of urgency, I will not sit around and be nursemaid to Gilda. There are plenty of assistant nurses who can do that. I want to be in the thick of things. Do you understand?'

'Yes,' he replied, 'I will approach them tomorrow.' And so it was that Hanna now worked with her 'husband' and his colleagues. She was in her element, the centre of attention as the only woman in the group and she was proving herself competent in her duties. She made it clear to the nurses who she was and who her 'husband' was, and they gave her the attention she felt she deserved.

A period of relative family tranquility and stability ensued in Salzburg. Luckily most of the hospital personnel spoke German as neither Vladimir nor Hanna spoke much English. Because of Austria's past political expansionist policy of annexing surrounding countries, most of the refugees at the hospital spoke some German. There were Hungarians, Serbs, Slovenes, Slovaks, and Czechs.

Hanna was delighted that everyone now called her Frau Doktor because she was 'married' to Herr Doktor Vladimir Dobinski. Austrian social custom dictates that the wife takes on her husband's credentials.

And so, the seed of a new history of Hanna's heritage and the Dobinski family started to germinate in her mind. Imagination took hold with full force. All of her past was being cancelled out, bit by bit. The Dobinskis were now a doctor's family, father, mother and child, and that became not only their present but also their future which would be substantially embellished and embroidered as time went on.

Most of the other expatriates were in the diverse medical areas offered by the hospital, a world Hanna found intoxicating. She mixed with exotic people in a profession she could only have dreamed of belonging to. As she was very attractive and knew it, she received a lot of attention. Flirting was a common pastime.

Perhaps Vladimir was aware of it, perhaps not, because he often lived in his own world. He loved medicine and his whole life revolved around how he could help people with his undeniable talent and skills. Apart from his politics, he wasn't concerned with daily matters and although he knew he was good at what he did, he was also modest about it.

Being medical people, numerous medical staff at the hospital showed a great deal of interest in what had happened to Gilda's eye and so it was a point of conversation whenever people first saw the little girl. Speculation as to how it could have been saved was always on the agenda. There were so many 'experts' with widely differing opinions. Many of these people did not have university medical qualifications; they may have just been okay on the Front, bandaging the wounded or doing on-the-spot amputations and other procedures to save a life. Nevertheless, they felt 'qualified'. The conversation always ended with Hanna saying pityingly, 'It is such a shame that her eye is so ugly, otherwise Gilda would be quite pretty.'

There was a sand pit in the hospital grounds where Gilda played alone as there were no other children in the compound, and certainly none in the surrounding area with whose parents Hanna would have socialised. Now and then Vladimir might come to the sand pit but he and Hanna were usually occupied with the other expats, chatting and drinking and engrossed in philosophical discussions although, they did stay near to keep an eye on her.

And so the days passed with an unremarkable sameness, until one day things seemed different. Hanna and Vladimir's tone and behaviour changed; they started to whisper to each other in private to ensure that their colleagues wouldn't hear what they were saying. Vladimir had told a trusted colleague who knew of his involvement with the Internal Macedonian Revolutionary Organisation (IMRO) that he would need to leave very quickly when the time came.

That time had come and he said to his trusted colleague, 'Vukasin, it is time for me to leave Salzburg. I have a letter in my top drawer that puts you in charge. Please pass on my best wishes to the administration and to the group and tell them, I am sorry not to have wished each of them goodbye but we must leave tonight. Can you drive us to the station at 7.30 PM, please?'

'Of course, dear Vladimir,' replied Vukasin, 'We shall miss you. 7.30 PM, yes?'

'Yes, thank you,' replied Vladimir as they shook hands.

That night, Gilda had been woken up by muffled voices outside her room and then her mother came in and told her to get up. 'Gilda, it's time to dress,' Hanna said, 'It's time to leave Salzburg.' Robotically, Gilda let her mother dress her and then she saw her mother put her belongings into one of the battered suitcases. It was 7.20 PM and in the dark they left their quarters.

'Mama, why in the dark?' Gilda asked her mother.

'We can't turn the lights on, Gilda,' Hanna replied, 'the hospital is under observation.' Gilda was too young to understand what that meant; she just did as she was told. They scrambled through a thicket, and then through a hole in the stone fence where Vukasin was waiting for them on a side road. He drove them to the railway station, shook hands with Vladimir and Hanna, squeezed Gilda's cheek, and said, 'Good luck, and I hope we meet again one day.' And with that he turned and left, clearly upset.

'Now, Gilda,' began Hanna, 'don't say a word until I give you permission. Do you understand? Not a word.'

'Ja, Mama,' replied the little girl. They waited in a darkened part of the station until a train arrived; they climbed into a carriage and it sped off. Again Hanna and Gilda were on the run, but this time with Vladimir. This time it had to be out of Austria as they had heard of executions of IMRO enemies in Vienna and so they headed west to Paris. They hoped that that would be far enough away to deter IMRO agents from following them. Time would tell.

Gilda had been happy in Salzburg, it was peaceful in the countryside where the hospital was situated and, as she was mostly alone, she could imagine and create her world the way she wanted it to be and continued to build her new and bigger castles in the air. Now she was heading to Paris.

CHAPTER 8
PARIS
1946 – 1950

The train trip from Salzburg to Paris had its share of heart-stopping moments. The first one was at border control into Switzerland. When the train stopped an official came on board to check passports. 'I hope they aren't looking for anything in particular,' Hanna whispered to Vladimir. 'Or anyone in particular,' he replied with a concerned look.

Glancing at Vladimir and Hanna, the official asked, 'Are you two travelling together?'

'Yes, Officer,' replied Hanna sweetly. He looked at them and then at Gilda. Both Hanna and Vladimir knew that their different surnames would cause attention. Hanna had obtained her divorce from Hermann as did Vladimir from his wife. They had the papers ready but they hadn't had time to get married. The officers quizzed Vladimir because his passport clearly showed an extended stay in Graz, the short stay in Vienna as well as the year in Salzburg.

'What were you doing in Austria?' the official asked stonily. Vladimir's explanation must have satisfied the official as he silently returned his passport.

'Hallo, kleines Mädchen, little girl, who do you belong to?' he asked Gilda with a smile. Before Gilda could reply, Hanna answered quickly, 'She belongs to me, Sir.' The official then moved on. Both Hanna and Vladimir sat still and waited till he was out of sight and hearing.

'Phew, that was tense,' Hanna said quietly, clutching her handbag.

'Yes,' was all Vladimir could muster and he sank in his seat.
A more terrifying moment occurred as they were about to leave Switzerland and cross into France. The train stopped in the middle of nowhere before arriving at border control. Two French uniformed officers went through the carriage closely inspecting all

passports and asking for other papers. Vladimir and Hanna were in the last seats of their carriage. One of the officers came up to them, while the other continued looking at the papers of another passenger in the seats in front of them.

Suddenly, the passenger rose, pushed the official out of the way, seized his passport, collided with the other officer before he jumped out of the train door. The other uniformed official yelled to his colleague and the two went in pursuit of the fugitive. Vladimir went white. Hanna looked at him and was terrified for him, her hand trembling as she held her passport. Both she and Vladimir realised what had happened. They sat waiting, Hanna praying to Mother Mary that the train would go before the men came back. It seemed an eternity till the train slowly started moving, the horn blew several times and the train picked up speed.

'The man who ran out must have been a fugitive….' Hanna ventured softly.

'Yes, yes,' interrupted Vladimir, 'Be quiet. Let's just hope they didn't get on in another part of the train.' They were on high alert for the rest of the trip, especially when the train needed to stop as the route was not yet completely cleared of war debris. They sat in silence, tensing every time someone entered the carriage.

It was not until the train was going full speed through the French countryside that they started to relax. When they arrived at the Gare de Lyon, despite the huge numbers of people and confusion at the station they at last found connecting city trains that took them to their flat. The Dobinskis had procured accommodation in advance, a two-room flat in the suburb of Les Lilas.

That night as Gilda slept, Vladimir and Hanna drank wine and celebrated their exit from Salzburg and their entry to this next stage in their life. Both were relieved that they had safely completed such a dangerous journey and hoped that they would now be safe. Neither Vladimir nor Hanna had a problem settling in Paris. Gilda, now two and a half years of age, had developed a typical child's habit of always wanting to know the reason "why" she had to do something or "why" things were the way they were, why, why, why... It wasn't because she was a difficult child; she was simply curious and wanted to know and understand things. It did drive her mother to distraction, as Hanna had to be the one in authority at all times. Being questioned impinged on this power play. It wasn't that Hanna was a bad person; it was that she had been brought up with strict guidelines of behaviour.

As a daughter, you were expected to behave in certain ways. As a mother Hanna believed that she had the right to demand respect and had these expectations of other people. As a doctor's wife, there were guidelines as well because people in different social standings had certain ways that they were expected to behave in a very strongly and inflexibly structured social system – such as that of the Vienna of Hanna's childhood and teenage years. Friction developed between Hanna and Gilda, particularly as Gilda's teachers encouraged her curiosity. She was affectionately known as 'La Petite Mademoiselle Pourquoi', "Little Miss Why". These French teachers nurtured Gilda's enquiring spirit.

Hanna had to find work. She wanted work that could be useful universally. She had received a glowing reference from Marta about her fictitious work in her clothing Atelier. Through this reference Hanna was able to obtain an apprenticeship with a French couturier, Germaine Schirrer of Boulevard Malesherbes, working there seven days a week to learn the dressmaking trade. The hours were long. Hanna could have worked fewer days but she and Vladimir needed the money and she was the only who could legally work. In any case, if she didn't work seven days, she would have been one of the first to be dismissed if there was a need to cut staff.

Hanna's Austrian background meant that she had to be careful because some of her colleagues, cautious about the political background of Austrians suspected that she may have had a Nazi background. In fact, some 'colleagues' openly suggested she was a Nazi.

At first Hanna couldn't speak French and had to rely on those who spoke German to translate for her. She was successful at the Atelier and at the end of 1948, received her Certificat-Diplôm from the Académie de Coupe de Paris, and continued working at the Atelier as a full-time First Class dressmaker.

Vladimir couldn't work as he had to lay low and in any case his medical qualifications were not recognised in France. He couldn't do manual work as it would have "ruined his hands" for when he could again perform surgery. Consequently, he stayed in the flat all day. He was a quiet person so Gilda had little to do with him when they were alone, notably when she returned home from school. Although he was a pleasant fellow, he had an annoying habit that Hanna and Gilda found difficult to get used to. He chain-smoked. Their flat being tiny quickly filled with smoke.

Hanna would come home after a hard, long day at work and would find burned out cigarette butts in ashtrays and ash on the table, and the stinking cigarette smell and smoke throughout the flat. 'Do you have to smoke so much?' she admonished. 'I work all these hours and most of the money goes up in smoke. And why can't you clean the ashtrays, wipe the table and open the windows? It stinks in here,' she continued.

He would then do as he was told but the next day the conversation would be the same. Hanna soon learned that in his culture women were regarded as the "servant" of the household and the men, even educated men such as Vladimir, were patriarchal figures, and as such were not used to, or inclined to, doing anything around the house. That was something Vladimir would learn he had to change.

When Gilda came home from school, she was sent to her parent's room and when her mother came home, she could often hear her and her father fighting in the other room. Hanna was always tired and Vladimir refused do anything around the two-roomed flat, including even some minor food preparation. Hanna was used to being pampered, not be the sole bread winner, as well as the maid servant. 'When this is all over, I will stop this. I know how to make a man do what I want.' she said. Gilda's parents slept in the bedroom while she slept where they ate, there was no other room.

Because of her age, Gilda was uninhibited about chatting with people, she quickly spoke everyday French. Her speaking skills were aided because every day of the week, from Monday to Sunday, she went with other children in the District to a little suburban co-educational pre-school run by Catholic nuns. On week days they undertook normal class-learning activities but on Saturdays and Sundays, the program changed. On Saturdays, the children would sit on a cart pulled by a donkey with one of the nuns holding the reigns and amidst loud laughter and singing they headed off into the woods populated by friendly "fairies and goblins".

'Alors, vite, vite, allez-y,' the nun on the cart would cry. 'Hurry, hurry, come on, the others on the bicycles will beat us there.' And the children would all squeal with laughter, hop onto the cart and with much cheering coax the donkey along to their forest adventures.

At the same time, the other nuns would ride their bicycles with their black head gear flying behind them as they left Paris. The day would pass with playing games amongst the trees and fields with the nuns chasing the children or, they would play hide and seek and role on the grass down the small slopes. When it was time to eat, the children would gaily lunch with the nuns.

Sundays were slightly different but still lots of fun. They started with a children's version of Mass, followed by games in the schoolyard and maybe a little walk around parts of the suburbs where destruction caused by bombing raids had been cleaned up.

On the way home, Gilda would pass the fruit cart of an old man in her street and, a couple of times a week he would give her a pear. She would greet him with, 'Bonjour, monsieur, ça va? Hello, how are you?' and the inevitable reply would be 'Ah, ma petite amie, oui, ça va, Ah, my little friend, yes, I'm well,' replied the pear vendor, 'Would you like a pear today?' he asked.

'Oh, oui, merci, monsieur, oh, yes, thank you very much,' she replied. Gilda told her mother about this kind old man, but Hanna told her not to speak to him. 'Oh, we don't talk, Mama,' Gilda replied. 'And you mustn't take a pear from him,' said Hanna, 'walk on the other side of the road,' her mother ordered. But Gilda always thanked the pear vendor for his gift and beyond these few words of gratitude Gilda never really spoke to him. To avoid Hanna's anger, Gilda ensured that the pear was completely devoured well before she returned home.

Soon, men and some women started coming to visit Vladimir and Hanna's tiny apartment. They spoke a language that Gilda didn't understand although she had heard something similar in Salzburg at the hospital. She found out as time went by that sometimes the language was Serbo-Croatian and at other times it was Vladimir's native language of Macedonian. Hanna didn't understand either language, but she had to learn it quickly, at least some words, as these people were frequently at the flat when she came home. To Hanna's disgust, these guests also smoked heavily. The Dobinski's flat was at the top of a very steep, long flight of stairs which scared Gilda and she always held on to the railings, however, she asked to be allowed to sit there, outside away from the noise and smoke. Hanna allowed her to sit there until she heard Gilda talking to one of the women who also lived on the same floor and then Gilda was now longer allowed to sit outside.

The arguing between Hanna and Vladimir continued, and Gilda often had to run errands or wait downstairs during the evening so that her parents could discuss things that were too grown up for her, such as their money problems, Vladimir smoking too much, his loud friends always being at their place when Hanna came home, and even denying him marital favours if he didn't comply with her demands.

Gilda would sit on the ground outside their building until Hanna called her up. But Gilda was never really alone, as passersby, usually older people, would stop and talk to her which she enjoyed but never told her mother about. It didn't take her long to learn French, and it soon became her preferred language. She would hear and speak German at home but French was now more natural. The old people liked Gilda as she was a sweet child, always polite and happy. Some would give her a sweet or a piece of fruit.

Gilda remembered how proud she was the first time her mother was called to the school to discuss her report. 'Ah, bonjour Madame Dobinski', greeted the nun. 'It is a pleasure to meet you. Gilda is such a wonderful child, Elle est une vrai mignonne, she's such a sweetie,' she told Hanna. 'Look at her results,' the nun said, 'In every subject she has the highest marks. It is all so easy for her. Even her behaviour is excellent and all her teachers like her very much. Even though she likes to talk a lot, she is never a problem.'

'Ah, but Sister, it is such a shame about Gilda's eye,' Hanna replied and lovingly looked at her daughter. The inward-turn of Gilda's left eye was becoming more pronounced as she grew. It annoyed Hanna when so much praise was lavished on Gilda and so she would bring this up; this was not how she was brought up. 'If you praise a child too much she gets lazy and gets a swollen head,' Hanna had frequently heard her mother say.

'Oh, but Madame Dobinski, c'est rien, it is nothing. Gilda is such a nice girl and so intelligent. In any case it can be fixed later on,' responded the nun.
'But she is such a tomboy.' Hanna countered strongly. 'Mais, non, she is an active child.' said the nun smiling at Gilda and patting her on the head. These report cards were the same for the three-and-a-half years Gilda went to school there, and each year, without fail, she received the "Prize For Always Being Cheerful and in Good Spirits", as well as other academic prizes.

Suddenly things started to change at home, Vladimir spoke with urgency in his voice that prompted Gilda to ask, 'Is something the matter, Papa.' Vladimir didn't answer at first, he just looked at her; he didn't know what to answer.

'You are too young to understand, Gilda,' her mother replied and then in a nicer voice, 'Just go and play in the bedroom.' Gradually, fewer people visited them, until only the same man would come and stay for a short time, speak in Macedonian as though something was wrong and then leave.

One day, Gilda came home from school and found all their belongings packed and their two suitcases were aligned near the entrance door.

'What's going on? Are we moving? Are we moving to another flat? Are we going somewhere else?' Gilda asked looking concerned.

She had heard her parents talking about a place called South America but she had no idea where that was. She couldn't understand why their belongings were packed, sitting at the entrance door. 'What is happening?' Gilda asked again with greater force when no one answered her previous questions.

'Oh, Gilda you will drive me mad with all your questions. Can't you just wait and then do as you are told. We are leaving Paris. You don't need to know any more.' Hanna replied impatiently. 'What? Leaving Paris? No, no, I don't want to leave! I won't go,' Gilda cried back. 'We are leaving and that is that, and if you keep yelling, I'll slap you, then you'll stop.' Hanna threatened.

Gilda was frantic, she didn't want to leave. She cried and pleaded for them not to go. 'If you have to go, you go, you can leave me behind. I can stay with the nuns.'

'Be quiet,' Hanna yelled, 'be quiet or I'll slap you.' Gilda was about to say something when she reeled in pain at the force of the slap across her face. She had never experienced anything like that before. 'Why did you do that to me? That hurt,' she cried placing her hand on her aching cheek. Her face burned, she was terrified, shocked. She ducked in case another slap came. Her mother had become volatile and often threatened to slap her, but she had never actually hit her before. Gilda sobbed and sobbed and made a last attempt to stay. She started to pull her things away from the rest of the luggage.

Hanna grabbed her wrist and glaring at her, bellowed, 'Leave your things alone, we are leaving and you are coming with us.' She then dragged Gilda into the bedroom and shut the door. 'Now, your darling nun should see how you behave. You're nothing but a trouble-maker.' Hanna yelled through the door.

Hanna saw Vladimir look at her. 'My nerves have had it, and then that child carries on like that. What else was there for me to do? Don't look at me like that. It's alright for you to be calm. You have been sitting home all day doing nothing while I have been working day and night.' she burst out.

Vladimir was about to answer when there was a knock at the door. It had become late in the evening and the frequent visitor came to collect them and their luggage. 'Hurry, we have to leave. The train will come soon.'

Hanna, still in a rage opened the bedroom door, grabbed Gilda by the arm and dragged her so fast down the long flight of stairs that Gilda fell down most of them. She was crying in pain. 'Arête, arête, stop. You're hurting me. Je ne veux pas; je ne veux pas aller; je veux rester ici! No, no I don't want to; I don't want to go; I want to stay here,' she kept begging but Hanna dragged her into the car and they drove off. The two men looked on helpless.

'Did you have to hit Gilda and drag her down the stairs?' Vladimir asked Hanna when they were in the car. 'Shut up!' she answered, 'if it weren't for you, we wouldn't be in this mess. Don't tell me what I can and can't do to Gilda, she will obey me. She's my daughter and I can do with her whatever I feel like, remember that.' Hanna shouted.

As they drove through the Paris's darkened streets, Vladimir kept looking back to see if they were being followed. He had panicked several times following reports of increasing IMRO assassinations in Paris. They seemed to have been driving a long time, going further and further out of Paris. After turning into a laneway, the car slowed and stopped at an isolated darkened railway station and as they left the car one of Vladimir's waiting friends greeted them. A tiny yellow light barely illuminated the deserted platform. Gilda wished she could go back to Paris, but that was not to be.

Very soon she heard the sound of a train horn and they moved closer to the edge of the platform. Vladimir and their driver shook hands; the latter muttered "good luck" and drove off as the train came to a halt.

Hanna, Vladimir and Gilda climbed in with their luggage. Gilda was in a state of shock and inwardly a part of her froze. She sat on her seat, staring into space, still holding her throbbing cheek unaware of anything around her, she was confused. Her mind was numb but her body was still in pain and her head ached.

The whistle blew, the train picked up momentum and rattled on to its ultimate destination, the Italian port city of Genoa. It was toward the end of 1950. Gilda was six years old.

CHAPTER 9
GENOA TO FREMANTLE
1950

The Dobinskis arrived exhausted at the port of Genoa in the northwest of Italy. Vladimir dropped the suitcase as he was bringing it down from the train. It was so worn that the latches broke open and he had to find rope to hold it together. It wasn't hard to find rope at a dock and the suitcase was quickly, but temporally functional again. They had to take their luggage wherever they went because they couldn't get a porter. In any case, Hanna was afraid that their belongings might be stolen if they were left with someone. 'You can't trust any of these people,' she said looking disgusted at the types she saw.

Hanna was not only a snob, but she also had a distorted view of people of certain nationalities. Her opinions were always based on their history centuries ago and so they remained barbaric, uncivilised and untrustworthy or whatever she heard about them growing up. She and Vladimir went to enquire about the next ship that left Genoa to any overseas destination, preferably a long way from Europe.

'Do you have a preference?' Vladimir asked Hanna.

'I don't really care, we just have to get out of here because of you, but I don't want to go to any of those strange countries. Those uncivilised ones in Asia, and certainly not Russia. What about America or Canada? Dora, who visited us in Paris at the beginning, went to Canada and she likes it there,' she replied with faux authority.

While they had lived in Paris, Vladimir had made enquiries with his compatriots so he had some idea about what ships could be sailing and their destination. There was no longer a chance of going to South America, because that ship had come in late from its previous voyage and consequently didn't have a specified time of departure. It was imperative that they leave Europe as soon as possible.

Vladimir was told that the next ship out would probably be to Australia.

'Oh, but that is at the other end of the world,' complained Hanna, 'I haven't heard anything good about it. It's also too hot there, only good for the natives. Oh, Vladimir, there must be somewhere else.' Hanna was beside herself. If truth be told, there were not that many reports about Australia, but Hanna always focused on the negative and liked to exaggerate to validate her usually uniformed opinions.

'We have no choice, Hanna, Darling,' affirmed Vladimir, 'It is the only one leaving this week that is some distance from Europe.' 'Yes, that's right, we have no choice,' Hanna repeated angrily at him. This once self-assured, confident, resourceful Viennese woman had changed. She was now nervy, aggressive and negative though she could be charming when she felt it suited her purpose.

There was too much that was out of her control and too much that she was not familiar with. Fortunately, there were still some vacancies on the Australian-bound vessel and because Hanna and Vladimir were paying for their passage they did not have to wait for official authorization for subsided fares. Vladimir and Hanna had married in Paris so all their documents now had the same surname.

The requisite official papers could be rapidly approved. However, they did need someone in Australia to act as a guarantor for them.

'But, we don't know anyone in Australia,' said a dejected Vladimir. An official who had been listening to their conversation came over and said, 'I'm sorry, sir, but I couldn't help overhearing. We have a list of registered people by nationality who can act as guarantors in Australia.

There is a Macedonian man in Townsville, north Queensland. We can contact him and see if he is willing to guarantee for you.' Vladimir and Hanna were to later discover that their Australian guarantor was a loyalist Macedonian, but not an IMRO member.

'Hanna,' Vladimir exclaimed excitedly to his wife, 'Did you hear that? That is wonderful news.' 'Yes, yes, that would be very kind, thank you, thank you very much,' exclaimed Vladimir. 'Come back at 10.00pm and we should have an answer by then,' added the official. 'Let's see first if it happens,' replied Hanna dubiously.

'What shall we do till 10.00 PM?' Hanna asked. 'I'm hungry,' complained Gilda, 'When can we eat?' Both Hanna and Vladimir realised that it had been hours since they last had a snack on the train. 'Yes, I'm hungry too,' added Hanna, 'How much money do we have?' They had been given some Italian Lira by Vladimir's friend in Paris. How much that would buy, they had no idea.

'Look,' said Vladimir, 'over there, there is a food kiosk. Let's go over and see what they have and what it costs.' Gilda held onto Vladimir's hand - the wharf was very busy and people were going in all directions.

They saw that the stand sold sliced bread with salami or cheese on it. 'That will do,' exclaimed Vladimir, 'We have enough Italian money for five pieces of bread, coffee and water.'

'Ciao, signore,' greeted the vendor cheerfully, 'Cosa le porto? What can I get for you?' Vladimir pointed at what they wanted; the vendor placed the breads on pieces of paper and with a flourish he made cups of espresso coffee. 'Certo, signor e signora, cinque pani, si? Due con formaggio e tre con carne, five breads, two with cheese and three with meat?' exclaimed the vendor as confirmation, 'E, un dolce per la piccola ragazza, eh, signorina,' he said with a smile as he gave Gilda a free sweet. 'Merci, monsieur,' said a smiling Gilda.

The Dobinski family ate contentedly beside the waters of the Ligurian Sea. It was late afternoon and the weather had become chilly but fortunately they had warm jackets. Never had a humble slice of dry bread adorned with a thin slice of sausage or an equally thin slice of cheese tasted so good. The strong espresso hit its mark and Hanna and Vladimir felt a renewed surge of energy.

Gilda gleefully watched birds vying for the food crumbs they dropped. 'Look, at the birds, they are eating our crumbs,' Gilda called excitedly to her parents pointing to the birds. 'Don't give them your food, Gilda,' scolded her mother, 'You won't get any more to eat until tomorrow morning.'

They walked along the wharf looking at the expanse of water that would provide the starting point for their long journey to Australia and take them far, far away from Europe. Each was engrossed in their own thoughts.

'Adieu, my beloved Vienna, will I ever see you again? Adieu, my dear, dear friends,' Hanna thought.

Hanna's shoulders drooped as she thought of what she was leaving behind. Vladimir's thoughts were similar as he sat looking into the distance. 'I hope we will be far enough away now to be safe, but I will be so far from my children,' he thought. 'Will I ever see you again, my darlings?' Gilda's thoughts were elsewhere. She was thrilled at the prospect of boat travel and enjoyed her immediate surroundings; the sea, the waves splashing up the side of the timber pier wall, sea birds swooping on fish and food scraps that lay on the wharf, and ships taking on cargo. Where to look first so not too miss anything?

Finally, it was 9.45 PM. They could wait no longer and they headed off to the Immigration building.

'You're in luck, folks,' said the official cheerfully as he saw them approaching, 'Your application for the guarantor in Townsville has been approved. If you haven't anywhere to stay the night you can now board the ship, the Flotta Lauro, and go to your berth. Dinner will be extra if you want to eat on board tonight but meals are included in the fare from tomorrow's breakfast until you disembark in Brisbane.'

They had recently eaten, and having no money to pay for a shipboard dinner, eating on board their ship was not an option. Hanna had kept a single piece of bread with cheese should Gilda get hungry later on.

Gilda had found the hustle and bustle of the activities in Genoa fascinating and was intrigued by the different-looking people at the port.

Gilda's ability to make the most of situations, to take life as it came, was a skill she'd been forced to acquire from the events in her short life to date. It was a skill which would see her through her growing years and later. She too had learnt not to let anyone or anything affect her for too long. Gilda had gone from being an open-natured child, to one who closed herself off from expressing herself, especially to her parents. She seemingly just tagged along, outwardly doing as she was told. Inwardly, however, her world was growing more and more interesting and real with all her new experiences and imaginings. And she loved talking to new people. New people didn't make demands and soon left again; this was a developing approach to relationships.

Hanna constantly warned Gilda of the consequences of disobedience. When the family first arrived in Genoa Hanna said, 'Gilda, you must behave and do exactly what I tell you or we'll leave you here and see if you can find your way back to Paris again.' Gilda retreated into her own self-contained world, a world she created with her imagination, a world made up of beautiful experiences, different places and people who were nice to her, just as the nuns in Paris had been.

The Dobinskis had nowhere else to stay so they gratefully boarded the ship. When they reached their lower berth, they saw that they were in small communal accommodation. Hesitatingly, they asked if anyone spoke German or French. No one spoke French but quite a few spoke broken German. After introducing themselves, Hanna asked, 'Does anyone know of someone who has gone to Townsville in northern Queensland?' No one knew of anyone who had gone there, but someone had heard of people who had gone to Rockhampton, which was en route and they said, it was a backward place. With that, Hanna and Vladimir concluded that because Townsville was further north it would be more isolated and primitive. 'Probably where black people live,' Hanna said knowingly.

Hanna was not at all happy with the accommodation nor with the people she would be 'living' with. Hanna and Vladimir had a fitful night's sleep; the ship at its berth rocked with the waves. They were not used to sleeping with a group of strangers and some of the men snored. Only Gilda slept well.

After the ship left port, life onboard took a turn for the better. Gilda was six and a half, and as Italians loved children, most of the Italian staff and sailors kept an eye on her. Because she was mostly on her own, Gilda soon started to feel relaxed and happy again. Shipboard accommodation for the Dobinski's was Spartan but being a child and lately being used to living humbly, that didn't bother Gilda. During the day, she participated in the deck activities, quickly falling asleep in her modest space in the evenings. She also had more freedom because her parents were engrossed in their distinctly separate worlds.

Hanna and Vladimir talked to other older people who were émigrés and who commiserated with each other about how bad life had become and debated and speculated about what the new country would be like. Also top of the discussion list was whether they would see their homelands again, whether any of their relatives were alive, and so on. Gilda, living in her own world walked around the ship all day and occupied herself as she had always done.

After they left Genoa, they sailed to Palermo, Sicily. This was followed by a short crossing of the Mediterranean Sea and the ship headed for Egypt's Port Said at the entrance of the Suez Canal. When Gilda had lived in Paris, apart from school, her life had been rather quiet so as not to be noticed. Even when they had visitors, doors were shut and conversation was always muffled. Initially, Gilda had found the noise on the boat a bit frightening but, when she got used to it, it was actually rather fun.

Arriving in Port Said, all passengers who were physically able could leave the ship for the afternoon and Gilda, bursting with impatience to get onto solid ground, could hardly contain her excitement. She couldn't wait; she was in awe. She could see from the railing all sorts of different people; men in light-coloured suits and straw hats, women in soft-flowing dresses holding pretty parasols against the scotching sun, men wearing 'dresses', some were coloured, some were white. There were animals Gilda had never seen before - camels, snakes, and bears on chains; even the dogs were different.

There were so many colourful things to buy. After Hanna and Vladimir took her ashore, Gilda didn't know where to look first. After Genoa, she wasn't surprised at the bazaar vendors shouting for people to buy their goods and coaxing them toward their colourful umbrella-covered stands.

Gilda loved the gaily-patterned clothing people wore, the camels and other animals being pulled along the laneways laden with buckets and all sorts of wares that crashed and clashed against each other as the animals swayed. Her eyes widened and it was so exciting; she took it all in. It was like she was the main character in a story.

'Mama, Mama, did you see those donkeys, they are so funny,' she would exclaim, pulling at her mother's skirt. 'Mama, Mama, look at that man with a snake,' she would shriek, now hiding behind Hanna's skirt. And so it went on. With each exclamation, she would tug at her mother's skirt pulling Hanna around with her.

'Enough now Gilda, that is enough,' Hanna scolded pulling her, 'Be quiet and stay close. You can't trust anyone here; they are not of our class; they are strange people just out to get your money.' She gripped Gilda's hand to make her point.

'Ouch, Mama, that hurt,' Gilda protested.

Gilda was too young to have prejudices; she just saw everyone and everything as wonderfully exciting. People all around the world seemed to love children and here was no exception. A vendor on the street gave her a little bracelet and excitedly Gilda said, 'Merci, monsieur.' 'Look Mama,' she exclaimed, 'Isn't it pretty?' Hanna wanted to give it back as she thought the vendor wanted her to pay for it, but when it was clear that he didn't, Gilda was allowed to keep it. Nevertheless, Hanna pulled Gilda away and they quickly went further in case he changed his mind or sent some men after her accusing her of stealing it.

As the afternoon wore on, the change in the skyscape was remarkable. From being blazing hot, the sun changed to an electric yellow rimmed with red arrows that faded outwards in a more demure blue sky. The air had changed and a slight breeze came from the waters of the Suez Canal. The animals were more alert yet calmer as they now had shade in which to take refuge. The gentle ripples of the water, especially where the barges glided, gleamed in the setting sun. Although still busy, there was a quieter buzz of activity.

After the ship left Port Said, the journey to the next stop, Colombo in present day Sri Lanka was long and monotonous.

To break the monotony of shipboard life for the children, the ship's crew organised games and other activities. Some adults would come on deck but many stayed below because they suffered sea-sickness and lay on their beds. The voyage was often rough but that didn't affect Gilda; she loved being on deck with the wind blowing through her hair and talking to anyone who would talk to her. She had had never seen such an endless expanses of water and yet, she felt completely safe when she first saw the ocean.

Colombo was very hot and had there was another stopover of a few hours. The sultry humid tropical heat was too much for most passengers so fewer passengers went ashore this time. However, Hanna and Vladimir decided to visit a famous Buddhist temple. Not knowing the custom about what to wear going into a temple, most of the passengers, including the Dobinskis, were inappropriately dressed and had to pay for the hire of a shawl to put over their shoulders and to cover their legs.

'Typical robbery to get money out of us,' complained Hanna, 'You can't trust these people; they would take your last penny from you.' When Gilda was given her covering, she couldn't believe how beautiful it was. 'Oh, look at the gold thread, Mama, isn't it beautiful?' Gilda's shawl was green with multiple gold threads through it forming a border and figures of people and animals. From that moment on, she decided that green was her favourite colour. On the way out of the temple, everyone had to return the shawls.

Hanna was furious. 'We paid for those,' she complained to the guide in German. He didn't understand and asked for the shawl back. Someone explained to Hanna that the fee was to hire the shawls not buy them. In German she said to Vladimir, 'These dammed crooks.' When Gilda wanted to return her shawl, the attendant gave it back to her and motioned that she could keep it. Gilda beamed. 'Oh, merci monsieur, c'est très belle; oh, thank you, sir, it's so beautiful.' Hanna had flirted unsuccessfully with the man to keep her shawl and was furious when Gilda could keep hers. 'She'll ruin it,' she shouted at the man who didn't understand her.

Hanna was still complaining about the Buddhist monks as their ship left Colombo for the final leg of their ocean journey to Australia. First stop was Fremantle near the Western Australian capital, Perth. However, to get into the southern oceans, they first had to cross the Equator.

There were great celebrations on board when the ship crossed the Equator; streamers and balloons were released, a feast was held on the top deck, with games during the day and music and dancing till the early hours of the morning. The ship was unusually quiet the next morning, except for boisterously playing children.

One Equator-crossing game stood out because Gilda won it. The first prize was a rag doll. She had never had a doll, in actual fact, she had never had any toys that she remembered. As a baby she had received toys from her grandparents and aunt and uncle, but as an older child she only had the bucket and spade from hospital sand pit in Salzburg and had to leave these behind when they left for Paris. Gilda was thrilled when she won the doll. When the sailor gave her the rag doll. Frightened that she might break her new toy, Gilda took it gently and cradled it in her arms.

However, danger loomed for Gilda. As she looked across to the far side of the deck, she saw the jealous glares and stares of some of the older girls. They were about 12 years old. Gilda was six and smallish for her age. They approached her menacingly; one of them came up from the side and grabbed her hand. 'Ouch,' screamed Gilda, 'Let go, let me go. Another girl caught her by the hair. Gilda was agile and quick so she was able to duck down, but then a third one caught her at the waist. By this stage, a couple of the sailors saw what was happening and came to Gilda's aid pulling one of the girls away. The other sailor took hold of the second girl. The third girl tried to maintain her grip. Other older girls who were coming to help their friends, changed their minds as they saw their parents come towards them.

'You stupid little thing, you'll never have that doll. I'll take it from you,' yelled the girl as she let her go. Instinct told Gilda that she would indeed soon lose her doll. It only took her a split second to decide what to do.

'You won't have her either,' she yelled and threw the doll overboard. She only lingered for a second before she began to run away. One of the crew was watching these events and saw that one of the girls was now chasing Gilda and catching up to her. He opened the door to another part of the ship so that Gilda could escape and halted the other girl. Gilda never saw any of them again. But, she was very sad about her doll. Maybe that was why she never liked dolls, preferring stuffed animal toys. It was on this voyage that Gilda realised how much she loved animals, even ones that looked strange and sickly.

After another long stretch at sea, made bearable by more activities, the ship arrived at its first Australian destination, Fremantle, close to Perth, the capital of Western Australia.

CHAPTER 10
FREEMANTLE TO TOWNSVILLE
1950 – 1951

Few people left the ship in Fremantle, so matters were settled quickly before the ship was on its way to the next Australian port, Melbourne.

The passage from Fremantle across the open water of the Great Australian Bight to Melbourne was rough and passengers were advised to stay below. Most of the passengers had heard of Melbourne, the capital of Victoria. Many people on the ship had relatives who had settled there and were going to unite with family and already well-established circles of friends. Only a few had no one to go to, and the Dobinskis counted amongst those few. Disembarkation in Melbourne took some time given the number of passengers who were making this city their new home.

After a long sea voyage, those who were leaving were jubilant; those who were still left behind stood looking stupefied, resigned to having to wait a little longer before they could start to put their roots down in their newly adopted homeland.

By now, everyone had had enough of the trip. People longed for privacy, space for their living quarters, clean clothes; most of all, they were impatient to start life anew. Many had become sick during the voyage, needing more sophisticated medical care than the ship could provide. Many passengers suffered from various ailments before boarding the ship in Genoa but had camouflaged them for fear of being excluded as a passenger.

As much care as possible had been given by the ship's medical staff, but the sheer number of passengers, their different states of health, different ages and language barriers made things difficult for the ship's medical staff. The passengers were simply fed up, not just from the voyage but from the many years of anguish accumulated during the war. This anguish spilled over into the immediate post-war years

It is really remarkable what a human being can endure. Many, like the Dobinskis, had been displaced for years and unsure of their safety. It was just the natural exasperation of people who had suffered more than the gentle human psyche was created to suffer. Some had reached their limit and were manifesting mental ill-health; others were close to their limit and had to be restrained from jumping overboard. Some mothers had given birth during the voyage, others had given birth and lost their babies. Some old people died and some not so old as well.

The people who disembarked had the opportunity to create their life on a new canvas. How would they create it? What prejudices would they hold onto and thereby, through frequent application, strengthen? Would they let go of malignant prejudices and open their hearts to the new experiences and respect others for being like themselves, having endured hardships to get to this point in their lives? Who will bemoan their fate, gripe and complain and blame others and circumstances beyond their control for their plight?

Who, on the other hand, will see that life will always give you what is best for you even if at the time that isn't apparent? The answers to these questions were as complex and varied as the people who needed to answer them at the end of 1950.

It was late on New Year's Eve when the ship docked in Sydney, the capital city of New South Wales. Most of the remaining passengers were making this city the starting place for a new life. Some who were disembarking looked frightened as they saw the large number of rowdy drunks on the pier they had to pass with their meager belongings. Those who didn't need to leave the ship, including the Dobinskis stayed on board. Their English was weak, and so they didn't feel confident.

Among those passengers who stayed on board some had musical instruments, which they brought out to serenade the arrival of the New Year, 1951.

Dancing started and the resulting merriment provided a release for some anxious and mixed emotions brought on by arrival in

Australia. Seemingly from nowhere passengers, brought out various national alcoholic beverages which assisted to create a jolly atmosphere. Dancing and singing and for those precious hours brought the remaining passengers together, albeit temporarily as a single united family.

The final stage of the journey from Sydney to Brisbane was choppy but uneventful, as the ship was by now comparatively empty. The Dobinskis were the only ones heading further north; others stayed in Brisbane or were going out west. From Brisbane, Hanna, Vladimir and Gilda took the Sunlander train for the 3-day long, slow trip to Townsville. To say that Hanna had a culture shock would be an understatement. She was aghast with what she experienced.

'It's all so primitive,' Hanna was fond of saying. And, indeed, things were very different from Vienna and Paris. 'The seats are wooden and hard, the heat immense, even the breeze is hot when the train moves. I am soaked in perspiration. In addition, when the train stops, the mosquitoes stick to me. How can I survive this?'

This was January 1951, Brisbane was hot and going north was even hotter, blazing heat, no air-conditioning, not even fans and, Hanna lived in her invented new "history" of being superior to common folk.

The train was so slow that in many sections of the route passengers could have outrun it. Then it would stop wherever it wanted to stop or wherever there were farmers selling pineapples along the rail tracks. When the train did stop at a station, there were limited foods to buy.

'What is this?' Hanna asked pointing to small things that looked like poo in red skin. 'Saveloys, love,' was the reply. 'Is it salty or sweet?' Hanna asked. 'I danno what ya mean, love,' replied the woman behind the counter. Hanna went over to Vladimir and complained, 'I can't get her to understand me.'

An old man who had been sitting in the corner drinking came up to them and said in German, 'They are sausages but don't eat them, you won't like them.' The Dobinskis looked at each other. The old man continued, 'Do you want a meal or a snack?'

'A meal, if you please,' replied Vladimir. 'Hey, Daisy, can you get these folk chicken and chips for two, and a child's size?' the man called.

'Gotcha, mate, on its way,' replied Daisy.

'Thank you very much,' said Vladimir. 'How long have you been here?' he asked the man. 'Oh, years and years, before those mongrels in Europe started fighting each other the first time. You'll be fine now. I gotta go. Good luck. Good place, you've just gotta give it a chance; it's not Europe.' And then he was off.

Hanna just looked on. She didn't know what to make of it. 'This is so strange,' she said quietly, for once it seemed she was almost speechless. She was still thinking about the old man's last comment, "you've just gotta give it a chance.'

Their meal came, they were surprised how good it tasted; all three of them ate everything on their plate. 'You know what, darling,' Vladimir said with a grin, 'We just have to give it a chance.' They burst out laughing. It was the first time in a long time.

Although the train was hot, day and night, and the outside air was hot, the Dobinskis became better settled and relaxed after that stop. They started to admire the vast landscape of sugar cane fields, the rugged bush, the mountains in the distance and at times glimpses of the ocean. They dozed as the train rattled on or they gazed into space each in their own thoughts.

As for Gilda, she loved the trip. The food caddie gave her a biscuit and spoke to her everytime he passed. Everything was so new again. She saw new animals including kangaroos as they hopped beside the train tack. 'They are racing the train,' she laughed to herself. 'Come on, faster, faster.' she encouraged them.

The surprise of arriving in Townsville was softened by the encounter they had had with the old man. Both parents were now more open to the new experiences they encountered. There they were met by the Macedonian man, Ilija, who had acted as their guarantor for them to migrate to Australia. From the Townsville Railway Station, he drove them in his old, battered utility vehicle to his house on stilts. He was dressed in shorts and a torn shirt, hadn't shaved in months, nor, so it seemed, showered. And there, Herr Doktor and Frau Doktor Dobinski, and their daughter Gilda were to stay until they could find alternative accommodation.

Gilda always loved chatting to people. In Paris, she never talked at home as she was sent to her parent's room and often ate alone there, especially when Vladimir's friends came over. When she went to school in Paris, she was encouraged by the nuns to talk as were all the children and that is how she learned French so easily. On the ship, she had mastered some Italian sufficient for daily conversation in the dining room and talking to crew members. And so, it was the same in Townsville, she would talk to anyone who would have a conversation with her. First the old lady next door to the guarantor would chat with her at the fence and they would talk for hours. School had not yet started for the year and so Gilda was glad of the company as was the old lady.

Hanna asked the old woman, 'What do you two talk about? Gilda doesn't speak English.' 'Oh, yes, she can, Hanna,' replied the old lady, 'She speaks English better than you do. I can understand everything Gilda says but I can barely understand a thing you say.'

Hanna recoiled when this simple woman addressed her by her first name. It just showed how primitive she was. 'She has no manners, no breeding,' Hanna thought, 'You just don't do that. I have not given her permission to call me by my first name.' In Hanna's defence, this was the custom in most European countries at that time.

As luck would have it, the Dobinskis only stayed a few weeks with their Macedonian benefactor. In any case, they were only staying in Townsville until the new University year started in 1952 in

Brisbane.

Although Vladimir had all his documentation, the Australian Government legislated that all people who had not studied in Australia or England were required to redo their study. No overseas qualifications, even if the applicant had the original, authentic documents that could be validated at the city of origin, would be recognised. So, Vladimir had to do his standard medical studies again, and not only that, he would then have to do his specialization again. The latter was out of the question because to get his primary medical degree would take six years and Hanna would need to support the three of them during that time. To make matters worse,

Vladimir had arrived too late in Australia to submit his application to study medicine in 1951 and no late applications were permitted. In order for the Dobinskis to have some income, Vladimir was given a job washing test tubes at the Townsville hospital. They soon recognised that he was who he said he was, a very skilled medical practitioner, and was given better work as much as they legally could give him. They contacted Brisbane for him but all hands were tied because of the new law and because of the unbending rules of the University of Queensland's rigidity regarding late enrolments.

Because of Vladimir's standing with the Townsville hospital, he and Hanna started to meet some of the local "better" people. They met a wonderful family, Mr and Mrs Hemming who had a daughter, Julia, two years younger than Gilda, and a baby son. Mr Hemming had a senior managerial position in a civil aviation company whose headquarters were in Sydney and they soon befriended the Dobinskis.

Their relationship with the Hemming family brought about placing Gilda in a good primary school. Also, because of this burgeoning friendship between the Hemmings and the Dobinskis, they boarded with the Hemmings until the Dobinskis left Townsville for Brisbane almost a year later.

Alice Hemming and Hanna became good friends, and stayed friends till their deaths 60 years later.

The relationship with the Hemmings brought wonderful days for Gilda; she started to feel like she belonged somewhere again. She had a happy home because the Hemmings were warm, welcoming people.

'Hey, Julia, do you want to come out and play in the garden?' Gilda would suggest.

'Sure,' replied Julia. Or Julia would ask to go out and play. If it rained, a swing was hooked up on the ceiling of the closed-in verandah where the girls could swing so high but never reach the ceiling. 'Come on, it's my turn,' Gilda would say if Julia stayed on the swing too long. 'Oh, okay, you can have a go.' Julia would reply.

The Hemmings frequently took the Dobinskis on picnics, garden parties and horse races. It was a world they had never known. Ladies wore colourful, pretty dresses and beautiful big hats and gloves every time they went out.

Gilda was also doing well at school. Despite the fact that her English was still at the early learning stages, she was well advanced in the other subjects because of the schooling she had had with the nuns in Paris.

'Gilda, would you ask your mother to come and see me, please,' asked the headmistress one day. Gilda looked shocked. 'It's okay, sweetie, you're not in trouble,' she reassured Gilda. The following day, Hanna came to the school.

'Good morning, Mrs Dobinski, please sit down. Thank you for coming to see me. How are you settling in?' enquired the headmistress. 'I am very well, thank you,' replied Hanna formally. 'It's not too hot for you, I hope?' continued the headmistress in a friendly manner. 'Yes, it is' replied Hanna in the same vein. 'When will she get to the point?' Hanna thought. 'Well, you'll get used to it, dearie,' the headmistress added. Hanna was getting beside herself, 'This idiot, what does she want?'

'I suppose, you're wondering why I've called to see you,' the woman said. 'Well, don't worry, Gilda isn't in any trouble.' she smiled sweetly. It was all that Hanna could do to stay patiently poised. 'I want to ask your permission to place Gilda into Grade 2. She's a very intelligent girl and a capable girl and, apart from her English, she is too advanced for Grade 1. Would you agree to that?' enquired the headmistress.

'Yes, that will be acceptable,' responded Hanna. 'Of course, the French education system is better than this primitive place,' thought Hanna, but smiled charmingly. 'Good, then that is settled.' eagerly agreed the headmistress. 'Tomorrow, Gilda will go into Grade 2. As we are such a small school, she will still be able to have the same friends. That is very important for a child, isn't it, Mrs. Dobinski?' Hanna just smiled. 'Stupid woman, Gilda has been fine all these years without friends. What does she know?' Hanna thought. And so the next day, Gilda went into a new grade. She was pleased as she was bored where she was and she loved to learn.

To add to their income, Hanna started to sew dresses for the ladies. Her sewing was very professional and no one in Townsville had seen dressmaking like it. She was soon very busy and life was good. Gilda was delighted too; Hanna made dresses for her from left over dressmaking fabrics. They were so pretty and Gilda had never had so many dresses.

'Thank you, Mama, for my pretty dresses,' she said as she gave her mother a hug.

Because Hanna was so busy with her business venture, Gilda often went grocery shopping with Julia and Mrs Hemming. Gilda loved it: it was as though she had an aunt and uncle now, as Mr Hemming was also very nice to her. 'I am so happy here,' she once said to Julia, 'I'm so glad to be your friend.'

Gilda was stunned when her parents mentioned in October that they would be leaving at the end of the November and going to Brisbane. 'Gilda, don't look so surprised,' Hanna said when Gilda started to object, 'You knew we would be leaving.' 'But that was when we first came here,' Gilda replied, 'Now we are so happy here, why do we have to move again?' 'I've told you why, and that's the end of the discussion,' Hanna replied and went back to her sewing.

While Hanna and Vladimir were in Townsville, they had heard of an organisation that had a list of people who were willing to take in boarders for a reduced rent than what was normally charged. These boarders had bedrooms of their own and shared the rest of the house with the host family. This sounded perfect as they didn't know what their income prospects would be while Vladimir studied.

And so the year came to an end and it was time to leave Townsville. Gilda didn't really understand why. Again, she was told they were leaving and that was that. This time she didn't cry or ask to stay behind. She was older now and knew what not to do or say. She liked living with other people, as her mother was so much nicer to her when others were around, or maybe it was because she was now older, after all, she was seven-and-a-half. She didn't seem to annoy her mother as much.

But Gilda was upset, very upset. Julia had been her first friend and they had been friends for months now. She was heartbroken to be separated from Julia, the best and only friend that she has within her short life-time.

The day to leave arrived. The Hemmings took the Dobinskis to the station. Mrs Hemming turned to Gilda and said, 'You've been such a lovely girl; I'm going to miss you, we're all going to miss you, especially Julia. See, she's crying too. Maybe you can come on a school holiday one day and stay with us.' she said, 'Would you like that?'

'Yes, oh yes, please, when, when can I come? Can Julia come to us too?' Gilda asked excitedly through her tears looking at her mother.

'That's enough,' intervened Hanna. 'You mean to say, Alice, you and Ben won't be sorry that Gilda is leaving, I know that she is such a turbulent child,' Hanna said charmingly. 'Oh yes, we will be sorry,' replied Mrs Hemming, 'Gilda is just an active, happy child; she is delightful.'

Then Hanna changed her tone and changed the conversation, 'Thank you so much, Alice and Ben, you have been very kind to us, until we see each other again. We will write each other, yes?'

'Off course,' replied, Alice. Then they shook hands.

Gilda boarded yet another train. She watched the disappearing station till she could see it no longer before going into the carriage to her parents. That numb, frozen feeling of just over a years ago returned.

So ended 1951.

PART 2

BRISBANE
1952 TO 1979

WITH
PAPUA NEW GUINEA
1957

CHAPTER 11
1952 – 1954

Mr and Mrs Williams, the Dobinski's new landlords in Brisbane, lived in a small wooden house built on stilts into the side of a steep hill. They had an adopted daughter, Karly, about a year older than Gilda, and so it seemed logical for the two girls to go to the same primary school, St Ita's, at Dutton Park.

'I'm not happy with this arrangement,' Vladimir said. As an atheist, he strongly objected to Gilda going to a Catholic school. 'I didn't mind it for the short time in Paris, but this is going to be for much longer.' Hanna responded with, 'Look, it's convenient for me. You'll be all day at the medical school. Gilda will go with Karly.' And that was the end of the discussion.

From one of the bedrooms, there was a squeal of joy. 'Oh Mama, come and see. I have my own room,' Gilda excitedly announced to her parents when Mrs Williams showed them their quarters. Her parent's bedroom was next to hers and both rooms led out onto a closed-in verandah where a swing hung from the ceiling.

Hanna was unimpressed and whispered to Vladimir, 'Du Lieber Gott! Good heavens, this must be the way houses are built here.'

The house was simple, and its small rooms were cramped with furniture. The hallway from the front door led through the house to the top of the high-raked back stairs at the other end of the house. 'What on Earth is that smell?' Hanna exclaimed as she held her handkerchief over her nose.'

'Oh, dear, the cat must have done his business behind the Pianola. I'll clean it up immediately,' Mrs Williams chuckled. To the left of the entrance was a small lounge with a Pianola, behind which the cat seemed to have permanent toilet. Unless Mrs Williams cleaned up the mess quickly, the smell permeated every room in the house.

'That is unbelievable! This is such a primitive country,' Hanna commented to Vladimir in German.

The remaining rooms before the back door were a small kitchen to the left, and to the right, a long thin room that contained a wooden table with chairs where the two families ate in shifts. Then another small bedroom for Karly. The toilet and bathroom were under the house, and entry was at the end of a long, steep flight of stairs. Because the house was located on a steep slope, the front of the house was supported by just two short stilts while the back of the house was supported by 12 feet long stilts. Immediately behind the house was undeveloped bushland. A man-made ladder enabled children to climb down the steep hill to play there.

Mr Williams was an unskilled labourer and his wife, Mrs Williams, a house wife. She was a wonderful woman, and a very strict-practising Catholic who was very kind and giving. She seemed to be constantly in the kitchen either cooking for her family or making cakes and scones for local church fêtes, fund raisers or for the nuns. She was very considerate when it came to sharing the kitchen with Hanna.

In the Brisbane of 1952, Hanna and Vladimir encountered Irish Catholic nuns who held a significantly different view to the more enlightened French Catholic nuns known to Hanna about the religious quality of relationships between a divorced Catholic woman married to a divorced atheist. In the penetrating eyes of these Brisbane sisters of the Church, this combination was a prescription for landing in hell, and if you were the child of such parent, you became subject to their scorn, as Gilda frequently found to her cost at the Catholic school she attended.

Had these sinners, Hanna and Vladimir, gone to confession that would have helped, although not enough to purge their sinful behaviour. Confession was out of the question given Vladimir's view of religion, so there was only one alternative left for the nuns to ensure their salvation. Because God could forgive if indulgences were paid to provide remission for sins, the nuns in turn could also forgive, for a time.

To ensure indulgences were forthcoming, they made Gilda's life at school miserable. After all, she was the child of these sinners, a nine year old girl also carried the moral blemishes of her mother and father. Gilda had no idea what was going on, she only saw that the nuns picked on her for things that either she didn't do, or that they didn't reprimand others for. On some occasions Gilda told her parents, but not always because she would have been in more trouble from her mother. Hanna would have believed that the nuns were right in their punishment if Gilda behaved as badly at school as she did at home. After all, in Hanna's view, Gilda was not an easy child. 'Gilda is so active, she gets on my nerves,' Hanna often said.

Gilda soon discovered that these nuns were different in other respects from the ones in Paris. They didn't like questions which they took as having their vocation and authority undermined. Children were to be seen and not heard. The common practice in those days was caning and belittling words supplemented with additional detentions. At lunchtime, on her knees, Gilda often had to polish the balustrades and floors of the convent.

This unjust treatment went on for months, then one day, when Gilda was unjustly treated, she stood up in class and proclaimed, 'I've had enough. I'm not going to put up with it any longer. You always pick on me, for nothing,' Gilda shouted at the offending nun. With that, she took the inkwell from her desk and threw it at the nun who continually contributed significantly to Gilda's misery. Blue ink streamed down the nun's white starched alb.

The nun flew at Gilda, 'You brazen girl,' she yelled while pulling at Gilda's ear, 'you brazen, brazen girl, that's what comes of having parents who are sinners; you are a sinner. Your behaviour is appalling!' She dragged Gilda to Mother Superior's office. 'Look what this brazen girl has done, Mother,' the nun ranted pointing a finger at her ink-stained alb.

'Thank you, Sister,' Mother Superior said calmly, 'Please go back to your class, I will deal with Gilda.' The nun stormed out still muttering. 'Sit down, please Gilda,' Mother Superior said kindly. 'What do you have to say for yourself?' In actual fact, the Mother Superior liked Gilda; she was lenient with her and usually just gave her a talking-to.

'But, it's not fair,' Gilda stammered through her tears, 'She always picks on me and makes up lies about what I have or haven't done. It's not fair.' She sobbed even more.

'Come to me, my child,' comforted the elderly lady and put her arms around Gilda's shoulders while giving her a handkerchief. 'Why have you not come to me before if that is the case?' Gilda looked at her astonished, 'Come to you? I can do that?' 'Yes, of course', replied the nun. 'You would have believed me?' Gilda asked. 'I would have looked at both sides of the situation,' responded Mother Superior and then she continued, 'This is rather serious, Gilda. I am going to have to ask your parents to come and see me.'

'Oh no, no please, no, just give me polishing to do, a caning. I'll do anything, just don't tell my mother. 'I see,' said the nun sternly but surprised, 'and why not?' And then Gilda told her what would happen if her mother found out. 'Um, all the more reason for me to see your parents,' she said kindly. 'And don't worry,' she added. Within the week, Gilda's parents came to the school. When confronted with what had been going on, they were shocked. Vladimir was incensed. Hanna tried to play the diplomat thinking that she could charm the head nun. She was used to charming people, but it didn't work. It was clear that Mother Superior was not going to be taken in by Hanna's behaviour.

After some discussion about the incident, the nun turned to Hanna and said, 'I do not know what the custom is regarding disciplining children where you come from, Mrs Dobinski, but here only God has the right to physical discipline when children have broken his laws. Do you understand me, Mrs Dobinski,' she said looking sternly at both Hanna and Vladimir. She reiterated, 'I repeat Mrs Dobinski, do you understand me?'

'Yes, Mother,' Hanna replied demurely, playing the role of the repentant sinner. 'Should I discover that not to be the case, I will need to take matters further,' threatened the nun.

Hanna loathed losing. She saw her encounter with the Mother Superior as a significant loss and a blow to her dignity. 'She can't tell me how to bring up my child. I'll get Gilda to obey me one way or another. Stupid country. That is how I was disciplined; that's how we did it,' she thought, 'and it hasn't done me any harm.'

'Hanna,' questioned Vladimir, "what did that nun mean about you and Gilda?' 'Oh, shut up,' Hanna admonished, 'what do you know about what I have to put up with? You go off to your medical school; you're getting your profession back. What do you think my life is like at the hospital and with these stupid, simple people we have to live with and that drunkard of a husband of hers? That's the way I was brought up. It made me disciplined. How do you think I got up so quickly in my profession while others stayed in the same job for years? Just mind your own business.'

For a while, things got a bit better at school for Gilda until it was donation time again. By now, Gilda had worked out what was happening and she did report home when the same nun started picking on her. Money changed hands and all was well again. She actually felt like she had hidden friends in the nuns now because it was the first time she saw her mother forced to do something she didn't want to do. Hanna was afraid of the Mother Superior. The yelling at home got worse but Gilda could handle that; she had learned to tune out, and in any case Mrs Williams was mostly home so her mother had to be careful.

Hanna had started a job as a night-shift floor cleaner at the Royal Brisbane Hospital. They lived in Dutton Park and the hospital was at Bowen Hills, so it was a long, arduous walk for her particularly as Hanna at first had the night shift. She couldn't afford to take the tram as she earned little, and with her pay she had to feed the three of them plus pay board to Mrs Williams.

Eventually Hanna was promoted to an assistant nurse position and later to nurse, which paid more and she only worked day shifts.

It was clear that Vladimir was making a name for himself at the hospital, especially during practical sessions. Even though he was a student, the doctors could see that his surgical skills were very advanced and he often demonstrated procedures. They had never seen such sutures. This meant that the Dobinski's circle of friends increased and widened with people who were more according to Hanna's perceived 'social class.'

Whenever Gilda played with the children in the street and they played 'Make-Believe', she would always play the role of a movie star. 'Come out to play, Gilda,' one of the boys called. 'Okay,' Gilda happily called back, 'be out in a minute.' And out she was in a flash. 'What will we play?' she asked. 'What do you want to play?' asked one of the girls. 'You know, I always want to play Make-Believe,' Gilda replied.

'Oh no, not again! Oh, alright, but not for long,' said another girl and then we'll play 'I Spy'…down the bottom of the hill.' 'Why do you always want to play that?' another boy asked Gilda. 'Ah, it sounds so glamorous. I heard some of the mothers talk at the tuck-shop about these beautiful women who were film stars,' Gilda said dreamily, 'And it sounded so wonderful.' She had never seen a film or a film star, but it sounded a world so removed from hers that she thought it had to be good.

'You'll never be a film star with your crossed eye; it's ugly,' one of the girls said.

Gilda tried to ignore that comment but it hurt and she cringed. 'Doesn't matter,' she replied stoically, 'That's why the game is called Make-Believe.'

Soon Gilda stopped playing with them. She also didn't have many friends at school because there was too much 'wrong' with her - her strange left eye for one thing, and then her family.
Also her lunches were pungent because of the salami and other weird sausages she brought from home. In addition, she had funny black bread when all the children had white bread, her parents were sinners, everyone said so, so it must be true, and on, and on…

All was not well at the Williams's house and one afternoon things came to a head. Mr Williams had been to the hotel as was his custom every Friday after work. When he received his weekly cash payment, he drank as much as he could before staggering home.

There was a swing under the house that Gilda used frequently. One afternoon she was swinging there when Mr Williams came home drunk. 'Ah, there you are,' he slurred when he saw her, 'Stay there, I have to go to the toilet.' When he staggered out again, he lunged towards her but fell flat on his face. Gilda jumped off the swing and started running. 'Come back you filthy piece of foreign shit. I haven't finished with you.' He tripped and his red face hit the dirt floor.

'Mama, Mama,' Gilda called out bursting with laughter as she ran upstairs. 'Mama, Mr Williams just fell over and landed in the dirt,' she shrieked with laughter, 'He looked so funny, his face was so red and he couldn't speak properly.' Gilda couldn't understand why her mother was horrified. When Vladimir came home, Hanna told him about the incident and the details she had gleaned after questioning Gilda.

'We must move out as quickly as possible before he hurts her,' said Vladimir, equally horrified. With his profession, he had seen the results of such incidents. Gilda had no idea why her parents were making such a fuss. She was told never to go under the house again. If she wanted to use the swing one of her parents had to be present.

A few months later, just before Christmas in 1954, the Dobinskis moved out. They had bought a rundown, old wooden house, also on stilts, a few kilometres away. They could ill afford it as Vladimir was not earning, but they felt they could no longer stay with the Williams family. It was only years later Gilda realised why her parents had been so shocked. She had started to develop a bust quite early and Hanna and Vladimir did not want Gilda to have any contact with Mr Williams - drunk or sober. He died not long after when he was hit by a motor cycle as he swayed, drunk, out of a hotel one Friday afternoon.

'I like Mrs Williams,' Gilda said when she heard they were moving, 'I'm going to miss her.'

Gilda would also miss two other people who had befriended her during the two years. About four doors down lived an elderly lady, Mrs Casey, and her 35 year old son, Arthur. She always asked Gilda to come in when she went passed their house to have some of Mrs Casey's home-baked cakes. Each time Gilda visited she saw Arthur sitting beside the gramophone player listening to beautiful music, 'What sort of music is that? I've never heard such beautiful music,' she exclaimed.

'It's called Classical music,' Arthur replied.

In fact, Gilda hadn't heard much music at all. The only music she had heard was when Mrs Williams or Karly played the Pianola, but that was different and Gilda didn't really like it. She had also never seen a gramophone record player and watched with wonder when Arthur would gently place the chosen record on the turntable, and carefully place the needle on the edge of the record. The music then filled the room. Each time she came, Arthur would sit motionless and listen to music. He would greet her nicely and ask her if she liked what she heard. But he never moved and always wore a brown suit as though ready to go out. He smiled at Gilda through his thick brown rimmed spectacles.

One day, Gilda asked his mother, 'Why does Arthur just sit there. Does he ever go out?'

'No, Dearie. He has very high blood pressure and the doctors can't do anything about it. If he exerts himself, he could die,' replied Mrs Casey. 'Is that why his face is so red,' Gilda asked. 'Yes,' replied Mrs Casey. 'Mr Williams's face is red too,' replied Gilda, 'Does he have high blood pressure too?' 'No, little one,' replied Mrs Casey, 'His face is red from drinking too much beer.'

'Oh,' replied Gilda, not really understanding what that meant. Gilda knew that her visits made Mrs Casey and Arthur happy. He always smiled when she arrived and the three of them would chat together and eat cake. The adults would have tea and Gilda had a cold glass of milk. Arthur would always have a particular piece of music ready for her to listen to and to then discuss it. 'I guess, I'm having my first music lessons,' she smiled to herself. But, it didn't feel like lessons provided at her school by the nuns. Arthur, like his mother, was gentle. Gilda loved these visits and she also loved hearing the stories that went with the music. He would tell her stories about Mozart and Beethoven and others as he played their music. Arthur especially loved these two composers.

'Mrs Casey and Arthur have such a simple, happy life. I wish ours could be like that too,' Gilda dreamed.

One day when Gilda came home from school, she heard Mrs Williams tell her husband that Arthur had died. Mr Williams commented in his perennially surly manner, 'That insipid bastard was good for nothing. Serves him right.'

Gilda had seen a cat die so she knew what 'died' meant. She ran out of the house to Arthur's place. Gilda knocked and Mrs Casey opened the door; she looked sad, her eyes were red from weeping. Gilda started to cry. Mrs Casey took Gilda into her arms and said, 'Don't cry little girl, he's where he will never be sick again. He'll still have his music. Arthur's with the Angels and God looks after him now.'

Gilda sobbed and buried her head in Mrs Casey's apron and continued to weep.

It wasn't long after that the Dobinski's moved away.

CHAPTER 12
1954 – 1957

'Finally, we have our own home,' Hanna said as she slumped exhausted on a box she used as a chair when their belongings were finally upstairs.

'Yes,' agreed Vladimir, 'It's amazing how moving few possessions could exhaust one so. It's going up and down all these stairs.'

The house was on a corner and also on stilts, 20 steps at the front and 20 steps at the back, but the land was flat. It had been tenanted and a court order was needed to have the previous tenants evicted. Neglect and filth meant that major cleaning was needed before it could be called a home.

'Once we have cleaned the house, this sunroom will become the patients' waiting room,' Hanna proclaimed, 'It won't need much furniture. We have to be frugal, you know, as I am still the only one earning. Your surgery will cost enough to furnish. It would help if you didn't smoke so much. Hopefully, you'll soon bring some money in.'

Vladimir winced. He always felt uncomfortable each time Hanna talked about money in that manner. Gilda romped from one room to the next oblivious to everything. She was thrilled to have a better room to call her own.

Over the past two years, Vladimir and Hanna had met many nationalities with different trades. Few of their fellow migrants had money to spare for extras, only having enough for food. Accordingly, bartering was the means of getting things done.

On the side, Vladimir would provide medical services to the migrant community, and in return patients offered electrical work, plumbing, roofing, concreting, installing new windows, decking, demolishing or moving internal walls and anything else that the house required. Whatever had to be done, there was invariably someone to barter with.

Some of these people became friends and it was with sadness that the Dobinskis would farewell many of them as they migrated to America. Nationalities who had fought against each other in the war were here the best of friends, and even people who didn't like an ethnic group within their own country were friends here. These became part of the Dobinskis large circle of acquaintances. 'I would not call them friends', Hanna would say, 'They are not of our class.' Vladimir was not class-conscious, having himself come from humble beginnings, but he let Hanna have her say.

It was a time in Brisbane's history when foreigners were not cordially accepted by the majority. Those who belonged to larger cultural communities such as the Greeks, Italians and Germans formed their own clubs and also lived in the same suburbs. New Farm became the suburb for Macedonians, and the Dobinskis would often visit there. This necessitated Hanna and Gilda becoming familiar with the language.

Gradually, the Dobinskis also participated in bulk-buying food with them. Food sorting became a social activity and Gilda loved these events. They were always happy, and there were children to play with. When these Macedonians met for picnics at a park, out would come the drums, a piano accordion, flutes and clarinets and everyone would dance. Consequently, music became an important part of Gilda's life.

When the medical examination results were released at the end of the year, Vladimir was called to a meeting of the Medical Board at the University. 'Mr Dobinski, thank you for coming,' welcomed the President. 'My colleagues and I have discussed the documentation you sent us last year when you applied to commence your medical degree. We made enquiries to Graz in Austria and they have confirmed your status as well as giving us a glowing reference of your ability and contributions. After observing you closely this past year, we feel that an exception can be made regarding your having to complete the full term of the undergraduate medical course.'

Vladimir couldn't believe what he was hearing. He sat glued to his chair leaning forward to better hear.

'You will need to complete the required assessments but you will only be required to attend certain lectures. If you complete the assessments which will include the written and the practical components, you will be granted your medical degree and licence to practice medicine in Queensland at the end of next year.'

Usually a self-contained man, Vladimir had to control his excitement and so he simply said, 'Thank you very much, Sir, that is indeed an honour and I thank you for your faith in me.'

The Chairman and Vladimir shook hands, Vladimir bowed slightly. When Hanna came home from work, Vladimir greeted her with the biggest smile she had ever seen on his face. Vladimir was not a smiler; he was a serious type. 'What's the matter? Has something happened?' asked Hanna. Gilda just looked, 'What is with Papa?' she also asked.

'Hanna,' Vladimir started, hardly able to contain himself, 'Hanna, I have some wonderful news.' And then he told her what had transpired with the Medical Board. 'Are you sure you understood correctly?' she asked. 'Yes, yes, very sure,' confirmed Vladimir. 'What about the written exams? How will you manage those?' she queried. 'The questions will be in English but most of the answers are Latin terms and they are the same the world over,' Vladimir reassured her and continued, 'They will also have an interpreter available should I need one.'

Hanna was never one to believe the good side of an idea or to be overly optimistic, and although she believed she was an optimist, she always first focused on what could go wrong. 'Hanna,' Vladimir said, 'Isn't that good news?' 'Well, we'll see at the end of next year how it all works out,' she replied.

'Hanna, I bought some wine, let's celebrate,' insisted Vladimir and Hanna finally let herself enjoy the happy moment. He led her to the dining room where he had set the table with wine glasses and plates and even put bread, cheese, sausage, olives and gherkins out for dinner. Hanna and Gilda burst out laughing at Vladimir's attempt at preparing dinner. That evening they laughed and were a happy family.

Indeed, Vladimir did graduate at the end of the following year, and he posed ceremoniously for a photo in the front sunroom in his graduation mortar board and gown. During the year, the sunroom had been enclosed in preparation for it being his patients' waiting room. The large front room was transformed into a surgery, resplendent with desk, chairs, patient examination bed, tools-of-the-trade and a sink. It hadn't taken very long for Vladimir's reputation to spread, and soon the little room opposite the surgery had to be converted into an additional waiting room.

The Dobinskis were now close to achieving financial stability. The loan on the house was decreasing and despite the hire of medical equipment and, because they lived frugally, their savings had substantially increased.
'We are now in a position for me to rent a shop and start my own dressmaking business,' Hanna announced. 'I have found a small vacant shop half-way between here and Gilda's school.'

For Gilda, it was quite a walk from home to her new school so her mother's shop would be a pleasant stop where she could do her homework, after which she and her mother could walk home together. Hanna always wanted to be independent and earn her own money, 'You never know what the future holds,' she maintained. She named her dressmaking shop, "Vienna Fashions", and soon had a steadily increasing regular clientele.

Gilda now 10 years old attended a State school and was in Grade 5. One Sunday Hanna said to Gilda, 'Now that we are settled and the fence has been repaired we can have a dog. Would you like that?' 'Oh yes, yes!' said Gilda excitedly. She had always loved animals. She would pass houses with dogs and cats on the way to school and would always stop and say 'hello' to them and put her hand over the fence to pat them.

'It will not be your dog, Gilda, it will be the family's dog, you understand?' her mother added. 'But I can play with it, can't I,' Gilda asked. 'Yes, of course, as long as you do exactly as I say to look after it,' replied Hanna.

In their recently bought second-hand car, mother and daughter drove to Redcliffe, north of Brisbane. Hanna wanted a Cardigan Welsh Corgi because that was the breed the Queen had. On the long drive Gilda couldn't stop talking, she was so excited. 'Gilda, please, will you be quiet? All your chatter is getting on my nerves,' Hanna scolded. Gilda could only stop for a short time before her excitement got the better of her, and Hanna had to repeat that she 'settle down order.'

With the purchase of a male puppy completed, Gilda cradled him in a towel on the way home. The trip home was much quieter as Gilda only spoke gently to the puppy, whispering loving words into his ear and stroking him gently. He was called Orion after the Great Hunter in Greek mythology and also the brightest star constellation. The following year they bought a female, a Pembroke Welsh Corgi, because the Queen had two Corgis. The new addition was called Venera, the Russian word for the goddess, Venus.

Vladimir's medical practice had steadily grown and most of Vladimir's patients were Russian, draw from the nearby large Russian community with its own Russian Orthodox Church nearby in the same suburb of Woolloongabba.

A major highlight in Gilda's life was that she was able to start piano lessons. Around the corner from Hanna's shop in Moorooka was an elderly lady, Mrs Daley, who taught from her home and Gilda went there once a week. Mrs Daley was a nice person but she did have the tendency to use her ruler to rap it over Gilda's knuckles for repeated technical misdemeanors. 'Gilda, I've told you many times, you must hold your fingers as though you were holding a tennis ball. That is the correct way to play,' Mrs Daley would say as she lightly but effectively struck the knuckles of the offending hand. Or, 'Gilda, how often do I need to remind you that the note is C sharp, not C natural.' Again the ruler would accompany this comment.

The ruler was merely a tap but it did cause discomfort. Nevertheless, Gilda liked Mrs Daley and she liked going to her lessons. She learnt about the composers of the pieces, the story behind the pieces she was learning, and about the history of the time in which the composer lived and worked.

'Mrs Daley, is what I'm learning called Classical music?' Gilda asked one day. Mrs Daley looked surprise and replied, 'Why, yes, Dearie. How do you know that?' Gilda then told Mrs Daley about her visits to the Casey's.

Hanna and Vladimir had bought an old iron-frame upright piano at a good price so that Gilda could practice at home. She was in heaven when she played, yet she made sure that she practised when her mother wasn't there because she could then play uninterrupted from Hanna's constant corrections. Hanna had played the zither in Vienna, and considered herself an authority on classical music and of the performance on any instrument.

After six months, Gilda completed her first examinations in pianoforte and theory of music which she passed with a high distinction. Mrs Daley told Hanna that Gilda was gifted and should continue studying both subjects for as long as possible. Sadly, Mrs Daley's comment about Gilda being gifted was a mistake as Hanna's expectations for Gilda were now excessive.

After one examination where Gilda passed with a distinction Hanna reprimanded her for not maintaining her record of high distinctions.

Consequently, playtime after school was shortened and replaced with more piano practice time. Gilda became very nervous when she played at home until one day Vladimir said, 'Hanna, do you think you might be a bit hard on the child?'

Hanna looked at him coldly, 'Mozart practiced for many hours in a day; if he could do that, so can she. Her talent will not be wasted on silly sporting games after school.' Vladimir sided with Gilda when Hanna asked whether Gilda had practiced enough that day. 'Oh yes, Hanna,' Vladimir would say smiling at Gilda, 'I made sure of that.' Hanna stopped asking and Gilda could relax.

For Hanna these early years in Brisbane were a period of enormous adjustment. Even though she came from a home dominated by an inordinately strict, despotic mother, Hanna knew the rules for behaviour and living in Vienna. She had made a few long-standing friends there, and knew she could count on them through thick and thin.

'I sometimes feel I'm too strict with Gilda; the parents here are so relaxed and easy in their upbringing. I can't see how that is any good.' Hanna's thoughts were in confusion at times. 'Here I'm not Frau Doktor, here I'm just Mrs Dobinski. In Vienna I would have been someone. I've paid a huge price to be here, leaving my beloved city and status.'

Suddenly she straightened up. 'I will be someone here too,' she pulled herself together. 'I will go to University and get a degree. None of these doctors' wives have one. It'll be easy to better myself here, they are still a colony. I'll bring up Gilda using the same discipline as my mother. Mama brought me up with discipline. It will make Gilda strong. She must learn ambition.'

By the time Gilda neared her twelfth birthday her physical appearance developed significantly. Mostly, Australian children went to her school and it was an area which had a small migrant population. The girls were flat-chested and it was unusual for a 12 year old girl to develop this way. Gilda told her mother that she needed a bra but Hanna said, 'No, girls don't wear a bra until they are 15 years old. You will get one then.'

'But, Mama,' Gilda begged, 'the children are making fun of me and deliberately pushing up against me to touch me. Please, I only need one; I can wash it in the evening and wear it the next day.' 'No,' exclaimed Hanna, 'Those children are just stupid.' 'Yes they are,' shouted Gilda, 'but I still have to put up with it.' 'Don't you yell at me; you yell at me again and you'll be sorry. This is the end of the discussion.'

Gilda constantly tried to flatten her bust but nothing worked and she had to put up with the continual teasing. She found the children at the new school different from the ones at the convent; they were more aggressive: 'You bloody wogs, your food stinks,' or 'Hey, you with the cross-eyes, what's your name? Your name's queer. How does your mother ever remember it?'

Another would then start another verbal attack, 'Your mother probably doesn't use your name and just says, 'Hey you with the cross-eyes', they would burst out laughing. 'How about we give her a name?' said another. 'Here's a good one, 'Cross-eyed Bill from Topside Hill.' Everyone roared with laughter, 'Yeah, that's a beauty; suits her. What do you reckon?' yelled one fellow as he lightly punched Gilda.

Gilda hit back. At first she would fight every time they called her that but she would then get into trouble with the teachers. The teachers would reprimand those insulting Gilda. However, the teachers stopped correcting the name-calling and effectively condoned the teasing. Because nothing more was done the insults and bullying continued.

Gilda had been doing well in her schoolwork at the convent but under the strain of these continued attacks she lost interest at school, and became defiant. Her grades on her report card became worse as did the comments. 'Gilda is an aggressive girl who picks fights with other pupils,' or 'Gilda could get better results if she applied herself more.'

The worse the comments on her reports were, the more she was in trouble with Hanna the more defiant Gilda became.

At the end of 1957, Gilda was to sit for the state examination for eligibility for high school entry called "Scholarship". The ever-socially-ambitious Hanna had booked Gilda into one of Brisbane's best private schools which would only accept Gilda if she was awarded high marks for this exam. Gilda was competitive by nature and wanted to do her best so she worked hard the last few months. Although bored at school, being intelligent, she found that cramming for the exams was no problem.

'Perhaps this new school will be different,' she thought. Because she was a foreigner, Gilda was required to write at the top of each answer page, 'I am a migrant,' so that the examiner would take that into account, especially in the History and English papers where some of the words had the same sound but a different spelling depending on the meaning: for example, 'England one or won World War II.'

'Thank goodness I can write that at the top of the history paper,' Gilda thought, 'I can't remember the difference.' Gilda passed the exam well and was accepted by her new school. But something even more exciting was awaiting her before she started the new school year.

Vladimir's surgery was thriving, as was Hanna's business so he and Hanna decided to treat themselves to a three-week driving holiday through northern New South Wales over Christmas and the New Year. To that end Vladimir had booked a locum doctor to keep the practice running while he and Hanna took their holiday. But Hanna first needed to make arrangements for Gilda to stay with family friends. She finally decided on the Hemmings with whom they had stayed in Townsville.

The Hemmings were now in Lae, on the north coast of Papua New Guinea. Unbeknown to Gilda, it was Mrs Hemming who had suggested that Hanna and Vladimir could use the holiday period as a type of delayed honeymoon and fly Gilda up to Lae.

Gilda knew that her mother and Mrs Hemming wrote to each other because she would sometimes write a few lines to Julia at the end of her mother's letters.

Initially, Hanna was completely against the idea; after all, Gilda was only 13. Vladimir however, encouraged Hanna to allow Gilda to go reasoning, 'Gilda will be well looked after by the air hostesses on the plane, and when she changes planes.' He added, 'And the Hemmings will be at the airport when she lands. It will be safe.'

Hanna considered what her husband said, 'Yes,' she thought, 'I need some rest from my trouble-making daughter. But I mustn't look as though I'm pleased about it.' 'Vladimir,' she said sweetly, 'Gilda is so immature, I'm not sure she'll know what to do.' Vladimir contradicted her, 'Gilda may be lively, Hanna, but she is not immature. She is quite grown-up for her age.'

This did not please Hanna, 'I will think about it,' she said and with that she ended the conversation.

At the beginning of December, Hanna called Gilda to her, 'Gilda, I must speak with you,' she said pulling the girl to her on the settee. 'Oh goodness, what have I done?' thought Gilda. 'Come here, child, you are not in trouble,' coaxed Hanna, 'As you know, I have been in contact with the Hemmings and because you have passed the scholarship examination, I am allowing you visit them for three weeks.'

Gilda listened, she waited, but that was it. 'You mean to Lae where they live,' she asked incredulously. 'Yes,' replied Hanna. Gilda leapt from her seat and hugged her mother, 'Oh, thank you Mama. When can I go?' 'You will leave just before Christmas.' Gilda was surprised, 'Oh, that means we won't be together for Christmas?' Christmas was always a big family celebration. 'You will be on your own with Papa,' said Gilda. 'Yes,' replied Hanna who wanted to terminate the conversation. Just then Vladimir joined them.

'Papa, Papa, I'm going to see Julia,' Gilda called excitedly.
'Ah, Hanna, you have agreed,' said Vladimir. 'But Papa, you and Mama will be alone here for Christmas. Can't I go after Christmas?' Hanna was eager to put an end to the discussion, 'That's enough now Gilda, go and play.'

'Yes, Gilda but we will also be away,' Vladimir said innocently. He looked over at Hanna and saw the furious look on her face, 'Hanna, you didn't tell Gilda?'

'You are going on a holiday without me?' Gilda asked looking bewildered from one to the other. 'I didn't want to tell her as I knew she'd be upset,' answered Hanna, 'See what you've done; you've upset her.'

Hanna tried to smooth things over, 'Come Here, Schatzi, darling, let me give you a hug. We had no choice,' she continued, 'That was when the Hemmings could take you and you have always wanted to see Julia again, haven't you?' 'Yes,' replied Gilda sulkily.

'Well there you are, now you will see her. We will miss you but we have to do what's best for you so that you can see Julia. Do you understand?' continued Hanna.

Gilda answered stony-faced, 'I'll take Orion and Venny for a walk.' She fetched their collars and leads and headed out the door without looking at her parents.

CHAPTER 13
PAPUA NEW GUINEA
1957

In December 1957, Gilda, now 13 years old, left Brisbane and went to the Hemmings in Lae, the capital of Papua New Guinea's Morobe Province. Their idea had been that by taking this posting, Mr Hemming would receive extra pay, income tax free status plus a living-away-from-home allowance, all of which meant they would then be able to save for a better retirement to supplement what he still earned when they returned to Australia.

However, this only worked if you were a teetotaler and very strict with your savings plan. Most people who went up there had a wonderful social time and many of those same people went back to Australia financially worse off. One four-year stint became another four-year stint and so it would go on until the Hemming parents realised they had better get back to Australia while Mr Hemming could still get work in the aviation industry back in Australia.

Towards the end of 1957, Hanna, Gilda's mother, had written to Mrs Hemming, 'Dear Alice, how are you? Vladimir and I are planning a holiday and we were wondering if you could take Gilda for the three weeks we plan to be away? It would be so nice for the two girls to see each other again, don't you think? Yours with best regards, Hanna.'

The Hemmings agreed and were more than happy to have Gilda. Vladimir and Hanna could go on a "delayed honeymoon" as Mrs Hemming put it. However, Hanna thought that a rather vulgar way of talking about the holiday. Any suggestion of sexuality in language offended her.

'It is how the peasants and the workers talk back home,' she thought. But she was glad they agreed to take her daughter while they went on their road trip. They planned to go south as far as Newcastle on the coastal route, and then through northern New South Wales where Vladimir wanted to visit Macedonian banana farmers at Crabbe's Creek. It would be a long trip as the roads were not good, but they were looking forward to it. Suddenly, a flicker of their previous adventurous spirit seemed to reappear.

The day for Gilda to fly out of Brisbane came; she was so excited and was beside herself, jumping for joy. Holding Gilda's hand, Hanna said, 'Now, remember to be a good girl. Do as Mrs Hemming asks and play nicely with Julia.'

'Yes Mama,' replied Gilda. Hanna let go of Gilda's hand, 'Off you go then.' Gilda hesitated for a moment and was about to go. 'Wait,' Hanna called and beckoned her daughter. She then gave her a long hug. 'I love you my little girl,' she said through her tears.
'I love you too, Mama,' said Gilda.

'Now, off you go,' said Hanna whose tears had suddenly dried up. Gilda ran up the stairs of the plane and at the top of the stairs she turned to wave to her mother again but Hanna had gone.

The flight was noisy but exciting. The air hostess brought Gilda food and drink and activity books, but Gilda was more interested in seeing everything that was going on in the plane and looking out at the clouds. She had never been in a plane and it was strange being so high. At first her heart beat quickly but then she forgot about it and enjoyed herself. She fell asleep and only realised that she had slept when the air hostess nudged her to ask, 'Would you like something to eat and drink?'

'Oh, yes please, orange juice, please.' Gilda had never had orange juice; it wasn't something they had at home; they mainly had water or milk.
Just before they were about to land in Port Moresby, the capital of Papua New Guinea, on the south coast, the air hostess said to Gilda, 'Now, when everyone leaves the plane, you stay in your seat. I will take you from this plane to another one that will take you to Lae, okay?'

'Yes,' replied Gilda. 'Are you sure you understand,' the air hostess asked. 'Oh, yes, I need to wait for you to take me to another plane,' Gilda repeated in her accented English. 'Good girl,' replied the air hostess. At first, when Gilda saw the smaller plane, she was a little concerned. She was going from a big plane to a little plane.

As they walked to the smaller plane, Gilda said to the woman from the airline who was with her. 'Excuse me, what happens if there are heavy winds?' 'What do you mean?' asked the woman. 'Well,' continued Gilda pointing to the plane, 'this plane is so small, if the winds in the sky are strong, can it still fly?'

The air hostess looked at Gilda and saw that she was serious and she had noticed an accent in her English. 'Haven't you seen a small plane like this before?' 'No,' said Gilda, 'I've never been in a plane before now. We came out to Australia on a ship. I've never seen a plane close up.'

It was soon time to board the next flight and the stewardess, who was with Gilda, said to her, 'Wait here for a minute, I'll be back soon,' and Gilda saw her go over to a man in uniform and speak to him. The man turned to look at Gilda, smiled and nodded. The woman waved Gilda to come over and said to her, 'This is Mike, he's the pilot. As the plane doesn't have many passengers and it's a short flight he said that you can sit beside him and see what he sees from the plane. You have to stay strapped in your seat like on the big plane though. Can you promise that?' asked the air hostess. 'Oh, yes, really, yes,' exclaimed Gilda and so it happened that Gilda sat next to the pilot. The plane wasn't up amongst the clouds so she could still see the ocean. Gilda felt like a bird, it was magnificent. 'Hold on tight', said the pilot, as they approached for landing in Lae, 'This runway is very short so we'll come to a quick stop.' Gilda could see how the pilot lowered the plane, straightened it a bit and then, one minute the ocean was beneath them, then a big cliff and then, bounce, onto the runway. She could feel the brakes pulling hard till the aircraft came to a stop. Gilda was so excited she could barely breathe.

'Hey, how was that, little Miss?' asked the pilot, 'Not bad, eh?' Just as she was about to answer, a woman came to open her door and in the distance she saw Julia. Gilda was so excited to see her again. She didn't have a girlfriend as there was no one who matched her mother's expectations. Although Julia and Gilda hadn't written to each other they each had made comments on the end of their parents' letters.

'Well, hello, Gilda,' said Mrs Hemming coming towards her, 'My goodness you have grown but then so has Julia. It's so wonderful to see you.' Gilda suddenly felt shy, but she didn't know why. Julia and Gilda looked at each other and didn't know what to do. 'Oh, my goodness, look at these two,' laughed Mrs Hemming, 'why don't you both start with 'hello, nice to see you?' With that, both girls burst out laughing and hugged and that was the end of silence. Then it was 20-to-the-dozen chatter.

Mr and Mrs Hemming looked at each other pleased. 'I was so thrilled when your mother said that she and your father were going on holidays and asked whether I would mind if you came to see Julia,' said Mrs Hemming. 'My mother asked you?' Gilda asked completely surprised. 'Yes, why do you ask?' replied Mrs Hemming. 'Oh, nothing,' responded Gilda. To herself she said, 'I don't care, I'm here and I'm happy to be here.'

From the small airport they drove through Lae suburbs, made up of low-set cottages, lush green trees and palms with coloured foliage. They passed a country club, two tennis courts, a race track, and then went onto another dirt road to a series of nicer houses. It was in this compound that the Hemming house was situated.
Gilda had seen different people when she travelled to Australia but, these were different again. 'These dark women aren't wearing anything on top and the men aren't wearing pants just a piece of material,' she noticed. 'Do they always thump the ground with their sticks,' she asked.

'Yes, we do as well; it frightens snakes away in case they want to come out of the jungle and cross our path,' replied Mr Hemming with a laugh. He knew that would terrify Gilda and he always liked telling that to visitors. Gilda pulled a face, 'I'll remember that,' she replied. 'It's very hot, isn't it? Is it always this hot,' she asked. 'Pretty much', replied Mrs Hemming. 'It's just not as humid in the winter months but it's always hot.'

After almost a week, Gilda asked Mrs Hemming, 'Does it always rain at lunchtime?' 'Yes,' she replied, 'There is always a deluge for about an hour and then the sun comes out again.'

Gilda's stay in Lae was a warm, happy experience for her. The Hemming family were welcoming hosts and she went everywhere with them, like just another member of the family.

One day, they were visiting friends when the hostess said, 'John why don't you take Gilda up to Goroka the next time you fly up?' 'Sure,' answered John, 'no problem. Are you game?' he jokingly asked Gilda. John had a plane, a Tiger Moth, which he regularly flew to Goroka, in the Eastern Highlands Province to do deliveries there. The following week, Gilda was again at Lae airport, but this time she would fly in an even smaller plane. The Hemmings waited to wave her off.

'Okay, Gilda, this is not like a normal passenger plane, there are no windows and you will have to sit at the back of me in your own cockpit, so it'll be a bit breezy but it's well constructed so that it's pleasant. Put this helmet on and if you want to speak to me you'll have to yell,' John informed her. 'Are you okay?' he asked. 'Oh, yes,' Gilda was so tense with excitement she couldn't wait to get going. She could barely swallow; she didn't know what to expect. 'Let me check if you're all strapped in', he said to her, 'Yep, all looks good. Okay, and we're off,' he yelled.

Looking back at the Hemmings, Gilda waved to them and they waved back. Just at that moment the plane started to roll slowly and then suddenly it picked up speed to take off from the short runway. Whoosh! And they were in the air. She could feel the breeze.

Looking down she saw the ocean and behind her and Lae airport. All she could hear was the rhythmic sound of the engine and the silence of the sky. The whirring was mesmerising, the little air pockets, oh so slightly lifted the plane and dropped it again.

Suddenly John turned the plane and, instead of an ocean of blue, all

Gilda could see was an ocean of green, an impenetrable dense forest of trees. The plane soared higher to avoid the mountains. With each change of direction or altitude, Gilda's heart missed a beat, not in fear but in in her appreciation of the sheer magnificence of what she was experiencing.

She and John didn't talk, there was no need to, as both loved where they were, talking would have been an intrusion into the other's private world. Although she could hear the engine, it felt as though the plane was drifting, it was so smooth.

Finally, she felt John commence the plane's descent. 'We're going down now, Gilda,' he informed her, and in no time John landed the plane on a grass airstrip. 'We'll be here about an hour,' he told her. 'Make sure you stay with me. I need to look for people, so you have to keep an eye on me. Okay?'

'Oh, yes,' she said feeling grown up. No one had ever talked to her like an adult before and she liked it.

They drove out of the airport, which was very close to the township and parked the Jeep near some buildings close to where a large group of people were gathered. Gilda now saw what John meant by keeping an eye on him; the area was filled with hundreds of native people from all around that part of PNG, all dressed in the traditional costume of their area with face and body paint. They were participating in the regional festival called a Sing Sing, a dancing feast.

'John,' called Gilda, 'Why do a lot of these people have red teeth?' she asked. 'Betel nut,' he replied. 'What's that?' Gilda asked. 'The locals chew the flesh of the Areca nut – the locals call it betel nut - which releases a mildly stupefying narcotic. When they add ground lime made from sea shells this increases the narcotic effect of the betel nut. As the juice from the Areca nut comes into contact with the ground-up lime powder, saliva turns bright red and stains teeth very badly. It is almost impossible to remove the stain and eventually it rots their teeth.'

John wasn't really comfortable with Gilda there. The villagers had been dancing and chewing betel nut most of the day. 'Here, take my hand and hold on to it,' he said. When John had finished his business, they left in time to get back to Lae before dark.

One day, Julia and Gilda decided to take a walk along a path that lead away from the house and into the jungle. Before they left, Julia warned Gilda about the strange sense of humour some of the older native men had.

'What do you mean?' asked Gilda.

'You'll see when we meet one,' replied Julia, 'and if we don't meet one, there's no need to explain,' Julia replied matter-of-factly. They were walking along when they came upon a small, old, bent man with a walking stick and a cloth covering his hips. He too had a stick. He spoke PNG TOK PISIN and said, 'Hello Missus,' 'Hello,' Julia and Gilda replied. 'YU LUKIM EM?' he asked and pointed to a coiled snake. 'Is it alive?' Gilda asked. NOGAT, MISSUS, SNEK EMI DAI PINIS, 'the snake is dead', replied the old man with a grin that showed the remaining two or three teeth in the whole of his mouth and these were stained red.

'Don't believe him,' Julia whispered.

'We have to do something. He and the snake are in the middle of the path,' Gilda replied. 'Touch the snake with your stick to show us he's dead,' Julia called as a suggestion. 'He dead, you see.' The old man touched the snake and it didn't move. 'Come on,' Gilda said, 'the snake must be dead or it would have moved.' They approached the old man and just as they were close, he lifted the snake with his stick and threw it in their direction. The snake uncoiled as it fell giving the impression it was still alive.

Julia and Gilda screamed and bumped into each other as they ran away from the fortunately dead snake. The old man burst out laughing, picked up the snake with his hand and walked off cackling away, very pleased with himself. Yes, the snake was well and truly dead. Now Gilda saw what Julia meant when she said that the local people had a twisted sense of humour. They both laughed, now that any danger was over.

One evening, after Julia and Gilda had come home from seeing a film, they sat and chatted for a while. It was nearing midnight so they decided to go to bed. It seemed like Gilda had hardly fallen asleep when she heard windows crashing shut, glass breaking, doors slamming and other noises of furniture being moved from one end of the room to another.

She ran into the kitchen and saw that a light was on. Mrs Hemming who was there held her close and said, 'It's okay Sweetie, it's just one of our regular but so-far-harmless earthquakes. We call them LIKLIK GURIA and we are used to them. It'll stop soon. All the crockery in the kitchen cupboards is secured into small sections so that it doesn't move when the house and/or land moves. Usually, there are some minor casualties but that is life here.'

'Really!' Gilda thought, 'You can have daily electric storms in the middle of the day, earthquakes at night, crazy people throwing dead snakes at you,' and then she burst out laughing.

She loved the experience. All too soon the three weeks came to an end. Gilda had been so happy in Lae. No one yelled at her, somehow she was never naughty, and no one ever reprimanded her. Everyone talked to her rather than shouted at her. In the Hemming's household there were none of the tensions generated by her family that Gilda was used to. She had forgotten all about that until now when she thought of going home.

Gilda bade a sad farewell to the Hemmings, 'Goodbye, Mrs Hemming, goodbye Mr Hemming, thank you very much. I had the most wonderful time,' she said hugging them both. And then she hugged Mrs Hemming again and started to cry. Mrs Hemming pulled her gently away and looked at her, 'Gilda, look at me and listen. You may not understand everything I say, but I would like you to listen, okay?'

'Yes,' replied Gilda.

'You are growing up into a fine young lady,' continued Mrs Hemming, 'I want to you believe in yourself and be true to yourself. It will not always be easy but you must remember. You have been very mature here and very easy to get along with. Believe in yourself and not what other people say about you or expect you to do if it doesn't sit well with you. Do you hear me?' Mrs Hemming said making the point.

'Yes,' replied Gilda again, remembering how her mother had lied to her about coming to Lae. With that Mrs Hemming let Gilda go. She went straight to Julia and they hugged amidst tears. It had only been three weeks but it was three wonderful weeks that she would never forget. Time had passed too quickly for her. At least, Gilda hoped, the next time they would see each other it would be in Australia. Little did she know that it would be a long time before they would meet again.

Back on the aircraft, Gilda was again well treated by the air hostess but this time her mood was down. 'Oh, well, at least I had this experience; no one can take it away from me,' she consoled herself. Then, sitting erect, she suddenly felt very grown up and resolutely thought, 'I'm going to live my life my way. No one will control me.' Gilda always bounced back.

CHAPTER 14
1958 – 1959

After Gilda returned from Lae, Hanna and she were busy getting all the formalities completed for Gilda to go to her new school, Brisbane Girls' Grammar School at Petrie Terrace, a private girls' school.

Gilda now went by bus to her new high school. This meant she had to leave home early and she returned home before her mother who still worked in her dressmaker shop. Thus she still had time to herself because Vladimir had expanded his medical practice with evening consultations. 'I love these times to myself.' she often said. 'I love the peace, no dramas.'

At her new school, Gilda found things quite strange at first. Not only was the school routine different in secondary school, but the teachers and students were also of a different calibre. Because it was a private school, there was more emphasis on decorum, speaking correctly, being ladylike and paying attention to 'British-style' manners. It felt odd. Apart from the year with the Williams family and her time at a Queensland Government State School, Gilda had barely mixed with Australians and even then only with children at school. The Dobinski's friends were all foreigners. Gilda didn't know much about Australian social customs and ways of behaving. It was confusing; sometimes she would run to a class and a teacher would ask her to go back to where she came from and 'walk like a lady,' and then be given a penalty for being late to class.

'I would have been on time, but….' Gilda started to explain. The teacher cut her off saying, 'There are no 'buts', it's is your responsibility to be on time. Keep this up, my girl, and you will get an after-school detention.'

Most of the girls seemed to know each other, having come from the same primary schools; Gilda initially was friendless. She knew no one. However, there was another girl, Elizabeth, also like Gilda, 'a loner' and soon they became firm friends. Elizabeth, known as Beth, and Gilda lived not far from each other and met up on weekends.

Beth's parents had died many years ago in a car accident and she lived with her only relative in Brisbane, her grandmother. Her heritage was German - similar to Gilda's, although Gilda thought herself as being more French than Austrian at that time. Given Hanna's rigid strictures about with whom Gilda could socialise. Some time elapsed before Gilda mentioned Beth at home. To Gilda's surprise, Hanna was prepared to meet Beth. 'Very well, yes, you may bring her home,' said Hanna, 'Her family must be well-to-do if she is going to the Grammar School; it's expensive enough. While we are on the subject of school, you don't seem to do much homework. 'Yes,' replied Gilda, 'I always do all my homework.'

Hanna left it at that as she was pre-occupied and concerned about another matter. 'I don't really like that Vladimir corresponds so much with his previous family in Macedonia,' Hanna thought.

Gilda was worried because she only did homework in the subjects she liked and understood. Mathematics which had been her best subject in Townsville had progressively become her worst subject. She couldn't understand much of the content of many of her first-year high school subjects. This contributed to her failing her initial 'in-class' Math's tests. In addition, she found French studies boring; her Australian teacher had a strange pronunciation and what the class was learning was well below Gilda's proficiency and fluency which earned her 100% marks in examinations.

Not long after the family had arrived in Australia, Hanna called Vladimir and Gilda together and said, 'We must make sure that we do not forget the languages that we speak just because we live here. At home, on one day we will speak German and the next day French and then continue that way. We will learn English by living here.' And indeed that is what the family did for many years. Years later, Gilda would acknowledge how grateful she was for the language immersion she experienced as a child and the stand her mother took about daily speaking those two languages. They also picked up some Russian as most of Vladimir's patients were from the Russian community. In addition, they frequently heard Serbo-Croatian or Macedonian because of Vladimir's compatriots who visited them or whom they visited.

Gilda decided to only speak English at home. It had become easier and she wanted to fit in. Her parents spoke distinctly foreign-accented English but Gilda worked at speaking English with no accent.

Unfortunately, Gilda's English results did not improve because she found reading school set novels and poetry challenging. At home, there was no one to help her. By contrast, parents of girls in her class sat with their daughters in the evening and worked through set texts with them. Gradually, Gilda fell behind and lost interest in her schoolwork. She found history and science interesting, but again, her English ability was the problem. She spoke English fluently now, but written English was difficult and she appealed to Hanna, 'Mama, can I have an English tutor, please?' 'Certainly not,' Hanna replied firmly, 'I never had tutors. If I found subjects difficult, I worked harder at them. Work harder and you'll see that you will improve.' Gilda knew better than to pursue the topic.

In the meantime, Gilda and Beth had made other school friends and Gilda met their parents at school sporting events. It was at these events that Gilda noticed, in contrast with Hanna, how differently the mothers spoke to their daughters and to her. These parents asked Gilda questions, listened intently to her replies and held lengthy conversations with her. She started to resent how she was treated at home and would deliberately do things to annoy Hanna. Not enough to get slapped, but just enough to get her angry. Gilda was immune to Hanna's yelling and started to enjoy the irritating effect that her questions had on her mother. It was one of the few ways she could get back at Hanna.

Gilda's music studies continued at her new school; she loved her lessons and her results were always excellent. 'Ah, I could stay here all day and play and listen to others play,' Gilda would say dreamily. Often at lunch times, she explored the music area, opening doors that appeared locked. 'Oh, what is this,' she asked herself when she opened a door and saw an instrument that looked like a piano lying on its side.

'What are you doing here?' a voice behind her asked. Gilda swung around and stiffened with fright when she saw a teacher. 'I asked you a question,' the teacher said gently. 'I'm sorry, I'll go,' Gilda replied. 'No, you don't need to go,' the teacher said, 'just answer my question.' 'I love this area,' Gilda started, 'I love listening to the music that comes from the different rooms. I didn't have class and as its lunch time, I thought I would look around. I didn't know I shouldn't be here.' 'I'm not suggesting you shouldn't be here. I'm Miss Ainsworth, Head of the Music Department,' explained the teacher.

Miss Ainsworth approached her. 'Isn't that a beautiful instrument,' she said pointing to the piece Gilda was admiring. 'Oh, yes, what is it?' Gilda asked. 'It's a harp. Run your fingers lightly over the strings,' suggested the teacher. Gilda had never heard anything so exquisite. Miss Ainsworth positioned herself at the harp and showed Gilda how to sit and hold her hands to produce the harp's shimmering sound.

Gilda did as she was shown and then got up and said, 'Thank you so much, Miss Ainsworth. I won't get into trouble for this will I?' 'Why should you get into trouble? Of course not. It's wonderful that you want to spend your lunch hour here. Come anytime and look at all the other instruments we have.' she said gently and then asked Gilda if she played and instrument.

'Piano,' Gilda replied.

'Come with me, I want to show you something.' Miss Ainsworth held out a hand to guide Gilda into another room. Gilda couldn't believe her eyes. 'This is known as a concert grand piano,' the teacher said, 'Sit down and play me something.' Gilda knew a few pieces by heart but her favourite was Frédéric Chopin's Valse - Op. 64 N° 2, so she played it. Miss Ainsworth was impressed and said so. 'You play well and with feeling. That is good. Come back and look around again.'

Gilda loved animals and wanted a dog of her own. Orion and Venny actually belonged to Hanna but Gilda walked them daily and fed them. She would bring home every stray cat and dog in the street that looked sick and asked her father to heal them. 'You're a doctor, Papa,' she would say, 'You heal people, so you should be able to heal animals.'

Very few cats or dogs that Gilda brought home ever survived. 'I'm sorry, Gilda,' Vladimir would say, 'That dog was too sick to heal, he died.' What Gilda didn't know was that Vladimir euthanised the animals. One day Gilda found a small, black puppy. It didn't seem sick but it had been abandoned and Gilda asked if she could keep it. Hanna was about to say something, when Vladimir said, 'Hanna, let Gilda keep it.' After a pause Hanna said, 'Very well, but it stays downstairs,' replied Hanna.

'But, Mama, it's so little and it's cold downstairs. He might go out onto the road. I can have him in my room; it won't be a nuisance.' 'No,' Hanna said emphatically, 'The dog goes downstairs.' 'But Mama, Orion and Venny stay upstairs,' Gilda replied. 'I said, no, Gilda, enough or I won't let you keep it.'
Gilda stayed with the puppy downstairs for as long as she could before she went to bed. As soon as she awoke the next morning, she went downstairs but found the puppy dead; it had suffocated in a pipe that it had fallen into. Gilda was beside herself with grief. She couldn't speak to her mother or her father. She didn't know what to think. 'How could she? She killed him.'

'Why doesn't he stand up to her? Why doesn't he stand up for me?' she asked cradling the dead pup in her arms as tears streamed down her face. 'They don't care about me. She hates me and he doesn't care. They can stop me having a dog but they can't stop me doing what I want to do. I'll find ways. They are horrible.'

Gilda developed a numbness, a shield that protected her from her mother's rage and her step-father's disinterest. She also became defiant because she realised that, as she was now almost as tall as her mother. When Gilda stood up to her mother, Hanna mostly gave in, and whimpered 'My nerves, my poor nerves,' she would exclaim. 'That girl will be the death of me.' Every now and then Hanna aimed a slap at her daughter but Gilda, most often, avoided the blow if she was quick. 'That girl will be the end of me,' Hanna would moan to her husband, 'My nerves are so weak and she has no pity for me. You do something,' Hanna pleaded with Vladimir, 'I do everything for her and this is how she repays me,' Hanna continued, squeezing tears from her eyes. Vladimir just stood silently.

Gilda censored what she told her parents about her school life. As the school year progressed, Gilda started to make friends with girls and boys who went to a local milk bar and they would all hang out there. Later, when Gilda took her mother's dogs for a walk she would return to the milk bar to talk with girls and boys who were about her age. Most of them went to a different school called State High. One of the boys, Jimmy, liked Gilda. He had a motor bike and would sometimes take her for a ride while her other friends looked after the dogs.

When Gilda's first year came to an end and the report card was sent home, Hanna was furious with the results and comments. It was the custom that parents went to the school and spoke with the Class Teacher and so Hanna and Gilda attended this meeting. 'Good evening, Mrs Dobinski,' began Gilda's class teacher, Miss Fletcher, 'It's a pleasure to meet you.' 'Good evening,' replied Hanna formally. Miss Fletcher continued, 'Is there anything in particular that you would like to discuss?' 'I cannot understand why Gilda's results are so bad,' Hanna replied. 'Overall, Gilda's results are satisfactory,' replied the teacher, 'She only has problems in two subjects.'

Hanna was not content with that comment. 'How is Gilda's behaviour?' she asked.

'Gilda is a very active and intelligent girl who needs to release her energy. She participates well in her sporting activities, however, she has problems in the Maths and English classes where she has difficulty understanding some aspects of the work,' replied the teacher. Hanna responded, 'If she is so intelligent, why is she not getting better results?'

Miss Fletcher responded, 'It is difficult in the beginning for children who come from non-English-speaking backgrounds. That is why we suggest individual attention such as tutoring. Gilda tells me that you are not in favour of this.'

'Oh, hell,' thought Gilda, 'Now I'll cop it when we get back home.' And she was right.

'What do you mean by telling the teacher what we say at home? You don't tell people anything, nothing more than they need to know. Do you hear me? No one can be trusted,' Hanna shouted while holding her daughter firmly by the shoulders and shaking her.

'Phew,' thought Gilda, 'That wasn't so bad.'

In November, the 1958 school year ended. The holidays were spent at home with trips to the seaside or on picnics. Beth, her friend from school, came to some of these outings before she left for Sydney with her grandmother to visit relatives. Christmas was celebrated as always in the traditional Viennese way on Christmas Eve, with a candle-lit tree and special baked and roasted foods. Hanna took a break from her dress-making business and Vladimir had a break from the surgery, only taking emergency calls. Gilda went along with what her parents organised although her preference was to spend time on her own. She loved to read and had discovered the Famous Five series by Enid Blyton. These books were helpful for Gilda in developing basic skills in English reading and writing.

Just after Christmas, Vladimir said to his wife, 'Hanna, in February next year, I would like to bring my daughter, Irena, out from Macedonia to stay with us for a few months. My son cannot come. He is tied up at his hospital in Skopje, in Macedonia. But Irena can manage the time during her University break.' This took Hanna by surprise. She knew he corresponded with his now adult children, but she thought she was safe from them ever coming out this far. 'I see,' was all Hanna could manage to say and then she pulled herself together, 'Of course, you must see Irena; she is your daughter. What are you planning?' 'I've made enquiries and there is a flight that arrives here on 1 February. She would stay until the end of April.'

'Oh, my goodness,' thought Hanna, 'Three months. I know what she's planning. She's planning to create a rift between Vladimir and myself so that, when we break up, he can then remarry her mother. 'What are we going to tell Gilda?' asked Hanna. 'The simple truth, tell her that Irena is s my daughter from a previous marriage'. Vladimir then laughed and said, 'I doubt very much that Gilda will ask anything about it. If it were an animal she would be more interested.'

On 1 February, 1959, Irena stepped off the plane to be greeted by an adoring father, a cheerful Gilda and a formal Hanna. From that moment on, the Dobinski household became firmly locked in the grip of continual emotional confrontation. It was clear from the beginning that there was a competition between Hanna and Irena for Vladimir's time and affections. Irena's motives were clear; she wanted her parents back together again. Hanna underestimated the power of parental love. Irena also made Vladimir feel guilty that he had abandoned her, her brother and their mother, and that for many years they were forced to live in poverty as a result of his fling with 'that woman,' as Irena always referred to Hanna.

'Look at how she treats you all,' Irena pointed out to her father.

Unfortunately, Hanna gave Irena a lot of ammunition to destroy her in her father's eyes, and to paint a beautiful picture of marital life and family bliss in Macedonia as one family again with her mother. Not even Hanna's advantage of the marital bed competed with Irena's portrayal of idyllic Macedonian wedded bliss. Sadly, Hanna, who took all affronts personally, made life even more difficult for Vladimir.

Gilda also took advantage of this feud between her mother and father. For once she wasn't the brunt of Hanna's explosive and at times irrational behavior. Another antagonist in the house gave Gilda more freedom and protection. By the time Irena left three months later, there remained a severe fracture in the relationship between Hanna and Vladimir.

However, there was another casualty, the close relationship between Gilda and Beth. If Hanna was miserable, so should everyone else be, and Hanna lashed out at Gilda and Beth's friendship. Gilda was told to stop seeing her friend. 'Gilda,' Hanna said, 'I do not approve of this girl; she has no background.'
'But her parents are dead,' Gilda replied, 'She lives with her grandmother who is very nice. You've met Beth, she's nice too.'
'No,' said Hanna, 'and that is that. You are not to go to her house again and she will certainly not come here again. Find better friends at school.'

Gilda shouted, 'You hate me. You don't want me to have any friends. You're just mean. You want to control me, well, you won't, never! I'll do as I please.' Hanna turned around and slapped her daughter so hard on the face that Gilda stumbled backwards, almost falling.

'Don't you dare speak to me like that! That tramp you have as a friend is teaching you that sort of behaviour.' She closed in on her so that Gilda was terrified of another imminent blow and moved away. Suddenly they saw Irena and Vladimir at the door. Irena went over to Gilda to help her but Gilda fled the room.

Gilda continued to lead a double life. It seemed like history was repeating itself. Hanna had lived two lives in Vienna, one to accommodate her mother, and the other when she was away from home. Gilda would make excuses such as taking the dogs for a walk on weekends and meet Beth. Or, she would say she had school sport practice if it was not convenient to take the dogs. Hanna was in the shop all day Saturday and Vladimir had surgery or house visits, or he took Irena to see other Macedonians. He asked Hanna to come too, but she preferred not to. She isolating herself with her behaviour. Beth and Gilda didn't meet often but they managed.

When Irena left at the end of April, Hanna started a charm offensive on Vladimir but it was clear that things were not the same between them. Vladimir was unforgiving about Hanna's tantrums and was as stubborn as a rock. When Hanna screamed and ranted, he became as silent as the Sphinx. Gilda profited from learning the benefits of his silent resistance toward Hanna, something that her mother couldn't handle.

One evening, Gilda was at the milk bar and she, Jimmy and another couple drove up to the Mt Coot-tha lookout. Gilda had never seen anything so beautiful as Brisbane by night from such a height. The two couples sat on a bench enjoying the view when Jimmy kissed Gilda. She didn't know what to do, but she just followed his lead. She felt a sensation within that she had never felt before, at times it was as though she stopped breathing. She had never been held like that either; it was so tender, so gentle. Jimmy had his arms around Gilda and in this blissful world they sat unconscious of time, sometimes chatting but mostly in silence, in the beautiful stillness of the evening. Suddenly Jimmy looked at his watch, and said, 'Oh God, it's 9.00 PM. I'm sorry Gilda.'

'Oh, no,' cried Gilda, 'I'm going to get killed.'

They left in a hurry. Gilda collected the dogs and hurried home. She was barely upstairs when her mother flew at her. 'Where have you been? We were worried to death about you.' 'I've been walking the dogs,' Gilda said hurriedly, terrified and shaking as she took the leads off the two dogs.

'You liar,' Hanna yelled and slapped her across the face, 'You've been with boys, haven't you, you slut. Tell me the truth.'

And so, protecting her face, Gilda told her parents who she was with and where they had gone but that they just enjoyed the view. Hanna was beside herself, Vladimir had to hold his wife back. 'Hanna,' he said, 'Let the child talk; there is no need to hit her.' 'You idiot,' she yelled at Vladimir, 'This is your field, girls who become pregnant because they were stupid with boys who took advantage of them.' 'Hanna, we don't know this. Give her a chance to explain.' he replied. Hanna screamed back at him, 'Look at her dress. It's crumpled and dirty. She's been in the bushes with a boy.' 'No, no, I haven't,' said Gilda was crying and pleading, 'We were only sitting on a bench. There was another boy and girl and we were chatting. We lost track of time.'

'Come into the surgery and get up on the bed to let your father examine you. At least if you are pregnant he can stop it,' Hanna ranted. Vladimir tried to reason with her but she was uncontrollable. 'Get up on the bed,' yelled Hanna as she dragged Gilda into the room.

'No,' cried Gilda struggling to get away.

'I'll make you get on that bed.' and with that she knocked Gilda to the ground and dragged her across the floor pushing her up on the bed.' Gilda was still struggling. 'Help me get her on the bed,' she screamed at Vladimir who then took Gilda by the legs while Hanna had her by the arms and they lifted her onto the consulting bed.

'Examine her,' she ordered Vladimir glaring at him. 'If she's had sex and is pregnant and you didn't examine her, I'll make life hell for you and your career will be over,' Hanna hissed.

'No, no,' Gilda cried wriggling to get free. Hanna held both Gilda's arms at her chest and with all her weight leant on her to keep her on the table, while Vladimir lifted her skirt. He put on his plastic gloves and inserted a cold metal instrument into Gilda's vagina.

'Ouch! That hurts,' she cried and tried to move but her mother had her nailed to the table. 'Then stop moving, you stupid girl,' replied her mother.

Vladimir examined Gilda internally to see if her hymen was still intact.

When Vladimir had completed his examination, he pulled the instrument out, pulled her skirt down, and said quietly with his eyes downcast, 'She hasn't been touched.'

Gilda was in a state of shock, and whimpering as she still lay on the table holding her stomach to make the pain go away. Looking at

Gilda, Vladimir said, 'I'm sorry, Gilda. I'm so, so sorry. We should have believed you.'

He tried to touch Gilda's arm but she pulled it away and lay on the hard bed sobbing. Her mother let her go without saying anything. Gilda curled up in the foetal position on the bed and stayed there for some time and then eased herself off it. There was a look in her eyes that expressed the disbelief at what had just happened.

Gilda stared at Hanna and Vladimir with contempt and then with a deliberate low tone in her voice said, 'I wish I could hate you. I wish I could hate you but I can't. Don't you ever, ever tell me what I can and can't do. I never want to talk to either of you ever again. You wouldn't have done this to anyone. You must hate me so much that you could do this.' She opened the door to her room, went inside, locked the door, and holding her stomach fell on her bed weeping uncontrollably until she fell asleep.

Vladimir looked at Hanna but couldn't bring himself to say anything. Hanna stormed off and slammed the bedroom door. That night, Vladimir went to sleep in the spare bedroom.

Things deteriorated rapidly in the Dobinski house after this. Vladimir continued to sleep in the spare room and the atmosphere was icy in the house. One Saturday, after morning surgery, Gilda was in the garden playing with the dogs, when she heard fierce yelling in the house. She ran in to see what the commotion was about. It was her parents yelling accusations at each other. She had never seen them like that. Gilda ran in and said, 'Stop, please stop. Mama, Papa, what is going on?' 'Oh?' said Hanna with a sarcastic sneer, 'Papa, is that what you called him? Tell her, Vladimir. Tell her, are you her Papa?' 'Hanna, please, there is no need to hurt the child, and this is between you and me.'

'What are you talking about?' Gilda asked alarmed shaking as she spoke. 'Go on, Papa dear,' Hanna mocked, 'Tell her who you really are.' Vladimir went over to Gilda, put his hands on her shoulders and distraught said, 'Darling, we should have told you this long ago but I am not your real father.'

Gilda stood motionless for a brief moment, pulled herself away from him and yelled. 'What is this? Have you two gone insane? First you fight like wild animals and now….this is not funny. If this is your idea of a joke or trying to get even with each other. 'IT's NOT FUNNY,' Gilda yelled, turning in one direction and then in another, not knowing what to do with herself.

'It's the truth,' Vladimir replied quietly while Hanna stood gloating at her victory. Vladimir started to explain. 'No, thank you. I think you've said enough. You've both said enough,' said Gilda stiffening, pushing him away and struggling to hold back tears. 'What else do I have to put up with? If you weren't such a doormat maybe she wouldn't carry on like she does. Or maybe she would.'

'You're mad.' Gilda said looking at her mother. Hanna went to make a move, 'Go on, I dare you, hit me. You hit me again and I'll hit you back. I'm done with the way you treat me, both of you.' She looked at her father and said, 'You're gutless.' Gilda then looked at both of them for an instant before turning and running away. She went out of the house and down the street. She was no longer able to control herself and the tears exploded.

So at the age of 15, Gilda's world was turned upside down for the second time. She walked and walked and walked. She didn't want to go to her friends at the milk bar. She wasn't sure that they would still like her if they knew what was going on at her house. She had no idea how long or where she walked. When she arrived home, Hanna came to her and started, 'My darling....'

'Don't, don't talk to me. Leave me alone. You're just as much to blame in this lie as he is. Nothing you can say will change that. You have lied to me all these years. He lied to me all these years. Do I matter so little in your lives that you had to have him tell me like that, so that you could get even with him?' With that Gilda went into her room.
While her parents were going through their own problems, Gilda became more and more withdrawn. Meal times had long stopped being a family affair. Vladimir would eat early as he had surgery from 3.00 PM - 8.30 PM, only having a cigarette break sometime in

between. Gilda would eat before Hanna came home so as not to eat together. She would also play the piano when both her parents were busy or away. Hanna would then eat after she came home from the shop. Otherwise, Gilda spent most her time in her room, leaving the house briefly to walk the dogs.

One day she stood at her window. 'If only I had the courage to jump,' she said to herself looking at the height of her bedroom window to the side street below. 'If I knew I would die, I would jump. I've had enough of this. It just gets worse and worse. I feel so helpless. I can't have friends because they would drop me if they knew of my family problems. So, she decided on a different method of ending this emotional rollercoaster she was on.

One evening, Gilda took her pajamas and slippers and a scarf into the bathroom to shower before going to bed. 'I'm more in control here,' she thought. She stepped into the bathtub, tied the scarf onto the external shower pipe and then around her neck and turned the shower on to full strength so that it was noisy. There she stood for a moment and then fell to her knees to allow the scarf to tighten around her neck. The pipe collapsed under her weight and fell into the bathtub. Water went everywhere. It made such a noise that Vladimir and Hanna came running into the bathroom. Hanna had just enough time to loosen the scarf and hide it in her slippers. 'What has happened?' Hanna asked. 'I don't know, Mama. The pipe just fell into the tub,' a terrified Gilda replied. Vladimir turned the water off. 'Are you alright, Gilda?' he asked. 'Yes, thank you, just a little shaken.' she replied.

Yes, Gilda was shaken; she was flabbergasted that she wanted to kill herself. 'I can't believe it. That was crazy. I'm becoming as crazy as they are,' she thought as she returned to her room. Suddenly, she became suddenly excited, 'There is a way out. I'll secretly get a job and then leave home. I'll make enough for rent and food. I can leave home when I'm 16.' Then she became sad, 'I'll have to give up the piano till I can afford to buy one. It's their piano and in any case I won't tell them where I live.' Gilda lay pensively on her bed until she fell asleep with a hope for the future.

Life in the Dobinski household went back to as normal as it could under the circumstances. The two Dobinskis led separate lives under the same roof. They played the happy couple when friends came, and all was temporarily healed when the whisky or wine flowed. Gilda saw that she could now play the one parent off against the other, because each was extra nice to her in futile attempts to win her over.

In August, Gilda went on her first official date. Her parents had established themselves with a nice group of Australians in the medical profession. One of these families had a son, David, two years older than Gilda and Hanna who was match-making, allowed Gilda and David to go to the Brisbane Exhibition together during the school holidays. They had such a pleasant time that David asked Gilda out for lunch the following week.

They went to Lennons Hotel in the city centre. In those days, meals in restaurants were always a formal affair – starched white tablecloths and multiple pieces of cutlery to fit with each course. They were shown to their table. When David held out Gilda's chair, she made sure that she sat down like a lady. There was no à la carte menu for lunch, only a set four-course menu. They were chatting happily and the waiter brought them their entrée, which was followed by the main course. Much to Gilda's horror it consisted of lamb roast, roast potato, roast pumpkin and… green peas!! She sliced a piece of meat and ate it, and then took a piece of potato on which to squash the peas in the English way. Suddenly, there was an explosion of peas that sprayed over the table and onto the floor. Gilda was aghast. She placed her cutlery on the plate, and lowered her head to hide her acute embarrassment.

David burst out laughing, 'Those little buggers have a mind of their own, don't they? Mine can even hit the ceiling. Stupid way to eat peas, I scoop my peas with the fork, makes more sense.' Gilda looked up at him surprised. 'You're not annoyed? You're not embarrassed?' 'Heavens, no,' David replied. 'No, really?' she repeated.

'Nope,' he repeated smiling.

With that Gilda breathed a sigh of relief and laughed too. The head waiter quickly appeared with his little dustpan and mini brush and cleaned the table while another waiter whisked up the recalcitrant peas off the floor with a broom.

'Please don't tell my mother. And don't tell your mother, she might tell mine,' pleaded Gilda. 'Good heavens, no. I never tell my mother anything.' 'Really?' Gilda asked incredulously opening her eyes wide. 'No, they don't really want to know. As long as everything appears okay, they're fine with it and can happily get on with what they want to do. Adults make such a fuss over nothing,' he replied cheekily. They talked and talked and had a fun lunch.

Gilda however, shied away from getting close to people. She would have friends until she started to get fearful and then somehow the relationships would evaporate. She didn't do this consciously, something inside her took over. There wouldn't be a disagreement; Gilda would just no longer be there; she would disappear. She didn't want to go back to the Grammar School, she wanted to go to State High where her other group of friends went. She and Jimmy had stayed friends and nothing more, again Gilda's decision.

'Papa,' she said one morning in December. You know how expensive the Grammar School is?' 'Yes, why do you ask?' he replied. 'Well, a few of the girls from my class are changing schools because their parents want them to go to State High; they say it's a better school for getting good results.' 'We'll need to speak to your mother about this,' Vladimir replied.

'Why?' Gilda asked, "She never asks you when she wants to do something. Why don't you stand up for yourself and do something on your own for a change? Come on, Papa. All you have to do is buy the uniform and then no more expenses.'

Vladimir looked at Gilda who was looking at him as sweetly as she could, 'Okay, but don't tell her,' Vladimir said, 'Once you're there, she won't be able to do a thing about it.'

Gilda gave him a big kiss on the cheek and a huge hug. She had learnt well from her mother!

CHAPTER 15
1960 – 1961

In the Dobinski household there was an attempt to use the coming Christmas festivities as a way of forgetting recent bitter memories sparked by the now concluded visit of Vladimir's daughter, Irena, and the bitter clashes between Hanna and Gilda. The turmoil sparked by Vladimir's daughter had receded but the wounds had healed. Family members took refuge in their occupations, Vladimir in his medical practice, Hanna in the shop and Gilda just tried to get on with her life and keep out of their way. Now there was an uneasy peace.

Strangely, despite the turbulence of her home life, Gilda, for a time, fared best. She was able to leap back into the world of joy through new-found experiences aided by a measure of freedom from her parents who were totally embroiled in their own misery and largely left her alone as long as she stayed out of sight. Her experiences to date had taught her that nothing is permanent and as a reaction, she lost sight of future opportunities and lived only for the 'now'.

As she grew older, Gilda discovered people who cared for her, whether they were her friends, or adults who were friends with her parents. But she didn't notice that she had learned to only believe in the permanency of herself. No one was able to get close to her. Although she was friendly and grateful, she guarded her inner being. Again, she didn't do that consciously. That was the way she had learned to survive. These friends could be male or female, young or old, married or single. If they tried to get too close, she would 'disappear'.

Until that point, they would have helped deliver her from the gloom of her home encounters, from the moroseness that could have swallowed her into melancholia or depression, which did happen at times. Gilda didn't know what these mood changes were but she became prone to nervous depression. What helped her through these was her ability to focus on the good and wipe out the bad, which was why she also couldn't hate. Was this also something that she had unconsciously cultivated to survive? Or, was she being protected and watched over by 'Higher forces'? Much later in life, she realised that she had always been protected by 'Higher forces'. When she recognised this, she learned to work with these and ask for guidance.

Depending on the situation, Gilda had learned to cope with the physical appearance of her damaged left eye. In photographs she would wink so that the left eye was shut, or she would hold her head sideways to 'hide' the left eye. She distracted attention from her left eye by becoming a highly animated, smiling conversationalist. She had also learned to adjust in many other ways, but these strategies could not compensate for her lack of self-worth that lay hidden behind her smiling façade. Outwardly she was very much in control, within was another story.

The first day of the 1960 school year arrived and Gilda waited until her mother left for the shop before she dressed in her new school uniform. Vladimir was on early morning house calls when Gilda left, and in any case, he wouldn't have noticed. He had forgotten the value of conversation: his work was his world. Gilda managed to hide her new school uniform for a week, but come Saturday, weekly laundry day, Gilda was summoned by an angry call from Hanna, 'Gilda, come here,' Hanna said, 'What is this uniform?'

Gilda kept a distance between herself and her mother. 'I am now going to another school. Papa said I could.' While Hanna was incensed that they had gone behind her back, all she could say was, 'We'll continue this discussion when your father returns.' Hanna hated not being in control.
The discussion resumed in the evening when surgery ended. 'Vladimir, Gilda, come into the lounge, I want to speak with you.' Talking to her husband, Hanna said, 'Gilda tells me that you gave her permission to go to another school. I want to know why I wasn't consulted.'

Gilda held her breath and waited for her father's answer. Much to her surprise, he calmly replied, 'Hanna, you always say 'no' to anything the child asks for. It has also become clear that you and I are not able to discuss anything with any civility. When Gilda asked me, as her father, I took it upon myself to make this decision.'

Hanna exploded, 'Can't you see what she is doing? She is playing us off against each other.' Continuing in a calm manner, Vladimir said, 'Then she has learned that well from you.' Hanna was so taken aback, she was momentarily speechless. 'Very well,' she replied with razor sharp steel in her voice, 'You will see that this is a mistake. If her school results are not to my satisfaction at the end of the first term, she will go to boarding school. I have had enough of her. I worked hard for you to get your medical qualifications back. The shop is not easy work and I do it so that our life in this new country can be what we want it to be. And now, I have both of you collaborating against me.' She stopped and waited for a reaction. No one said anything. They had both learned to stay silent and that ended the discussion.

But Hanna wasn't finished. She liked to repeat herself in an altered dramatic way. She looked at Gilda and said, 'I want to repeat, you may stay at the new school for this term but if your results, in my estimation, are poor, you will go to a boarding school. I have been talking to the priest we know and he can get you into a good Catholic school.'

Gilda looked over at her father. 'Do you know about this?' she asked him. 'No,' he replied stunned. Gilda turned to her mother. 'So, you've already been talking about putting me into a boarding school. When were you going to tell me, tell either of us? It's my life. I have a right to know.'
Hanna looked at her haughtily and sniggered, 'Until you can prove to me that you are responsible, you have no right to make decisions about what you will do. I am your mother and you will do as I say. In any case, you have so ruined my nerves, the boarding school will be the best for both of us.'

Gilda knew that irrespective of her term results she would be going to boarding school next term so she decided to make the best of it. Throughout the term, she went to classes that interested her because she loved to learn. She tried new subjects and she was fascinated by Physiology and Zoology, except she didn't like dissecting frogs or other living things. Maths she skipped as she got more and more behind, and some English classes also, though strangely she loved the grammar lessons and saw that as a means for her to improve her written English because she loved to write.

Sadly, Gilda's music lessons stopped because they hadn't been organised at the start of the term. Nevertheless, she still played piano at home. Most of the time at school, she hung out with friends who also skipped classes. They would go to the park next to the school and chat and laugh till they heard the school bell. The school would telephone home and Vladimir would receive the message. All he would say was, 'Gilda, the school rang and said that you are not going to some classes. You know what your mother said about your results.'

'Yes, Papa, she said that she had to be pleased with the results. You know she would not be pleased if I received 100 percent in all courses. So why bother? I bet she's already enrolled me at the boarding school. You know Papa, I will succeed in doing what I want after I leave school, but on my own, not what she says. I want to make music my career.'

Needless to say, in Hanna's estimation Gilda's school report was unsatisfactory and Gilda was sent to a boarding school 15 minutes from where they lived.

On the morning that it was time to go to her new school, Gilda mused, 'I wonder what this place will be like. The nuns are Catholic like at primary school. Oh, well, I'll cope, I'm also older now and not as clueless as I was in primary school.'

It was clear that the Mother Superior and Hanna had spoken well before this meeting because the nun made comments such as, 'Don't worry Mrs Dobinski, we'll make sure your daughter studies,' and 'We do not tolerate such behaviour here.' During the interview, Hanna was superficially sweet and loving towards her daughter and charming to the nun. Gilda sat quietly only speaking when asked a question.

'Is Gilda prone to being sullen?' the nun asked looking over at her. Before Hanna could answer, Gilda replied, 'Oh, no, Mother Superior, I'm just quiet because I'm listening. Otherwise, I'm very lively, aren't I Mama?' She smiled sweetly at Hanna.

As Hanna left she gave her daughter a kiss, hugged her dramatically and said, 'Now darling, be a good girl, and I'll see you when the school allows me to take you out for the day on Boarders' Day Out.'

Gilda couldn't wait for her mother to go. She knew she could handle any situation. Another nun was waiting to show her to her room in the Year 11 and 12 dormitory. For Gilda, her new surroundings seemed pleasant.

The dormitory block was Spartan, but clean. Gilda thought, 'This is good, at least I have my own room,' when shown her allotted cubicle. The cubicle was too small to be classified as a room but a curtain could be drawn for privacy. Outside the cubicles were showers and a long bench with six washbasins and mirrors. Apart from the curtain at the entrance to her cubicle door and the showers, there was no privacy.

From the beginning, the students in Gilda's classroom made her feel welcome. Compared to other schools Gilda had attended, class numbers here were comparatively small. In all, there were 20 girls - 8 boarders and 12 day girls. One of the boarders, Zara, was allocated as Gilda's mentor, but it was clear that her role was also to get Gilda to obey the rules and inform the nuns about Gilda's behaviour.

Nevertheless, Gilda and Zara became friends and Zara would always speak on Gilda's behalf and save her from any trouble.

Many of the day girls were interesting. One of them, a Pacific islander, had a sublime singing voice and sang with a blues band on weekends. The day students would often have jam sessions during lunch to which Gilda was also invited. This was the first time she saw and heard vocal and instrumental improvisations, which she thought were marvellous. She tried to devise her own improvisations at home during vacations but was told sharply by Hanna to stop wasting time and practice her scales, exercises and pieces.

Some of the boarding girls were also interesting and very friendly. One of the country girls invited Gilda to stay for a week at her parent's property in western Queensland during the long summer vacation. It was here that Gilda saw what life was like in the Australian outback. 'All these animals,' Gilda exclaimed, 'I love horses; they are so beautiful.' Other invitations were extended to Gilda to visit the homes of other school-friends and it was easy for Gilda to contrast the wide differences in the warmth of her school friends' parents toward her and the emotional frigidity of her own immediate family circle.

At school, the nuns were mostly fine, but with one notable exception, Gilda go along well with them. The exception was the nun responsible for the academic department. It was clear to Gilda that this nun disliked her intensely. Gilda wondered, if it was because of her 'sinning' parents, or was it because she simply disliked Gilda? This nun seemed to believe that Gilda was the personification of evil and her criticism of Gilda was unremitting. The criticism was so sustained that it penetrated Gilda's dreams, in one of which Gilda threw her nemesis into the river from the swimming pool steps. 'Oh, heavens,' Gilda said to herself when she woke up, 'Not again. God, I'm so sorry I dream this way but she is really mean.' However, Gilda as she prayed recollected that other students had similar problems with the same nun. Nevertheless, Gilda did find support, from her piano teacher, Sister Leona.

For Gilda, Sister Leona was a gift from God. From the time of her first lesson to when she left the school, she adored that Sister and her music lessons. 'Sister Leona has opened up so much more for me of what it means to be a pianist,' she thought, 'I love going to her, I love my lessons, I am so happy. I love improvising, although I'm no good at it. I could sit all day and just be with music. I love playing for her.'

One day, Sister Leona said to Gilda, 'At the end of each year, the school holds a concert for parents and friends. It consists of a choir, instrumental soloists, a small chamber ensemble, solo singers and a short theatrical production as well as the prize-giving celebration. Would you like to play the piano?'

Gilda was horrified, 'A solo, on my own? NO, no Sister, not on my own.' 'Then would you play in a duet?' the nun persisted. Gilda thought about it, 'Yes, as a duet if I have the second part.' She figured she wouldn't be so visible to the audience. 'Very well, that is possible,' Sister Leona replied smiling at her.

And so, at the end of 1960, Gilda had her first experience of performing before an audience. She and her duet partner stood behind the closed curtain; it opened, the audience clapped and they sat at the piano, played their piece, bowed again, and people clapped enthusiastically. The curtain closed. Gilda had never had such an adrenaline rush' 'Oh, I feel like I could burst!' she said to no one in particular, trying to restraining herself from jumping up and down in joy at her performance.

Gilda's parents came over to her at the end of the concert but Gilda didn't want to get into a conversation with them, especially with Hanna. She hadn't seen much of them during the year; they were now part of another world, a world she would gladly leave behind if she could. 'My mother would only find something to pick on,' she said to herself with a giggle. 'I won't give her a chance.' 'I have to go,' Gilda told Hanna and Vladimir, gave them a quick hug and promptly disappeared behind the stage curtain.

In this concert Gilda also sang on stage with the school choir and received the French Prize and the Sports Cup. She appreciated the audience applause as she went up on stage to collect her prizes. 'I've never experienced this in my life before. People praise me; they tell me how much they enjoy what I do.' Sometimes she felt bewildered by the attention and had to go off on her own. She had made many friends and had also met their parents. Being at that school meant that she had less to do with her parents and by the end of her first year at the boarding school, Gilda was detention-free, and she strongly felt that control of her life rested with her rather than her mother.

Gilda's reprieve from the aggravating academic nun occurred in 1961 when she was in Grade 12, her final secondary school year. Once a month, on a Sunday, the Archbishop of Brisbane would visit the school, and three of the Grade 12 boarders would go with him in his chauffeur-driven limousine to the local chemist to fill prescriptions for the school's Sick Bay. The first time Gilda met the Archbishop, he held out his hand and as is the custom when someone extends their hand, she took the Archbishop's hand and she shook it. The driver saw this and went into a flutter. It was unheard of to behave with such informality toward His Grace.

The Archbishop laughed. 'What is your name?' he asked. 'Gilda,' she replied. 'Which country do you come from? 'I was born in Vienna but I went to school in Paris before we came to Australia,' she replied. The others were still trying to get Gilda's attention but couldn't without being rude because the Archbishop continued to speak with her. 'It's alright, girls,' he said holding up his right hand in a stop movement, 'This is rather amusing. He turned back to Gilda and said, 'Do you see this ring?'

'Yes,' she said, 'it's beautiful.' 'This ring is the symbol of my position, and when I extend it, people bow and kiss it.' 'Why,' asked Gilda, puzzled. 'It's tradition, a mark of respect,' he replied. Gilda looked at his old finger and the big ring and asked, 'Does everyone kiss it,' she asked. 'Yes,' he replied with a smile. 'I hope you won't mind if I don't, it must be really dirty.' Gilda commented.

With that, the Archbishop roared with laughter till his belly shook. 'You know, I never thought of that,' he managed between laughing. 'May I just shake your hand?' she asked. 'Of course it is,' replied His Grace.

The Academic Head Nun was not amused, and Gilda received a detention for her behaviour. The following month, the Archbishop came again. He had already pre-arranged for Gilda to be one of the three girls every month. He affectionately called her, 'The little foreign girl.' When she learned that, she took the opportunity of telling her 'new friend' about the Academic Head Nun. Miraculously, the harassment stopped.

Life was good for Gilda, Year 12, in 1961 and it was her last high school year. The results at the end of the year determined what she would do when she left. Apart from playing the piano, Gilda had no idea what she wanted to do. Hanna wanted her to be a lawyer or a doctor because they were 'good professions.' 'No,' said Gilda, 'I want to be a concert pianist and maybe a conductor one day.'

'You'll never be a concert pianist; you don't want to play solo in front of other people,' Hanna told her. 'In any case, you have to be better than excellent to be an international pianist. You are good but not excellent and also, you never stick at anything.' Although it would sting every time Hanna spoke to her in this manner, Gilda would brush it off.

While at school, Gilda discovered she was good at sport and she rapidly mastered the rudiments of most competitive sporting activities. In those days, there was no designated time for sports training and Gilda could train freely, especially during classes she didn't like.

At the end of year 12, Gilda's social life centered on school social activities. It seemed as though Catholic girls' schools and Catholic boys' schools were intent on making sure that each generation intermingled only within their faith. Girls like Gilda who had no Catholic boyfriend connections were paired off with 'suitable beaux'.

For each ball, Gilda had a different partner and so her education in how the opposite sex behaved was accelerated. Having seen her mother in action she knew how to flirt.

Gilda had also found a new passion, dancing. She loved to move to the music. Her dates used to have to get up for each and every dance regardless of whether they knew the correct steps or not. Although, she had never learned dancing, Gilda just moved instinctively to the rhythm of the music. She learned dances such as the Pride of Erin and Gypsy Tap at school during dance classes in preparation for the Ball Season. 'Feels like the boys didn't have dance lessons,' she complained about numerous partners in the Pride of Erin. She inwardly winced as they 'danced' on her feet.

The final event of the year was the School Picnic at Dunwich Point. The class took a boat over and then spread blankets on which the placed a mountain of food. 'Pass me a bread roll,' called one girl. 'Who's got the sausages?' came from another direction. 'Who's got the tomato sauce and mustard,' called another. 'Gilda, will you stop taking photos,' complained another. Gilda always had her camera ready.

After they had eaten and the pile of left-over food looked like a stampede of wild cattle had gone through it, Gilda said, 'Okay, group photo everyone. Come over here; we can fit everyone in.' They all scrambled to be at the front, laughing, squealing and bumping each other. 'Okay, first photo, everyone with a sexy look,' ordered Gilda. 'Next one, with a silly pose.' And so it went on. By the end, they all collapsed on the ground in fits of laughter.

On the way back on the boat, they sat in their respective groups talking quietly. Some sat silently knowing that they would never be as care-free again; knowing that it was soon time to face the big world outside of school. In a way, Gilda was clueless about the big wide world. Apart from her school in Paris, Gilda's life had largely been a series of being uprooted from one place to be planted in the next and living with extreme familial volatility interspersed with wonderfully, memorable times. For her, leaving school was just another such episode. However, the difference now was that she had a greater possibility of exercising her control over the direction of her life.

During the year, Gilda had seen little of her parents. Hanna came to pick her up for the day if Gilda had no other school commitments. This suited both of them. Hanna only went up to the school to fulfill her duty and Gilda didn't miss seeing her mother, although she did enjoy it when they picnicked together. Both Vladimir and

Hanna were surprised when Gilda came back to live with them and found, with uneasy surprise, that they now encountered a young woman with definite views. She would appear to obey, but both knew that she would only do so much of what they asked, and then, when out of sight, she would do what she wanted. Hanna couldn't treat her as before; Gilda was now possessed of a determination that was stronger than Hanna's.

Gilda passed her Senior Certificate and qualified for University entry. She still had in mind to get a job and move out. When school ended, unbeknown to her parents, Gilda successfully applied for a job at a chemist shop in Brisbane's city centre.

One day, as Gilda swept the footpath outside the chemist shop her mother came up to her. 'I knew you'd be up to no good so I followed you in. So, this is what you want to become, a street cleaner.' Hanna grabbed Gilda's hand, pulled her into the shop and went to a man behind the counter,

'Gilda, give the man the broom,' she ordered and then turned to the man, 'My daughter will not be returning.' Hanna stormed off with Gilda protesting, 'Sweeping the footpath was just a small part of the job, otherwise I help customers and learn what it means to work in a chemist shop.'

Hanna was stony silent for a while but then couldn't help herself, 'You will not work in a shop.' When they arrived home, Hanna said to Vladimir, 'I found this tramp sweeping streets.' Turning to Gilda she said, 'Count yourself lucky that I don't slap you. Don't think you are getting too old for that?'

Gilda tried desperately to control herself but then she yelled with tears streaming down her face, 'I wish I had killed myself in the shower. You'll always keep trying to ruin my life. I'll never be able to do anything for myself. You're a bully,' and she stomped her foot for emphasis.

Vladimir went pale and stood between Hanna and Gilda as he asked, 'Gilda, do you mean you tried to suicide?' Gilda realised what she had said; there was no way out. 'Yes,' she replied calmly, 'But then I thought, I'm not going to let her win. I'll live even if it's just to annoy her. Then turning to Hanna she said, 'You hate me so much that you wouldn't care except, with me out of the way, who you would pick on?'

'The girl is crazy,' an agitated Hanna responded. 'I always knew it. My nerves have taken as much as they can bear.' Vladimir pointed to two chairs and motioned for the two women to sit down. He also sat down. 'Gilda, for your sake, for a better future, your mother and I would like you to go to University.' Hanna was about to interject. 'Wait please, Hanna,' he said, 'Gilda will be 18 in a few months, a young woman, it is time that she is allowed to be treated as such. Children never do things the way parents wish it. We didn't do what our parents wanted. Slapping is not a part of upbringing here and frankly I don't see the value of it.'

By now Hanna had had enough. She rose from her chair and in a rage said, 'I have had enough of this modern psychology. I will do as I see fit and you will not tell me how to behave.' With that she stormed off. Vladimir and Gilda looked at each other. Vladimir was the first to speak. 'Your mother and I want you to go to University. Please go for one year and give it a chance. I believe you will enjoy it.'

'Papa, thank you,' Gilda said softly as she went up to him and gave him a hug. He gently returned her hug and they stayed like that for a few moments to celebrate their accord.

For Gilda, many university study options were not attractive. 'I don't want to be a teacher because I never want to see the inside of a school again,' she said to herself. 'Nursing? Oh, no, I hate the sight of blood. Get married and end up like my parents? No thanks, I'd love to travel,' she said, 'I'll ask and see what happens.'

And so one morning at breakfast Gilda broached the issue, 'Mom, Pop, the parents of one of the girls in my class are letting her go for a year to England as an au pair. Can I do that too? All you have to pay for is the return airfare and then I get paid for looking after the child of the family which employs me. Board and lodging is included.'

"You mean you will be a servant to a family?' Hanna responded sitting up straighter. 'No, it's more like a guardian, a governess, looking after their child, helping them learn to read and so on,' Gilda added. 'Definitely not,' said Hanna, 'you can't even look after yourself. You will get a proper education at University and have a career.'

'But, Mom...' Gilda persisted.

"NO, end of discussion. No. Do you hear,' interrupted Hanna looking malevolently at her daughter.

And so it was decided that Gilda would attend the University of Queensland and study for an Arts Degree.

'Nothing's changed,' Gilda thought to herself, 'I have to get out of here.'

Hanna had bought a rundown Maisonette duplex apartment, which she let to two tenants. Vladimir was somewhat surprised to learn that she had bought it in her name but as she said, 'It's money I earned from the shop.' To which Vladimir replied, 'I don't mind that you have bought a property, but we are living in a house that I am paying for from my income and I cannot buy another investment property.'

'Are you complaining that we are living in your house,' Hanna said tartly. 'It's impossible to talk to you, Hanna,' Vladimir replied. Not long after this conversation, Vladimir said to his wife, 'Hanna, it is quite obvious that for some time we have been having difficulties in our marriage. I suggest that as one of your tenants is moving out, you move in there and we can see if we can sort out what is going on between us. Living with you is like living on top of a volcano waiting for the next eruption.

She looked amazed at him. 'You mean I move out of here?' Hanna quickly collected herself and asked Vladimir, 'What about Gilda?' 'Gilda can decide for herself. She can stay here if she wishes.' 'No, she will come with me.' Hanna snapped. 'You will want me back,' Hanna said under her breath.

By Christmas, Hanna and Gilda had moved into one of the Maisonettes. Gilda just took it in her stride. 'It's all the same to me,' she said, 'I don't care; it's fun moving.' Vladimir paid for the piano to be moved. Except their clothes, because the apartment was furnished, the piano was the only item to be moved from the house. Gilda's room was a small built-in section of the outside verandah of the single-bedroom Maisonette. She was able to lock her door but always felt scared being out there on her own. Neither Vladimir nor Hanna told anyone about their separation. Always enterprising, Hanna was on a mission to enjoy her new circumstances and Gilda had no complaints about that. They went to the theatre, concerts, ballet, opera, and whatever else was on. They cut a good looking pair and were often photographed by The Courier Mail social page photographers as they walked down Queen Street going to a theatre.

Gilda had blossomed. Her thick mass of long brown hair swept to one side fell languidly in soft waves below her shoulders. She knew how to dress stylishly and sophisticated. This was one area in which Hanna never interfered. Gilda also always wore stiletto shoes, as they lengthened her legs and added to the pertness of her walk. She knew how to be attractive.

Life at the Maisonette was not always glamorous however. Its walls, doors, ceilings and verandah rails needed painting. While Hanna painted, Gilda would play silly tunes like chopsticks on the piano or practise sensibly, depending on Hanna's mood. She was given smaller painting jobs and was responsible for feeding her mother, 'the worker.' It was fun.

'Why can't Mom be like this all the time,' Gilda thought. She now called her mother Mom, a term which she picked up in American films. Papa had become Pop because 'Mummy and Daddy' sound so kindisch, childish, and Mama and Papa just don't suit anymore.'

Because Hanna had no time to cook, Gilda took over those duties. Her cooking skills were limited, but she soon became an expert in grilled toasted cheese and tomato. The dogs had come with them which added to the merriment in their little home.

At the end of December Vladimir visited them. They chatted, drank wine and ate toasted cheese and tomato as they sat on the patio.

Time would tell where this visit would lead.

CHAPTER 16
1962 - 1963

The turmoil of the previous years had taken its toll not only on Hanna and Gilda's home life but also on Gilda and her music studies. Now enrolled at the Queensland Conservatorium of Music in South Brisbane Gilda had two different teachers, one for piano practical and another for theory of music. Gilda was intensely drawn to playing Chopin's music, which for her had become an emotional refuge. The melody and harmonies of Chopin's music helped make her emotionally complete and through this she was able to enter into an inner world that she loved.

She met with her theory of music teacher first, a well-known Brisbane harpist, and they got along very well. She was gentle, kind and understanding, and Gilda felt good attending her lessons and progressed well. The practical teacher was a well-known pianist. During her first lesson, he asked Gilda to play scales and pieces to assess her strengths and weaknesses. At the end of that lesson, he said, 'You certainly have a feel for what you are playing but we need to work on your technique. From now on it's no more Chopin and more Czerny and Hanon exercises. Please buy 'Hanon: The Virtuoso Pianist in 60 Exercises, Books 1 and 2 and we will start with these for your next lesson. Concentrate on these in your practice schedule. Your pieces you can play for leisure.' And so, this was the direction her lessons took.

She began to loathe her lessons with him. 'I have a tyrant at home and now I have one for music,' she complained. This went on every week for four months but the die was cast. She came to a lesson and after she had played the requested exercises, he looked at her and said, 'If you don't improve, you'll never pass the next exam and without it you cannot study for the AMUSA exam. I've spoken to you repeatedly about your technique. I don't see it improving sufficiently.'
Gilda got up off her chair and said, 'You know what Mr Lorrie,' she started with tears welling, 'I once wanted to make music my career but clearly I'm so bad that's not possible. I used to love practicing, I used to love my lessons with my previous teachers and

I love my theory lessons, but I hate my lessons with you. You won't have to suffer me ever again. I'm not coming back.' And with that she stormed out and indeed never returned.

Sadly, he had just been the wrong teacher for her at the time. She was going through enormous emotional turmoil. After that day, she would play on and off at home just for fun but, with time and the turn of events in her home life that followed, playing gradually became a thing of the past. She still often listened to music but never played. Oddly enough, she would not part with the piano which always moved with her wherever she lived. Gradually, her skill level deteriorated and whenever she sat down to play, she became frustrated at not remembering pieces she used to play well from memory. This lengthened the gaps in her attempts at playing.

Despite its simplicity and frugality, Gilda enjoyed the stay with her just her mother. Hanna was occupied with getting their living quarters up to standard, and she had taken time away from the shop and was calmer. Mother and daughter had never got on so well although Gilda was always wary as she never knew when her mother would get into a temper. Even when Vladimir visited them it was a pleasant time for all three of them.

However, Gilda was constantly engaged in fulfilling some exaggerated expectation that her mother wanted of her. While she was growing up, she had never learned to be herself. Instead, praise and love had conditions placed on them. Words of love may have been spoken but they were not shown and there was more punishment than affection.
Hanna's self-worth never had the opportunity to mature and become steadfast. Compliments from others were what she depended upon to make her feel confident and she constantly needed external validation. She was emotionally immature and had no role models. Because of her harsh upbringing Hanna saw expressions of vulnerability as a weakness. The older Gilda became, the more Hanna saw her daughter as a threat and would emphasise Gilda's 'weaknesses' and her so-called poor examination results compared to what Hanna maintained she had achieved at the same age in Vienna. Even Gilda's High Distinctions in Piano and Theory

were not good enough. 'The standard in this country is low; you would never receive those results in Vienna,' she constantly told her daughter.

Before the university year started, Gilda had her left eye surgically straightened. It was a difficult operation for those times and not as successful as Gilda would have wished, but it was a significant improvement. The eye specialist told Gilda that the straightening may need to be repeated, and that success would depend on how the strength of the muscle and stitching held the left eye in place as it moved in synchronization with the right eye. The eye surgeon explained that it was is better to have it move than to have the eye static.

Gilda had lived with the previous "look" for so long that she thought the result of the surgery was wonderful. However, she still thought she was ugly though it didn't bother her. Gilda wasn't trying to impress anyone, and life, at that time, was good.

Vladimir visited them more often; sometimes Hanna would go out with him, other times the three of them went out together. When he brought Hanna home one day, she announced, 'Gilda, Pop and I have decided to reconcile. We will all be one family again.' Gilda wasn't too sure she liked that as life had been so much more pleasant when they were on their own. 'That's nice,' she replied. 'Gilda,' Vladimir addressed her, 'you don't seem very pleased. Don't you want me to come back?'

'It's not that pop; sure I want you back, but things have been so simple and happy. No arguments, yelling or fighting. Mom hasn't once wanted to hit me. I'm old enough, maybe I can live here. You can pay the rent at the beginning and I'll pay you back when I get a job and I can study at night.' 'Out of the question,' Hanna replied, 'What will people think? We will be living across the road from you and you will live here?' 'What do you mean 'across the road?' asked an astonished Gilda? 'Yes,' replied Hanna smiling sweetly at her husband, 'to start our new life together, we have bought a large house not far from here.'

'Oh, boy,' thought Gilda, 'Here we go again.'
And so, the previous house was sold, the Maisonette rented and the Dobinskis' new house was larger than the combined area of the original house and the Maisonette. The downstairs area was remodeled for Vladimir's surgery and waiting room, leaving plenty of room for two cars and a laundry. Patients entered the surgery from the side street without disturbing the Dobinskis' home life. The interior of the house was magnificent. The first time Gilda walked through the house she was in awe, 'I love these high ceilings with decorative plaster work, picture railings, and chandeliers. And look at those gorgeous transparent stain-glassed bay windows.' The polished wooden frames and dividing swing doors also had translucent, multi-colored stained-glass windows and elegant drapes hugged the windows.

Hanna was in her element because the final stages of the Dobinskis' ascension into high society were being established. She could invite anyone here and feel proud. The upstairs section of the house needed some renovations; the back verandah was enclosed, and the kitchen and bathrooms modernised. The bedrooms, lounge, dining room and the enclosed front verandah were adequate as they were. Two bedrooms opened onto the closed-in carpeted verandah. These were taken by Hanna and Vladimir, and Hanna converted the verandah into a study for herself. She had started a part-time Bachelor of Arts degree at the University of Queensland and wanted to get a university German qualification to teach German in a private school. Hanna closed Vienna Fashions because it wasn't in keeping with her newly-created public image but, always one to have her own income, she now offered German tutoring at home in her newly acquired study.

As a consequence, Gilda was given the main bedroom which was in the style of the other parts of the house – elegant. It was a large room in which she often danced. The only drawback was that the external door led out onto the open front verandah which in turn led in from the front gate. Main Street was a major traffic thoroughfare and so to feel comfortable Gilda always locked her door to the veranda.

University had started at the beginning of March. Gilda needed to Take two buses to get there. She was enrolled in a Bachelor of Arts degree, a three-year full time course which could be taken as an evening student if she worked full-time during the day. What she would do with it she had no idea because it only opened up a teaching future which she was adamant she would never pursue. 'Hell, I hated school. Why would I ever want to go back to one?' Gilda went to Orientation Week and met students who would attend the same lectures and tutorials. She and these new friends met at the Cafeteria during breaks and this became a bigger part of Gilda's day than did the lectures and tutorials. She had never met such talented and interesting people. Most of them had evening or weekend jobs. Soon she was invited to parties, picnics, barbecues where she met their parents and other family members. It was intoxicating. 'There is so much to do and see, places to go, and they are all so nice.'

There was no control on students in those days in terms of attending lectures. Tutorials were optional and students were encouraged to there was no compulsion to attend. Gilda led a whirlwind of social life and it didn't occur to her that there could be consequences for not attending lectures. During her time in high school, Gilda had always been good at 'picking' what topics would be on an exam paper. She did the Assignments and passed them, 'Exams will be no problem,' giving them little thought. Life was a buzz.

November arrived and marking the end of the academic year, and with it university examinations. Gilda sat for her exams and then the results came out – German, Pass, History, Pass, Psychology, Pass Conceded, with the latter counting as a Pass. However, she couldn't go on with that subject at the next level unless she sat for the exam again in January and obtained a full Pass; with another History, a similar result. Gilda was shocked; she hadn't expected these disastrous results.

'They aren't going to be pleased,' she thought to herself about her parents. And they were not. 'What happened?' Vladimir asked when he saw her results. Gilda couldn't answer, he wouldn't have understood and she could not blame him. 'I had no idea what was involved,' was all she could say, which was the truth. Hanna was about to say something but he stopped her. 'What do you think we should do?' Vladimir asked.

'In January I can resit the exams for the Pass Conceded subjects. I know I can pass them.'

'And then what?' Hanna said to Gilda as a prelude to a verbal assault on her daughter, 'Will we have the same next year of your good-for-nothing behaviour?'

'Hanna, please, no,' Vladimir intervened, 'Can't you see Gilda is just as upset as we are?' 'Gilda is upset,' Hanna repeated. 'I'm too ashamed to tell these results to anyone.' 'Well, don't,' Gilda replied. 'What did you say? You, abomination. I'll show you what happens when you talk to me like that.' Hanna was about to lunge at Gilda when Vladimir intervened. 'This sort of yelling will not solve anything.' he said.

Gilda could not believe her ears. 'He's standing up for me,' she thought, 'I can't believe it.' 'Pop, I'm truly sorry. There were so many interesting things to do at Uni. Apart from the interesting people of my age I met, there were theatre productions, subject committee meetings, debating clubs and so many other clubs. I, I just got carried away by the new experiences,' Gilda explained. 'Yes, that's what happens when I don't have you under my control,' said Hanna, shaking with rage.

Gilda continued, 'People like me, Pop. I mix easily with everyone. I've never had so many friends.' 'What utter rubbish,' said Hanna, 'these friends distracted you from your goals.' Hanna continued in the same vein as before, 'We will find the right type of friends for you.' Vladimir looked softly at Gilda and asked, 'What would you really like to study next year?'

'I'd like to get a qualification so that I can go to work during the day and go to Uni at night,' Gilda suggested, 'There are colleges in town that teach office skills. It's a 12 months' course but I'm sure I can finish it sooner. Then I can earn money and won't be a burden on either of you.' 'Money is not the issue here,' her father added calmly, 'The University is free and you will always be able to live here for free with us.'

'No, she won't,' interrupted Hanna, 'As soon as you get a job, you'll pay board.' Vladimir looked at her astonished, 'But Hanna…' he started to say. 'Yes, she will. I had to pay board to my mother so Gilda will pay board here.'

'Hanna, your home situation was different from ours.'
'There was nothing wrong with my home.' Hanna was almost frothing at the mouth, 'I came from a better background than you.' Vladimir knew that it was hopeless to continue. Gilda couldn't wait to get away. 'There's something wrong with her,' she thought, 'There must be. She flies off the handle, you can't talk to her. I wouldn't want to be in Pop's shoes now.'

Gilda passed the two subjects in question, and so passed all her first full-time year university courses. She had enrolled in two subjects as an evening student and also enrolled in a Business Training College during the day. The first day there Gilda looked at the schedule and thought, 'Yes, I can finish this before the 12 months are up.' At first she went every day to the College and as the work was self-paced, she was soon further ahead than required so she able to relax by the Brisbane River, or walk through the Botanic Gardens and daydream or read her university lecture materials.

'This is ridiculous,' she grumbled to herself after sitting by the river for a couple of weeks, 'I'll be able to do this in six months if I want to… and I want to.' With this self-generated determination Gilda rigorously applied herself and indeed before the end of the half year, she received her Office Skills Certificate. Gilda had kept in contact with her university friends and some who worked in the city would join her for coffee when university lectures were over. She told them, she had completed her business studies and was now looking for a job.

One friend advised, 'Did you know that the Commonwealth Public Service is holding selection tests for entry into the CPS? 'What does that mean?' Gilda asked. 'It means that you have to do a series of tests/exams, English, Maths and General Knowledge and if you are good enough, they give you a job. Are you interested?' Gilda was very interested, 'How do I find out what to do?'
'I'm going up to their head office to get an application form this afternoon, so come with me.' The two girls went to the Head Office together that afternoon and collected the necessary documentation. 'You will need to bring your birth certificate,' Gilda's friend pointed out. Gilda shuddered when she thought of asking her mother for it and thought that an alternative route was preferable, 'I'll ask Pop, it'll be safer.'

'Make sure you get the form in by the closing date,' her friend emphasised, as she headed off to catch her bus. 'Sure will and thanks so much,' Gilda replied waving her off.

Gilda completed the Application Form and asked her father for her birth certificate. He had to ask Hanna but that went smoothly because Hanna now vowed to have as little to do with Gilda as possible, notably since Vladimir had stood up for Gilda.

In any case, Hanna was not interested in anything where she could not be in charge. She now felt that there was contest between her and Gilda for Vladimir's attention and she was simply waiting for an opportunity to exact revenge on her daughter. Gilda had no idea why her mother was staying out of her way but the reason would soon reveal itself.

Gilda looked at her birth certificate and for the first time it hit her that the name she was using was not her birth name. After the fiasco when she earlier discovered Pop was not her real father, Gilda hadn't given the incident another thought. She looked at her birth certificate and saw, Gilda Hollar.

'Gilda Hollar,' she said out loud, 'Gilda Hollar,' she repeated. She looked away from the piece of paper and stared into space, it was surreal; she felt like she was talking about another person. 'Yes, that's my date of birth, the city of birth. It's all about me,' she said silently and slowly. Gilda continued to read the document, 'Father's name: Hermann Hollar.' Transfixed by the information concerning here real identity and transfixed at the name, Gilda started to weep.

Gilda couldn't understand why tears were running down her cheeks. Tenderly she held the document away to make sure she didn't wet it with her tears. 'I wonder what he looks like. I don't know anything about him. Why hasn't he contacted me? He probably doesn't care and has forgotten all about me. He probably has another family, just as I have,' she thought as she gazed at her Austrian birth certificate. 'Oh, forget him, don't be silly,' and she suddenly and fiercely reprimanded herself, 'Just forget him. He hasn't existed till now and he won't ever exist. You are Gilda Dobinski.'

But deep within something had been activated that not even her ability to push things aside would erase.

In August 1963 Gilda received a letter informing her that her Application for a position with the Commonwealth Public Service had been received and announced the dates of the tests and the addresses where they would be held. On the allotted dates, Gilda was at the examination centre with hundreds of other applicants of all ages. The English and General Knowledge tests were fine but she knew she had failed the Maths test. She only answered 40 of the 100 questions. 'Oh, well,' she thought, 'I'll just have to wait and see.'

Gilda's parents often went to the German Club at Woolloongabba on Saturday night for the weekly dance night. A band played all types of music from popular European hits to rock n' roll and dance music from various nationalities. Men would ask Vladimir if they could dance with Gilda and, if he thought they looked acceptable, he would nod. He mostly agreed because it took courage for a man to come and ask for a father's permission to dance with his daughter. Gilda loved to dance and was always on the dance floor. She had an innate sense of rhythm and could quickly pick up the steps of any dance.

One Saturday a man she had never seen before was clearly fascinated with her and he repeatedly asked her to dance with him. He was very tall, wore a well-cut dark suit, white shirt and tie. Strong and well built, he was even taller than Gilda in her high heels. Gilda was an energetic dancer but he had no trouble holding on to her and twirling her around whatever the rhythm or speed of the dance. At first they didn't talk much; they just danced and smiled at each other. He stayed close to Gilda's table to ensure that he was the first to ask her father when a new dance began. When the evening concluded he left with another girl and a man.

Excitedly, Gilda waited for the following Saturday, but he didn't come, and nor did his friends. Gilda danced with others but she was disappointed. 'Oh, well, that's the way it goes,' she thought. Nothing was permanent for Gilda, so when this fellow didn't turn up, it was nothing new; she accepted it. The following Saturday she wore a new skirt she had made especially for dancing. Gilda made most of her own clothes; a skill she had learned from watching her mother.

Gilda's skirt was black crêpe cut into 10 panels, hugging over the hips and then flaring out to the hem, perfect for dancing. It would cheekily flip up to just above the knees, showing the red lining sewn to the crêpe. It was risqué, but discrete. With that she wore a black sleeveless halter top which she also had made. Long drop diamante earrings and black high heels finished off the outfit. Her long brown hair was down and flew when she danced. 'Men love long hair on women, Gilda silently remarked. Hanna did not approve of the outfit, but there was nothing she could do now. 'What would you like to drink?' Vladimir asked after they had seated themselves at their usual table near the dance floor. Just then the music started. Gilda saw her father look away, nodded and then she looked up to see a hand extended towards her. She smiled and her heart skipped a few beats. It was the man from two Saturdays ago.

As they started to dance, he said, 'I'm Giovanni, what's your name?'

'Gilda,' she replied. 'I'm sorry I wasn't here last week I had a family gathering,' he said.
'That's okay, I did miss dancing with you though,' she replied innocently. He held her a little tighter but still at a discreet distance. They danced together all evening and Hanna became more and more agitated and told her husband to separate Gilda and Giovanni. 'Come, Hanna, what can go wrong? We are all here. In any case, he seems a nice young man. That is his sister over there and her boyfriend. I know him; he is German.' 'How do you know?' Hanna asked surprised. 'I have already made my own enquiries,' he smiled sheepishly.

When it was time for the band to have a break, Giovanni brought Gilda back to the table and said to Vladimir, 'I am sitting with my sister and a friend over there; could Gilda come and sit with us during the break, please?' Hanna was about to answer but Vladimir replied, 'Yes, as long as we can see her.' 'Thank you,' Giovanni replied, I will bring her back after the next dance.' Vladimir nodded his assent.

Gilda was shy when talking to Giovanni's sister, Natalia, and her boyfriend, Hans. Natalia was very confident and loud. She and Hans were also older than Gilda. 'Giovanni must be about 25,' Gilda thought. She was almost 19.

Gilda and Giovanni met up for the next three Saturdays at the German Club. On that last evening he said, 'I have booked a trip to go back to Italy for six months. I leave this coming Friday.' 'Oh,' Gilda's heart sank, 'I hope you have a wonderful time. I will miss you.' 'I will miss you too, Gilda,' he responded and looked deeply into her eyes, I would cancel the trip if I could but I must go. My relatives expect me. 'Of course,' Gilda replied. The rest of the evening they danced holding each other as tight as they could without being obvious. He held her extended hand tightly till she had to wriggle her fingers to get the circulation back. Gilda, pressed her hand on Giovanni's shoulder tighter than usual.

Giovanni told Gilda his surname and what ship he would be on. 'I'll write when I get to Italy,' he said as they parted. 'Yes,' she replied,

'Bon voyage.'

Gilda thought a lot about Giovanni, and even thought of writing to him on the ship but then she decided against it, 'Don't be silly. Why should he care about you after such a short time? Wait and see if he gets in touch when he returns.'

Although Gilda had many friends, she didn't want to seem silly and tell them about what was going on in her life. She wasn't really sure how she felt; she had never had friends and didn't know what it was like to have friends or confide in someone else. Hanna had always said that if you never tell people anything about yourself or how you feel then they can't take advantage of you. Gilda had also closed her heart off from hurt, but she didn't know that; it was something she did automatically and further reinforced each disappointment and hurt.

While Giovanni was away, Gilda started to go out with boys as she now had a lot of friends, both male and female. Apart from David when she was 15, she had never been on a date. If a boy started to get 'fresh' and want to kiss her, she'd pull away.

Although her father was a Gynecologist, anything to do with boy-girl things were never discussed. Hanna found such topics sordid and distasteful, so they were not spoken about. Even when Gilda got her period the first time, she was shocked, not knowing what was happening. She asked a girlfriend what it was. The friend's mother then explained it to her.

Later in the year, Gilda received news that would change the direction of her life. She was offered a position as Base Grade Clerk in the Commonwealth Public Service and was asked to make an appointment with 'Charles', a recruitment clerk. When she told her parents, she received a warm response from Vladimir, and a hug. 'That is wonderful, Gilda, congratulations.' 'Well, we'll see if anything good comes of it,' was Hanna's response. 'We'll also see if you continue with the University studies,' she added.
Gilda went to the interview to discuss the finer details of her appointment and the logistics for her first day. Hello Gilda,

congratulations, well done,' said Charles from recruitment. 'Thank you very much,' answered Gilda, 'I'm very excited.' 'You'll be working in the Department of Census and Statistics. It's an up-and-coming department for which only University undergraduates were considered. You will be continuing with your University studies I assume,' Charles asked. 'Oh, yes, definitely,' Gilda replied enthusiastically.

'Currently, it's a small department in Brisbane but it will quickly grow. The department has expanded in Canberra and the Government has many new plans for it. Consequently, the work you'll be doing will become more and more important.' 'I have a question,' said Gilda, 'How is it that with my Maths you've put me into statistics?' 'Actually, you may not have answered all the questions,' said Charles, 'but those you answered were 100% correct. There were no mistakes. But, we really want you because of your language skills.'

'Oh,' said Gilda surprised. She didn't think it was anything special being able to speak three languages and understand the basics of two others. 'Yes', Charles continued, 'We're planning to expand our trading with South American countries, and your ability to understand how languages work will be an asset when we get correspondence from them.'

'That sounds interesting,' Gilda said animatedly. She didn't realise it then but she loved speaking other languages and would study many other languages in later years.

'Now for the paperwork,' Charles said, 'I see that your surname is different on your birth certificate.' 'Yes', replied Gilda, 'I didn't know about that name till I saw it on the certificate. I have never used it.' 'I see," he replied, 'I'll have to see what we can do as normally you are known by the name on that document and all your correspondence has to be in the same name. Leave it with me.' As it turned out, Gilda could keep the Dobinski surname for daily communication but official documents would need to be addressed to Gilda Hollar. Gilda could barely contain her excitement when she left Charles. 'I'm going to be independent.' She realised she must have said that rather loudly when a man next to her said, 'I beg your pardon?' 'Oh,' she said, 'I was just talking to myself,' and skipped away.

Gilda didn't immediately want to go home so she went to her favourite coffee place in the city, 'Primitif', a Queen Street trendy coffee bar set in semi-dark gypsy-style décor. There she sat and drank coffee while listening to a guitarist play soulful gypsy music. She felt exhilarated. 'I am so happy; I could jump for joy. Without my doing anything, things are happening to me. I will be working and studying. I love to study but I want to have my own money so that I can move out. Pop and Mom won't mind. I'm getting older.'

When she arrived home, her mother said while sarcastically waving a letter, 'Here's a letter here from your boyfriend. Do you want it?' Gilda looked at her puzzled, 'I don't have a boyfriend,' she added quickly and feeling uneasy. 'My beautiful Gilda,' Hanna read sarcastically from the opened letter. 'What?' Gilda exclaimed. 'Yes, my beautiful Gilda, here you are,' repeated Hanna giving Gilda the letter. 'My personal letter has been opened,' Gilda exclaimed. 'Yes,' said Hanna, 'I read it.' Gilda raised her voice, 'You have no right to open my mail'. 'Gilda, I can do whatever I please,' Hanna replied with a sneer.

Gilda decided to contain her anger and went into her room. As soon as she started to read the letter, she forgot her anger. It was so beautiful, 'Mia bella Gilda, how I wish you were here with me. Every day when I walk the streets of Florence, I make believe that you are by my side and every evening as I promenade in the moonlight along the River Arno, I feel my hands on your shoulders keeping you warm. Then as I cross the Ponte Vecchio and see couples dancing in the lantern light of the small piazza, I remember how we danced together..." And so on. Gilda read and reread the letter until she knew it by heart.

'Tomorrow, I'll get a post office box,' Gilda vowed. 'She'll never read my mail ever again. I'll tell work and I'll tell my friends to send everything to the box.' She then took pen and paper and replied to Giovanni, 'It feels as though we have known each other for a long time,' Gilda thought. And so she started, 'Mio Caro Giovanni…, My Dear Giovanni…'.

It was now the middle of November and Vladimir said to his daughter, 'Gilda, my receptionist would like time off in December till the end of the first week in January. Would you be interested in replacing her? You would train under her till then to learn the surgery routine. I would of course pay you a wage.' Gilda looked at him questioningly raising her eyebrows, 'Are you serious?' 'Yes, I mean it,' he replied with smile. 'Oh, yes, I would like that very much,' answered Gilda. 'Good, can you start tomorrow morning and work with Louisa?'

Gilda stood motionless and pinched herself to make sure she wasn't dreaming.

Vladimir's surgery was thriving. Hanna was making a name for herself as a tutor of German and in the following year she would be teaching German a few hours a week at a nearby Catholic college. The Dobinskis now had a full-time housekeeper. The parents met at the end of the day, dined together or, as was mostly the case, entertained or had professional meetings.

It had been a good year for Gilda. She obtained her Office Skills' Certificate and her appointment in the Commonwealth Public Service was confirmed. Her home life had improved and her encounters with her mother were less painful. Inevitably, with her parents separately occupied each evening, Gilda had greater freedom to enjoy her increasing circle of friends. Giovanni's letters were of course, a highlight, as were her university studies. Gilda obtained Credits, a higher level than a Pass, for both her University subjects.

CHAPTER 17
1964 - 1965

Gilda had now come to terms with the fact that Vladimir wasn't her biological father and working in her step-father's surgery filled Gilda with exciting new experiences. She was able to put into practice skills she had learnt at the business college, and proved to be a very competent receptionist. The patients were mostly elderly folk from a nearby Russian community and she loved talking to them. From them Gilda learned some of the basics of the Russian language. Every Easter and Christmas, the Dobinskis were invited to the Russian Orthodox Church to celebrate traditional religious events.

Gilda had already experienced how festivities were celebrated in other cultures. One thing was clear, it was always the women who did the work while the men sat around, talking, smoking, ordering the women around and, depending on the festivity, quaffing large amounts of their national liquor. However, at these celebrations, everyone knew what was expected of them and everyone just did what they had to do without serious complaints. The children ran around laughing, playing, squealing and crying, depending on the experience they were having in that moment. The boys would chase the girls, who would make a weak attempt at objecting. Everyone knew what to expect and everyone was content.

Gilda exhibited to others quite a few good attributes about herself which she, regrettably, didn't recognise. By now, she unconsciously focused more on the many things her mother said were wrong with her, and overlooked her many good qualities. Personal skills that came easily to her, she didn't notice at all. Gilda had streamlined various areas of the business side of her step-father's medical practice, such as the filing system, record keeping and how medical supplies and drugs were ordered and recorded. Procedures that were not visible to the public, such as rearranging how her step-father placed instruments in the disinfector, were now logically laid out. Gilda unconsciously showed initiative and drive. Had she been cognisant of the value of what she did, she would have seen that she had excellent organisational skills and leadership qualities.

Gilda's step-father was very happy with her work and said to Hanna, 'Gilda absolutely amazes me. The waiting room hasn't run this smoothly before, the patients say what a delight she is.' Hanna made out as though she hadn't heard what Vladimir said. 'Would you like a coffee?' she asked. 'Yes, please.' Vladimir replied. 'Did you hear what I said about Gilda?' 'Yes, but it won't last, so don't get excited about it. She doesn't stick at anything.' Vladimir shook his head without responding or pursuing the topic.

Something Gilda did acknowledge from her experience at the surgery was that she would not be suited to any profession that entailed blood. Because she loved animals she had toyed with the idea of becoming a veterinarian, but now, after an unfortunate experience, Gilda was convinced that that was not for her.

One day, it was necessary for her to assist Vladimir in the surgery. 'Come in here, please Gilda', he asked as he opened the door to the waiting room, 'I need you for a short while. Mrs Krapivnikoff has a small lump on the side of her head and I need to remove it.' 'Coming,' replied Gilda cheerfully. She went into the surgery and noticed that her step-father had shaved the hair around the lump. She picked up the kidney tray and placed it under the ugly protrusion. He had anesthetised the area and started to make an incision. Gilda looked away as she wasn't sure she should be looking at the procedure. Unfortunately, she did peek to see if it was soon over as her arm was getting tired from holding the dish. That instant, Gilda fainted and the kidney dish fell to the floor. Vladimir took another dish and the patient held it while he completed the removal.

Fortunately, the patient and her step-father saw the funny side of what happened, and Gilda only had to clean up the bloody mess from the floor - no reprimands - but for the rest of her temporary tenure at the surgery, there was no more assisting with even minor surgery.

In January 1964, at 8.30 AM, Gilda started her new job. She walked from her house in Kangaroo Point along Main Street to the ferry that crossed the river. From the ferry she walked up Edward Street, turned into Adelaide Street to the Commonwealth Bureau of Census and Statistics office, and then, in the afternoon, at 4.50 unless she went out after work, she did the return trip. Gilda loved that walk and the boat ride. 'What a wonderful way to start and end the day,' she thought to with the breeze blowing through her hair while she herself leaned on the boat's safety rail as it crossed the Brisbane River.

The Bureau of Census and Statistics was an interesting department. There were older men who clearly resented the introduction of young women simply because they went to university. The men had started in the Bureau as young boys and had worked their way upwards, though not very far, over 35 years, and were still only two levels above Gilda's entry. They had wives who stayed home, ran the household, knitted their cardigans, vests and pullovers and daily made lunch for them to take to the office. The Brisbane office was managed by a woman, Carolyn, about 10 years older than Gilda. Gradually, they became friends and even did a train trip together to Sydney for a holiday.

Gilda's social life outside of work flourished. She didn't meet many boys of her own age in her department, but she did meet men of her own age, mainly from other government departments, who frequented the rooftop restaurant for breakfast.

By March, Giovanni had returned from Italy and they were seeing each other again. Although by now, Gilda's parents had little control over her, Hanna's snide remarks persisted. Gilda would come home from work and suspect that her mother had rifled through her drawers because things were not placed how she had placed them. One afternoon Gilda came home from work and saw that her dressing table drawers were partly open. She went to the back eating table where Hanna and Vladimir were sitting and asked her mother, 'Did you go through my drawers today?' 'You mean your dressing table drawers... yes,' Hanna calmly replied but avoiding eye contact with Gilda.

'Why?' Gilda said incredulously raising her voice slightly. 'Why? You have no right going through my things.'

Hanna turned to look at Gilda with a stony look on her face, 'You think you are an adult now. You think you can do as you please. But you forget, I am your mother and I will always keep an eye on what you do. You think you can outsmart me by getting a Post Office Box. Well, you should hide your letters better as I have read all of them. Such stupidity they contain. They prove that you are still a silly child and as for your friends… Idiots!'

Gilda couldn't believe what she was hearing and was speechless. Vladimir took over. 'But, Hanna, you can't do that. The child is entitled to her privacy.' 'So, you're just as stupid as she is.' Hanna replied, and then added, 'Where would either of you be if it weren't for me? I am the only sensible one here.' 'You had nothing to do with my getting a job.' Gilda responded almost yelling. 'Yes, it's a job, but it is not a profession,' Hanna replied coolly, 'You are an office assistant, nothing more.'

'I'm studying to improve myself,' Gilda continued through tears. 'Unless it's an academic position at a university, it is nothing,' came Hanna's response.

'I don't want a Uni position,' she almost screamed at her mother, 'Oh and by the way, I will outsmart you, as you put it, because I will leave this house. I'm old enough, you can't stop me.' With that Gilda stormed out and into her room, took her handbag and left the house.

Gilda was starting to assert herself, and Hanna was desperately trying to maintain control. What Hanna didn't realise was that Gilda was a conservative young woman and was not a rebel. She longed for a good relationship with her mother and, in a sense, Gilda felt protective towards her, however, being constantly attacked by her ill-tempered mother, she had to defend herself. There was no way she was going to go under Hanna's thumb. Hanna and Vladimir had their own problems but managed to sweep them aside while they each pursued their careers. They participated in the local medical social circle. Hanna was making a name for herself teaching German while continuing her university studies.

On weekends, Gilda, Giovanni, Natalia and Hans would go out together. Giovanni had a Plymouth convertible, and drove the huge car safely with great confidence. Gilda was childlike and yet sophisticated. She had an innocence about her and people felt protective towards her. Everyone always had a good time around her; she laughed frequently and was always happy. Gilda was appreciative when nice things were said or done for her, and would openly express this. On the surface, there was nothing complicated about her.

Towards the end of 1964, Gilda started to get symptoms of being physically ill. Whenever she ate, she was unable to control her bowels. It seemed that whatever she ate she had to dispose of. She didn't tell her parents as she was afraid to. Her friends told her she should tell her father. 'No, he'll only tell my mother and it'll be my fault whatever it is and get into trouble,' Gilda replied.

One Sunday afternoon, Gilda went to Giovanni's home. His parents had invited her to visit them. She had never seen an entire front garden cemented over as well as a large part of the back garden. The only part of the back yard that was still soil was a large vegetable patch which also contained fruit trees.

'Why did your parents cement the garden?' Gilda asked Giovanni. 'Oh, it's an Italian thing,' he laughed, 'less work for the man, no mowing I suppose.' 'But what about the vegetable patch, enquired Gilda. Again Giovanni laughed as he replied, 'That's also the woman's job; it's part of the kitchen.' 'Are you like that?' she asked looking him in the eyes. 'No,' he replied holding her face. 'I'd do anything for you.'

Just then his mother, Mrs Tibaldi, came to the front door, 'Ah, ciao, Gilda.' she said kissing her on the cheeks, 'So nica you come. Come insida, Giovanni's fada he watcha TV.' At that moment, Mr Tibaldi came towards her, 'Ah, ciao, bella,' and also kissed Gilda on the cheeks and pointed to a chair for her to sit down.

Gilda spent a wonderful afternoon with Giovanni's parents. Mrs Tibaldi produced all sorts of Italian delicacies such as rice and polenta dishes with chicken and veal, different sweet pastries, fresh fruit and chocolates. She was concerned that Gilda hardly seemed to eat anything. When Giovanni explained the problem in Italian, Mrs Tibaldi responded in Italian and Giovanni then translated, 'Mum is worried about you, about your problem, and she thinks it is nervous stress. I'm afraid I told her how your mother treats you, I'm sorry, Gilda, I hope you don't mind.'

Gilda was taken aback. She didn't realise people noticed. In fact, she was so used to it that she took it for granted that that was the way things were in her house. Suddenly, she burst into tears. 'Oh, cara mia,' Mrs Tibaldi embraced her, 'My darling girl.' Gilda had never cried like that before, and it was as though the flood gates of an inside vault had been opened and she released her pent up emotions. Giovanni stood helpless. He wanted to take her in his arms and take her away from it all and be with him but he just had to look on.

Unfortunately, the result of that outburst meant that Gilda closed herself off even more emotionally. 'I feel so stupid,' she said to herself when she returned home. 'How did that happen? It will never happen again. I have to be careful from now on. I'll go to a doctor and get a prescription to control my bowels and take tablets when I know I have to go out'. Before she could get to a doctor that condition nearly took her life.

One morning in 1965, Gilda was walking to the ferry and, although she had eaten only a small, dry breakfast it aggravated her stomach. She was halfway along Main Street, Kangaroo Point when she had to urgently go to the toilet. She made for the service station on the other side of the busy main road. She saw that traffic was stopped at the lights and so she ran across the street. As the lights turned green, the first car on the extreme inside lane accelerated so fast that it hit Gilda as she was almost at the kerb. She was hurled into the air hitting her head with full force against a telegraph pole before falling to the footpath.

She lay motionless on the road. People came to her but she didn't move. A service station attendant rang the ambulance and she was rushed to hospital and regained consciousness several hours later. She was immediately put through various tests and heavily drugged. When the results were returned, the doctors and the police were amazed that there was no serious damage to her head. She had severe internal bruising and had to stay in hospital under observation, but no bones were broken and no organs damaged.

It wouldn't be the first time that 'Higher forces' took charge of her. 'To this day, I still have a chip out of a bone in my head. It just goes to show how stubborn you can be,' is always the humorous reply. The hospital doctor gave her a prescription for her bowel condition. After she was released from hospital, she and her step-father were alone at home when he asked her, 'How long have you had an issue with your stomach, Gilda?'

'Oh, I'm fine now, Pop', she replied flippantly with a wave of her hand, 'Nothing to worry about.'

'Gilda, be honest with me, please. If it is from stress..." she interrupted him and said, 'No, really Pops, it's okay now.' She smiled at him as she gave him a hug. He just looked at her but there was nothing he could do if she dismissed the issue.

The discord between Hanna and Vladimir was increasing. One day Vladimir informed Hanna that he was bringing his daughter and her family to Brisbane. 'Permanently or just for a holiday?' Hanna enquired. 'Permanently,' he replied. 'I see,' was Hanna's reply, 'and where will they live?' 'I will buy them a house. They cannot stay here - there is not enough room.'

Vladimir's daughter, Irena, was now married with two children. Hanna realised that she needed to make plans for the future should it become necessary. 'I remember all too clearly what happened the last time that bitch was here.' Hanna decided to sell the Maisonettes in order to have money for a deposit on a house should that become necessary. She reasoned, 'I need to be prepared should he tell us to move out again.'

Nothing more was said. Hanna's problem was jealousy wedded to her paranoia. If she had, to a certain degree, embraced Irena and acknowledged her as a significant part of her husband's life, she would have made it easier on herself and harder for Irena to influence her father against her. Had she allowed her husband to have a relationship with his daughter, and not forced him 'choose' between them, she would have been in a position of power and things would have turned out very differently.

All her life, Hanna had chosen force, and that was why she was always fighting some person or circumstance and even fighting herself. The problem was that she never learned from these experiences. She dismissed them as all being the other person's fault. She wanted to control and consume her men and whoever was in her life. When she couldn't have total control over them or anyone else, she would discard them. When she consumed people, she considered them weak and stupid. The reason for this behaviour became clearer over the years: it was a behaviour that blinded her to the ramifications of the chaotic results of her actions. There was a big party for Gilda's 21st birthday. Giovanni was still on the scene but it was becoming evident that Gilda was shutting herself off. She liked him very much but she was afraid to become involved in deeper relationship with him. Giovanni sensed what was happening but didn't want to say anything because he didn't want to create a situation that could end their relationship.

During this time, Gilda joined two prestigious organisations, the Royal Commonwealth Society and the Victoria League. Each organisation consumed a great deal of her after-work time. Before long Gilda was on the organising committee of the former and then an office holder. She attended meetings at the premises at Brisbane's Wickham Terrace and acted as a compere at fashion parades and fancy dress evenings. Frequently her photos were in the social pages of 'The Sunday Mail' or 'The Courier Mail', dressed in long gowns, as a movie character if it was fancy dress event, or holding a microphone when she compered official functions.

One evening a group of members went on a boat trip. On the way back in the dark, the boat ran aground on a sand bank and the water police rescued them. The party arrived back in Brisbane after midnight. Everyone on board thought the event hilarious. This made the front pages of The Sunday Mail... 'Gilda Dobinski, daughter of Dr Vladimir Dobinski of Kangaroo Point in miraculous boat rescue'. It was quite a topic of conversation for weeks.

CHAPTER 18
1966 - 1967

Gilda's executive position in The Royal Commonwealth Society resulted in her receiving invitations to cocktail parties, some of which were hosted by captains of visiting Royal Australian Navy ships or visiting ships from other Commonwealth countries. At one of these cocktail parties on a British ship, Gilda met Bill.

'Well, here goes,' she thought as she parked her father's car and was signaled by an attendant's torch to follow him. When they arrived at the official entrance, he turned to her and said, 'Have a nice evening, Miss, and might I say how lovely you look.'

'Oh, thank you,' replied an embarrassed Gilda.

It was a magnificent, clear, starlit night. The gangplank was illuminated with multi-coloured lanterns and as Gilda walked up the vessel's gangway to board the brilliantly lit warship. She started to fidget with her dress to make sure it was sitting correctly, 'Why am I so nervous? I've been to these before. Maybe not as formal but, it's still just a cocktail party.'

Artificial lotus flowers glowed with light bulbs on the deck and Gilda passed through a decorative archway of blooms and, as she boarded the ship, a red carpet led to where the party was being held. It was a magnificent, clear, starlit night. Because the reception was a formal affair, Gilda wore a fitted but flowing pale lilac crêpe sleeveless dress, with a low cut back to the waist. A large bow at the waist with two tails dropping to the floor was the only ornament at the back of the frock. The cut-out back was bold for those times but she had seen it in a fashion magazine, liked it, made a pattern and then re-created it.

A waiter came immediately with a tray of champagne glasses but before Gilda could take a glass, an officer took one for her and said to her, 'Allow me,' and then smiling handed her the champagne flute.

'Thank you,' she replied and then added coquettishly, 'What made you think I would like a glass of champagne?' 'I thought to myself, a beautiful girl like that is sure to drink champagne,' he replied. They laughed. 'Kind sir,' she answered with a smile, 'I fear you are mistaken. I don't drink champagne, in actual fact, I would prefer orange juice.'

Bill looked at her as he took the champagne glass and replaced it with an orange juice. 'You mean you don't drink?' he asked surprised.

'If you mean alcohol, no. We have it at home and I have tasted wine but that's it. It gives me an unpleasant feeling which I don't like.' Bill and Gilda spent the whole evening talking with each other, he finding out about her and her background, and she learning about him and what it was like in England and about shipboard life. Bill was an engaging conversationalist and showed her around the publicly open areas of the ship including its nerve centre, the bridge. As the function came to an end Bill said, 'I've been delighted to meet you. Tomorrow we leave for Singapore. Could I write to you?'

'Yes,' Gilda replied, 'I would like that.'

'I'll be back again in three months. Perhaps we could meet again.' 'Yes, I can show you our beaches at Surfers Paradise,' she suggested. They exchanged addresses and then shook hands before she went to her car. She could still see him on the ship as she reached her car. They waved to each other before she drove off. Some weeks later, a letter arrived from Bill in Singapore and they started corresponding. Each time his ship docked in Brisbane they would be together as often as they could. Between visits, the letters became more and more frequent and contained photos. They would hold hands as they walked. He would put his arms around Gilda's shoulders when they sat on a bench, admired a beautiful view and kissed. Despite the distances that kept them apart on a daily basis, they had become a couple.

On one visit, Bill looked sad and said to her, 'This is my last trip to

Australia. The announcement was sudden so I couldn't tell you before I came. We are returning to our home base in Southampton'. Gilda was shocked and fought back her tears. He embraced her gently saying, 'I love you, Gilda. I want us to continue together. We can make it work. When I get back to our UK base I'll get a plane ticket for you to come and so you can be with me.'

'Yes,' was all she could say, trying to convince herself.

Gilda, you can also come to London when I'm on leave. It'll be a bit awkward at first but when we are married, it'll be easier.'

'Married?' she asked surprised. 'Yes,' Bill said, 'You do want to get married, don't you?' 'I've never thought about it. We have never discussed it,' was all she could say.

'We haven't had to till now,' he replied. Getting down on one knee he said solemnly, 'Gilda Dobinski, I am here on bended knee. Will you marry me?' He looked so funny, she burst out laughing and said, 'Yes, you nutty Pom.' They kissed and enjoyed the rest of the time together. However, in the cold light of the next day, Gilda, without knowing it, had already compartmentalised Bill in the 'it's over' category. 'Nothing lasts,' she said but her heart ached for many months. 'I want to write to him but I can't. I don't want to string him along.' she said sadly wiping tears away. 'But I don't want to get hurt either.'

Mid-year, Vladimir's daughter, Irena and her family arrived permanently in Brisbane but lived in another part of the city. Initially, Vladimir and Hanna were invited to dinner on weekends. Hanna mostly declined to go, 'I will show them who the superior one is. I will not mix with them.' That was a mistake. There is the saying, "Know thine enemy and keep them at your side." The invitations increased and included days when Hanna was at work or at the University and on other occasions in the evenings when she genuinely felt too tired to go out. On these occasions Vladimir visited Irena and her family, usually with Gilda. It didn't take long before Hanna and her husband only discussed business and house matters and the atmosphere between them grew icy. They lived in the family home but became estranged from each other.

At the beginning of 1967 Gilda was still going out with Giovanni but it was very much an, on and off relationship. She liked him very much and sometimes scolded herself about why she couldn't feel more for him. 'Why can't I feel for him like I did at the beginning? He hasn't changed, in actual fact he is even nicer to me. I know I can trust him in everything. What's wrong with me?' Gilda also had other male friends whose company she enjoyed until things became serious and then she backed away. Gilda especially liked the cocktail parties on the visiting ships because there she was in control. If she liked one of the officers and they went out together as she drove her father's car and so controlled where they went and for how long and what they did. She felt safe. Mostly, she just enjoyed the first few hours of parties, but then left alone. 'It's a lot less complicated that way,' she would say, remembering her heartache after Bill.

At one of the Royal Commonwealth Society functions, Gilda met a young man called Andrew who came from an old and distinguished Brisbane family. He lived in Nundah, one of Brisbane's northern suburbs on the opposite side of Brisbane from where Gilda lived. They were soon dating and it was in this relationship that her lack of self-worth feeling became painfully obvious. She would never have admitted it, but having been accepted as Andrew's girlfriend was something she could have only dreamed of. It was in essence the same situation that her mother experienced when she first met Hermann in Vienna in 1937.

Gilda didn't have her own car, and could borrow her father's in the evening. During the day, he needed it for house calls or emergencies. Hanna never lent Gilda her car. Andrew would say that Kangaroo Point was too far for him to drive and that Gilda had to come to where he lived. She would take a bus and then a tram, about an hour's trip one way. Andrew would then pick her up and they would go somewhere. This went on for months and Gilda was proud of being his girlfriend. 'He's not worth it,' her friends warned her but she refused to listen.

However, Andrew did take Gilda to interesting places. They went glider flying in Beaudesert. A winch hauled the glider up into the air and released it to find an air pocket. They also went to another gliding club at Kingaroy, famous for its peanuts, a 2½ hour drive north-west of Brisbane. They would silently fly for about an hour. 'Oh, it is so quiet, so peaceful,' she sighed to herself. 'Why can't life be as simple as sitting up here in the air?' They were both going for their glider pilot's licence, and Gilda would go off alone for walks while Andrew had his lesson. She would disappear for the hour and no one knew where she was.

'Where do you go when I'm up in the air? Who goes with you,' Andrew questioned her one day. 'What do you mean?' she asked. 'You know exactly what I mean? Tell me. You never know with you foreigners.' Gilda was shocked. No one had ever made a reference to her having come from somewhere else. Andrew held her arm tightly. 'Let go. You're hurting me. No one goes with me. I go alone. And if you continue to act like this, I'll head home.' 'I was only joking,' he laughed, 'Sorry if I hurt you. I'm stronger than I realise.' One day Andrew announced that he wanted her to meet his parents. She was simultaneously pleased and terrified at the same time. 'Oh, no,' Gilda silently thought, 'He is from this important family and they are strict Catholics. I hope they don't ask me about my family.' Gilda needn't have been concerned. The day came and Andrew introduced her, 'Mother, Father, I'd like you to meet Gilda Dobinski'.

'How do you do, my dear,' each parent said to her. 'How do you do,' Gilda replied not sure whether to shake hands or not.
'Andrew has told us about you. It's so nice of him to be kind to you to make you feel welcome in Australia. It must be so difficult not knowing anyone. He's such a good boy to people in need.' his mother added looking sweetly at her son.

Gilda glared over at Andrew who looked expressionless straight ahead. 'What the hell has he been saying?' She was furious. She suddenly realised that what her friends had said about him was true. Ignoring him, she went over to the parents and said resolutely, 'It was so lovely to meet you but I must go,' and headed for the door.

'Oh but my dear, we have prepared afternoon tea, delicious scones, you know, with butter and jam.' 'Thank you, that is very kind, but I really cannot stay,' Gilda said sweetly. With that, she headed for the front door with Andrew quickly following her.
'Gilda, where are you going,' Andrew asked. 'Away from here, and I never want to see you again,' she said firmly and continued walking. 'What do you mean? Stop. Wait. I don't understand.' 'No, you wouldn't understand. I'm this poor little foreign creature you rescued and brought to your high and mighty world. Your parents seem to think that I am like a stray dog that should be grateful for a meatless bone. Well, you know what. This foreign kid doesn't need rescuing. You stay with your well-bred crowd. I'm catching the tram home and I never want to see you again.'

"But...okay, but, I wish you'd explain what you mean.' It was Andrew's turn to be flustered and not knowing what to do or say. 'Oh, I thought,' said Gilda, 'it is very clear. It seems that you're the one who has a problem understanding English.' 'At least let me drive you near your home.' Andrew said.

'No, thanks, to think I was so grateful that you looked at me, talked to me, deigned to go out with me. I travelled all those times by tram to see you, months of it. I can't believe I was so stupid. Go away and never come near me again.' She glared at him threateningly and he stopped in his tracks.

She had gone a few streets before she slowed down. 'What a prig!' she exclaimed. 'I can't believe it.' She stopped for a moment, saw a bench at a tram stop and sat down. 'Okay, girl, this was a good experience but I never want to go through that again. I need to have more pride in who I am. I was such a doormat. No idea why I was, but I was. He wasn't even fun most of the time. Oh well, move on,' she philosophised.

'I've been coming to this area for so long and have never been into the large shopping centre,' she thought as a tram arrived. 'To the shopping centre please driver.' She took her ticket and change and

announced inwardly, 'Shops sound like a good idea at the moment.' She alighted from the tram and explored the centre.
As she passed a newsagency, she saw a table outside containing books. She could never resist books and stationery. As she fossicked through the books Gilda came across a thin paperback with a strange red drawing on the cover and the word "Taoism" printed on the cover. 'What can this be? It's too small to be an art book, and what does Taoism mean?' she thought. She went to the back of the book and read the Blurb. She read entranced, 'Oh, my goodness,' she said to herself. She then looked at the chapter headings in the book's contents page. 'I must have this book'

After she bought the book, she sat on a bench in the centre and started to read it and then whispered, 'So, in a nutshell what this philosophy says is that all life forms are connected on this Earth - humans, animals and nature; the same energy unites all of these and we are dependent on each other for survival. Each life form has yin and yang energies that is, female and male energies. The way to live life is through love, compassion and humility. Love means loving all that has been created, and not even an ant is killed. Love and peace are everything; it is the Way, the path to life.' She stopped for a moment to digest what she had just said. 'Do people really live like that? They must, otherwise there wouldn't be a book on it,' Gilda reasoned.

Gilda sat immersed in her thoughts and skimmed parts of the book, 'I want that sort of life. That's how I want to live. I don't like all this arguing and fighting,' she silently declared. It was not going to be an easy path for her. She had no role models. It was still a survival of the fittest in her home. 'I will carry this book around with me and when I feel lost and unsure, I will read from it.'

And that's what Gilda did, or at least tried to do. The book was always with her. 'I can't leave it lying around as my mother will surely find it and take it away from me.' More often than not, she erred from the Way but it was always in her consciousness.

Gradually however, the realities of her life were too strong and the book was forgotten, except, on a subconscious level where seeds had been planted. Books would always be Gilda's friends, and a book title would always appear that helped her in whatever she needed at many times in her life.

Andrew didn't give up easily. He was obsessed with Gilda. 'I don't think it's me that he likes. I just think he has a case of severely wounded pride.' He would wait for her at the lift to talk to her when she started work or finished work. Gilda was obdurate, 'I told you I never wanted to see you again, and I meant it,' she firmly reminded him. But it didn't help. He would still come to see her. She didn't know what to do. Finally, she called Giovanni. Andrew was tall, skinny and weedy. Giovanni was tall, muscular and had a presence. To look at him, you wouldn't know he was so gentle. A gentle giant.

One day, as Giovanni was waiting at the lift standing away from Gilda. Andrew was present attempting to reason with her. The lift came. Gilda made out she was about to enter, Andrew and Giovanni went into the lift together and Gilda went back into the hallway. When the lift returned, Andrew was pale and as he stormed past Gilda he said, 'You wogs are all mad,' and that was the last time she saw him. 'Oh, my goodness,' Gilda laughed, 'What did you say to him?'

'I stretched the truth. I told him I was part of an Italian clan whose headquarters were in Sicily and then I rambled off something in Italian and waved my hands around. I think he was about to shit himself. Luckily the lift door opened and you saw the rest.' They burst out laughing.

'Come Gilda, let's go for a coffee,' Giovanni suggested. Arm-in-arm they walked down the street, giggling all the way. They sat in a cubicle so they could talk in private. 'Gilda,' Giovanni started, 'You know I love you.' Gilda gently put her index finger to his lips to stop him from continuing.

'Giovanni, please don't go on,' she said softly. 'I know how you feel about me and I love you too, but not that way. You deserve better than me. You are a good man. You deserve a wife who can return your love and who will have your children. I am not that woman. I don't even know if I can love. And I don't want children. To be honest, Giovanni, I don't really know who I am or where I fit in. I'll be leaving Brisbane soon. I just want to get away from my mother. Until I do that, I'll never know what I can really do. I'll be going to Canberra where I can better my career chances. Can we still be friends?' she asked.

'Of course we can, but it will be very tough for me,' Giovanni replied.

'Yes, you are right, it isn't fair of me to ask that. It is best we don't see each other anymore, so that you can find someone else.' They were both emotional and silent. Suddenly Gilda rose and said, 'Goodbye Giovanni, thank you for all the wonderful times we had. I have never been happier and I love you in my way. I wish the very best for you and I will miss you.' With that she kissed him on the cheek and hurried away.

Gilda was miserable for weeks but she knew it couldn't be any other way.

During the Christmas break, she took holidays from work and met up with friends. On one occasion she was having drinks at the bar of the National Hotel in Queen Street. By now she drank rum and coke, the then 'in' drink of those days. A group of them were sitting at a table when a man came up to them. 'Hello Jack,' he said to one of Gilda's friends. 'Hello, Mark,' Jack replied unenthusiastically. Mark had been drinking.

'Hey, Jack, is that your girl?' pointing to Gilda, 'Aren't you going to introduce me?' Jack ignored Mark, and pulled up a chair next to Gilda. 'We were just leaving,' Jack said curtly. 'Na, stay and have a drink… on me, mate.' The others at the table didn't know what to do. In order to avoid a scene, Jack sat down. Everyone sat in silence except for Mark who persisted, 'I know all of Jack's girlfriends, but I've never seen you before. She's not a bad sort, mate. What's her name?'

To placate Mark, Jack replied, 'Her name is Gilda.' 'That's foreign. Where are you from, honey,' Mark asked. Gilda told him. 'What's your last name?' Mark wouldn't let up. 'Dobinski.' replied Gilda. Mark looked at her briefly and said, 'The doctor, Dobinski? You're Dr Dobinski's daughter?'

'Yes,' she replied. Mark roared with laughter. Jack rose from his chair and the others did the same. 'Come on, Gilda, it's time to go,' he said earnestly. 'No wait, not so fast,' said Mark raising his voice. 'So this is Dobinski's daughter? The guy who helps ladies who have got themselves into trouble get out of trouble, he's your father. Well, well.'

'Come on Gilda,' Jack implored. 'No, wait,' she said sternly. "I don't like the way you are speaking about my father,' Gilda challenged Mark.

'Oh, dearie, dearie me, she doesn't like the way I'm talking about her Daddy. Well, honey, ask your dear father. He can tell you better than I can. He's the one who does it,' he said sarcastically. Jack pulled Gilda away and the others at the table held Mark back and waited until Gilda and Jack had disappeared.

Gilda waited until she and her father were alone before she confronted him with what she had heard at the hotel. She didn't understand what was said but she had a horrible feeling about it. Vladimir said it was true but he begged Gilda to let him explain. 'Part of my work is helping mothers who have lost their child as a fetus within the womb, and to be able for them to give birth again to a healthy child in the future I clean out that area.' Vladimir continued, 'The same procedure is used to remove an unplanned pregnancy. For various reasons which I believe we are not in a position to judge, women can get pregnant and it is financially, and sometimes emotionally, unwise to continue the pregnancy. Sometimes it is also unwise for their health and they wish to terminate it. I help these women. If I turn them away, they will go somewhere else. With me, it is a safe, hygienic and a properly performed procedure. If women go to a 'backyard' unregistered medical practitioner, they could be internally mutilated or even bleed to death. I have helped many women in Europe where it is legal and accepted. Here, I help migrant women whose situations are such that they don't have enough food for themselves, their husband and their existing children. They felt horrible about having to resort to prematurely terminating the pregnancy but there was no other way. I do not charge these poor people. I also never want to take the few vegetables they grow in their garden that they want to give me but, they insist on paying me what they can. For them to keep their self-respect, your mother and I take the vegetables.'

'So, my mother knows about this as well,' Gilda interrupted. 'Yes,' her step-father replied softly. 'But please let me continue. I find this very hard. When Australians came who clearly simply see fun sex having gone wrong, I charge them, yes.' Gilda knew how respected and loved her step-father was amongst the migrants, and now she knew one of the reasons why. 'It's okay Pop,' she said when he had finished, 'It's not for me to judge either. I believe you would only do what you felt was best for them. But, you better be careful. I have found out what you do through some drunk in a hotel. My friends knew and wanted to protect me from it. You could get caught by the authorities and your career would be over and you would go to jail.'

'By the way, where do you put the money that you charge,' she asked. 'In wall boards,' he replied without going into detail. Gilda felt uncomfortable about the situation. 'I'm never going to know what people are thinking when they are introduced to me. Who will know about this and more than likely judge me? Oh, well, I'll just get on with my life and, at least, I'll be aware of it when it comes up again.'

It was almost three years since she started at the Commonwealth Bureau of Census and Statistics and had received two promotions. Gilda had passed all her Uni subjects to date and only had three subjects remained to be completed. The regulations only allowed an evening student to enroll in two subjects per year. Gilda thought, 'If I can only find a way to do the three this coming year, I could finish my degree. And, in true Gilda fashion, she found a way. She obtained a letter from a superior in the Bureau to say that she was taking time off for study and her university allowed her to enroll for the final three units.

As Christmas approached, it became clear to Gilda that continuing angst in the Dobinski household meant it would not be the site of happy and joyous festivity. Carolyn, Gilda's boss at the Bureau, decided to go to Sydney for two weeks. 'How about a train trip?' Carolyn suggested. 'Sure, why not?' Gilda agreed, 'It'll be a lot of fun.' And that's what they did.

CHAPTER 19
1968 - 1969

In 1968, Vladimir's younger brother by two years, Dragi, with his wife, Gabriella, and three children arrived in Brisbane from Macedonia. The two older boys were from a previous marriage and the teenage daughter, Lindana, from his current marriage. The two Dobinski families were often together and Hanna got on well with Gabriella, who was a very cheerful, optimistic person, although she didn't think her sister-in-law was educated enough to converse with except for daily pleasantries.

Hanna and Vladimir's marital problems intensified and they had slept in separate bedrooms for months. Vladimir spent most of his time with Irena and her family and Hanna had friends amongst whom was a Hungarian, Stephan, who she found interesting. One Saturday after morning surgery, Vladimir approached her, "Hanna, could I please speak with you?' 'Yes, of course,' she replied. 'Hanna, what I have to say will not come to you as a surprise. I think it is best that we separate with divorce in mind.' She was taken aback by his bluntness, but then she remembered how Hermann, Gilda's father, had ended their marriage. 'It's obviously the direct way a man does it,' she thought. 'Very well, I have seen this coming. Ever since your daughter arrived, you have changed.'

'No,' contradicted replied Vladimir, 'Please do not bring Irena into this. You and I have had problems for years. Getting back together again to work things out after the first separation seemed a possibility, but it has not worked. This happened before Irena arrived.' Vladimir added, 'I hope we can discuss this with civility.' 'Well, I certainly can,' responded Hanna.

'I will get my solicitor to prepare a document for us both to peruse,' Vladimir replied and left for his daughter's and did not return that evening. Gilda, sitting in her room, had heard everything. When Vladimir left, she came out and spoke to her mother who was sitting staring at the chair that he had vacated.

'Mom, I heard everything,' Gilda began. Hanna burst into tears. Gilda was not unaware of the theatrics her mother could turn on depending on who was in her presence or whom she wanted to influence. 'What did she expect,' thought Gilda, 'that she would go on forever living in this chaotic angry relationship?' Instead, she put her arms around Hanna and let her cry it out. Hanna collected herself quickly and Gilda went to get tissues for her. 'Mom, what will happen now? What will you do,' she asked taking over the adult role.

Hanna shrugged. She wasn't really surprised but needed to play the helpless, friendless wife and mother. What she couldn't believe was that this had happened to her again and once again she hadn't been the one in control of the situation. Hanna's reason went along these lines, 'I am always in control. I am the strong one. Without me, Vladimir wouldn't be where he is today. I am the one who sacrificed everything by leaving Vienna. Once he leaves me, he will see, he will be nothing. That bitch cannot give him the life I gave him.'

Suddenly, Hanna she sat up, looked at Gilda and stated, 'We will move to St Lucia, near the University. We will live then be living in Brisbane's best suburb. Vladimir and his precious relations can live in a low-class suburb. It will suit them.'

Gilda couldn't believe what she was hearing. 'She's deranged. She must be in shock. I need to take over.' And so Gilda did. On the weekend, she asked amongst her friends what happened when parents divorced. Her friends were shocked; they didn't know that things were so bad between Gilda's parents. Divorce wasn't common in those days. People stuck it out or lived separate lives under the same roof.

'Oh, the man gets everything,' said one. 'The woman is always worse off because the courts favour the husband,' said another. I know a lady who had to go cleaning because she didn't get enough to live on. He got the house and she had to go on the pension,' added another and so it went on.

Gilda was horrified. This was something she had never encountered. None of her friends had parents or grandparents who had divorced. 'Oh, no, that's not going to happen to my mother,' she vowed. And so Gilda embarked on a mission. On Sunday morning when she was alone, Gilda went into action. 'I know where he hides money. I'll take that for her. At least that'll get her started.' She found the wall panel 'treasury' and took out all the notes and hid them. 'Goodness, who would have thought he had that much money there,' said Gilda. 'I don't know how long I've got before they see a solicitor, but I should think that I have at least a week.'

On Monday morning, Gilda went to the two largest department stores in Brisbane, Myer and David Jones, in the City Centre and bought all sorts of clothes for her mother: dresses, hats, gloves, slacks, blouses, hosiery, and underwear - whatever she could think of. 'It's too bad she has such big feet, so I can't risk buying shoes,' she thought. Then she bought the latest kitchen appliances using her subsidiary credit card, which was attached to her father's.

On Wednesday, the stores rang the house to check that the purchases were legitimate. Gilda answered the phone and in a formal voice assured them that all was in order. 'Oh, yes, we are having a special occasion and it is a surprise. Thank you for checking.' 'It really is a special occasion and two people will certainly be surprised,' she thought, giggling. 'At least she'll feel good in her new clothes and if we have to live in a dump to begin with, she'll have new kitchen things.' 'It won't take him long to make up the money,' Gilda rationalised.

It was quite a job hiding all the purchases. The domestic purchases she hid in some of the spider-infested storage cupboards under the house. 'No one goes there. They should be safe', she hoped and crossed her fingers. To hide the new clothing, Gilda piled them up in her wardrobes by squashing her clothes up and then locking her wardrobe doors. 'That's in case anyone snoops in my room,' she hoped as she pocketed the keys.

No one guessed what had happened. In any case, both her father and mother were hardly home as they were making final arrangements for the cessation of married life as they knew it, and they concentrated their planning and organising for the separate new life ahead of them. Vladimir was mostly at his daughter's, and Hanna just wasn't home.

On the following Saturday, Gilda was alone at home when she heard her father at the wall panel. She quickly opened her door to the front verandah for a quick get-away if necessary. 'Oh, hell, he's going to be furious when he sees that the money has gone.' At that moment, Vladimir stormed in. His face was white. Gilda stood at the door to the verandah.

Vladimir shouted, 'Did you take the money?'

'Yes, I did,' Gilda replied simply but firmly.

'Where is it? Give it back to me. It's my money,' he demanded trying to contain himself.

'No, sorry Pop, it's not anymore,' she replied, 'It belongs to my mother. I'm giving all of it to her.' Vladimir glared at her in disbelief. She continued. 'Pop, listen, you have a career that pays well. Mom only has part-time work at the moment which means she doesn't get paid during school holidays. That's two months without any income. My salary isn't much either, so, I can't help her. I made enquires amongst my friends and they all said that the woman always loses out in a divorce settlement, I'm just making sure that she's looked after as best as I can'.

'I'll make sure she gets half of everything.' her father said.
'Half? You know that isn't a fair deal. Because I'm older and working, she won't get alimony. Yes, don't look so surprised. I've made enquiries,' said Gilda. 'Look, Pop, Mom hasn't got anyone but me. You have your family behind you. She has no one for moral or financial support should she need it, even if only temporarily. Be reasonable. You two once loved each other. Look what you two went through to get to where you are now. Doesn't that count for

anything?'

'She's got the Hungarian,' Vladimir said loudly 'she can go to him.' 'What are you talking about? He's a friend, that's all. I've been with them, there's nothing going on. Gosh, you grownups can be stupid.

'You're not going to use that against her for the divorce, are you? Because if you do, look out,' Gilda looked at him in a knowing fashion as she paused slightly, 'And now, please leave my room.' She stared at him until he left and then thought, 'I know it's not over but at least it's out in the open. I'll keep my doors locked in future even when I'm asleep and when I leave the house I'll take the money with me. I need to put it somewhere safe. But where?'

Suddenly she had a revelation, 'I know. I'll post it registered mail to myself at my post office box. That'll keep it safe.' Then, with a smile and as an afterthought, she said, 'Mom is never around these days, maybe Pop's right,' she thought, 'I don't care if she is having a fling with the Hungarian. While she's occupied, she's out of my hair.'

By the end of the year, Hanna and Vladimir were divorced. It had gone quicker than normal. Hanna had received a cash settlement for half the value of the Kangaroo Point house. Although this money wouldn't buy much, fortunately, Hanna sold the two Maisonettes but by the time the mortgage had been paid off, not much of the sale money remained. She hadn't had the property long enough to make much of a capital gain to be of value but she was able to buy her dream, a house in St. Lucia, which was only a 10 minute walk from the university. Transport to the city centre was convenient as the bus terminus was across the road and there were frequent buses to and from the University of Queensland.

Vladimir hadn't told Hanna what Gilda had done with his cache of hidden money so she had no idea. He wasn't at the house when Hanna and Gilda left. 'It's weird,' Gilda thought, 'It's as though no part of our life together existed. No one matters, nothing matters. All you can do is live your life. It's best not to get attached to anyone because people come and people go. Family also means nothing. I've had fewer problems with friends than I've had with my family. The saying 'Blood is thicker than Water' is nonsense. Gilda was sad, but not for long.

Mother and daughter now lived together without another person acting as a filter. As they unpacked the items the furniture removalist had brought, Hanna saw the packages that Gilda directed to be put into the lounge.

'What is all this,' Hanna asked when she saw box after box being piled into the room. 'Surprise, Mom, they are all yours,' Gilda declared triumphantly. 'What do you mean? I've never seen those items before,' a bewildered Hanna replied. 'Seriously, it's all yours. I bought it. It's all for you,' Gilda announced and flashed a smile. 'Where did you get the money to buy all this? Is some of it for you?' Hanna still couldn't understand what was going on. 'No, as I said, Mom; it's all yours. Nothing is for me. It's for you,' she repeated with an even bigger smile directed at her mother. 'It's a parting but unwilling gift from your ex-husband,' Gilda joked.

'What do you mean? Vladimir has given me this?' Hanna asked incredulously. 'Well, not directly. Indirectly, yes.' Gilda replied having difficulty controlling her mirth and then, she told her mother what she had done. Hanna went over to the lounge filled with an assortment of brand new articles of clothing and unopened boxes of kitchen-ware.

'Oh, and by the way,' she added taking a small package from her handbag, 'This is yours too.' Hanna opened the little parcel containing a large envelope. She opened the envelope, looked inside, and gasped, 'Was ist das? What is that? Gilda told her about this too. 'But Gilda that is a lot of money,' an astounded Hanna said. 'Not that much for Pop, it's not. He'll soon make that up but it is a lot of money for you. Enjoy.'

Hanna was surprised when she heard what Gilda had done for her, Vladimir was out of his mind when he got that month's credit card statement for around $4,000 worth of goods that Gilda had bought for her mother. But all in all, he didn't hold it against her; Gilda hadn't bought anything for herself. In a way he admired her loyalty and she had continued being nice to him during the unpleasant divorce experience. He had also seen how Irena would have deprived Hanna of receiving anything and consequently he stopped her attending solicitor's meetings with him.

The Christmas festivities were a forced affair. The Christmas tree was erected and decorated and lights and candles were lit. Presents exchanged but it was clear that neither Hanna nor Gilda had anything other than their blood relationship in common. Hanna's relationship with the Hungarian had stopped, and Hanna was on her own again with nothing to distract her attention, except finding fault with Gilda.

Desperately Hanna sought avenues where she could feel important. Her imagination, her make believe world was not enough; she needed actual people so that she could display and puff out her feathers. Gilda on the other hand had lots of friends, both male and female, and she made sure that she was at home as little as possible.

The bickering between the two women was constant provoked by Hanna's desire to assert herself. Meanwhile, Gilda's stomach problems had subsided for the time being. They had not been cured and flared up unpredictably and at times, with catastrophic consequences. The problem would not go away under the current circumstances of intensive intra-family discord.

It was 1969 and Hanna maintained her university her studies in German, which gave her enormous satisfaction, and she developed close contact with some members of the German Department at her University. But this and her tutoring and part-time teaching work were insufficient for her to feel 'important.' She didn't have a group of people where she would be recognised as a pivotal, controlling nucleus.

Hanna wanted to belong somewhere, but she was also fiercely independent and would pull away at the first sign of people becoming too demanding on her time. It also irked her that Gilda had numerous admirers, lots of girlfriends, and that she went to see Vladimir every so often. It was clear that the visits were pleasant which made Hanna jealous; she didn't like being excluded, unless it was her choice. Gilda was open about visiting her step-father and told her mother whenever she went to see him.

Hanna's unceasing barrage of complaints against Gilda rapidly escalated, 'If you spent more time helping me in the house and less time flittering around, I would also be able to go out more often. And then she would always add, 'I'll be penniless with all the amount of phone calls you make.' Gilda countered with a simple truth, 'Every time I make a call, I put money in the box to pay for the call, Gilda responded. 'You aren't paying for any of my calls.' Money was always an issue with Hanna. Even if the change was a cent, Gilda always had to give it to her mother or Hanna gave it to Gilda. Hanna insisted that each paid for herself whenever they went out together, tram or bus fare, or half of any expense that they had accrued together. The one would never take the other for a coffee; Hanna didn't allow such frivolity with money. 'Everyone pays for herself,' was her mantra.

Hanna was relentless in her criticism of Gilda, 'I can never go out because you go out so often.' 'What has my going out got to do with you not being able to go out,' a perplexed Gilda asked. 'Someone has to be home for the dogs,' was Hanna's reply. 'Oh, for heaven's sake, lay off. I take the dogs for a walk every morning and afternoon. They have each other when we are out,' Gilda said in her defence, and to bring some sanity into the conversation.
'But you are seldom home. You are never home,' Hanna nagged on. 'Mom, you are impossible. It's impossible to reason with you. One of us has to move out, we can't live together and since it's your house, I'll move out as soon as possible.'

And so it went on, anything that came to Hanna's mind at any time would be brought up and would end up in an argument. Gilda would at times not answer back. Although Gilda tried to live friction-free, Hanna simply became worse. If things became too heated, she would take the dogs for a walk. They now had a male and a female Weimaraner. The intention was to breed from them. After a visit to her step-father, Gilda said to her mother, 'Pop is very sick.' 'Oh rubbish,' replied Hanna, 'he's always been a hypochondriac, always had headaches, or had an ache somewhere.' 'No, really, he is sick,' replied Gilda.

'Oh, so now you'll side with him, will you? Well, I don't need any of you. I can make my life for myself. Heaven knows you probably see him behind my back. Oh, my poor nerves,' she added, 'No one cares about my nerves.'

'Oh, geez, leave your nerves out of this, it's wearing thin. If they are so bad, go and see a doctor. You lived with one for a long time, what did he say? As for when I go to see Pop, I always tell you when I visit him,' an exasperated Gilda replied. But Hanna continued, 'I suppose the whole family has free rein of the house now that I'm not there,' Hanna went on. Gilda could see that there was no point in continuing the conversation so she didn't answer. 'Answer me,' screamed Hanna.

'No, not always and, even if they were there, so what? The house belongs to their father, they have a right to be there if he's fine with it and why shouldn't he be, they are his children and grandchild? For what it's worth, they aren't always there when I'm there,' replied Gilda raising her voice to match Hanna's vocal excesses, and said to her mother, 'For God's sake, do you always have to yell at me?'

Hanna had successfully applied for a full-time teaching position for the following year at a respected private girls' school in Ipswich. She made arrangements go to the school in January before the academic year began to check on her classroom and procure any texts and stationery she might need. 'Congratulations, Mom, that is wonderful. I'm so excited for you. You'll now have a permanent position with greater security and you'll earn more money.' Hanna replied in the queenly manner which she adopted addressing people she regarded as her social and intellectual inferiors. 'Thank you, Gilda, but it's nothing unusual and, I had no doubt I would be selected. No Australian here can equal my qualifications as a German speaker,'

'When will I ever learn,' thought Gilda and brushed it off.
Gilda also had good news. She completed her Bachelor of Arts Degree having received Credits for the final three subjects and she had been accepted to begin a Master of Arts (Qualifying). 'I've now graduated. I'm so thrilled. Pop will be proud of me,' she mused and allowed herself a small self-congratulatory smile. Hanna didn't say anything but then Gilda didn't expect that she would. 'She's just jealous now because we've got the same academic qualification. She can't say that I don't finish anything I start and she can't say that the system is easy here because we both did the same study.'

By the end of October, it was obvious that something was wrong with Liesel, the female Weimaraner. Gilda took her to the Vet who diagnosed that she was pregnant. 'Oh, but she's so young, Gilda commented to the Vet. 'Yes,' he agreed, 'she is, this would have been her first season, the first time she was in heat. It would have been better to have waited another six months till her next season.' 'But we didn't see anything,' Gilda replied.

'It would have happened when the dogs were alone. You and your mother are both inexperienced in these matters. I'll tell you in detail what you need to do till she delivers her litter and what to look out for,' the Vet offered. 'Dogs know what to do so Liesel, although very young, shouldn't have any problems when she delivers'. Liesel was a healthy dog so she was fine during her pregnancy. Gilda often directed her anxieties verbally to her, 'Liesel, my little girl, you are doing so well. I'm so proud of you and how you are handling this. You're still just a puppy yourself. Blasted males, they're the same in all species, aren't they? One thing on their mind. Look at him over there, not a care in the world, and you have the whole bother'.

As it came closer to confinement, Gilda stayed home in the evenings and on weekends just in case the puppies arrived. One Saturday night, she was alone at home and as she did her regular checks to the laundry where Liesel slept, she noticed that Liesel was heaving and pushing. 'Oh my goodness, she's giving birth,' Gilda cried out simultaneously excited and anxious. She had read and re-read the instructions from the Vet in the event that Liesel needed help. 'Oh, no,' Gilda cried as she saw the first puppy come out dead. Liesel was clearly distressed and Gilda felt helpless. 'Liesel, darling, it's okay, you can do it. We'll do it together, she lovingly said to her pet. 'Oh, no, this can't be,' Gilda cried out again as the second pup came out, also dead. This completely unnerved Liesel, who had started to lick the pup.

Gilda saw that another pup was coming. It was alive when it arrived. Liesel was so exhausted by this stage she wasn't taking notice of this pup. 'God, if I don't pull that cord the pup will die and maybe Liesel too. Oh bugger, here goes,' and with her bare hands Gilda took the cord and pulled it freeing the pup. 'I've no idea what I'm doing', Gilda thought trying to stay calm and weeping at the same time. Liesel had recovered slightly, had taken charge and licked her pup till it was clean. Gilda looked on in awe at the beautiful picture of Liesel with her one surviving pup. Gradually, both mother and pup settled and the pup was sucking at Liesel's teat. Liesel just lay on her side while her baby fed itself. Her eyes were glazed but looked at Gilda.

Gilda watched this with a full heart as Liesel looked at her. 'For as long as I live, I'll never forget the love in her eyes as she looked at me. It was a look of love and gratitude.' Gilda said with tears streaming. She then kissed Liesel on the top of her head and stroked her gently so as not to disturb her or her pup. When the puppy had finished drinking, mother and baby fell asleep. 'Isn't it incredible what love, real love can do and overcome,' Gilda said pensively to herself as she watched the two now slumbering animals. 'I didn't like the sight of blood in the surgery but when it came to saving my darling Liesel and her helpless pup, the blood and guts didn't matter.'

She looked over the two into space and quietly said, 'That's the proof, isn't it? Whether you love or whether you don't.' The tears became heavier until she fell asleep on the laundry floor.
Gilda stayed with them that night and for the ensuing week. She slept on a chair curled up in her eiderdown. Gilda kept Liesel's miracle pup and called him Benno after a German poet she liked at the time.

CHAPTER 20
1970 - 1971

Gilda's career with the Bureau of Census and Statistics was going well and she loved what she did. She was now only half a day at the office and then did field work for the remainder of the day, going go to the Queensland State Government department responsible also in Adelaide Street to gather the latest information about companies registered in the State of Queensland. Her plans to transfer to the Bureau's head office in Canberra had started. 'I'm so excited. I can hardly wait and it's a good time to leave. I don't think I can bear to live alone with my mother any longer. She's so unpredictable, flies off the handle at anything. Her and her bloody 'nerves'. Why doesn't she go and get them checked?'

Hanna fitted well into her new school. The head mistress and staff were delightful and welcoming people and she could now play the 'grande dame' and bask in the accolades she received. She played the role well and was extremely charming. Now in charge of a German Department, Hanna at last had the opportunity to wield her impressive knowledge and expertise to good purpose. She was dedicated to her work and to her students, and she lived her life through their successes. Ipswich was then still a country town and Hanna was a novelty who played up her created upper middle-class Viennese background, aided by personal history that she had invented and exquisitely embroidered.

Hanna never said she came from the Austrian aristocracy but if that mistake was made, she allowed it to be perpetuated. When asked about her husband's occupation her reply was always, 'My husband is a doctor, a specialist from Vienna.' It was an evasive reply. Women in those days were judged according to their husband's profession. Hanna carefully hid the fact that Hanna was now divorced from Vladimir. As far as Hanna was concerned, she was still a doctor's wife.

Gilda had received an invitation to another cocktail party, but this time it took place on board an Australian ship. It was not a formal evening, so she wore a knee-length, pale blue satin cheongsam with

a Chinese collar, sporting cheeky slits up above the knees on both sides of the dress, silver stilettos and her trademark flowing hair and diamante earrings. As she boarded, she was greeted by the ship's captain, and Kenneth, a Lieutenant Commander in the Australian Naval Reserve. At first she thought that Kenneth was just being polite by staying with her so she said, 'You don't have to stay with me if you need to mingle with other guests.'
'I'm not staying with you because I have to; I'm staying because I want to,' he replied moving a little closer as though telling her a secret.

Gilda was surprised and said flirtatiously, 'Oh, I am flattered, kind sir.' Nevertheless, she was also embarrassed. After that, they chatted and walked on the deck like old friends, 'It's really easy to talk to him,' Gilda mused. Kenneth had his own secret thoughts, 'I've never seen such a gorgeous, interesting woman.' The cocktail party was a two-hour affair and on the dot of 8.00 PM people were going down the gangplank.

'Are you doing anything after this,' Kenneth asked. 'No, just going home.' Gilda responded.

'Would you like to go and have coffee nearby?' he suggested. Gilda was suddenly terrified. 'Don't be stupid,' she said to herself. Calming herself, Gilda replied, 'that would be lovely, but not for long. I have an early start tomorrow morning'.

Over coffee Kenneth responded at length to Gilda's questions. He was an accountant by profession and was in charge of a large firm in Hobart. He loved travelling, was passionate about the Navy and enjoyed his compulsory time at sea as a reserve commissioned officer.

It was 10.00pm before they looked at their watches, 'Oh, goodness, the time has flown.' Gilda said. 'Well, time flies when you're having fun,' said Kenneth and immediately added, 'Gilda, we are still in Brisbane for the rest of the week. Can I see you again?' 'Yes,' she replied. 'How about dinner tomorrow night,' he asked and Gilda agreed. 'Good' replied Kenneth, 'I'll meet you on the ground floor of your building at 5.00 PM.' Kenneth paid for the coffee and as they left he said, 'I'll catch a cab back to the ship.' He gave Gilda a peck on the cheek and she drove off.

'5.00 PM for dinner?' she repeated inwardly as she left, 'That's an early dinner.'

They saw each other every day after that. Kenneth waited for her where she worked and they strolled around the city to Anzac Square, King George Square and to the Botanical Gardens where they sat gazing at the busy river traffic while talking and joking. Kenneth linked arms with Gilda. 'I love walking arm-in-arm,' she thought to herself suffused with a warm comforting feeling, 'It's so much more intimate than holding hands. It can easily lead to a snuggle, giggling inwardly as she realised what she had thought. Gilda and Kenneth talked a lot and learned more personal things about each other. Dinner was always at the Steak House of the National Hotel and they were recognised there as a couple. Each afternoon and evening was the same. They walked, chatted, had dinner and then he would take a taxi back to the ship.

On their last evening before the ship sailed for Sydney, Kenneth said, 'The ship goes more often to Sydney than it comes to Brisbane, so perhaps you could come down to Sydney sometimes so that we could meet more often.' Gilda looked at him and thought for a moment before she asked, 'Are you sure you want us to get more serious about each other?' 'Yes, very sure, Gilda,' pulling her gently to him and kissing her lips gently before releasing her. 'I don't want to rush you,' he added, 'I want you to feel comfortable and safe with me.'

'No one has ever spoken to me like that,' she thought. 'Maybe it's because he's 12 years older than me and more mature.' 'I do feel safe with you even though we've only known each other a week' she replied, 'Let's keep in touch and see how we go.'

'I mean it, Gilda. From the moment I saw you, I knew there was something special about you. I won't rush you that would push you away. But, I also want you to know how I feel so that you can see

I'm genuine,' he said earnestly. 'A lot of the guys meet girls at ports and they have a fling. This is not a fling for me.'

By March it was evident that Vladimir was seriously ill. He was bed-ridden and had 24-hour nursing assistance. Gilda hadn't seen him for two months and was shocked when she saw him. 'What's wrong Pop,' she asked frowning. 'Give me your hand, Gilda.' Taking her hand, Vladimir answered, 'I have cancer… in two places… stomach and colon.' Gilda had heard about cancer but didn't know much about it.

'Is it serious Pop,' she asked, 'you look so different from the last time I saw you.' 'Yes, Gilda, it is serious,' he replied and not wanting to say more that could alarm her, he added with a slight smile, 'But I am being well-looked after.'

On leaving Vladimir, Gilda went to see her mother. When Gilda saw Hanna, she said solemnly, 'Pop's got cancer, stomach and colon.' Hanna looked at her saying, 'Are you sure? 'Yes, he told me himself. He said it was serious.' 'If that is true then, indeed, it is very serious.' Hanna replied. 'What do you mean, 'if that is true'? Why do you always have to doubt what people say? Do you think Pop would lie about something like that? You're unbelievable. It's as though you're the only perfect person in the world and everybody else is flawed,' Gilda snapped at her mother. 'Don't you have any compassion for him? He was your husband for God's sake and you both went through hell coming out here and setting up a new life. What is wrong with you?' With that Gilda left and slammed the door behind her.

'When are you coming back,' Hanna called after her opening the door again. 'No idea Mom. Never if I can help it,' Gilda replied. 'Damn,' Gilda grumbled annoyed at herself, 'Why did I yell like that? I'm so bloody upset and she can't lay off her carrying on.' And then she burst into tears. 'It's so unfair. Why does he have to die?' she thought angrily. 'It's bloody not fair.'

Hanna was on her best behaviour for the next few days but she couldn't sustain it. 'So when are you seeing him again,' she asked.

Gilda responded curtly, 'You know what? I've just worked it out. You're jealous if anyone else gets attention, even if that attention is because they're dying. I don't need to tell you every time I go. I tell you when I visit Pop because it's the right thing to do and I've no need to hide it. But, keep this up and I'll choose what I tell you. You can blame yourself. I don't need to tell you anything!'

Gilda went to see her step-father a couple of days later. He had been moved from the bedroom and a mattress placed on the lounge floor so that he was in an airier and cheerier room. She knelt down beside him and then sat on the floor next to the mattress, 'How are you feeling, Pop?

'So so,' he replied. 'You're wearing that lovely ring again,' he said as he fingered her white-stoned ring set in a gold loop. 'Be careful the loop doesn't get caught somewhere and you lose the stone,' he added. 'I'll be careful,' she replied desperately holding back tears. 'His mind is still so alert,' she thought, 'Why does his body have to be so sick?'

He sighed and suddenly looked exhausted. 'I'll go now Pop but I'll and come back tomorrow.' 'Yes,' he whispered as he smiled at her. He continued to hold her hand not wanting to let go, but gradually he released it when he dozed off, the result of a morphine injection. As she left, Irena stopped her on the verandah, 'Gilda, this may be the last time you see him. I'll be in touch should things change.'

'Thanks,' said Gilda smiling slightly through her tears.
It was the last time Gilda saw her step-father. He passed away that night. 'Pop's dead,' Gilda informed her mother when she put the phone down after Irena's call, 'He died during the night. The doctor had given him extra morphine because of the pain and he died in his sleep.'

Gilda waited. There was no response from her mother. She looked at her but as there was no response; she didn't pursue it. Gilda went to the funeral, Hanna didn't. There were a lot of people there. Vladimir had been loved and respected by many. After the service, Gilda went up to Irena, 'Thank you for the invitation to the wake but, please excuse me if I don't come.' Irena just looked at her and nodded. That was the last contact they had for many years. Years later they would see each other at other funerals but would greet each other politely, that was all. Their common link, Vladimir, was gone.

Instead of going to the wake, Gilda went to the Kangaroo Point cliffs where she had often taken the dogs for a walk. The cliffs had a 90 degree view of the Brisbane River and over-looked Brisbane's city centre. It was now dusk and the lit up buildings on the other side of the river made a beautiful, surreal picture, 'Isn't that just like life? Pain and beauty, all at the same time,' Gilda philosophised. She sat there for hours silently staring into nothingness. By the time she rose to leave, it was dark and the fairy-tale view had intensified. As if walking in her sleep, Gilda slowly walked to Main Street and passed the house she had lived in and where Vladimir's wake was still being celebrated. She observed it and moved on to the next bus stop.

In a way, Gilda and her step-father had been very similar. Both were loyal to a fault until provocation proved to be the last straw and their termination of such situations was calculated and absolute; both took things as they came yet preferring peace and harmony; both wanted to get on with living and not get involved with squabbles - he, with his medical practice and she, because of her youth, building her identity and life. It was only towards the end of Vladimir's life that each really understood the other. Kenneth and Gilda's relationship did continue.

They were in regular correspondence, and barely a week went by that one or the other didn't write. When his ship was in Sydney, Gilda would sometimes fly down on Friday evening after work and return Monday morning in time for work. They went dancing and saw shows. She would pay for her flight and for her hotel room and he stayed on his ship. Gilda didn't want to be beholden to him financially, 'It's okay that he pays when we go out, but that's all,' she reasoned. Kenneth took her to places that she didn't know existed; theatres with the latest shows from abroad, night clubs, expensive restaurants, luxurious seafood eateries at Circular Quay, and cocktail lounges and other ritzy places with the most extraordinary indoor decoration and views and as well as extraordinary views of Sydney harbor.

They also went for long walks together. Gilda had never been to these parts of Sydney before and so they explored the city together, 'Doesn't it bore you to see places you've been to before,' she asked. Kenneth's response was, 'I've never seen them before like now. You bring a whole new life to them; you bring a whole new meaning to life itself.' He wanted to kiss her but every time she would gently push him away and say, 'Can't we just be very special friends, Kenneth?' He looked at her tenderly and said, 'Yes, for as long as you want. I can wait till you are ready.'

When she was back in her hotel room, she stormed, 'What the hell is the matter with me?' she said taking the pillow from her bed and thrashed it multiple times, 'What the hell is wrong with me? Why can't I even just kiss him? He's not asking for anything else and I really like him'. She continued bashing the pillow and wept. 'I've pushed Giovanni away. I stopped writing to Bill. And what about the others? I don't let anyone get close to me. What is wrong with me,' she asked in desperation. But then she paused. 'Maybe they just aren't the right ones,' she consoled herself. 'I don't know. I just don't know.' Gilda replaced the pillow on her bed and went out for a walk on her own. She wasn't to meet Kenneth for a couple of hours. 'Oh, what a beautiful city,' she said looking across to the Sydney Harbour Bridge, and the impact of her previous outburst began to fade.

Each time the plane landed in Brisbane and the door slid open Gilda stood at the top of the stairs and felt she was on top of the world. The wind would blow through her hair and she would walk down the steps feeling like a movie star. Returning to Brisbane she wore an outfit that was the latest fashion in Sydney. In those days, it took months before fashions moved to other cities; Sydney was always ahead.

One Saturday morning when Gilda was home alone, she answered the phone. A woman's voice at the other end said, 'May I speak with Gilda Dobinski, please?' 'Speaking,' Gilda replied. 'My name is Miss Kensington and I am the Principal of Champion College. I'm ringing up about your application for the teaching position we advertised.' 'I beg your pardon,' Gilda replied. The voice repeated what she had previously said.

'I'm sorry Miss Kensington, there must be a mistake. I'm Gilda Dobinski, but I haven't applied for a teaching position.' 'Well, that is odd,' Miss Kensington said. Suddenly it hit Gilda; her mother had applied in her name. 'She doesn't want me to go to Canberra, she thought, 'Damn, Damn, Damn.' 'Look, Miss Kensington, I think I know what's happened,' and then explained it to the Principal. 'I see,' said the woman, 'How odd, I thought it strange that the application didn't enclose a copy of a University degree or academic record.'

Gilda enlightened her, 'My mother doesn't have a copy.' 'So it is you and you have majored in History and German?' 'Yes,' replied Gilda. 'You know Gilda, I would still like to meet you,' Miss Kensington replied. 'Look, Miss Kensington, I don't want to waste your time. I hated school and vowed I would never set foot in a school again,' Miss Kensington countered by saying, 'I find you and the situation interesting, Gilda; if it isn't too much to ask, could we meet?' countered the woman.

Gilda thought, 'She sounds nice, oh why not? 'Okay but I have no idea where Champion College is and I don't have a car.' Miss Kensington said unperturbed, 'That's quite alright. We can meet in the city at the Peoples' Palace Hotel. Shall we say tomorrow at noon?'

'Yes, that's fine,' Gilda affirmed. After they hung up, Gilda said, 'This is weird. Oh, what the heck.' She didn't tell her mother about the incident. In fact, she had learned that her mother's motto of 'tell people things only on a need to know basis' was prudent, especially when it came to divulging anything to her.

The following day, Gilda dressed nicely and when she entered the Peoples' Palace, she saw that it was a teetotaler's hotel with accommodation. A middle-aged woman sat and looked expectantly toward the revolving entrance door. She rose and approached Gilda with a smile, 'Gilda Dobinski?' she enquired.

'Yes,' replied Gilda smiling and they shook hands. 'Come, sit here. Would you like tea or coffee?' 'Yes, please, coffee would be nice,' replied Gilda looking surprised that a headmistress would buy her coffee. After Miss Kensington placed the order, she said, 'Right, so tell me about yourself, Gilda.' 'This took Gilda completely off guard; no one had ever been interested in her enough to ask such a question. 'What would you like to know?' 'Let's start with where you were born and other details to the present day,' was the reply. 'Goodness, how long do you have, Gilda said laughing and summarised her life to this point. 'Very interesting, and why did you hate school?'

'I loved the learning, well, most of it. Some I didn't because I kept getting more and more behind due to my then lack of English. It was the silliness of some of the rules and most of all the lack of caring that seemed to go into teaching. It seemed to be all about obeying rules and doing whatever the whim was of the particular person in charge. Also, it was as though what we had to learn was more important than who we were. I feel both are important.' As Gilda continued, it was clear that Miss Kensington was really listening to what she said, and asked for more details.

When she finished, the Miss Kensington said, 'Gilda, I have looked carefully at the application and I have also rung the number that was given as a reference at an Ipswich school. I spoke to a lady with an accent.' 'Oh, that would have been my mother.' Gilda looked crestfallen. Miss Kensington noticed this and said hurriedly, 'Oh, she spoke very highly of you.' To herself Gilda thought, 'I bet she did. She wants me to stay.' 'Your mother is Senior Mistress of German at the school, isn't she?' 'Yes,' replied Gilda.

'Gilda, this is what I suggest,' said Miss Kensington, 'How about you give us a chance and take on the position of German Language Mistress? You would control the department. The other subject, Citizenship Education, will be easy for you to pick up. Some of your history studies may even come in handy. What do you say?' Gilda just looked at her bewildered, 'Do you mean that you will give me a chance?' An emphatic, 'yes' was the reply and Miss Kensington went on, Gilda, I like the way you think. I like that you want the best for the students. I too believe that the student comes first. We are here to nurture these girls, give them self-confidence and then they will want to learn. I know you will be firm with your students because you have a strong will, but just being compliant and upholding the status quo does not work. These are 'modern' girls, the old ways are no longer effective, nor right for them. We and the system are not bringing out the best in these students. They are good girls, and rarely are there any discipline problems. If you have any difficulty with developing the curriculum, I'm sure your mother could help you.'

'When would I be required to start?' Gilda asked.' 'In four weeks. We still have two weeks of school; next week is exams and the final week is sport. Then there will be two weeks' holiday. The Secretary will be at the College during that time for you to get texts and whatever else you will need, and I shall be there at times also. Should you need me, I don't live far and can come to the school, as I am not going away.'

'I'm sorry but why? Why would you be interested in me and be so kind to me?' 'Because I believe in you,' came the simple reply, 'and you are wasted in the Public Service. You will be of greater value to our girls. I believe you are indicating that you want to accept the position. Correct?'

After a momentary silence Gilda replied, 'Yes, correct.' That was all Gilda could say. With that the interview ended. Miss Kensington smiled, shook Gilda's hand and was about to go but added, 'My Secretary will send you the necessary paperwork.' Gilda, mindful of Hanna's liberal approach to reading other family members personal mail said, 'Would you mind sending it to my post office box?' 'Ring my Secretary and give her the details,' was the response and with that, Miss Kensington left.

Gilda stayed seated and stared after her, 'What just happened? I've just agreed to become a teacher.' She was overjoyed and could barely contain her happiness - that at last someone, in this case, Miss Kensington recognised Gilda's special gifts.

Gilda left the Commonwealth Bureau of Census and Statistics with many happy memories. It had been her first work experience; it had given her a taste of freedom and she had loved working in the city. However, as would be the pattern in her life, once Gilda left a place, she never stayed in touch, even if they had been friends there. For Gilda, the past was the past, something to be forgotten and the future was still unknown. She still didn't believe in a long-term future. All she saw was what was happening now and in the immediate future. 'Even that can be taken away at a moment's notice though,' was Gilda's belief.

During the school vacation, Gilda went to the College and collected everything she needed to prepare for the first day of the new school term. From the start, she felt at home. But then, she never had issues fitting in anywhere new. The staff was friendly and helpful and the students were wonderful. 'I wish I'd had teachers like these when I went to school.' Gilda thought about her colleagues. 'They are a fun bunch of people.'

At her first staff meeting, Gilda was officially welcomed by Miss Kensington. Each of the Department Heads had to make a short speech about their goals for the current school term, and as Gilda was a Department Head, she also made a short speech. She worked closely with the French Department Head, Mrs Polis, and together they were responsible for the foreign language contributions to Fêtes, Open Days and Continental Cafés, which were fundraising events that Gilda later initiated. Gilda and Mrs Polis worked well together, and eventually, when Mrs Polis left for Melbourne to take on a school Principal position, Gilda became Head of Foreign Languages.

It was 1971 when Hanna, who had become highly involved with her school's activities, began staying the week nights at the Boarding House, a part of the school designed to house students from abroad and interstate. She found this preferable to driving for an hour in the dark to get back to Brisbane, and then returning to Ipswich early the following morning.

This meant that Gilda often stayed alone at home during the week which suited her very much. When Hanna did travel daily to the school, she often took the school bus that picked students up from Brisbane. This meant that Gilda now had Hanna's car during the day and at night when Hanna stayed overnight at the school. Gilda loved the freedom of having a car to visit friends' places and to parties during the week. When Hanna came home at the weekends, tensions increased. Gilda was now used to living her life on her terms. Hanna continued to expect her autocratic controlling style to be obeyed.

Gabriella and Hanna kept in touch; they had an affinity, both being the second wife of brothers, and both being of a different nationality than their spouses. The rest of the family, including Gilda and Lindana also kept in touch.
Lindana was now engaged to a Russian, and they planned to marry later in the year; Gilda was to be her bridesmaid. 'It's a pity Pop can't be at the wedding, but that's the way it goes,' she thought. 'At least his family will be there. Mom's not going to like that, but, too bad.' Hanna was not looking forward to the prospect of seeing Irena who she now saw as an opponent.

Gilda made great strides at the College. Her students competed in annual Goethe Verse Speaking Competition and did well. She was elected to the District Teachers' Advisory Board for German. 'I love teaching,' Gilda once told a friend over coffee, 'I love the kids, particularly the girls, because they are so receptive. When I took on this job, I vowed that I would be the sort of teacher I would have liked to have had, a person who inspires and doesn't think the worst from the beginning.' At district meetings, she stayed away from the politics of other language teachers. 'I can't stand when a language teacher boasts that her language is the best one for students to learn. I know it's a numbers game, and if you don't get the numbers, you don't have a class, and if there are not enough classes, then the language may eventually be dropped because there is such a demand on the student's time. But then the teacher needs to be as inspiring and self-confidence-building as possible to instill a love of the language in the student. It's as simple as that.'

At a language teachers' meeting Gilda was asked to share how it was that she had such large numbers of students in all grade levels. This was her explanation. 'At the beginning of each year, in the first lesson, after the preliminary notices have been read and logistics relayed, I chat with the students to build rapport with them. I'm genuinely interested in each one and ask them to briefly tell me about themselves. I inform them that this class is individual and different from other classes, even if they are largely the same girls in other groups, consequently, I ask each child to express an opinion on how they would like the class to function.'

Gilda continued, 'Different subjects bring out differing class dynamics. One of the students records the comments and reads each comment out for accuracy. I then take the responses home, type them up and put them on an Overhead Transparency to be discussed at the beginning of the next class. We look at them and, as a class, prioritise them. The top 5 to 10 become the class rules, with the remainder sub-rules to be used as needed. Therefore, each student has ownership of the rules and knows them in advance. It has happened that the class has taken me to task when I have wanted to be lenient with a good student who 'broke' one of the rules, even if that was her only time, ever.'

The girls would say, 'Miss Dobinski, a rule is a rule' and I would have to agree,' she laughed as she finished her presentation.
It was indeed a democracy.

CHAPTER 21
1972 – 1973

Gilda was restless. Something was missing that produced this discontentment. It wasn't that she didn't have a lot on her plate, she did, but it was keeping busy for the sake of being busy. 'What is the point of everything?' she asked herself one day. 'Nearly all my friends are married, some even have children. I don't fit in with them anymore. Maybe I'll go overseas at the end of the year during the long holidays,' she thought, 'I love my job and I love my studies, but there's just something missing. I've no idea what. If it weren't for Kenneth and the Sydney trips, I'd go nuts.'

Because she was teaching, she decided not to proceed with the Master of Arts (Qualifying), but instead enrolled in a Bachelor of Educational Studies degree, as an evening student, which was more appropriate for her new career.

'It makes more sense to do a Bachelor in Education now,' Gilda reasoned, 'rather than specialise in German for a Masters. Also, later I can always do a Master in Education.' However, she found going to lectures dull. 'The lecturers just walk up and down the stage and pontificate. It's so boring. I can get the information from text-books.'

And so, although she lived in Brisbane and external enrolments were supposed to be for students living outside of Brisbane, Gilda convinced the University that she often worked outside Brisbane and would miss the weekly lectures. On that basis she was permitted to enroll as an external student. This also reminded her how self-motivated and self-sufficient she had become. 'I can study on my own,' she thought, 'and it certainly suits me better.'

Miss Kensington was always eager to see what fashions Gilda wore when she came back from her Sydney trips. She would jokingly say to Gilda, 'It forewarns me as to what the students will be wearing on uniform-free days, and at dances. 'It's also hard to keep up with skirt lengths these days. Sometimes they are just above the knee then they drop to the ankles, only to go back to being shorter than ever, before they go three-quarters down the leg. Halter-neck tops become gypsy tops. It's hard to keep up with fashion nowadays,' Miss Kensington would laugh.

In February, Lindana became engaged. It was at this party that Gilda's life would take another interesting turn. She had recently broken up with a suitor and was not really interested in going to the party. 'I won't know anyone as they are all her and her fiancé's friends. At least I'll know her parents and her brothers; I can always talk to them for a while and then I can help with serving.'

At the party, while talking to Lindana's older brother, Larry, he called another fellow over, also a Macedonian, and introduced him. 'Gilda, this is my friend, Alexei Milosevski. Alexei, this is Gilda Dobinski. My uncle, Dad's brother, was her step-father. The one who died.' 'Hello,' they nodded to each other. Silence reigned as Larry walked away. 'So where do you fit in with all these people?' Gilda asked to make conversation. 'I am Larry's friend,' Alexei replied,' 'I know who you are,' he volunteered.' Silence. 'Well, that's exciting, I don't think,' Gilda thought to herself, 'That's that. I don't need to say anything now. End of conversation.'

She was about to walk off when Larry said, 'Would you like to go for a walk?' 'Oh, well. I've got nothing better to do,' she thought. 'Sure,' she replied. He walked ahead down the few steps to the garden and opened the gate. They headed for a park at Bulimba where a Brisbane River Ferry stopped to take passengers to any of the many stops along the river.

Alexei offered Gilda a cigarette, she declined. He lit his. 'I've never been out with a smoker before,' she said, amused. 'They all smoke, these people. Pop smoked like a chimney, as does his family.' They walked silently most of the time. 'He must be shy probably because his English isn't all that good,' she thought. It was a lovely evening, the moon was out, the Brisbane River's lapping waves rippled to the shore as a ferry berthed to let passengers off, and then took on new passengers heading for the other side of the river.

It was a Saturday night and people were either out or others stayed home and were watching TV. Gilda and Alexei were the only people in the park. Shortly after, they were joined by a couple walking their dog; they stopped every now to kiss. Gilda and Alexei gradually headed back to the house but before they arrived, Alexei spoke, 'Can I see you again after this party?' Gilda hesitated a few seconds before replying, 'Sure, I'll give you my phone number.' As soon as they entered the house and Alexei had walked away, Lindana's brother pulled Gilda aside and asked, 'Has he asked to see you again?' 'Yes, he has,' she replied. 'And what did you say,' he asked. 'I said, yes. Why?' 'Nothing,' he replied.

'Gosh, I hate it when people answer that way. Why ask if it's 'nothing'? 'Listen, you can't just say 'nothing'. Why did you ask?' And then he told Gilda a little about Alexei, but not enough to satisfy her curiosity. Two days later, the phone rang just as she arrived home from school. 'Hello, Gilda speaking,' she answered puffed from running up the stairs.

'This is Alexei. You remember, we meet at Lindana's party.' 'Oh, yes, of course, how are you?' she asked.

'Can you come for drink tonight? I pick you up at 7.' 'Who rings up and asks you out the same night?' she thought for a moment. 'Okay, but I cannot stay out late, I have to work tomorrow.' Alexei arrived punctually at seven and they drove to the Jindalee Hotel close to where Gilda lived at St Lucia. Not much was said during the drive. Monosyllabic replies were the responses to Gilda's questions and silences followed when she said something about her day. 'Boy, was this a mistake,' she thought, 'I'd have been better off staying home marking essays or watching TV.'

When they arrived, they sat outside in the beer garden. It was a balmy evening with just the hint of a breeze. Alexei went inside to the bar to get the drinks; gin and tonic for Gilda and scotch and ice for himself. 'How long have you been in Australia,' Gilda asked just to say something although she already knew he had been in Brisbane four years. 'Four years.' Alexei replied, lighting a cigarette, 'Oh, so you came straight to Brisbane from Macedonia?'
'Yes.' 'This is going to drive me insane,' an exasperated Gilda

thought. 'It's really lovely here, isn't it,' she persevered. 'Yes.' 'Isn't it a beautiful evening?' 'Yes.' 'That's it,' she thought, 'When I've finished my drink, we're going.' And so they did.

When Gilda arrived home, they said, 'goodnight' and Alexei drove off. 'Holy, bloody, Moses, that was like squeezing water out of a stone. Never again.' About 30 minutes later her phone rang. 'I bet it's him, well I'm not answering the phone.' And she didn't. For the rest of the week, she didn't answer the phone. 'Friends know my work number, if they can't get me at home, they can ring the College,' she said resolutely.

On Friday evening, Gilda was getting ready to go out when the front door bell rang. She walked down the stairs, 'Probably some Jehovah's Witnesses or someone like that.' She was ready to be abrupt with them. She opened the door and there stood Alexei. 'Can I speak with you?' he asked, 'I have tried to ring but no one answers phone.'

'I'm going out shortly.'
'Oh, I see.'

'Oh, bugger, I'm just going to a party,' she thought feeling guilty. 'Look, I'm going to a friend's place, she's having a party, if you like you can come too. There'll be lots of people there. We can go in two cars and when you want to leave, you can.' 'We can go in my car. I not want to go early,' was his reply. She looked at Alexei briefly and replied, 'Okay, but if I want to go, I'll leave and take a taxi, okay?' 'Okay.'

Just like the last time, not much was said in the car. When they arrived, the party was in full swing, people were laughing, talking and drinking. The music was loud and some were dancing. 'You like to dance?' Alexei asked.

It was a slow dance. Alexei was not much taller than Gilda who wore stilettos. 'Another guy wearing Old Spice aftershave,' she thought, 'not very original.' Alexei tended to stay in one spot when he danced, Gilda was used to Giovanni who accommodated her more expanded style of dancing that covered the dance floor. 'Is he ever going to move,' she thought. Finally, a samba sounded from the record player and she was ready to move. Although he had good rhythm, again he moved in an area the size of a postage stamp. 'Let's get a drink and talk,' Gilda said moving off the dance floor. 'I can't dance like that', she thought, 'it's boring.'

Gilda had brought gin and tonic and offered some to Alexei. 'How do you like it?' she asked after he tried it. 'Very nice, I like better than scotch and ice.' They took their drinks and went to sit on the veranda, 'Okay, you want to talk,' Gilda started. 'You don't like me.' 'Oh, crikey,' she thought, 'here we go, Weeping Willy, confession time,' and then said to Alexei, 'Look, I don't know what the custom is where you come from when it comes to talking to girls, but single syllable answers is not talking. It's also not the way to get to know each other.'

'But my English is not good,' stated Alexei. 'Your English is good enough. It's up to you,' said Gilda. But you strike me as the sort of fellow who calls all the shots with girls, like most of the guys from your country.' 'What is 'calls all the shots,' he interrupted. 'It means you sit back and the girl chases you. Some guys here can be the same, but that's not for me. We both have to work at getting to know each other. Do you understand?'

'Yes, I understand.'

'Lindana's brother asked me if you had suggested we see each again and when I said you did, he told me a little about you. Judging by what he said, you have no problems being with women any way.' There was a short silence. 'Alright, I will tell you about myself,' said Alexei 'Let's get another drink first. I have a feeling we'll both need one,' Gilda replied.

And so Alexei began. 'My parents come from very small village in Macedonia. My father has small business and my mother is village girl, no education, she cannot read. They marry and move to the capital Skopje. My father make good contacts and become quite rich by standards there. In time my father take a mistress and, when

I a few months old, he and mistress go live America. Leave my mother with five children and no money. The only work she can do is clean and that is how she look after us. Through snow, storm any weather, seven days a week, she go cleaning.'

Gilda was fascinated. She had never come across such a story. Although Alexei and Vladimir had the same nationality and she had met many Macedonians in Brisbane, they were all hard workers with established families. They had succeeded in taking on different lives from that in Macedonia.

She was about to hear more that would astound her. 'Time for another drink,' Gilda suggested. Having taken care of their thirst, Alexei continued, 'My oldest sister and older brother look after me but then other two brothers also look for me. I was not good student and often not go to school. My brothers and sister marry when I young so, I only with mother and she work long hours. In Skopje, I not work, I can only do labour work and I not want that so, I have women. They take care for me, feed me, give me money when I want.'

'You have got to be kidding,' Gilda interjected. 'Are you serious? You were a 'kept' man, a gigolo?' 'That is true. I not come Australia if I have work over there. I love life there, friends, food, music. Is my culture. But my second older brother in Brisbane, he have plastering business here and say, he teach me trade and I can make life for me here. Old life is no more for me, is true. Even in Skopje, I not bad person, I let me be looked after, is easier.'

Gilda put her hand up indicating that he should stop talking. 'Okay, let's get one thing straight and, I don't even know why I'm bothering to tell you this because I don't see any future in our relationship.' But you would never be like that with me. I would leave you as soon as I suspected something.'

'I not be that way with you,' replied Alexei. Gilda looked at him in amazement. That was the first time he expanded on something that was said and on something so personal. 'I don't like the direction this is taking.' she thought. 'Come on, let's go inside and dance.

That's enough talking.'

He rose first and extended his hand to help Gilda out of a canvas bucket chair. 'Thank you,' she said. The mood in the party had become louder and merrier, some people were drunk, some couples were canoodling and others were smooch-dancing and kissing. 'It's time for me to go. I can get a taxi if you want to stay,' she told Alexei.

'No, I too think is good idea to go,' he affirmed.
When they arrived at Gilda's place, he jumped out of the car to open her door. As they reached the front door, Gilda said, 'Good night, Alexei' and was about to open the front door. 'No wait, please, can I come in to continue talking?' 'No, it's late and I don't feel like talking anymore.' 'Can I see you again?' 'I'll let you know. I'll call you. Good night and thank you for a nice evening.' With that she hurried through the door. He heard the front door lock engage.

That weekend, Gilda was busy and she didn't give Alexei another thought. She and a couple of girl friends went to the races on Saturday and then to a post-races party at a plush house at Greenslopes, the home of a mutual friend, Gerard.

'Thank goodness it's Sunday,' she thought when she woke up the next day. Suddenly she realised the phone had woken her. 'No, I'm not answering it. I said I'd ring. If he thinks he can pester me and I'll give in, he can think again. I'm going to have a quiet day at home, Mom isn't here. I'll take the dogs for a walk around the Uni and we'll sit under a tree while I read a book.'

School was busy as usual the following week. Thursday, she was called to the phone at lunch time, it was Lindana's brother. 'Gilda, why are you not answering the phone when Alexei rings you?' 'I don't know he's ringing me. 'Why', Gilda said, evading the question. 'He is very keen on you and is very upset.'

'This is a turn in events; you were the one who told me to be careful about him and now you're trying to match us up?' 'No, it's not that. He really is upset.' 'Look, it's really none of your business. I said I'd ring and that's that. Don't you dare give him this number otherwise I will tell the school not to call me to the phone. Do you hear?'

'Yes,' he responded in a low voice.

Two weeks went by and Gilda was occupied so she didn't think of Alexei, but restlessness and discontent wouldn't go away. 'I'm sick of these parties. There isn't anyone I find interesting, even just to talk to. Kenneth is on an assignment overseas and won't be back for at least three months. He's out at sea and can't even get or send mail,' she complained to herself.

Gabriella had invited Hanna and Gilda to afternoon tea one Sunday. As they were chatting, Gabriella's two sons arrived with Alexei. Lindana had brought them over to her place. Gilda felt uncomfortable for two reasons; firstly because she hadn't told her mother about Alexei, not that she needed to, and secondly, because she had never phoned him as she said she would. 'I didn't say when I would ring,' she thought defiantly making herself feel better.

Lindana spoke first, 'Hello everyone, I think you all know each other. Oh, no, Aunty Hanna, you don't know Alexei Milosevski, a friend of my brother's. 'How do you do?' said Hanna and shook Alexei's hand. Looking at Gilda she asked, 'And where do you know him from?' Before anyone could answer, Gilda replied, 'We met at Lindana's engagement party.' Hanna looked suspiciously at her poker-faced daughter looking her straight in the eyes. Everyone started talking and Gilda took the opportunity to go alone out into the garden. 'Bugger, I feel trapped. What the hell is going on? It'll be like the Inquisition in the car and when I get home.' Unbeknown to her, Alexei followed her into the garden.

'Hello Gilda,' a voice behind her said. Gilda swung around to see Alexei there. 'Please don't say anything. I would like to say something first, I like we learn to know each other better but if you not interested, just tell me you not want see me again and I go,' he said quietly. Gilda sat down on a bench and he approached her.

'No, please don't come near me. I need to think. You can sit over there on that bench.'

And so Gilda thought, 'What's the point of carrying on like this? Nearly all of my friends have their own lives now with their families. Even though my mother isn't home much, she still believes she should control my life. I may as well give this guy a chance. The odds are the same either way; stay as I am and be discontented or give him a go, and who knows.'

'Look, Alexei, I'm sorry I didn't ring when I said I would, it was rude of me and I apologise…' He interrupted her, 'Please, not apologies, it difficult for you when you hear about my past. Now you know, perhaps can we start again?"

'Yes, let's start again.'

'Good, then you answer phone now, he asked with a grin on his face. And they both laughed clearing the strain from their relationship.

Gilda and Alexei's relationship developed quickly after that. They saw each other daily and both recognised that they had the same attitude to having fun in life. This was evident on the surface as Gilda did not know herself yet. She thought that life was a party, going out, drinking, flirting and dancing. With these activities, she sustained the self she knew - her true self, the one she didn't yet know was trying to break free and was being nurtured during the week by the profession she loved, teaching, and the place where she worked, the College.

Hanna was shocked about the relationship, 'What do you think you are doing? Going out with a plasterer? Do you think I sacrificed everything bringing you to this country, marrying a doctor, so that you could marry an uneducated tradesman from a primitive place? I brought our social standing up and you will now drag it down.' 'We're just going out. We're not talking about marriage.' 'You will marry him because you have no pride. You do not fit into the social milieu I have created for us. I can tell you one thing, you marry him and I disown you.' 'Well, that's a good enough reason to marry him,' Gilda replied defiantly. She suddenly reeled with pain as Hanna's hand slapped her face. 'You bitch', Gilda shouted in her fury, 'You bloody bitch. I'd marry the devil just to get away from you.' Hanna was about to repeat her performance when Gilda ducked and Hanna landed on the floor as a result of the forceful blow which failed to connect with Gilda's face, 'I'll get even with you, you slut,' she yelled as Gilda took her handbag and left the house and ran to the bus stop.

Gilda telephoned a friend and asked if she could stay the night at her place. Even before she heard what had happened, her friend agreed. When Gilda arrived her cheek was red and swollen. The friend took ice from the freezer, put it in a tea towel and gave it to her to treat her cheek. The following day was Monday. Gilda called in sick at the College and went home when she knew her mother would have left.

The episode was never mentioned, but both Gilda and Hanna were making individual plans. Gilda and Alexei were in their third month of courtship, although differences were emerging, which Gilda thought she could ignore. Gilda loved going to the theatre, the opera, symphony concerts and other performing arts. Alexei had never been to such events and thought only snobs attended them. Gilda went with friends but, little did she realise that would cause problems later on.

'It doesn't happen often,' she thought, 'I can deal with that,' and indeed, mostly they had a lot of fun together. Into their fourth month together, Alexei said, 'Why don't we get married?' 'Sure, why not, replied Gilda. 'Good, then let's plan it for as soon as we can,' replied Alexei. 'Okay, I'll make enquiries as to what we need to do and as soon as the paperwork is completed, we can marry'. Shortly after, Gilda received a letter from Kenneth saying that he was coming to Brisbane. The ship would be in the day after tomorrow for a couple of days and he would ring her when he arrived.

'Oh, good heavens, I didn't expect that. I'll be so glad to see him though.' she said. Two days later, Kenneth rang. 'Hello, Darling,' he started, 'how are you?' 'Hello Kenneth, great, how about you? How did you get this number?'

'I rang the other number and your mother answered. I told her where I was staying for her to give you the message in case I couldn't get hold of you,' he replied. 'Can we meet tonight?'

'Kenneth, there's something I have to tell you before we go on. I'm getting married.' There was silence at the other end.

'Do you love him?' There was silence at Gilda's end. 'You don't, do you?' Still silence. 'Then why, Gilda? Why waste your life? Marriage isn't a date.' 'Oh, please, Kenneth, let's not talk about it, please. We can still be friends and meet for coffee.'

There was a pause in the conversation. Kenneth finally said, 'I'm not sure I can at the moment, Gilda. You know how much you mean to me. Please give me time to adjust to this. I'll get over it, but I need time to adjust. You do understand, don't you?'

'Yes, I'm sorry, Kenneth.'

They didn't meet up on that visit and their letters became infrequent. Then, one day, when it was her turn to write, she thought, 'Why are we continuing with this? If Alexei finds out, he'll be furious. I've experienced what he's like when he gets jealous and it's not pleasant. He won't understand we've always been just friends. I won't write back, it's for the best.' But she was sad, as she thought about it tears started. For a long time, she sat immobile staring at his letter. Suddenly energised, Gilda rose her chair, seized the letter, tore it to shreds and put it in the bottom of the bin.

Gilda and Alexei needed their birth certificates to complete the marriage application paperwork. However, Alexei did not have his and it had to be sent from Skopje. The family didn't have it so it was necessary to contact the relevant Skopje government department. Given the inefficiency of most of the government departments there, they decided to ask a relative in Skopje to procure the document. They sent over a quantity of money sufficient to cover the cost of a government official to expedite the birth certificate, and enough for the one of Alexei's relative to keep as payment for his troubles. It still took two months for the certificate to arrive. When it finally arrived, Gilda could no longer postpone telling her mother that they were planning to marry. 'I'm a coward; I'll tell her when Alexei is with me.'

The doorbell rang, Gilda opened the door and Alexei entered. He greeted Gilda first and then, seeing Hanna in the kitchen, said hello to her.

'Mom, we have something to tell you.' Hanna continued chopping onions in the kitchen. 'Alexei and I are getting married in two weeks' time.' Hanna stopped chopping, looked at her then moved her glance to Alexei before looking at her daughter again. 'Unfortunately, I will not be in Australia.'

'What do you mean? You aren't going away.' 'I am now,' said Hanna. 'You don't honestly think I would go to your wedding? I will be away and that will save you from embarrassment when people will see that I, your mother, am not present at your marriage. You can say with honesty that, 'she is not in the country'. 'But, why don't you want to come?' Hanna looked disdainfully down her nose at Alexei and then at Gilda before returning to her onions. Nothing more was said.

Neither Alexei nor I have much money so we'll have a party in the evening of the day before we marry. We can use money that Mom gave us for our honeymoon,' thought Gilda.
Hanna had given her daughter some money because she knew people would talk if she went away and also didn't contribute to the wedding. 'Money always buys a favourable impression,' Hanna smirked.

'After the wedding, we'll go to dinner with Alexei's brother who is in Brisbane, and his wife and then we'll leave the next morning for our motoring trip to Whyalla in South Australia to see Alexei's sister and family before then going on to Melbourne and Sydney, and coming back to Brisbane. That should be fun,' and Gilda continued planning.

Hanna was leaving for Vienna on Gilda's wedding day. 'I don't need you to take me to the airport. I have called a taxi,' she told Gilda who offered to drive her there. 'You and your husband can rent the old house I have in Taringa. Leave the rent cheque in the letterbox because I never want to see you again.'

Gilda stood stunned. 'What do you mean, you never want to see me again?' 'Surely you should be able understand what that means? After all, you are so brilliant,' Hanna said sarcastically. 'Now go away, I need to finish, the taxi will soon be here.'

Gilda and Alexei married as planned. They packed the car and food for Benno, Gilda's dog, who was also coming on their honeymoon. Alexei loved dogs which meant a lot to Gilda.

Alexei's family was wonderful to her; she was immediately one of them, as was Benno. The two newly-weds had a happy adventure taking turns in driving, sight-seeing and staying at quaint motels. Even in Melbourne they found a hotel near the city centre that accepted Benno. Gilda always went into reception first without Benno and talked nicely to the desk clerk. When she brought Benno, who was very well trained, desk clerks fell in love with him. At the hotel in Melbourne, when she went to register, the man at reception said, 'Lady, we've just had a football team here. Your dog will never make as much mess as those fellows.'

The honeymoon was two weeks of fun, sun and merriment. Alexei resumed work when they returned, but Gilda still had three weeks' vacation. They moved their few personal belongings to the old house Hanna had bought as an investment property. Gilda spent her 'holiday' cleaning the house and making it their home. Fortunately, it was furnished.

For one large item they did need a removalist; it was for Gilda's beloved piano, an old steel-framed upright with yellowing keys.

She hadn't played for years, but every now and then she would sit on the piano stool, open the lid and stroke the keys with much love in her heart. She would try to play pieces she once knew but that skill had gone. Despondent, she would close the piano. 'Now that we are alone, I'll play when Alexei is not here and get back to some semblance of my past standard,' she thought. 'I love you darling piano, even though I don't play you. You are so important in my life,' she would tell it gently dusting it with a soft cloth.

Hanna returned at the beginning of 1973 in time for the new school year. True to her word, she didn't contact Gilda, and if Gilda rang, she just hung up on her. Soon, Gilda stopped ringing. For Gilda, the sadness of the distancing between her and her mother eventually decreased and the impact of the ruptured relationship lessened. She had built up ways and means to cope with estrangements. Gradually, Gilda's friends dropped away. 'When did it happen that I lost touch with everyone,' she asked herself. She asked a friend with whom she had been particularly close why they no longer saw each other.

'Gilda, this is going to be very hard for me to say and please don't be angry with me but it's Alexei. Whenever we're all together, he criticises everything and everyone. We can't go to a restaurant altogether because he picks on the waiters and makes sarcastic remarks if things aren't like he's used to. He has such a chip on his shoulder. Gilda was silent. 'Please don't be angry,' her friend repeated.

'No, I'm not angry with you, I've seen it too, but he doesn't mean any harm by it.' 'I'm sure he doesn't, but it doesn't make for a pleasant evening. My husband will never come again and I know he's not the only one. You and I and the girls, we can still meet up without the men.' 'Yes, sure, of course,' Gilda replied but she knew that they never would, 'It's just another thing that's over,' she thought, 'I'll get over that too.'

That first year of marriage was challenging for Gilda. Something new was introduced that she hadn't experienced before and that she didn't find pleasant, sex. 'What is all the fuss about,' she asked herself. 'Movies make it out to be this wonderful thing. Sure, the orgasm is nice but the rest of it, the before and after, is not. Actually, come to think of it, there isn't any foreplay. It's such a damn nuisance, everytime he sees me in my underwear or in a petticoat, it turns him on. I can't get dressed in the bedroom without him wanting to touch me which leads him to wanting sex. When I say, 'I don't want it, he sulks for hours.' There was a further off-putting aspect. 'Whenever we are in bed together, he wants to lie close to me and I can feel him getting all excited. Bloody hell, I want to sleep.'

The bed they had in the old house when they moved in was an old double-bed with a sinking mattress so when it came time to buying a new bed, Gilda said, 'Alexei, it's so hot in this house. How about we buy two double beds and we put them together for when we have sex and otherwise it's cooler to sleep in individual beds.' And so they bought two double- beds and placed them together. Gilda could then sleep right on the edge of her bed away from the middle. Alexei didn't like it, but that's what happened.

A further irritation, which was not so easy to remedy, was Alexei's total disinterest in helping with household chores. He was a typical male from his culture; it was women who dealt with cooking and cleaning the house. Gilda had an interesting career and to come home to be a servant without any help didn't appeal to her. Alexei would sit and watch TV as soon as he had cleaned up after a day's plastering and leave her to prepare dinner. Gilda also earned significantly more than he did at the time which didn't help when he played at being 'lord and master'.

'Do you think you could help by at least setting the table,' she would ask. 'Soon, I just want to watch the end of this soccer match,' he would reply. One time she didn't prepare dinner and sat watching TV with him. When he asked when dinner would be ready, she replied, 'I don't know. Who's cooking it tonight? I certainly am not. I've had a big day.' He stood up, went to the fridge and took out feta cheese, olives, ajvar, chilies and bread. He then returned to the TV. She looked at him. 'Is that for you?' 'Yes,' he replied, 'Would you like some?'

'No, thanks,' She went into the bedroom, took her handbag and the car keys and said, 'I'm going out to have dinner. You've clearly looked after yourself and won't want dinner after those nibbles so I'm going out to eat. See you later.' 'What do you mean?' he asked getting up. 'Exactly what I said. This cook is having the night off. See you when I get home.' And out she went.

Later the phone rang and Alexei answered it. 'I'm at Marilyn's place. We've had some wine so I'm not driving tonight. I'm staying here. See you tomorrow after work.' She waited for his response. He was so stunned; he didn't know what to say. 'Bye, bye,' she said cheerily, 'Have a nice evening.' When she hung up, the phone stayed off the hook. Marilyn was a friend of Gilda's from way back who was unmarried and planned to stay that way. She didn't like Alexei.

The two friends burst out laughing and poured another glass of wine.

CHAPTER 22
1974 - 1975

Whatever Gilda did, she went all out to achieve the best result. She never asked for help, because she was always able to do whatever it was, always managing to figure it out and going further than the minimum that was required. Everyone at her school could see how competent she was. Her students were very loyal, and worked in her classes, even if they didn't care much for the subject, a compulsory one. As a teacher, she had a special relationship with them. She treated each one as the special person she was. 'I know what it feels like to be different, and not be liked or get into trouble because of it. No student of mine will ever feel that way.' She took on more responsibilities at the College, such as being in charge of staff stationary requirements, stationery distribution and orders.

When Gilda came home, the different dynamics in her home environment became increasingly pronounced. At school she was a respected professional, but at home she was a domestic. Despite discussing this with Alexei, it made no lasting impression. One Friday afternoon, she came home and prepared a meat and vegetable casserole for the evening meal. As she took the hot dish out of the oven, it slipped from her hands and all the meat, vegetables and sauce splashed onto the floor. The glass dish was smashed by its impact on the linoleum floor and needle pointed glass splinters were strewn everywhere.

'What's happened?' Alexei asked coming into the kitchen from the lounge where he had been watching TV. Gilda looked at him and asked, 'What does it look like?' 'Oh, okay.' said Alexei and proceeded to go back to the lounge.

Gilda took off her oven mittens, threw them on the bench top and followed Alexei into the lounge. 'Is that all you have to say? Would it hurt you to ask if I'm alright? I could have burned myself. Clearly, you have no intention of helping me clean up the mess, have you?' 'Why you can't offer to help me...' she said glaring at him. Alexei stayed seated in the lounge chair, took a sip of whisky, and then drew on his cigarette, glancing intermittently at the TV.

Gilda waited but there was no change in him.

'Right,' she said walking over to the TV and turning it off. 'I've had enough of this. Pack your clothes and get out of here. Call a taxi and get out.' He looked at her raising his eyebrows and said, 'What do you mean?' 'You heard. Get your belongings and get out of here. We are finished. I did not marry to become a slave to you. You may be able to do this in your culture but not here, not with me. This marriage is over. Is that clear enough?'

'Oh, come on Gilda, you're upset, let's talk about this,' Alexei foolishly said. 'Alexei, we have talked about this many times before, today is the last straw. Pack up your stuff and get out. You've really only got your clothes, the rest I paid for. So in 30 minutes you can be out of here. I'm serious, get out… and give me your keys.'

What could he do? He packed his clothes, Gilda called the taxi and he left. After Alexei left, she had an incredible sense of relief. She went to clean up the mess so that her dog, Benno, didn't try to lick up the sauce and eat the meat on the floor that was covered with broken glass. She then sat in the lounge with a glass of gin and tonic and listened to music for about half-an-hour. Dinner that night was Brie on crackers for entrée and a tossed salad with a glass of wine. 'Gosh, isn't life simple without a man? Well, I've tried marriage. Like a lot of things in life, marriage certainly isn't what it's cracked up to be.' Gilda raised her glass toasting to her freedom and continued listening to music. Much later she went into the bedroom.

'Ah, peace at last,' she sighed. It was as though a heavy crushing weight had been lifted from her body.

The next day, Saturday, Gilda phoned her friend Marilyn. After the usual greetings, Marilyn asked inquisitively, 'What's going on? I can hear something in your voice.' 'You'll be really pleased with what I'm about to tell you.' she paused, 'Alexei has left, I asked him to go.' 'You mean you kicked him out?' Marilyn could hardly contain her joy. 'No, I asked him to leave. Might be semantics, but it was civilised.'

'Okay, honey, do you have any plans for today?' 'No, not yet. I thought you're sure to make plans for us.' 'You're dead right. Get out your finery and we're heading for the races. There's a big meeting on at Eagle Farm racecourse today and I just happen to have box seats. I'll pick you up at midday.'

Right on midday, a taxi pulled up, the driver sounded the horn and Gilda saw Marilyn waving to her. 'Is this what you meant by picking me up?' Gilda asked her jubilant friend. 'Absolutely, you didn't think I was going to drive? It would have interfered with the champagne. It would be rude not to make full use of Charlie's box and all its perks.' she said coquettishly and then burst out laughing. Charlie was one of Marilyn's affluent friends, high up in the racing fraternity.

Gilda wasn't a gambler but she loved seeing the beautiful horses, getting dressed up and seeing everyone else looking glamorous. 'You know, Marilyn, I can't remember the last time I got this dressed up. It's fun and it feels good.' 'There'll be more of it now that you've thrown out your 'ball and chain'. Incidentally, where has Alexei gone'? Gilda replied, 'Don't know and don't care!' Marilyn laughed, 'You can count on me to get you back in the circuit. We've missed you. Gerard has missed you too.' By the way, he's coming this afternoon.' Marilyn said with a wink. Gerard was an old flame of Gilda's who still held a torch for her although she was now married.

'Oh, no, Marilyn, I'm not ready to date. In any case, I'm still married.' 'Who's talking about dating, he's just an old friend and he knows you're married.' 'We'll see.' was all Gilda said.
At that moment a voice behind her said, 'Well, this is a surprise. Has he let you off the leash for the afternoon?' 'Hello Gerard, please don't talk like that about my husband.'

'Come on Gilda, I can understand that you weren't interested in me, but him…?' Gerard saw the look on Gilda's face. 'Oh, alright, I'm sorry. I won't say another word about him. I'm just glad to see you again. Friends?' 'Yes Gerard, friends.' replied Gilda with a smile.

The old crowd was back together again. Marilyn, a self-declared Bachelor Girl and feminist, Charlie, wealthy, flirtatious, always with a new girl, Gerard, steady, charming and also wealthy, and then, of course Gilda, whose life at the moment was in transition. All were glad to see her, and were making plans for her renewed social life. 'The social butterfly has re-emerged from her self-imposed chrysalis,' joked Marilyn.

As the afternoon wore on, everyone pressed their claims to what they should do, and where they should go when the races finished. Gerard came over to Gilda and said, 'How about coming over for my famous Crêpes Suzettes when we leave here? You used to like them.'

'I don't think I should, Gerard.' she replied. Gerard smiled and said, 'I promise to behave myself and you know I keep my word.'
'Well, I certainly don't feel like going somewhere as a noisy group, and I don't want to go home yet.' She thought for a moment. 'Okay that would be nice, and I do love your Crêpes Suzettes, especially the amount of Grand Marnier you put in the sauce.' she said with a grin. Gilda went over to Marilyn and said, 'Marilyn, I won't be going with the group, I'm going to Gerard's for a bit.' 'Oh, really, ummm, I like the sound of that.'

'No, it's not like that, not at all, we're just going to catch up. I feel like a quiet evening. I'm not feeling very gregarious or sociable'
'Okay, you can't blame me for being hopeful. Well, have a lovely evening, and I'll call you first thing tomorrow.' Marilyn pecked Gilda on the cheek and gave her a hug
.
When Gerard opened the door of his Mercedes convertible, he said, 'It's like old times, isn't it Gilda?' but she didn't answer.
They reached his beautiful, spacious house, set high on a hill at Greenslopes. The lights of the city views were stunning on such a clear night. 'Drink?' he asked. 'No, not yet, thanks,' she replied and watched as he pulled out the crêpe pan from the kitchen cupboard, retrieved some ingredients from the pantry and then took some Grand Marnier liqueur from a glass cabinet, took out two liqueur glasses and poured a glass for each. 'Just to get the palate ready,' he

joked. She laughed as she took her glass. He walked up to her and said, 'I know it's premature but, welcome back.' She ignored that, but they clinked glasses before taking a sip.

'And now, the Chef has work to do,' he proclaimed cheerily as he started to make his culinary masterpiece. They chatted as old friends do, as she looked wistfully at the superb view. 'Um, this does remind me of the past,' Gilda said as the aroma of the cooking crepe suzettes mingled with the crisp evening air.

On the deck overlooking the city they ate, talked, laughed, and drank champagne. Gilda then said, 'I must go Gerard. It's been a very special evening.' 'But not special enough is that right?' 'Gerard, please, this isn't easy for me and I know it isn't easy for you either. It's not even a day since I asked my husband to leave. I'm not sure how I feel about anything at the moment.' 'Sorry, Gilda, that wasn't fair of me. You know you can always ring me and I promise, I won't get heavy with you. I would rather we were friends than not see you at all.' With that he came over to her and gave her a goodnight kiss on the cheek. 'I'll drive you home.'

'No, thank you, Gerard, I'll go home by taxi.'

When Gilda arrived home she half expected Alexei to be waiting at the front steps, but fortunately he wasn't. What she didn't see, was a car standing around the corner parked in the shadow of a large tree.

Early the next morning the phone rang. Gilda hesitated answering it but she thought it might be Marilyn. Gingerly she lifted the receiver, 'Hello, Gilda speaking.' It was Hanna.

'Have you gone insane? Are you out of your mind? Alexei rang me last night and told me what you've done.' shrieked her mother. For an instant, Gilda was shocked but she quickly pulled herself together. 'Hello Mom, how are you? That's not much of a greeting after all this time.' 'You idiot!' was the reply. 'Can't you make up your mind whether you want to be married or not. I knew it wouldn't last.' 'Well, I would have thought that you'd be pleased, after all he is only a tradesman in your eyes, not worthy of being in the family.'

'Don't be insolent,' snapped Hanna. Gilda snapped back, 'Look Mom, either you are civil to me or I'll hang up. I don't need you bellowing at me.' 'I'll speak to you as I please. Let me remind you, you are living in my house.' 'I am paying you rent,' Gilda pointed out.' 'A pittance,' her mother screeched, 'I would get more from a stranger.' 'Okay, then I'll move out and go somewhere else. I don't mind, and I won't give you my phone number.'

There was silence at the other end. Hanna had hung up. Gilda also replaced the receiver on the arm. 'Damn, why did Alexei have to ring her? What a louse, coward! He's a tittle-tattling coward.' Gilda composed herself and rang Marilyn. 'Listen, my mother rang. Alexei contacted her. I can't stay home and I also won't answer the phone anymore. I thought I'd tell you, just in case you phoned and there was no answer.'

'Come over here and we'll work out what we'll do. Stay the night as well. You can go to school from here Monday morning.'

'But I have Benno.'

'That's okay, he can come too. He's no problem, and the house is fenced for during the day.'

'Okay, thanks, I'll get some things together and come straight over.' Gilda went around the house like a whirlwind getting Benno's food, his dishes and blanket, her clothes, school books, and gathered up everything she would need for the next few days or so. She drove off and just as she turned the corner, she saw her mother's car coming from the other direction. Alexei was with her.

Marilyn was waiting for Gilda as she drove into her street. She had the driveway gate open for Gilda to drive to the back of the house so that her car was not visible from the road. 'Hello Benno. Yes, I love you too, but please don't lick me.' said Marilyn as she was greeted by an enthusiastic Weimaraner. 'Gilda, I'll help you take your stuff into the house.' Marilyn offered. Once all Gilda's belongings were in her temporary bedroom, Marilyn made tea and the two friends sat in the lounge.

'You know what, Marilyn,' Gilda began, 'I'll never be rid of them.' And she burst into tears.

Marilyn came over to her, putting her arms around her she said, 'It breaks my heart seeing you like this. You're such a sweet person; you don't deserve a mother like that. Alexei is an angel compared to her; she's a demon. I hate to say it but Alexei is probably trainable. He's at least a good person. I wouldn't have wished him for you, but you are married to him and you are going to have to make a choice eventually.'

'Yes, I know,' Gilda replied wiping her eyes, 'But not yet.' Benno came over and snuggled up to comfort her.

'I have an idea,' said Marilyn, 'Let's go to Cleveland for a seafood lunch. The ocean view is divine there and if we sit outside, Benno can come too. By the way, does Alexei know where I live?' 'Not sure, why?'

'I think we should go in your car, just in case unwanted visitors come. There won't be any evidence of you being here, as Benno will be with us.' The friends drove off and unbeknown to them at the time, 15 minutes after they had left, visitors did arrive.

The weather was magnificent and the blue sea gleamed under the sun's rays. The seafood platter they shared was fresh and scrumptious, lobster, crab, King prawns, scallops, fresh grilled fish, fresh oysters and oysters Kilpatrick, accompanied by hand cut, fresh hot potato chips; a side salad completed the serving. Benno ate up the prawn tails and had the soft lobster and crab innards, and for dessert, some chips. Here, by the sea, Gilda's problems seemed far away.

When they arrived back at Marilyn's, she suddenly exclaimed, 'The bastards, they've been here, they didn't shut the gates properly.' Gilda was furious. 'This is it. I'm not taking this. I will not be intimidated.' She went into the house, rang a friend of Alexei's to see if he was there and he was. When he came to the phone, she got stuck into him. 'Listen Alexei, I don't know what you were thinking when you contacted my mother, but it was a big mistake. An even bigger mistake is you and her stalking me. I know you were at my friend's today. You keep this up and I'll get the police onto you and my mother. If you want to have any chance of us MAYBE getting back together, you are going about it the wrong way. Don't you dare stalk me anymore! You can also tell her to mind her own business. This has nothing to do with her. How could you crawl and whimper to her? You make me sick. You know she doesn't like you. Where is your pride?' Gilda paused. 'Did you hear what I said?'

'Yes,' Alexei replied. 'I want to talk to you.' 'Well, I don't want to talk to you. Your behaviour has been disgusting. Do you honestly think I want to talk to you? Bugger off.' And she hung up.

'Yikes,' said Marilyn in amazement. 'That's telling him! Wow, if he doesn't get the message, he's either got thick skin or a death wish.' Gilda stood still for a moment and then laughed loudly. 'Boy, oh boy, that felt good. I think I just released a whole lot of pent-up tension.' Marilyn laughter with Gilda. Benno had no idea what was going on, but he joined in and bounced around Marilyn's lounge. 'Come on, let's take Benno for a walk. I always feel great after a walk.' Gilda said. Off they went, and Benno swam in the nearby creek temporarily dispossessing a flock of ducks using the creek banks as an afternoon resting place.

Gilda went to school from Marilyn's place on Monday. No one at school knew what was going on in her private life. In actual fact, she was more excited than usual to be at school. She had been toying with the idea of going to Europe at the end of the year and the now increasing tensions between her mother, Alexei and herself made this even more pleasurable. Gilda's desire to distance herself from it over the Christmas and New Year period prompted her to activate her ideas of organising a school trip to Germany to give her language students real-life experience in using their newly acquired German language skills. She had already prepared a detailed itinerary and costings and went to Miss Kensington with the proposal and to ask her permission.

'This is a very ambitious undertaking, Gilda. You have certainly thought it through, and I agree that it will do the girls the world of good to see how other people live, and to practise the languages they are learning. Leave it with me and I'll get back to you.' Gilda was happy. The school's principal hadn't said no and was actively considering it.

At the next staff meeting, Miss Kensington tabled Gilda's proposal. It caused a lot of discussion, as it was something that had never been done at the school, nor was it common for those days. 'I suggest that we present it at the next Parents' and Friends' Association meeting and gauge their reaction,' Miss Kensington said. Everyone agreed with that. The Association approved the idea in principle, and suggested a special meeting for the proposed trip. Parents had also been asked for expressions of interest as to whether they would consider the possibility of their daughter or daughters participating. Students from years 10, 11 and 12 were eligible. A minimum of 12 students were needed for a cost effective quote.

Before the special meeting, Gilda refined her proposal. The itinerary was more detailed, an interim airline booking had been sealed, insurance quotes provided, examples of accommodation were included, and a list of German winter clothes needed formulated, other luggage items and family approval forms to sign. Nothing was omitted. She created an overhead transparency presentation. Gilda even had well-known German songs playing as over sixty sets of parents and their daughters took their seats in the school's Assembly Hall.

After the formalities and introductions, Gilda took the floor and spoke to the visitors. During refreshments as the evening was coming to a close, a couple with their daughter came over to Gilda. 'Hello Miss Dobinski, I mean Mrs Milosevski.' the student said. 'Hello, Denise, how lovely to see you? Did you enjoy the evening?' Gilda replied 'Oh yes, I want to go.' Denise said. 'I'd like you to meet my parents, Dr and Mrs Pankhurst.' 'How do you do,' Gilda said shaking their hands.

'Denise has told us so much about you.' began Mrs Pankhurst. 'We felt it was time we met this 'wonderful Mrs Milosevski'.' Everyone laughed and they chatted for quite some time until they noticed they were the only ones left.

Back at school the next day, Mrs Kensington called Gilda to her office. 'Well, my dear, it looks like the trip is on. The parents were delighted, and my Secretary's phone hasn't stopped ringing with parents saying that their daughter will be participating.' Gilda was thrilled and said. 'I'll send a letter to the parents and give them details as to how to contact me so that your Secretary isn't bothered anymore.'

Friday came and it was almost a week since Alexei had left. In the evening the home phone rang, it was Alexei. 'Gilda, can I come over so that we can talk? We can go out if you don't want me in the house.'

'Yes alright, you can come over, it'll be more private. But you cannot stay.' 'Is 6.30 PM okay?' 'Yes,' she replied and hung up. Alexei arrived promptly at 6.30 PM with a big bunch of flowers and champagne. The atmosphere was awkward at first but gradually it relaxed. They talked, accompanied by champagne. After a few hours, they ordered take-away to be delivered, and they continued talking. 'It's getting late,' Alexei said at midnight, 'I should go.' 'Yes,' Gilda replied. 'Thank you, it was a nice evening and thank you for the flowers.'

'Gilda, they were my idea. I have not spoken to your mother since you called me last weekend. She has rung me but I have told her there is nothing for her and I to discuss.' Gilda just nodded. They said goodbye at the door and he left. She sat silently with Benno beside her for some time. She wasn't thinking anything, just sitting. An hour later, she went to bed. Benno jumped onto the bed. During the next week, Gilda and Alexei met a couple of times for coffee. 'Gilda, what have you decided? Anything yet?' Alexei asked two weeks after their separation. 'Give me another week, please, Alexei. I can't give you an answer yet. If we were to get back together again, things would have to change dramatically. I expect us to be equal, and that we share the house work. If not, then it's over for good.' 'I know, Gilda, I can change and I want to change.' The following weekend, Alexei was back. Gilda rang her mother to tell her, but she hung up on her. 'Oh, well, that's that. Better anyway.'

For Gilda, life took on a different focus, it was as though she was performing a duty. She was keeping her end of the marriage bargain and was being a good wife. Alexei for his part kept his word and did help Gilda around the house. They enjoyed themselves and their relationship seemed to have gained from the separation.

Gilda resumed giving Alexei English lessons. Despite Gilda's efforts, Alexei was incapable of writing even simple English notes and his reading was poor. He had never been used to studying, and found it difficult. He would get impatient with the many irregularities in English writing and pronunciation. In the end, they both decided to stop for the time being.

Plans for the December/January trip to Europe had progressed well. By now Gilda was teaching two of Dr and Mrs Pankhurst's children, and the two families became close friends. They were of similar ages and often went out together or went to each other's home. They had the same passionate approach to having fun, and always enjoyed themselves whether it was a sophisticated ball or a barbeque in the back yard.

Meetings for the end of year trip became more frequent, final details fell into place. All who were participating could barely contain their excitement – five weeks in a European winter which included Italy, Switzerland, Austria, Germany, Luxembourg, Belgium, Holland and France, and finally a week in London and environs before flying home. The group would have the same bus throughout Europe, take the ferry over to Dover and collect another bus for the rest of the trip in southern England. Christmas would be in Vienna and New Year in Amsterdam.

Gilda took the trip on her own as Alexei couldn't take time off work. The trip was a raging success.

When she arrived back at the College in January 1975, she presented a report at the first staff meeting and finished her report with the following comment, 'I would like to say what an honour it was to accompany the girls on that trip. Wherever we went, they made a wonderful impression. They behaved so well and were so much fun to be with. I would repeat the experience. The College can be very proud of them.'

Until now, Alexei had been working with his brother who had sponsored his migration to Australia. They were always busy with new customers, continually had new referrals and repeat customers. Nevertheless, at the end of each trading month after all bills were paid there was never a credit balance in the business account. Gilda knew it was a sensitive subject, so she decided not to bring it up again but go for a different tactic. One Saturday morning, she said to her husband. 'Why don't you work for someone else on wages? You would have a regular amount each week without the burden of the partnership, and it would be easier for our own monthly budget.' Not long after this conversation, Alexei went to work for a large company. As Gilda and Alexei only had one car, and he now needed it to go to work, they moved out of Hanna's house in Taringa and moved into a ground floor town-house in Clayfield. This meant that Benno could be accommodated and the town house was only a 10 minute walk for Gilda to the College.

Hanna, who was still not speaking to her daughter, had made the acquaintance of a Latvian man, Ivan, a few years younger than her. By day he was a clerk, but his hobbies showed him to be an interesting and talented fellow. Ivan was an accomplished artist, painting in oils and had frequent exhibitions where the majority of paintings were inevitably bought by discerning collectors. In addition, he was deeply interested in philately, and was a national and international stamps judge in all categories.

Ivan had arrived in Australia with his then wife and little daughter, Danika, but after some years the marriage broke up. Both Hanna and he had been on their own for some time; they became friends, which lead to a deeper relationship.

Hanna was busy renovating, raising and extending the house where Gilda and Alexei had lived. The idea was that once the refurbishments were complete, she would sell where she lived in St Lucia and she and Ivan would move in together. 'Hanna, you told me when we met that you have a daughter but you never mention her.' Ivan said one day. 'I would like to meet her if that suits you.' 'She and I are estranged, and I prefer not to go into details about that.' And so the subject remained closed.

CHAPTER 23
1976 – 1977

Gilda found living in a two-bedroom town house quite different from living in a three-bedroom house with back deck, veranda and large garden and she felt as though she was suffocating in the town house. There was nowhere for her to escape to when Alexei was home constantly watching TV. 'The noise of that stupid TV will drive me around the bend,' she thought. 'Alexei, can't you find something to do and not watch TV all the time? Why not read?'
'You know my English is not good enough.'

'My step-father used to read Carter Brown mystery stories to improve his English. They are supermarket-type books with a good story in simple English, and they are short books. That's how he picked up everyday vocabulary and sentence structures. He didn't do any courses.'

'I'm not educated like your step-father.'

"Oh, lay off this 'poor me' stuff; it wears thin after a while. It's more like you're afraid.' 'What you talking about, I not afraid of anything,' he bellowed expanding his chest and taking another puff of his cigarette.

'No, you're not afraid of anything physical; you'll punch up anyone who gives you shit, but you're afraid that someone will see how poor your English is, and you believe they'll think less of you. Well, you're wrong. Everyone when they learn something new has to go from not knowing anything to the degree of mastery they want to achieve. All my students do that; I do that with my studies. But the truth is that you think you're better than everyone else. Why, I can't imagine.'

Alexei got up, went to get a gin and tonic and lit another cigarette. Irritated, Gilda spat out, 'And now you're going to sulk. That's your usual technique, isn't it?' Without answering, he went back to the TV. 'I wonder how long this sulk-session will last,' Gilda thought. Gilda came to realise that it was impossible to have a discussion with Alexei. If he felt out of his depth, or he felt he was personally being attacked, he would sulk, drink, and smoke even more than usual. But Gilda wasn't the type to just take it. Communication was everything to her. The trouble was that she could put up with things for a long time, and she would leave issues till they really bothered her. Then, she would pursue them to the end, often exasperating the other person.

Alexei did not speak to Gilda for two weeks. He slept in the spare bedroom, made his own lunch, took food from the fridge that was cooked or he cooked his own meals, and ate alone watching TV or he went out. In the meantime, Gilda would ask him things as needed, but he would still not reply. Gradually, after two weeks, Alexei would reply in monosyllables and gradually his responses were longer. The truth was that he missed sex and the only way to get that back was to talk to her again. The incident was not brought up again, and life went back to normal. 'I sure was an idiot to go back to him,' Gilda thought. 'Too late now I suppose.'

In the middle of the year, her dog Benno became ill. She took him to the Vet who recommended that he stay at the clinic for tests. She agreed. 'Please do whatever is necessary to get him well. I don't care what it costs,' she repeated to the Vet, 'I'm serious; I don't care what it costs.'

"Now, now Mrs Milosevski, don't worry. We'll do our best; he'll be fine.'

Everyday Gilda rang the Vet and each time she was given the same news. Tests showed nothing conclusive. 'We may need to operate on him, open him up to discover what is going on,' Dr Harris, the Vet, suggested.

'Yes, please, do that, do what you have to do,' Gilda pleaded.
The next day she was in an afternoon class when she heard over the loud speaker, Mrs Milosevski, please go to a phone urgently.' She excused herself from her class and asked the students to quietly work on their own.

'Hello, Mrs Milosevski speaking.'

'Mrs Milosevski, it's Dr Harris. Are you sitting down? Benno is here on the operating table and I have opened him up. I'm sorry to have to tell you that he is consumed with cancer. There is nothing that can be done. There is no....' Gilda gasped. 'Are you alright, Mrs Milosevski,' Dr Harris enquired. 'Please go on doctor,' Gilda said almost inaudibly.

'There are two alternatives. I could stitch him up and he might live at the most another two months. I cannot say how much pain he may be in as he gets worse. The alternative is that I can euthanise him now on the table. What would you like me to do? Please don't feel you have to hurry with your decision. I can keep him in this state for a short while.'

Gilda's heart took a dive; she could not believe what she was hearing. The Vet had to repeat what he said and then she asked, 'Is there nothing, nothing at all that can be done, Doctor? No new drugs that are on trial. Anything?'

'No, I'm sorry, only what I have just suggested. I am truly sorry Mrs Milosevski. I wish my news was better, but he is riddled with cancer. I'm surprised he hasn't shown symptoms earlier.' Summoning her courage, she whispered through tears, 'Very well, Doctor, I don't want him to suffer just because I don't want to let him go. You have my permission to euthanise him.'

After a pause, Dr Harris asked. 'What would you me to do with his body?' 'Please cremate him.' Moments later, the school bell rang announcing the end of the lesson and the end of the school day.

A teacher walked past and saw Gilda crying as she clutched the phone. 'What's wrong, Gilda?' Can I help?' 'No, thanks,' Gilda said shaking her head. 'Your class is next to mine, I'll look after the girls,' offered her colleague.

Gilda went to her staff room and closed the door, sat down and sobbed uncontrollably. She had suffered terribly when Liesel had to be put down, but now Benno. It was more than losing another pet. Of all the pets she had, Benno was her favourite. 'I helped give birth to you my darling; you are too young to die. You've been such a good dog. You never caused me any problems. You were so human, better actually. How can I face going home and you're not there? I love you so much.' She sobbed and sobbed.

Exhausted by grief, Gilda still stayed in her room. 'I really don't want to go home. How can I face that place without him? Benno, I will never forget you. Thank you so much for the happy, wonderful years together. You were the only one I could ever rely on. Why, oh why….?' Night had fallen when she left her room to walk slowly home.

Before Alexei could ask why she was late home, he saw that something was wrong. Gilda told him briefly. He too was very upset, 'Would you like to go out to eat? Can I get you a drink,' he asked. 'No, thank you,' and she walked into the spare bedroom and closed the door. She lay on the spare bed in the dark, and stared till she eventually fell asleep.

It took Gilda all her strength to get through each day. Her heart was broken and she felt as though she were choking. Difficulties with Alexei increased and Gilda decided to minimise contact with him. So that she had a reason for leaving the town-house earlier and arriving home late. She offered before and after school catch-up tutorials for students who were having difficulties.

It was now for the first time in a long time that she yearned for her old friends. 'We were always there for each other; life is so empty now. If truth be told, I don't love him, and he doesn't love me. We're two emotional misfits who found each other and got along, well, more or less. No one else could really put up with either of us.' After a pause, she continued, 'Oh, well, could be worse.' Her survival mechanism had clicked in.

Gilda and Alexei still went out quite a lot with the Pankhurst's and with other people in their circle, but they were mostly Gilda's contacts. Alexei brought no friends into the marriage. It wasn't that he didn't know some nice people from his own culture, he did, and Gilda liked them, but Alexei was extremely judgmental. He would place people on a pedestal and as soon as they did the slightest thing he didn't like, he would cut them off. However, for Gilda there were enough external distractions to keep life moving. She needed to be careful that she didn't think of Benno when she was out in public because she would get teary. In private, that was another matter; she could cry as much as she liked, which she did.

One evening, Alexei said, 'My family back in Skopje ask me, why we not come to see them. What you think? Can we go over this December?' 'Yes, that's fine,' replied Gilda. 'It would be nice to meet them. This meant that she had something to occupy herself with - making the travel arrangements. They would first go to Skopje for a week, then go for a week to Vienna followed by another week in Skopje. In the end, she decided to leave it to a travel agent, as the trip involved visas, flights with stopovers, different currencies, and so on.

The old saying, 'time marches on' certainly applied, and as humans, we learn to cope with loss. The familiarity of daily routine superimposes itself over what we'd really like to do, and deadens discontent as numbness sets in. This is what happened to Gilda. 'I can see why people stay with each other or stay in a job they don't like, it's a case of 'better the devil you know,' and that's basically what I'm doing. I love my job but if I had the old fire I used to have, would I stay with Alexei? Probably not but, I don't know anymore. Things would need to get intolerable to make a change now,' she thought.

If we don't take the initiative, life tends to take it for us. It would still be some time but eventually, things would become intolerable in an unexpected way. Another marvel of life is that it has a knack of bringing people and situations into your life out of left field, just as you need them.

Until now, all the people Gilda had met were in mainstream professions and relationships. At a State-wide language meeting, she met some interesting people from the northern coastal areas of

Queensland known the Sunshine Coast, notably a German teacher who practiced numerology and healing. Over a lunch break, she told Gilda what she did and gave her more details about these two fields. Gilda was fascinated by both skills and researched them in the public library. When she researched about healing, she was reminded of the little Chinese book she had bought years ago on Taoism. 'Goodness, I'd forgotten all about that.'

She started meeting more people, men and women, who had left married life to lead the life they wanted and work in 'alternative' fields. It was the first time she heard the concept, 'live your life's purpose'. All these people had children and otherwise lead a normal life.

'This is weird,' she thought, 'Meeting these men and women is opening up a completely new way for me to see life. It's also making me feel more peaceful, more self-confident, and more 'normal' for wanting more out of life.'

The end of the year approached with all the stress, tension, and the countless traditional tasks that occur when the academic year winds down. Students panic about exams and teachers are bogged down with marking exam papers, finalising assessments, and writing reports.

The itinerary and other necessary finalities for the trip to see Alexei's family were completed. Two weeks before Christmas, Gilda and Alexei left Brisbane and flew to Skopje. Again, his family made her instantly feel at home and a part of their world. She especially liked her sister-in-law, Kate, who was a happy, intelligent lady married to a drunken unfulfilled husband, Alexei's brother. He would eventually drink himself to death. She also saw what a close-knit community could achieve to counter the ineptness and lack of government infrastructures.

Few government utilities could consistently pay their employees their weekly wages and accordingly, it was up to the community to help each other out with food and with money when bills had to be paid or fuel was needed for heating and for the car. 'I think these people are amazing,' thought Gilda. Their government stuffs things up and they help each other out.

The buildings were grey in the winter season and most buildings looked like they could do with refurbishment and safety maintenance. Inside however, you could tell that people cared for where they lived; it was spotless.

After their first week in Skopje, Gilda and Alexei took the train to Vienna. The contrast between the two cities was monumental. Vienna was adorned with Christmas decorations and the magnificent historical buildings were beautifully maintained, inside and out. Many shops and hotels had glass walls and flower pots to brighten the grey of the season. There were many 'Christkindelmarkts'. These Christmas Markets glowed with their decorative products and the aroma of Glühwein (hot spiced wine) wafted through the winter air.

Looking at people's attire and clothes advertised in store windows, it was easy to see there was money in the city. Gilda and Alexei crammed in whatever they could see in that one week and vowed to return for longer. They took the train back to Skopje, but at the border town of Maribor, in Slovenia, they were stopped by customs control.

Gilda couldn't understand what was being said but it was clear there was a dispute. 'The idiot is telling us that we don't have a visa to enter,' Alexei informed her as he nodded his head looking over at the official.

'We had a travel agent do our booking and she would have done all the necessary documentation,' Gilda told the customs official in English. Alexei translated. 'He insists that we don't have a visa,' Alexei repeated.

'Let me see your passports, please,' said the border official who looked at them and pointed out pages in each passport. 'Look Alexei, we had a visa to enter, which we used up when we flew in from Brisbane to Skopje, but the travel agent didn't get us another one from Vienna. She booked the train but it mustn't have occurred to her that we needed another visa to re-enter. He's right, we don't have a visa.'

The customs officer then spoke to Gilda and Alexei translated, 'He says that you don't need a visa as you were born in Vienna and Slovenia has a friendly neighbour agreement with Austria, you can go to Skopje but I need one. I told him I was born here. He just said that I should have brought my Jugoslav passport instead of using my Australian one. I told him it was expired. This idiot says that's my problem.'

Gilda burst out laughing and said cheekily, 'So, I can enter into the country but you can't. If it were the reverse and I would go back to Vienna, I'd do that, but for me go to Skopje while you stay in Austria, no way.' He looked at her horrified. 'I'm kidding', said Gilda. 'Come on, we'll have to go back to Graz. It's about three hours away one-way by train; it's the closest large city with a consulate. You can get a visa there.' Thank you," she said to the border control officer. He shrugged his shoulders and then saluted.

By the time they obtained the necessary visa and returned to Maribor, the last train for Skopje had departed. They had to sleep at the station overnight as it was too late and too far to go the city centre. Exhausted from lack of sleep, they caught the train the next day and Alexei's family picked them up from the station.

New Year was celebrated with the family. Gilda and Alexei took them to a traditional restaurant that had music and dancing. Although there was no actual dance floor, there was room to dance. Gilda coaxed Alexei to get up and dance, and others followed suit. The music was magical and great fun. When the week was over, they said their goodbyes with promises of returning. Gilda was very glad she had met them, 'Such very, very nice people,' she told Alexei.

On their return to Brisbane, Alexei decided that he now needed the car. Gilda then bought herself a Moped to ride to school. She had never learned to ride a bike so it took her somewhat longer to get her balance. 'I can't see why you're having trouble. It's easy,' Alexei would say when he saw her persevering but struggling.

'Okay smarty pants, if you think it's easy, I'll take the car and you can ride the Moped.' And that's what happened. Needless to say, he didn't often need the car when Gilda did. One day she was in the Taringa area and drove past an almost derelict house on a large block of land with a 'For Sale' sign on it. Gilda couldn't get that property out of her mind and the following day she drove past it again. This time she saw that the old house had been removed but the 'For Sale' sign was still there. She quickly jotted down the afterhours phone number and address of the agent. 'I'll risk it, even though it's Sunday, I'll go to the agent's office. Perhaps he works at the weekend.' She climbed up the steep narrow stairs to his office, saw a door ajar and knocked. 'Hello', came a man's voice, 'Come on in.'

Gilda opened the door and said, 'I hope I'm not disturbing you.' 'You're lucky,' came the reply, 'I was about to call it a day. What can I do for you, young lady?'

'I saw the house, well it's now a block of land, that you have for sale in Alpha Street, Taringa, and I wondered how much it is going for.' 'Oh yes, the one that had the house removed, $14,000. It's a quarter of an acre block. Bloody beautiful if you ask me. Won't last long.' 'You're right,' said Gilda, 'that is a great price. How much deposit would you need to hold it?' '$50 and a signed contract should do it and the remainder in 30 days.' 'Do you mind if I ring my husband?' 'Nope, here's the phone.' Gilda told Alexei what she had found and what she wanted to do. 'Are you okay with that?' 'But we don't have any money till we both get paid. I won't get paid till I start work again at the end of the month, same with you.' 'Never mind that,' said Gilda. 'Do you like the idea?'

'Well...' 'Good,' she said, and hung up.

'It's a deal." she told the real estate agent, and gave him a $50 cheque and signed the contract. 'My husband can come on Monday

after work and sign so as not to hold you up today. Is that okay.'
'Yeah, sure. I'm going home now and I'm not answering the phone anymore. Time to have a beer and relax,' he laughed.

On Monday afternoon both Gilda and Alexei went to the real estate office. 'You know what, folks, some bloke offered me more today but I told him it was sold. You were a lucky lady that you caught me in the office yesterday. Today would have been too late.'

They left the office and Gilda was jubilant, 'We are now land owners,' she said excitedly to Alexei. All he could think of was that they didn't have the money. 'Oh, come on, we'll get the money. I'll go to the bank and get a loan. It's prime real estate. The bank will love it. I have a good steady income, and you're full-time employed. Let's go home and celebrate. We've got food and drink, and we'll light some candles and make it special.'

Sometimes, Alexei just couldn't keep up with her.
Alexei was a very good plasterer and always did a high-quality, clean job and was reliable. If he said he would be at a customer's place at a certain time, he would be there or ring to say he would be late. Recommendations were soon prolific and he began to get weekend work. They had spent all the money they had on their holiday overseas, and now they had a loan to pay off. The extra he brought in from weekend work helped supplement their income. They could now easily handle the repayments and start saving as well.

One weekend when Alexei came home on Saturday after a job and he and Gilda were having a drink on the patio she said, 'Listen, Alexei, I have an idea.' 'I never like when you have these ideas,' he said looking warily at her.

'Oh, come on, don't be such a scaredy cat,' she replied, this is a great idea. Why don't you go into business for yourself? The job you've got pays less for 5 days' work than what you get on a weekend. You have enough weekend work to fill a few weeks and in the meantime more work will come. What do you say?'

This was something quite unexpected for Alexei. Given his upbringing, he would never have dreamt that he could one day have his own business. He lit a cigarette and took a gulp of his drink. He started to fidget, 'Gilda my English is not good enough to run a business.'

'Has your English been a problem with the customers to date?' she asked. 'No,' he replied, 'but that's different.' 'What's different? 'You'd still be saying the same things to customers,' said Gilda, 'We'll set up a business bank account. I'll help with writing the quotations and receipts. Once you set up trade accounts with the plaster and equipment hiring places, I'd do the book-keeping and pay the bills. It's all really simple. Then you wouldn't have to work all weekend. You would at least have one day off.'

He went to get them another drink and lit another cigarette. 'Do I have to decide now?' he asked. "Why not?' she replied, 'Now is as good a time as any. If you don't decide now, you'll keep putting it off. Just agree and I'll get everything ready, business cards, and advertisements in the local paper. You can call it Alexei's Plastering Service. Sounds good, eh?'

'Okay, Gilda. It does sound good and I'm sick of working hard and getting the same wage as the other fellows who are sloppy and lazy.' 'Bravo!' Gilda exclaimed. 'That's right. Think how much happier your customers will be.'

Gilda knew that when Alexei started his own business it would have to be in an area where they wanted to live. She decided that it was time they had their own house. 'Rent money is wasted money. If we have our own place, the long-term mortgage payments will pay off the house. We would need too much to build on our land at the moment but a rundown house which we can redecorate is possible.'

On weekends while Alexei worked, Gilda looked for another house in the area and other Western suburb locations. In those days, real estate agents came to collect the client, so not having a second car didn't matter.

When Alexei came home one Saturday afternoon, he found an excited Gilda waiting for him. 'Quick, get back in the car. We're going to a little house I found in Toowong that will suit us. There is a lockable downstairs area for all your work gear and upstairs there are three bedrooms, an enclosed sunroom, upstairs toilet, and so on. You'll see.' And so he went back to the car and off they went.

The property was situated on a corner, opposite a park. A bus stop was nearby and the train station was only a five minute walk from the house. The main road was a busy thoroughfare but the living areas were at the back of the house. Alexei agreed that with some plastering and painting it would be livable. It was already fenced and had a lockup garage.
All they needed to do was build a deck at the back. Two months later, they moved in.

They now, really, needed a second car. Gilda bought an old FJ Holden for $500. That was all they could afford. The car coughed violently black smoky clouds from the exhaust pipe. On the downside, Gilda now had a longer drive to the College, but she was happy to be living back in the Western suburbs.

As predicted, Alexei had so many customers that he needed to employ a plasterer to assist him. Gilda did the book work which she loved, and Alexei found that he was fine with anything to do with the practicalities of the business.

In 1977, Gilda completed her second degree, a Bachelor of Educational Studies. Most of this work was done before and after school in her school staff room. Now she considered completing a Master of Education degree. It wasn't so much that she was ambitious for university degrees, but she loved studying and enjoyed the mental challenge it gave her.

Gilda and Alexei had been married for almost five years and one evening Alexei said to her, 'Do you think we should start a family?' She looked at him amazed. 'Why,' Gilda countered, 'Why should we start a family?'

'Well,' said Alexei, 'we've been married for some time and that's what people do. They have children.' 'Just because people do it doesn't mean it has to be. Do you mean to say, you married me with the intention to procreate?' 'Well, no, but it's the thing to do', a perplexed Alexei said. They had never actually spoken about having children, but for Alexei, it was a foregone conclusion that they would have children.

'Listen, Alexei, to be perfectly frank, my childhood was no picnic and I wouldn't want to bring a child into that sort of life. Furthermore, our marriage, while it's okay, also has its turbulent moments. Again, I wouldn't want to bring a child into that either. Gilda then added, 'getting pregnant will take me out of the workforce. How we will we pay our mortgages?'

Alexei didn't know what to say. At last he ventured, 'So, you don't want to have a child?'

Gilda didn't know why she couldn't categorically say, no, but she couldn't. She hesitated and again, didn't know why. Finally, she replied. 'Okay, I'll make you a deal. I have long service leave that I can take from the beginning of next year. We'll go overseas for three months, and when we return, it'll be that night or not at all.'

He looked at her to see if she was serious. He saw that she was. 'Alright, it's a deal.'

Life took on a new energy. Not only were Gilda and Alexei occupied with renovating the house, she now also had the three-month trip to arrange.

CHAPTER 24
1978 - 1979

Gilda taught for the first term, from the end of January until the Easter break at the end of March, she and Alexei then left for their three-month trip to the Continent.

Mrs Kensington was, as always, very supportive and called Gilda into her office. 'Gilda, I just wanted to wish you a safe and happy trip. I know what your attitude is to having a child, but please allow me to make this comment. I don't know exactly what your childhood was like but I can imagine it was not easy. You have such wonderful qualities with children and your child would truly benefit by you being its mother. Promise me that you will just enjoy yourself on this trip and that you will allow yourself to be open to whatever comes to you, even if it's unusual.'

Gilda look enquiringly at her Principal for a moment, and then she went over to her and gave her a hug. 'You have been so supportive from the beginning Miss Kensington. I want you to know how much it has meant to me and still means to me. If it weren't for you, I wouldn't be here. The College is my home. Thank you.' Gilda started to get teary and quickly left her Principal's office.

Alexei's business was looked after by his employee who had shown himself to be trustworthy and reliable.

It was also Gilda's first extended stay away from Brisbane since she arrived as a migrant child. She and Alexei were not seasoned travellers, and there were many situations that could have taxed her had she not possessed the ability to 'float' over difficulties. Alexei didn't fare so well; he was often short-tempered with the oddities of certain peoples and cultures, such as the long siestas in Spain, foods not being served with bread, small glasses for alcohol, weak alcoholic drinks, hotels they stayed in not having a bar fridge or coffee-making facilities, to name a few.

After landing in Frankfurt-am-Main, Germany, they took the train to Paris and stayed a week before travelling to various French towns as they headed southwards toward the Atlantic Ocean coastline. They stopped for two days in Biarritz, then the playground of the rich, 'Goodness, it's freezing here and this is their summer,' Gilda exclaimed as the wind blew a gale from the ocean. 'Look at all these steps to go down just to get to a rocky beach below.'

Alexei hated the strong wind. 'I can't even light a cigarette because the wind is so strong. Let's go into a bar and have a cognac to warm up,' he suggested.

Despite Biarritz not meeting her expectations, Gilda was exhilarated to be there. 'I've always dreamed about coming here ever since I watched a film with ladies in their long-legged coverall swimsuits and bonnets on their heads running into the water with waiters bringing drinks on trays down the steps to people lying on the sand.'

Leaving France behind, they toured Spain before leaving Madrid to head by train to Portugal. Gilda spoke German and French, and had a smattering of Italian. The only place they would have had language difficulties would have been Spain. Consequently, she had taken a six-month immersion course in Spanish before they left Brisbane. She was able to make good use of language study, and had an amusing experience at the Madrid railway station when she bought tickets to Lisbon.

When it was her turn at the cashier, she asked for the tickets they wanted. In Spanish, she said, 'Two adults, window seats, first class return, no smoking to Lisbon, please.' However, Gilda's Spanish was somewhat jumbled but the cashier became so excited to hear a foreigner speaking Spanish he decided to help her fix up grammatical errors. In a flash, a cashier from another window came to help out. Suddenly the third cashier came over, and the three men worked with Gilda until she had the sentence grammatically and pronunciation perfect. Those standing in the queue cried out jubilantly with the cashiers when Gilda had the sentence right. It was a hilarious scene. 'Gracias Señores,' she called waving her hand as she and Alexei boarded the train.

From Portugal, they went to the Spanish Mediterranean coastal cities of Valencia and Barcelona. In Valencia they had booked a room with shower. When they entered the room, after the landlady left them, they burst out laughing. The room contained a large bed against a wall, a small open toilet on another wall and the shower was a coffin-size prefabricated structure in the middle of the room. When Alexei was inside, he could barely move. The photo of Alexei naked trying to take a shower was a highlight photo of the trip; he looked like Auguste Rodin's sculpture, 'The Thinker'.

On their first evening in Valencia they booked a table for two in one of the many large tented booths that lined the sandy beach. The booths were romantically lit with flickering candles and the tables were placed on sand. They sat with their feet in its softness. In this romantic, beautiful place they ate a traditional Paella dish that was unequalled in its taste and appearance. Their pre-dinner drink was a glass of Cava, the Spanish equivalent to French champagne, and to accompany the meal, Rueda, a white wine. After their meal, they went onto the beach and walked passed many such beautiful tents, with lovers sitting watching the partly illuminated, gentle waves lapping the shore.

Barcelona was extraordinary. They stayed in a quaint hotel with a balcony overlooking the Las Ramblas Avenue. The same floral pattern was used on the wallpaper, carpet, and bed coverings. It was floral overload. Even the tiny bathroom had the same print. On their first day wandering along Las Ramblas they found themselves caught up in an anti-nuclear march. People wore gas masks and carried slogans while chanting in chorus their opposition to nuclear weapons.

It was somewhat unnerving with all the marchers wearing gas masks covering their faces. Gilda and Alexei left the march and did a pilgrimage of Antoni Gaudí's architectural masterpiece, the Sagrada Família, the magnificent cathedral named after the Holy Family. From there they went to Park Güell, where they spent a day walking, listening to buskers and watching street performers and pavement artists. Finally, they walked past Casa Milà, Casa Batlló, two colourful apartment blocks. 'We really need to come back to

Barcelona,' Gilda said, 'I didn't realise how much there is to see and do here. This place is so alive.'

Alexei was not as impressed. He couldn't get used to the long siesta closure of all shops, bars and restaurants. 'It's uncivilised not to be able to get a drink in the afternoon,' he complained. If he wanted a drink, he had to have it then and there. Expensive hotels were open, but that wasn't where he wanted to go. Other than tiny, off-the-beaten track places that only locals knew about, most others closed from 1.00 PM to about 5.00 PM, but then stayed open till about 5.00 AM. Consequently, most places didn't open till 10.00 in the morning.

Leaving Barcelona, they caught the train which meandered along the south of coastal France hugging the Mediterranean Sea. They stayed a few days in the Côte d'Azur cities of Nice and Cannes before overnighting in Monte Carlo, the capital of Monaco. 'Have you ever seen a more magnificent marina than this?' Gilda was overawed at the sight of huge luxury yachts in a harbour at the base a curved mountain.

Switzerland was next on the agenda, and it was here that Gilda had an experience that would alter her perspective on what exists outside the obvious world. She and Alexei took a cruise on Lake Geneva. It was a brilliant day, with a blue clear sky, and the fountain in the middle of Lake Geneva hurled water skywards with huge force. The lake cruiser glided smoothly along the lake's shoreline until it came time to disembark.

Gilda stepped onto the gangplank to leave and at that moment a voice said softly, 'It's going to be a girl and you'll call her Angelique.' Gilda looked around to see who spoke those words. No one was in front of her and Alexei was behind her. She kept hearing those soft words for a few seconds and then the voice left. She felt as though she had been 'elsewhere'. She had no idea what had happened, nor why she felt so serene. Naturally she kept her experience to herself and gradually, over time, she forgot about it, but something felt different. She had changed.

From Switzerland, they explored the northern part of Italy before heading southwards to Brindisi where they crossed the Ionian Sea to the Greek port of Piraeus. It was the first time Gilda saw a 'loch' in action. The ship was placed on a platform that ascended and descended depending on the flow of the river. The large stone walls on either side cocooned the ship in its voyage. It was like being in a futuristic movie but the stone walls traced their heritage back to antiquity.

In Greece they did a classical tour of Greece and some of the Greek islands. In Athens they watched a breath-taking night-time Sights and Sounds display in the Acropolis. This southern part of Europe was unexpectedly hot, and they had to buy appropriate clothes at the Monastiraki Markets. Watching waiters navigating through the unmarked busy, wide, circular streets bringing drinks from hotels to customers sitting on the other side of the road was an unbelievable sight. They wove through fast moving cars without any fear. It reminded Gilda of the traffic going around the Arc de Triomphe in Paris.

While they were in that part of the world, they took the opportunity to spend ten days with Alexei's family before going up the Adriatic coast to Dubrovnik, Split, and Sarajevo and then over to Austria and its capital, Vienna.

Gilda always loved going to Vienna. Before she left Brisbane, she noted the address of her birth father, Hermann, on the off-chance that she might be able to find him. They were to stay 10 days in Vienna and after a couple of days she said to Alexei, 'Would you mind if I checked whether we could meet my father?'

'No, of course not,' he replied.

Gilda was now 34 years old and she had never corresponded with her birth father. She looked up the phone book and found a listing for Hermann Hollar. The address she had was correct so she dialed the number. While she waited for someone to answer, she said to Alexei, you know it's odd, I don't feel at all nervous.' 'Well, why should you be?'

'Hallo, Herr Hollar am Apparat,' said a man's voice. 'Hallo,' replied Gilda, 'Hier ist Gilda aus Australien.' There was a moment's silence. 'Gilda? Meine Gilda,' the surprised voice asked. 'Ja, deine Gilda, I'm here in Vienna with my husband and I was wondering if we could meet.'

'But of course,' her father replied, 'where are you?' 'We're in the city centre but we can catch public transport to meet you anywhere.' 'No, that's fine. Do you know the Aida Konditorrei, cake shop Am Graben? I can meet you there in an hour.' 'Yes, I do know it. Okay. Till then.' They hung up. She was now shaking and tears filled her eyes. She turned away and couldn't stop weeping. In an hour, a tall, slim, elderly man in a well-cut, light camel-coloured coat entered the Aida coffee and cake shop. They recognised each other immediately. Gilda rose from her chair and they embraced. He hung his coat on a hook. 'This is my husband, Alexei.' The two men shook hands. Hermann looked at Gilda and said. "I can't believe this. When you didn't reply to my letters, I thought you didn't want to have anything to do with me.' 'I never received any letters.' she said astounded. 'When did you write?' Hermann, didn't reply directly saying, 'Do you remember Dora, the one who went to Toronto?

'Yes, she died a few years after getting there.'

'Yes, but before she died, she was in contact with one of your mother's friends here in Vienna, Mara. Mara learned from Helga in Kirchberg-am-Wagram of your mother's whereabouts in Brisbane. Hanna had written to Helga and she was then able to tell Dora who told me. I then contacted Helga, we knew each other before the war. Helga came to Vienna and showed me some photos of you.'
'Well, it's obvious Hanna kept that from you,' said Alexei matter-of-factly, 'Typical.'

Gilda and her father just looked at each other as though they were checking that this was really happening. 'When I didn't hear from you, I wrote again on your 16th birthday, but it was returned to me. I recognised Hanna's handwriting. She tried to camouflage it, but it was hers. I then knew there was no point in writing again.'

'I don't know what to call you,' Gilda began, 'I'm sorry but I can't call you Papa or Vati, it feels strange.' 'Call me Hermann; we are meeting as two adults.' 'Okay, thank you. Tell me about you and your family.'

'I'm still married to the same woman. I have three children, Silvia is 25, Hermann Jr is 20 and Sonja is 16. Silvia is married and Hermann has a fiancé. Sonja is still at school.' 'Now, please tell me about yourself.'

And so Gilda provided a précis of her life to date. 'I have an idea,' Hermann said when she had finished, 'Why don't you come over to my apartment on Sunday and meet the family?' 'Yes, that would be nice,' Gilda replied.

On Sunday afternoon, Gilda and Alexei arrived at the appointed time. She rang the bell of the outer wooden door that led to the courtyard. Hermann came out onto one of the balconies and was all flustered, 'Look, can you come back another time? Now is not convenient for my wife.'

'What do you mean?' Gilda asked.

Hermann was flustered and clearly embarrassed and after a long silent pause he said, 'My wife is not prepared.'

'Oh, that's okay. She doesn't have to prepare anything.' Then she saw the look on Hermann's face and heard loud talking from inside the room.

'So, she doesn't want us to come in, is that it? Come on Alexei, let's get out of here. I've never had a father, and I sure don't need one now.' Her stone wall was erected and nothing could penetrate it.

'Wait,' Alexei pleaded, 'Maybe it'll sort itself out.'

'Can't you see what's going on? She's terrified that I may want to make a claim on what they have here when he dies. They all think the same way. My mother thinks that way too. What his wife doesn't realise is that we already have more than they can even dream of. He's a car salesman, an employee on a wage, and his wife has never worked. They have three children and live in a three room apartment. It's not a three-bedroom house. It's three rooms; one bedroom, kitchen and small lounge. There are fold up bunks for the children to sleep on. If he had any guts, he'd stand up to her, but my mother only ever latched on to gutless men because then she had power over them and that's what she wanted. 'Come on, we're off.' Gilda then strode away.

Hermann left messages at her accommodation but she never returned his calls. 'I've managed very well without him all these years, nothing has changed.'

The subject of her father was never brought up again.

They enjoyed the rest of their stay in Vienna, and it was as though the meeting with her father had never happened. Gilda was used to pushing things aside. They did a day trip to the Seegrotte, a subterranean lake at Hinterbrühl outside of Vienna.

Another day was spent on the beautiful Danube River taking a boat ride to the Melk Abbey, a Benedictine Abbey said to have the largest church library in the world, with over 80,000 volumes. A day trip to Salzburg, Mozart's birthplace, completed their out-of-Vienna excursions. Vienna is a city you can amble and walk around for hours without ever going over the same territory, so that is just what they did.

Munich was their next stop, with visits to alpine villages such as Garmisch-Partenkirchen and to the Castle of Neuschwanstein, the home of King Ludwig the Second of Bavaria also known as Ludwig the Mad. He is famous for financing the operas of Richard Wagner which bankrupted him. He was found dead in Lake Starnberg in his castle shortly after he had been forced to abdicate his throne.

To have a break from train travel, Gilda and Alexei took a trip up the Rhine River. Leisurely they cruised, visiting villages, sampling their cuisine, sighting ruined castles made famous by haunting fairy tales, and then heading up the Rhine towards Germany's northern sea ports. They then crossed the border entering Denmark for a few days in Copenhagen.

The duty-free, cross-channel ship going from Denmark to Norway was a floating refrigerated supermarket with fresh-frozen fish, sausages, cheeses and other delicacies. Another section of the ship was a gigantic, duty-free liquor store. A cruise of Norway's northern fjords was a highlight, as was eating fresh-cooked prawns while sitting on the harbour steps of Oslo.

Their visit to Stockholm, Sweden's capital, was brief. There they took part in the large annual Mardi Gras before crossing the Baltic Sea and returning to mainland Europe. On the way back they saw the contrasts between Holland, Belgium, and Luxemburg before motoring to Frankfurt-am-Main to catch their return flight to Australia.

Gilda and Alexei had an extraordinary three months away. They travelled well together and barely had a disagreement. Gilda made sure that no cultural activities such as going to the opera in Vienna were discussed. They did go to a performance of the Spanish Riding School's Lipizzaner horses in the Hofburg, the Winter Palace, in Vienna, of Austria's last monarchy.

Back in Brisbane, life went back to normal, Gilda taught and Alexei ran his business. Gilda would often reminisce alone about the trip. 'I loved that trip. I love travelling and especially talking to people in different languages; that is so much fun. There are so many beautiful places in the world.'

All this time, Hanna and Gilda were still not in touch. Ivan and Hanna were still a couple.

By July it was clear that Gilda was pregnant. As soon as she found out, she stopped drinking alcohol and was very careful about what she ate. By the end of the third month, her gynecologist said, 'Gilda, your blood pressure is abnormally high. You will need to stop working.' She was horrified. 'You can't be serious,' she said. 'I love my job. I'd go nuts staying at home. Besides, we need my income.' 'Very well. If you insist on going to work, then this is what you must do. As soon as you arrive home, you are to rest, no cooking, nothing. You are to lay horizontal, propped up with pillows. Do you understand?' The doctor looked so serious that she agreed with him.' 'And I want to see you every two weeks,' he added.

The kitchen had been renovated into an open-plan room with a window overlooking the new back deck. Alexei placed a couch at the window so that Gilda could lie comfortably and watch while he prepared food for the evening meal. Every two weeks she went for a checkup and all was going well; her blood pressure although still a little high had stabilised. She was able to do her exam and assessment marking from the comfort of her couch.

Miss Kensington was thrilled that Gilda was pregnant. 'Gilda, I would like to give you something for your baby. You know how my friend, Mrs Francis, crochets so beautifully. I have asked her to crochet something for your little one. What would you prefer, 12 crocheted coat hangers or a large bunny rug?' Gilda was touched, and was speechless. 'Oh, Miss Kensington that is such a lovely thought. A bunny rug, please.'

School ended mid-November and Gilda enjoyed staying home. Her baby was due mid-to end January so she was quite large. Suddenly on 24 December, Gilda called Alexei, 'I think the baby is ready to come. I'm getting contractions.' He called an ambulance and she went to hospital. There a nurse gave Gilda an injection to arrest the contractions. 'Geez, she must have been a horse Vet before she became a nurse,' Gilda said, 'She was so heavy-handed when she stuck that needle into me.' However, generally patients and nursing staff in that ward were a happy lot. It was the 'holding place' for women who were not ready to confine but were all healthy and happy at the prospect of their impending new born. Because it was Christmas Day, the hospital put on a wonderful celebration. There were decorations, festive food and Christmas carols. A very happy place to be.

At the start of 1979, except for her attempt to emerge from Gilda's womb at Christmas time, Gilda's baby had been very quiet. It rarely moved, and when it did, Gilda quickly called Alexei but by the time he came, the baby was again immobile. Gilda had not experienced morning sickness, and her sleep at night had never been interrupted. Towards the end as she became heavier, it became uncomfortable, but that wasn't too bad.

It was the middle of January when Gilda's gynecologist said to her, 'If the baby doesn't make a move, we are going to have to induce you.' 'What does that mean?' asked Gilda. 'We'll have to force her out with forceps. Gilda's response was immediate, 'That sounds terrible. Just wait.'

On 24 January the specialist insisted that Gilda be taken to hospital and to be placed under close observation. On 26 January, he said that she must be induced as there was now a risk to the baby. Gilda was wheeled into the delivery room and decked out in the gown. She lay on the bed with her legs strapped up.

'Push', ordered the sister' 'Will you push! Why don't you push? I'm telling you to push,' she kept yelling at Gilda. 'Will you stop yelling at me, I AM pushing?' 'For heaven's sake, doctor, will you tell her to push?'

By this stage, things became very uncomfortable for Gilda and she was in a lot of pain. 'Listen you bitch, don't talk as though I'm not in the room. I am pushing. Can't you do anything else other than tell me to push?' 'We'll have to give her an epidural injection to ease the pain,' the doctor said pleasantly and patted Gilda on the shoulder. He came over with an injection and said, 'Gilda, please lay very still. It won't hurt.'

Thirty minutes later, still no change. 'We'll have to give her another. Gilda, can you try pushing again, harder, please,' the doctor said kindly.

'I am, doctor. I really am.' The doctor gave her another epidural but there was still no sign of the baby coming and she was still in a lot of pain. 'I will have to induce the baby,' the doctor said to the sister.

Suddenly, Gilda was aware of people going backwards and forwards; there was a lot of activity. She was also aware that she was going into an altered state of consciousness and things were getting faint, sounds were at a distance and her vision was blurred. And then, the doctor's voice sounded alarmed as he spoke to the nurse. 'What are you doing? We're losing her. What the hell is going on? Her blood pressure is dangerously low. Give her oxygen. Quickly.' A momentary silence, then the doctor said, 'We've lost her. I'll get the baby out.'

All at once, Gilda found herself looking down at her limp body on the table. The doctor and all the theatre staff were frantic. She observed this scene with tranquility and serenity. She was encased in a glowing white light; there was a feeling of limitless expanse around her. Looking down she thought, 'It's so magnificent here. My body is dead, and they're all panicking down there.' The doctor was giving instructions and the sister looked shocked. "Serves her right.' Gilda said from her vantage point above the commotion.

But then she saw a nurse give the baby to Alexei. 'Oh, no, no,' Gilda cried as she watched him hold her. 'No, I have to go back. I can't leave her with him; she'd have no chance, no future at all.' After Gilda's marital experiences, she had no doubt as to how Alexei would bring up her little girl. 'She'll just watch TV all the time. Hell no, I've got to come back!'

Gilda's body wriggled on the table. 'Quick, she moved,' someone called, 'give her more oxygen, keep up the oxygen, she's regaining consciousness… She'll be fine now. Phew, that was close. What the hell happened? No idea what went on but it's okay now.' said the doctor.

Gilda had regained consciousness, and now took her baby in her arms and whispered to her.' 'I'm going to need your help but you and me, together, we're going to create a beautiful life. You are an

Angel. You know what happened before, don't you? It's our secret otherwise people will think I'm nuts.'

This was 6.03 AM, 26 January, 1979.

It was good that Gilda gave birth to a girl, as she and Alexei could not agree on a boy's name. They both agreed to 'Angelique'. Gilda still didn't recollect the experience in Geneva until some weeks later when she thought about her 'death' and it suddenly hit her. 'Holy Moses, I'd forgotten about what happened on the lake in Geneva, and now this experience! I know I'm not crazy. What is all this? Where does it come from? Do I have friends 'on the other side'? That would certainly explain a lot of other things that have happened in my life. This opens up a whole new way of looking at life. There's more to life than meets the eye. Hell, where do I start to find out about these things. I'm sure they're not in mainstream libraries.'

This was the beginning of a journey for Gilda that would be exciting, as well as at times causing her confusion and conflict. She was still very much a product of her upbringing and conditioning.

Although she rebelled against the status quo if it didn't make sense to her particularly if it meant obeying rules simply for the sake of obeying them, Gilda hadn't learned that there were ways of establishing your individuality without conflict. All she had known was conflict, and this was still a dominant modus operandi for her. Subtlety and diplomacy were not tools she used when she was annoyed about something.

Angelique's existence 'softened' Gilda, and she gave her a new meaning to life. There were times though that Gilda felt increasingly unworthy. It was the age-old syndrome of 'Who am I to deserve this blessing?'

A couple of months after Angelique's birth, Gilda and Alexei held a 'Welcome Angelique Party' for all their friends. Many of Gilda's students came and it was a battle as to who would hold Angelique. Miss Kensington came, as well as friends and family from the past.

Miss Kensington presented her with a bunny rug that became one of Angelique's most treasured possessions. She had it until all that remained was a minute speck of woollen fabric.

Angelique was a healthy, happy baby. Gilda stayed home for the first six months and then she 'imported' Alexei's mother from Yugoslavia to look after her for the next six months. The ground rules were laid; as soon as Gilda came home, she did everything for and with Angelique. Angelique quickly caught on to the routine and slept all day and woke up when her mother came home. She then stayed up till around midnight or later. Gilda didn't mind, she loved being with her.

This routine started to cause tension, as Alexei's mother would complain that she never had any real time with Angelique, who slept all day. This was to become an issue with Alexei. 'Gilda, do you think you could let my mother play with Angelique when you are home, she never has time with her.'

'Alexei, we had an agreement. It's up to Angelique when she sleeps and when she's awake.' Gilda replied, smiling at Angelique who seemed to know exactly what was going on. After six months, Alexei's mother went home. It had been a good arrangement and Gilda did actually get on well with her mother-in-law.

Gilda had researched child care centres and found a good one in a suburb on her way to and from school. The director, Theresa, was about Gilda's age and had a daughter the same age as Angelique. Theresa was Dutch and her husband, Wolfgang, was German. Theresa was also keen that children learn another language as early as possible. Gilda and Theresa became good friends and the two families often socialised.

Angelique accompanied her parents everywhere. They loved to go Greek dancing and, as a baby, she would be covered up in her bunny rug in a basket and slept soundly through the music. The same applied when they went to a restaurant. Angelique learnt to sleep whether it was noisy or silent. She grew up to be socially mature and adept at mixing not only with children of her age but with all adults.

Gilda also noticed that her daughter was an observer. Others called Angelique shy but she wasn't shy with people she knew. She merely observed and discerned whether she would converse or listen.

'I can see that I can learn from you, my little Schatzi, Darling,' Gilda remarked as she watched her. 'She really is behaviourally more mature than I am in many respects.' She picked Angelique up and said, 'You are, aren't you? Mum can learn a lot from you. I bet it's going to be like that throughout our life together – we learn from each other. I love you so much, Schatzi, darling; you're very, very special.'

Part 3

Brisbane
1980 - 2013

CHAPTER 25
1980-1981

When Angelique was born, Gilda telephoned her mother to let her know that she had a granddaughter, but as soon as Hanna heard Gilda's voice, she broke the connection. 'Oh, bugger her then, I don't have the time nor am I in the mood to deal with such antics – her loss,' Gilda thought. But it did upset her for Angelique's sake. 'It would be so nice for her to have a grandmother and I'm sure Mom wouldn't be the same with her as she is with me.' At this point, Gilda didn't know that Hanna was the same with everyone, she had an undiagnosed condition over which she had only minimal control. Had Gilda known this, she would not have been so keen to build a relationship between Angelique and Hanna.
'I'll go and visit her,' Gilda thought, 'Maybe that will make a difference. She can only shut the door in my face, and that's hardly new for me.'

Angelique was a year old when Gilda went to see her mother. She rang the front doorbell. Hanna always answered with a stern and haughty, 'Who is it?' before she opened the door. Gilda didn't answer till she knew her mother would see them when she peered through the lattice door. 'What do you want? I told you we were finished. I never want to see you again,' was Hanna's greeting. 'That's fine with me,' Gilda replied, 'I just wanted to be able to truthfully tell my daughter, Angelique, that I tried to contact her grandmother, but she wasn't interested.'

Silence and then...Hanna half opened the lattice door - the other half was always latched, 'You have a child?' 'Yes.' 'Obviously,' Gilda thought. 'I didn't know you were pregnant.' 'How could I tell you? You hung up on me each time I rang. Would it have made a difference?'

Hanna softened a little, 'Now that you're here, you may as well come inside.'

With Angelique in her arms, Gilda followed Hanna into the lounge. At the same time, Ivan came in from another room. Ivan was a reserved man with an expressionless face until he got to know you. Now, he had a smile on his face.

'This is my daughter and her child.' 'Hello, so glad to meet you,' he said extending his hand to Gilda. He then gave Angelique a pinch on the cheek which was customary amongst Europeans. Gilda had always hated that as a child because adults didn't realise how hard they pinched.

'Hello, nice to meet you too,' Gilda responded while shaking his hand. Angelique smiled at Ivan and looked straight at him with her beautiful big, brown eyes. You could see this six foot three inch tall, solid man melt. He gave an embarrassed giggle which shook his large frame.

'Would you like to sit down?' Hanna suggested. 'Yes, thanks,' Gilda replied placing her daughter on her knees as she took the offered chair. 'Would you like to hold Angelique,' Gilda asked her mother.

No reply, Hanna just looked stonily at the child.

Silence.

'I like the renovations you've done to the house,' Gilda commented, 'A huge improvement.'

Gilda's words sounded louder than intended in the quiet of the room. Not even Angelique made a sound. 'The carpenter has to return, the deck is not done properly,' Hanna replied. Ivan rose from his chair and asked, 'Would you like a coffee?' 'No thank you, Ivan.' Ivan sat down. Silence again. 'So, what's her name?' asked Hanna. 'Angelique.' At hearing her name, Angelique looked up at her mother and smiled.

'When was she born?'

'This is like extracting a tooth,' Gilda thought, '26 January last year. Mom you're looking well,' she said to her mother. Hanna just shrugged her shoulders.

'That's it,' Gilda thought. 'Okay, we had best be going,' she said getting up from the chair. 'Nice to meet you, Ivan,' Gilda said. She shook hands with him and went to the front door and said 'Bye Mom.' She opened the door and went to her car. 'Well, no one can say I didn't try.' She took Angelique to play in the park near their home to cool off. 'See that block of land over there, Schatzi, darling, that's ours. One day we'll build a house with a pool on it. You'll have a beautiful home to invite your friends.' Angelique snuggled up to her mother and Gilda felt her heart take a joyous leap. 'I love you so much. You make life worthwhile now. Nothing and no one will stand in the way of my being able to give you the best and happiest life; no one, no one.'

When they arrived home they took Oskar, their Weimaraner dog, for a walk in the park across from their house. Angelique was fond of Oskar but he didn't reciprocate the feeling. He was a spoilt dog and regarded Angelique as an unwelcome interloper. Until Angelique's arrival Oskar had been 'an only child'.

Gilda arrived back home shortly before Alexei, and decided a stiff gin and tonic on the deck was required. She didn't admit it but the way her mother had treated her upset her. Her usual means of survival was to push things aside as though they didn't matter but, with Hanna, it clearly wasn't working. Angelique was happily playing with a mobile swinging from a beam in her playpen.

Angelique picked things up very quickly. All sorts of new words were coming from her; Macedonian words she had heard from Alexei's mother when she was in Australia, and German words that Gilda taught her. Gilda would sit her at the piano and Angelique would tinker on the keys and giggle as she looked to her mother for approval. Gilda would reply with, 'Mummy's clever and beautiful little girl. I love you very, very much.'

When Alexei arrived home she told him of the abortive visit to Hanna and Ivan. 'I went to see Mom today to show her Angelique.' 'What did she say?' 'Not much. I met Ivan, the current man in her life; seems nice enough. Hanna wasn't very communicative. In actual fact, it was tortuous, so we didn't stay long' Alexei didn't say anything. He couldn't understand Hanna. Although his family was dispersed around the world, they were still close.

They sat for a while enjoying the view of the park. Suddenly Gilda said, 'Lindana's older brother, Sergei, is applying to be a registered builder. He has to build three houses and when they are completed and approved he can get his Builders' Licence. I went to see the block after I visited Mom this morning and I think that now would be a good time to build a house. He would build it at a reasonable price to be able to use our house as one of the three to qualify. What do you think?'

Alexei thought for a time and then replied, 'Yes, that's a good idea. How about I get a quote from him?' The quote was acceptable and accepted. It took about six months for the house to be completed and then the pool, retaining wall, a long concrete driveway and front fence and gate were completed two months later. Close to the end of the year they moved in.

'We'll be able to have a pool party at Christmas.' Gilda thought,' 'I'll invite Mom and Ivan but I bet they won't stay long even if they come.' There had been no contact between Gilda and her mother since that first and only visit with Angelique. Hanna never telephoned to enquire about her granddaughter. 'Every time I ring her she's too busy.' Gilda had stopped ringing her mother until she invited Hanna and Ivan to the Christmas Party.

Angelique continued to blossom. 'She's a very easy child, always happy, eats well, and sleeps well'. Gilda sometimes spoke German and French to Angelique. As Angelique grew, Gilda made sure that Angelique was exposed to a variety of children's cultural activities such as ballet, dance and music. 'I want her to have a smorgasbord of activities to choose from when she is older. Later, she can learn the piano and violin. They are good for a girl.'

Nevertheless, to ensure she was doing things correctly, Gilda took Angelique to a State Government-run child health centre where a nurse assisted new mothers with the correct principles of child rearing. The nurse weighed babies and suggested eating and upbringing pointers.

As soon as Gilda heard the nurse, she was hesitant about her decision to bring Angelique there.

The nurse was a proponent of toweling nappies I hope you only used a disposable nappy because you came here,' the nurse said looking disdainfully at a soiled nappy.

'I only use disposable nappies,' Gilda replied honestly.

'That is shameful,' the nurse replied waving her finger at Gilda like the witch from the story of Hansel and Gretel. 'Do you realise that she'll get nappy rash? You should ONLY be using towelling nappies.' 'I'm sorry, but I don't see how that can be true. Ever since she was born, Angelique has had only disposable nappies and she's never had nappy rash. Frankly, I don't even know what that is.' The nurse glared at her and said, 'If you don't know what it is, how do you know she's never had it? Nappy rash is when a baby gets a red rash on her bottom from dirty nappies.'

That was it. Gilda was fuming and it was all she could do to not to pick Angelique up and leave. 'You, stupid idiot!' she thought. 'I didn't know what nappy rash was because she's never had a problem with her bottom. If she was going to get a rash, Angelique would have had one by now – it's been over a year,' she snapped at the nurse. The nurse snorted and continued as though Gilda hadn't spoken, 'Now let's get to what she eats. Are you giving her vegemite?'

'No, we don't eat vegemite.' Gilda and Alexei were Europeans and ate mostly European foods. 'Well, I'm not talking about you, young lady,' the nurse said in a superior tone eyeing Gilda sternly. 'I'm talking about your daughter.' 'Why should she have vegemite?' 'Because it's good for her.' 'What's so good about it?' 'All children need to have vegemite before they go onto solids,' repeated the nurse.

'That's not telling me why it's beneficial,' Gilda thought but she didn't want to persist with her question. Instead, she asked, 'Will there be any side effects?' 'She may get wind,' replied the woman. 'She doesn't have wind now, so why should I give her something that gives her wind and you can't tell me why it's good for her?' 'This woman is a lunatic,' Gilda thought and then added, 'In any case she's already on solids; she loves sucking and 'biting' on soft steak.'

'What! You are giving a one year old steak?' The nurse huffed and puffed and was quite beside herself with indignation. She'll get the runs.' 'No, she never has the runs, her stool is perfect.' Gilda thought, 'I have to end this,' Gilda thought, 'Look, can you just weigh her, please?' She couldn't wait to leave. The nursed weighed her Angelique and pronounced that her weight was perfect. 'Thank you,' said Gilda, 'I must be doing something right,' said Gilda sarcastically as she picked up the smiling Angelique and went out the door. 'I'm never going to her again. I'll go to the chemist to have Angelique weighed, the rest I can do. This woman is still in the Dark Ages.'

In 1981, Gilda's stomach problems had started to surface again. She had mostly been free of them, and only every now and then did she need to take tablets. One Saturday, the Dobinski family was in the city and Gilda had to suddenly go to the toilet. She was desperate. She left Alexei with Angelique in the pram outside the store and raced upstairs to the toilet, but too late. Added to the catastrophic outcome, her stomach hurt fiercely and she felt abnormally hot. When she was inside the cubicle she cried uncontrollably. Two women to came to her aid when she came out. To one of the women she gave some money to go downstairs and buy products so that she could clean herself and then change her underwear. The two women stayed with her as she sat on the sofa in the powder room until she felt better. It took some time for her temperature to come down and the slight dizziness to settle.

'Thank you so much,' Gilda said weakly, 'I so appreciate what you've done.'

The two women looked at each other and then one of them spoke, 'You need to see a doctor,' she suggested and asked, 'Does this happen often?'

'I used to have it a lot a few years ago however, I didn't have it when I was pregnant but about six months ago it started again. It's never been this bad,' Gilda replied with shoulders stooped and holding her stomach.

The other woman said, 'Please don't think me impertinent but are you happy? Do you have a lot of stress in your life?' Gilda was surprised at the questions. She had never thought about stress, she was indefatigable, and as for being happy, what did that really mean? 'Life is fun, what more is there to it?' Gilda thought. She never went into her feelings; she just took things as they were and learned to live with them one way or another but this incident shocked her. She had never felt so ill or had such embarrassing consequences.

'I really can't answer those questions,' she replied softly, 'I really don't know,' and burst into tears again. Then Gilda thought of Angelique and tears streamed uncontrollably until she finally said with eyes downcast, 'I'm fine now, please don't think you have to stay with me any longer. I'm sorry I held you up.' The two women looked at Gilda with concern but each one gave her a kind smile and left.

A short time later, she went downstairs and joined Alexei and Angelique. 'Are you alright,' asked Alexei? You've been gone a long time. I didn't know where to come looking for you' 'Yes, I'm fine,' Gilda replied. 'Sorry I took so long,' and with that she dismissed any further conversation. 'But I need to go to a chemist,' she added. From that day Gilda took a tablet whenever she went out.

Sometimes she took a tablet for weeks on end without interruption. Her system got used to it and regulated itself.

At the end of the year the three of them went to Vienna for a three week holiday. They spent the first 10 days in Vienna seeing favourite old sights and exploring new ones. Hundreds of photos were taken of Angelique.

Before they left for Vienna, Gilda had started corresponding with one of Helga's daughters, Eva. Helga, who still lived in Kirchberg-am-Wagram and Hanna were still writing to each other and Hanna had met up with her on trips to her home city. Eva, Helga's daughter, had moved from Kirchberg-am-Wagram to Vienna when she married her first husband. Now she lived with her second husband, in a village just south of Kagran, one of the outer Districts of Vienna. Living with them was Sally, a daughter from her previous marriage.

The remaining ten days were spent with them. Gilda and Eva got on famously from the beginning as did the men. Angelique made friends with their fat, ginger cat called Whiskee Whiskee would often sit with Angelique on her bunny rug, the one crocheted by Miss Kensington's friend. That bunny rug travelled everywhere. As it was the Christmas holiday period, the three of them happily drove with Eva and her husband, Gregor, to outlying parts of Vienna and then to Lower Austria. Although it was winter and some of the days were grey and bleak, the weak sun sometimes peeked through the clouds - just enough to take some wonderful photos. Outside Vienna snow was plentiful.

In the evenings, they all watched the TV news and some Austrian sitcoms together. This improved Gilda's day-to-day colloquial German language skills. Often, after the men and Angelique had gone to bed, Gilda and Eva sat in the kitchen and chatted, and Gilda learned more about her mother's past because Hanna and Helga, Eva's mother, were close.

Gilda also learned the fate of some of the other friends. 'I'll give you Fritz's phone number. He is still around. He remarried after his first wife, Agnes, died'. Hanna had seen Fritz over the years whenever she went to Vienna. 'When did she die?' Gilda asked. 'Agnes became very ill before your mother left Vienna and was taken to hospital. It was the night before Fritz met your mother at the Hotel Sacher when she met her boss, Herr Grünbaum. Fritz had been up all night and took her to the hospital. Apparently, Agnes lost her baby. There were complications and she died not long after. Fritz remarried about 10 years ago.'

One evening as they were sitting in the kitchen having their usual chats when Eva asked, 'Gilda is something wrong? I don't know you very but I can sense something.'

Gilda looked at Eva and then looked away and hesitated before she said, 'Oh, Eva, no, it's nothing but thank you for asking.' Eva waited and looked questioningly at her new friend, 'It's Alexei, isn't it? Eva persisted in her typical straightforward manner, 'There's something not right, isn't there?'

Gilda stared out the curtained window into the dark of the night. Snow had fallen that day and was still resting on the window sill with droplets coming down the window pane from the roof awning. It was 1.00 AM. Again Gilda hesitated. She never liked talking about herself. She felt it was a sign of weakness. 'I'm not sure what it is. I don't think about it. I just try to get on with things,' Gilda sighed before she continued, 'Yes, you're right, something hasn't felt right for some time. Maybe it never was right. I guess I believed in fairy tales and that a marriage is forever and that things would improve. Why, I don't know. No one in my family had just one marriage, even after two marriages, they didn't last. I guess I'm not making much sense.'

Eva put her hand on Gilda's to reassure her. 'Gilda, you know that I was married before I married Gregor. I was young when I first married and I also thought that love lasts forever but, it didn't work out. Tomas, Sally's father was immature and unfaithful, and finally he left me. I had a very hard time working and looking after Sally. Gregor became a good friend and he helped me a lot. It was a natural progression that we became lovers. Now, this marriage is good but there are still things that I don't like but they're not bad enough for me to leave. I can't say I love Gregor but he has been very good to me and I know he loves me. He is also much older than I am and I like the stability of an older man. But, if leaving would be the best course of action for you, then leave. Once a marriage is over, it's over.'

Gilda and Eva were silent for a while. Gilda was digesting what Eva had said. She had never heard Eva's perspective before.

'I don't think Alexei loves me and I guess I don't love him. I don't know, I honestly don't know. Until Angelique came along, I didn't know what love was and even so, I'll have to see how I may need to 'protect' myself when she gets older. I don't know whether Angelique will love me when she can think for herself. All I know is that people hurt each other. So, I may as well stay where I am because, it'll be the same no matter who I'm with. At least, I've got to know Alexei now.'

'But what about your stomach problems?' Eva asked.
'How do you know about that?' 'You left your tablets in the bathroom. I put them into your cosmetic bag.' 'Oh, I wondered how they got there. Thanks.' 'Well, Gilda what about your stomach problem?' Gilda knew she was cornered' 'Let's change the subject. Enough on this one, too depressing.'

Eva knew there was no point in continuing. She had observed Gilda and when a topic was over, it was over. They sat pensively sipping their Chamomile tea and turned to chatting about fun things they had experienced that day. These long chats with Eva, always when the others had gone to bed, showed Gilda that she didn't have to put up with the way things were if they were not in her or Angelique's best interests. She had never consciously said, 'I don't like things this way, I'll change them.' Instead, she would put up with situations until something inside her erupted and then it was like a volcano with molten lava and debris everywhere with everyone in shock at her emotional eruptions.

It would still take her many years to develop the skill of expressing what she felt as circumstances arose and deal with them rationally and calmly.

Finally, the ten days with Eva and Gregor came to an end. Both Gilda and Eva had tears in their eyes as they parted and after a prolonged hug Eva whispered, 'Alles Gute, und schreib' mir. All the best and write to me.'

Gilda nodded.

They wrote a couple of times but, as usual, the connection wasn't sustained between the two women. In this respect, Eva was similar to Gilda, once something was over, it was just that, and was forgotten. However, something had stirred up in Gilda, active evidence of which would surface later.

Gilda devoted her life to introducing Angelique to interesting and fun experiences, outings, games, activities, and visitors coming to the house for pool parties so that the little girl could have friends to play with. All of Gilda's lifelong interest in opera, symphony concerts, plays, theatre productions, and pre-concert talks had been abandoned due to Alexei's philistine approach to the Arts coupled with his sheer lack of interest and his conviction that these activities were attended only by snobs.

Gilda decided to resurrect her abandoned cultural interests and to include Angelique in these activities. 'She's not going to miss out on these wonderful experiences just because her father is totally disinterested. It was okay for me but not for her. I want her to know that she has choices. I want to make better decisions for her until she can make her own. You, my darling Angelique, will be able to make informed decisions and not just 'fly by the seat of your pants' like I have done, and still do a lot. You, Schatzi, darling, you will create your life.'

And that's exactly what happened. Alexei would continue to complain and sulk but that no longer worked on Gilda.

CHAPTER 26
1982-1983

Gilda's career at Champion College went from strength to strength. However, she was never really aware of her own value and the good work she did. She was popular with the school administration, teaching staff and students.

Gilda's home-life with Alexei was becoming troubled and he behaved like a masculine version of Hanna. He constantly tried to dampen Gilda's spirit with ceaseless put-downs. On and off, she attempted to revive her pianistic skills with practice when home alone. Sadly, this wasn't often because she rarely had sufficient personal time and was too embarrassed to play in front of him or anyone else. 'How can my technique be so bad when it used to be so good? Now, it's pitiful.'

Once when she and Alexei sat having a drink, Gilda without thinking said, 'You know, Alexei, I so miss not playing.' 'Well, why don't you?' he responded, 'the damn thing gets lugged from one house to another and you never play it. You can't be that bad if you studied for so long. It's like riding a bike, you never forget.' 'It's not quite the same,' Gilda replied, 'My fluency isn't the same and I don't remember my pieces, certainly not by heart, like I used to.' 'That's ridiculous,' Alexei said scornfully. 'Go and play something now.'

Gilda should have seen what was coming. Alexei was not the type of person to be supportive but, her need for encouragement was higher than her common sense. As she sat down on the piano stool she felt herself shaking and thought. 'Why are you so nervous, you idiot; it's only Alexei.' Slowly and apprehensively Gilda started to play. Her fingers felt stiff, cold and sweaty, her heart was pounding; she felt uncoordinated. After several wrong notes Alexei yelled out, 'That's terrible! If I were you I'd give up! No wonder you don't want to play in front of anyone.'

Gilda went from being shocked to being livid, furious at herself for having left herself open to ridicule and furious with Alexei for being so insensitive. 'I told you I haven't played for years. You and your stupid analogy of riding a bike! Shows how little you know about learning an instrument!' she yelled.

Alexei shouted back, 'You only think you could once play, you never could or you wouldn't be so bad now. The gypsies back home have never had a lesson in their life and they can pick up their violin and play. They don't need to practice. They can play without music, by ear. You can't play a thing without having to practice and have music in front of you. Give up,' he said disdainfully.

Gilda couldn't believe what had happened. Still shaking but with deliberate movements, she closed the music book, gently placed the piano lid down, rose from the stool, returned the music inside the stool and went over to Alexei, towering over him as he sat. Looking him straight in the eyes, and speaking in a low voice Gilda said, 'Don't you EVER, EVER dare speak to me like that again, because I tell you what, I'll be out of here and I'll be taking Angelique with me. I had to put up with that crap from my mother but I don't have to put up with it from you. I don't need you and your put-downs. The good life we have today is a result of me. I don't need you and your put-downs.'

Gilda loved the ocean and she and Angelique drove to Cleveland. They sat looking over Moreton Bay and strolled along the walkway beside the water, 'The sea is so calming,' she thought, and then she addressed Angelique, 'Look, Schatzi, look at the beautiful seagulls. Do you see the sailing boats,' she asked her. Angelique was now three years old and was good conversational company and Gilda had learned to also brush away Alexei's insensitive comments. After several hours, she drove home. When she returned, Alexei came to hug her but she brushed him aside knowing what was on his mind. 'He thinks by having sex with me, all will be forgiven and forgotten. That's always his solution.' She went into the kitchen and made Angelique's dinner.

'What are we having for dinner?' Alexei asked.
'I'm not eating,' Gilda replied, and poured herself a drink. The next morning, she left with Angelique to go to the Child Care Centre and

then to Champion College. By the evening life went on in the Milosevic home as usual. The incident was never referred to but Gilda never played the piano again in front of him. She would play a little at school in her lunch hour if one of the music rooms was vacant, but that was all.

The Milosevic's had been in the new house for just over a year. One afternoon, while sitting by the edge of the swimming pool Gilda said to Alexei, 'Our parcel of land is very big for us to manage and unless we get a gardener it will soon become unmanageable. You can't attend to it as you're busy with the business and I can't either. What if we buy a smaller block of land in Chapel Hill and build on it and then, with the remainder of the money buy a small house at the beach in Southport?'

'You really can't stay in one place for long, can you?' Alexei replied. Gilda ignored his comment; she had an agenda and wasn't going to get into an argument about his silly comments so she continued, 'It would be financially better. At the moment, we have all our money tied up in one property. Chapel Hill is a new suburb not far from here and it will soon increase in value. The same thing will also soon happen at Southport. Look at what happened when developers discovered Surfers' Paradise, prices skyrocketed, and Southport is next door.'

Silence from Alexei, so Gilda continued, 'I'll start looking at what's available at Chapel Hill. Once we've found what we want there, we can go for a weekend down the Coast and check out real estate there.'

'Okay,' replied Alexei with a complete lack of interest.
When Gilda thought about things, actually she mulled over whatever she was focused on but once she came to a decision, she was a whirlwind. She knew what she wanted, and went for it. It wasn't long before she found the perfect piece of land; a level, corner block that didn't need much excavation work. Alexei liked it also and they bought it. One day, she was at the land when a man approached her, 'Hello, have you bought this block?'

'Yes, my husband and I,' she replied. 'I'm your neighbour,' he replied as he approached her.

'There's something odd about this fellow,' she thought as he came very close to her. 'I don't like it when strangers invade my space.' 'Oh, hello,' she replied as she extended her hand. He ignored it. 'I just thought I'd tell you that I'm building a pool and will want a seven feet high fence.' 'No problem,' replied Gilda, 'We'll certainly pay our half of the four feet fence that is required by law.'

'No, lady, you've missed the point. I'm building a seven feet fence and I'll be expecting you to pay half.' 'But the Law stipulates that a four feet fence only is required.' 'I'm warning you lady; I'll take you to Court if you give me trouble over the fence.' He then walked off.

Gilda stood where she was for a moment. 'What just happened?' she asked herself. 'That guy has a few screws loose.' She went home and told Alexei. Sure enough, a week later a letter came from his solicitor with a quote for the seven foot fence. 'We'll have to get a solicitor as well,' Alexei said nervously.

'No way,' Gilda replied defiantly, 'I'll answer his letter.' A reply came two weeks' later with a Court hearing date. 'Now we'll need a lawyer,' Alexei announced. 'Nope, I'll go to court,' she replied. 'But you're not a solicitor. His solicitor will make mincemeat out of you.' 'I don't care about his solicitor; the judge will be on our side because we're prepared to do what the law says.'

The hearing date arrived. Gilda went to Court. The neighbour and his solicitor were huddled together, whispering and looking over at her. She felt confident as her sense of justice and fair play assured her that all would be well.

They were all called into the room. The Judge spoke to Gilda, 'Who is representing you?' 'I'm representing myself, Your Honour,' she replied politely. There was a snigger from her neighbour and his solicitor. The Judge looked at her and said, 'Let's proceed! Am I to understand that this is a dispute about a fence line?' Gilda clarified the situation, 'Not quite your Honour. It's not about the fence line; it's about the height of the fence.' 'Your Honour...' the solicitor said in a haughty voice feigning exasperation.

The Judge waved his hand to silence him, looked at Gilda and said, 'Continue.' 'We are happy to pay half of the required four feet fence but our neighbour wants to build a seven feet fence and expects us to pay half of that. I don't think that's fair. He can build his seven feet wall......" The judge raised his hand to silence her, and addressing her neighbour's solicitor asked, 'Is what has just been said true?'

The solicitor began with a smile on his face, 'Your Honour...' 'Yes or no?' asked the Judge. 'Well, your Honour...' 'Yes or no?' repeated the now irritated Judge. 'Yes, your Honour,' quietly replied the solicitor looking sideways at his client. 'You and your client approach the Bench,' ordered the Judge and as the two men approached he snapped at them, 'Get out of this Court room before I charge you with contempt of court and wasting my time and tax payers' money. You and the defendant will get quotes for a four feet fence and she will pay half of that cost. Case dismissed.'

'Oh, thank you, Sir,' Gilda said excitedly. With a slight smile on his face the Judge waved her away.

Gilda was elated; she could barely contain herself, 'Wow, I've just won a court case,' she said as she giggled to herself.

When Alexei came home they celebrated. 'You know what Alexei, I don't want to have a guy like him as a neighbour.' Alexei agreed that he wouldn't be a pleasant neighbour. Gilda continued, 'He's a pain and who knows what he'll think up next. How about we sell the land and buy a house on the other side of Taringa.' 'Houses there will be dearer,' predicted Alexei.

'We can buy a small, run down house and renovate it. If we need to extend it, we can get a contractor, and still buy a place at Southport.' And so, Gilda was on the hunt for a house. She found the perfect place with great potential, including a nearby primary school for

Angelique. The land was large and flat, and installing an in-ground swimming pool would be both easy and relatively inexpensive. There was a lock-up garage by the house and there were several thriving banana trees at the back. The other house sold quickly so in no time they moved again. This time they had more belongings and so friends of Gilda's from school helped them. Bit-by-bit they made the renovations and had the pool installed.

In 1983, when Angelique was 4 years old, Gilda enrolled her at the Pre-School of Champion College adjacent to the College. 'She looks so cute in her school uniform,' Gilda thought, 'And so grown up with her school backpack.'

When Gilda told her students that her daughter was now at the College pre-school, they all wanted to see her. Angelique looked pleased when laughing girls came to her at lunchtime to chat and play with her. She had no end of students looking after her when Gilda was busy with fêtes or other school functions.

By now, Gilda was the foreign languages Senior Mistress. She and the new French teacher, Vicky, quickly became good friends. One day Vicky approached her. 'Gilda, what do you think of the idea of taking a group of French students to Noumea for some cultural immersion during the mid-year holidays?'

'What a fabulous idea, Vicky! Yes, I'm all for it.' Vicky and Gilda organised a 10-day trip in the May school holidays. Parents were welcome. It was a memorable holiday with more enjoyment than French spoken by the students but they did see Pacific French culture at first-hand. Angelique who also loved to travel had a wonderful time. 'Reminds me of when I lived in Paris, but hotter and more humid,' Gilda reminisced.

Gilda's strong interest in new teaching fields saw her immersed in multiple school activities. As long as she was kept busy, she didn't think about her life at home. Alexei was happy just sitting at home and watching television unless she organised a family outing. She had tried again to help him learn English spelling and encouraged him to read simple, but interesting fiction to expand his command of the English language. However, he lacked both patience and interest. English was summed up and dismissed, 'English is a stupid language. The way it is written and the way the words are pronounced doesn't make sense.' His spoken English did improve from long hours spent in front of a TV set but that was it. Alexei was happy to leave decisions to Gilda and tagged along.

Angelique, on the other hand was the direct opposite. Gilda would mention activities to her and she would immediately want to try them or would suggest her own from talking with her school friends. Often, she would have three or four activities going on at the same time.

As the year came to an end, Gilda said to Alexei, 'I've enrolled Angelique at the primary school up the road so that she can develop friendships near where she lives. I'm happy to drive her to friends at the other side of Brisbane but I can't expect the parents of her friends to drive all the way to here.'

'Okay,' he said without moving his eyes from the soccer match on TV.

Gilda was exasperated, 'Do you understand what that implies? Can you please stop looking at the TV, you've seen that game multiple times. I'm trying to have a serious conversation with you about our daughter.' He turned the TV off. 'What did you say?' he asked. 'I said that Angelique will be going to school locally, and that that means you will need to pick her up from school or she'll have to stay at after-school daycare or, I'll need to resign from Champion College.' 'Well, do what you have to do,' Alexei replied.

Gilda looked at him in disbelief. 'Have you understood what I've said? It's not as simple as that. Will you be able to pick her up or will she need to go daily to after school care which I would not be happy about.' 'Why does she have to go locally? Why can't she go to Champion College with you like she does now?'

'Because next year she goes into Grade 1. For continuity, she'll need to be at the same school till Grade 7 which means, she won't have any friends in this area. I grew up with no friends because we moved around so much; I don't want that to happen to her.' Alexei now understood. 'Well, you'll need to resign from the College because I can't look after her after school.' Gilda knew that this was the only option. 'The College has been the only place where I've felt at home and felt that anyone cared about me, Gilda thought sadly.' Instantly she dismissed such thinking and replied, 'Yes, that's the only thing to do.'

Miss Kensington, the students, her colleagues were also sad that Gilda was leaving. She received a wonderful reference from the Board with an invitation to return at any time.

Lifting Angelique in the air, she said, 'Schatzi, dearest, next year is the beginning of a brand new life direction for both of us. We'll do lots of interesting things to do, and you'll have friends close to home to play with during school holidays.' Her daughter gave her a big hug before Gilda placed her on the ground again. Gilda was excited about the year to come.

CHAPTER 27
1984 - 1985

At the end of January, 1984, Gilda said, 'Good morning, Schatzi! Rise and shine! Time to get up! Today's your first day at your new school,' Gilda sing-songed as she woke Angelique and opened her bedroom curtains. This was her daughter's first day in Grade 1. Rubbing her eyes, the little girl sat up slowly. Gilda took her in her arms and gave her a kiss on the cheek. Angelique affectionately returned her mother's hug.

Gilda put on a brave front. 'I'd really have preferred Angelique could have stayed at Champion College but, I guess this State School will be good for her, toughen her up. As for me, I've not been in unknown waters for years. I felt so secure at the College, more so than anywhere in my life previously. Now I'm out on a limb and, I don't have a profession. I'm totally dependent on Alexei's money, not that he sees it that way; it's always our money but…. Frankly, I feel like terrible this morning.' She felt her stomach play up; it had been unsettled for months. 'I'd better take a tablet.' Gilda had been to see a number of doctors but they couldn't find anything wrong. 'Something isn't right, I know that. I'll have to do my own research.' But she never did. It was easier to just take one of the little tablets. When she took them, she felt fine and forgot about her discomfort.

Gilda then left her daughter to dress while she prepared her lunch box. Suddenly she heard an 'Uhum!' behind her. Turning around she saw her daughter beaming, and now dressed in her new uniform. 'Schatzi, don't you look gorgeous and as for the hat, it's adorable,' Gilda enthused lifting her daughter up at the waist and whirling her around until the little girl laughed with delight. 'Hey, easy Mum, my hat will fall off,' said Angelique as she held on to her hat with one hand. 'Okay, my little schooler, time for breakfast and then we'll be off. Are you looking forward to going to your new school?' 'I'm sure she can see right through this act but I have to keep her spirits up. No use both of us being down,' Gilda thought.

Angelique was five years old and only just made entry into Grade 1 because her birth month was January, the start of the school year. Grade 1 was normally for six year olds. When Gilda met the class teacher the latter was quick to point that out and because Angelique was so young there was a possibility that she may need to repeat Year 1. Gilda thought, 'This woman knows nothing about Angelique and she's already talking about her having to repeat a class. Not if I can help it she won't, unless I can see there's a good reason.'

School was only a five-minute car ride from home. 'Bye, Schatzi, have a wonderful day. I'll be here at 3.15 this afternoon to collect you. Love you lots.' Gilda embraced her daughter and they briefly clung to each other. Gilda then pushed her daughter gently in the direction of the school gate entry. Angelique turned, waved to her mother as her teacher led her and some other children away.

When Gilda returned home she slowly opened the front door, stepped into the empty house and looked around. The house still felt strange; she neither liked nor disliked it. Slowly, she walked from one room to the next, standing at the door of each room, looking inside. Then she walked through to the back yard. There she saw her daughter's toys on the grass and burst into tears. Gilda had no idea why her tears flowed but it seemed to her that she had fallen into a pit that was steadily getting deeper and deeper. She felt she was slowly drowning in quicksand. She fell into a chair on the patio and motionless stared into thin air.

After some time, she thought, 'I have to do something. I can't just be at home all day or I'll go crazy.' 'Gilda,' she scolded herself, 'Snap out of it!' and leapt up from the chair saying aloud, 'You've been through worse than this. You'll be fine. Some of the mothers at the College have party-plan businesses, I can do something like that. And so Gilda became a distributor for various organizations including a cosmetics company, personal care products and foodstuffs, health supplements and food containers. Daily she walked the streets knocking on doors, leaving catalogues and order booklets, and later returning to collect orders when she returned to collect the printed material.

After some months of intense working these systems Gilda rationalised, 'This is for the birds, people say they'll turn up and never do. The poor hostess is left by herself and maybe one other person. I have to find something else to do.' She then had an idea. 'When Angelique is in Grade 6, I'll go back to teaching. In the meantime, I'll be a stay-at-home-mum and be there for her when she needs me. But, I won't suffocate her.' Gilda wanted to give her daughter the kind of life she would have liked with her mother - to feel love, to experience being cared about, to have fun with each other.

In the interim, until she went back to teaching, Gilda decided that she would do tuck shop/canteen duty at Angelique's school twice a week. She was surprised how much she enjoyed serving the children. It also meant that she saw her daughter during the day, even if for only for a short time. 'Good heavens, what a crazy bunch they are! These children are quite different from those at the College; they are so rowdy, especially the boys, mind you the girls aren't much better,' she thought smiling to herself as she served them pushing each other aside for service.

One day when after she had finished her shift, Angelique came up to her mother and introduced her to a girl. 'Mum, this is my friend Denisha.' 'Hello Denisha, how lovely to meet you.' 'Hello,' responded the little girl shyly. This friendship proved to be wonderful; both girls are still very close 30 years later even though they live in different cities.

Gilda filled her days with activities around the house, frequently going to the nearby large shopping centre and browsing around the shops. The evenings were spent drinking gin and tonics at the pool until it was time to go inside. In actual fact, Gilda was markedly drinking more and more in the evenings. Alexei would watch TV also drinking but Gilda was always available if Angelique needed help with her homework.

One evening Angelique asked her mother, 'Mum, can you come to school tomorrow afternoon?' 'Yes, why? What's on?' replied Gilda. 'Tomorrow it's cross-country racing. I'm in Carter House and we are competing against other Houses for the Cross-Country Cup. It starts at midday.' 'Of course, do you need anything special?' 'I have to wear my sports uniform and I need to bring my school hat, a water bottle and some money if I want to buy an ice block.'

The following afternoon, Gilda arrived at the school and saw her daughter amongst a group of girls dressed in red waving pompoms and streamers; boys were blowing whistles, everyone was shouting; teachers were trying to make themselves heard to give instructions and a voice over a loudspeaker was bellowing the details of the next race and the names of the competitors.

One of the senior girls gave Gilda a map of the cross-country run. The sun was blazing hot: the temperature was 31 degrees Celsius. The children had to sit in the unshaded heat. Added to this, the run itself was in full sun, all the way from start to finish, over rocks, torn-up tree roots, dirt, and pools of muddy water. 'I wonder when Angelique trained for this,' Gilda asked herself, 'There must have been times during school because she never went before or after school to any training.'

Just before Angelique was to run, her teacher came over to Gilda and said, 'Angie will have to run with the six year olds as there are only a couple of girls her age.' Gilda looked at the teacher and said, 'Her name is not Angie, it's Angelique, I would appreciate it if would you call her by her proper name.'

'Oh, we all call her Angie, Angelique is too long,' replied the teacher flippantly. 'Who has given you permission to change her name? Angelique?' Gilda said as she looked directly at her. By now the teacher was not so cavalier. 'No, Angelique hasn't, but she hasn't corrected us.'

'No, she wouldn't. She is a child and won't correct a teacher. But, I insist that she be called by her proper name,' Gilda replied calmly.

'Yes, of course, Mrs Milosevic, I'll see to it.'

'Now to the matter of five year olds competing against six year olds, there is a substantial physical difference between those two age groups, don't you think?' It was obvious that the teacher had never given it a thought nor did she seem to care. And, when do they train for this sport? I've never heard it mentioned in the notices.' Gilda continued.

'Some of the boys and girls go before school and after school to Clubs to train,' replied the teacher.

'So, that means that children who don't train compete against children who do training outside of school hours? 'Yes,' the teacher had to concede after a pause.

Just at that moment, the runners returned. At the very back, some distance from the last runner, Gilda could see her Angelique struggling to finish the course. She was bright red, panting and sweating as she came over to her mother and was clearly despondent. Gilda comforted her daughter, wiped her face with water and gave her a drink. 'Come on Sweetheart, let's go.' 'Oh, no, I can't go. I have to wait till it's over,' she said still breathless.

'No, you don't. I'll tell your teacher I need to take you now. She'll agree.' Gilda thought to herself, 'I bet she'll agree. She'll have no choice.' She turned to Miss Dunstan saying, 'I hope you don't mind but I need to go and Angelique will come with me. That won't be a problem, will it?'

'No, that's fine, Mrs Milosevic. See you tomorrow, Angelique,' the teacher replied sweetly.

The next day, Gilda had a phone call from the Principal's Secretary asking if she had time to see the Principal that afternoon before picking Angelique up. When Gilda met her, the Head Mistress apologised for abbreviating her daughter's name and addressed the issue of the different ages running in the same event. The situation would change for the following year, she said. The school was also going to introduce training for all competitive sports within the school curriculum.

When the Principal had finished Gilda thanked her and they shook hands.

'I'll find a sport for her where she doesn't have to run in the blazing sun. It's madness.' The school had a program whereby if students competed in a sport outside of school they didn't need to do school sports; it was then their choice.

At the end of the year, the class teacher called Gilda for a meeting. 'Thanks for coming Mrs Milosevic. It's about Angelique going into Grade 2. I feel that as she is so young, it would be better for her to repeat Grade 1 so that she is better prepared for Grade 2.' 'I see," replied Gilda. 'Are her marks low?' 'No, her marks are actually very good, she is in the top five of the class." 'So, what is the problem?' 'I feel she is still socially immature and the extra year would help her gain maturity.'

'Miss Dunstan, thank you for your concern however, my daughter is not socially immature. She mixes with a lot with adults, always goes out with us, and has many friends of her age outside of school and has been overseas three times, twice when I took students to Europe when I was teaching at Champion College. I think I know better my daughter's level of social maturity. If you do not allow her to go into Grade 2, I will move her to another school.'

'Oh, I see, I didn't know that about Angelique. Why didn't she tell me these things?' 'Unless you talk to her and ask her about herself, you couldn't know. She's not a child who pushes herself onto you or seeks attention.'

Angelique's report was good and no mention was made of her social interactions.

When the school year finished, Gilda took Angelique to children's theatre productions, watched pantomimes at shopping centres, went to the movies or picnics and just they enjoyed each other's company. Angelique's friends also came over to play and swim in the pool. Their parents also came and all enjoyed a barbecue there. Sometimes the Milosevic's would go to their friends' places.

Two weeks before Christmas Gilda and Angelique erected the annual Christmas tree. From the time Angelique was a baby, Gilda introduced her to the festive traditions of Vienna that she had grown up with. Alexei didn't celebrate his own cultural traditions and like anything else he participated in, if it was arranged he attended.

The following January, 1985, Angelique went into Grade 2. She had a different class teacher who understood her better and school hours became more enjoyable. She and Denisha maintained their burgeoning friendship having gone to each other's homes over the summer vacation. They also made more friends with new girls who came into their class. They befriended mostly children from other migrant families because the Australian children ignored them because their customs were different. Angelique's results continued to steadily improve and she started private piano and theory of music lessons which she enjoyed. Each evening, Gilda would sit and enjoy her daughter's playing.

As usual, Alexei watched TV but one evening he appeared in the room where Angelique was playing and said, 'That's a lot of mistakes I'm hearing tonight.' Gilda responded saying, 'Don't take any notice.' Gilda attempted to be jovial, 'Dad has been watching the soccer and hasn't really been listening. It's just his idea of a joke.'

After Angelique had gone to bed, Gilda called Alexei outside.

'Don't you ever do that again, criticise her when she's learning something. I was stupid enough to let your put downs get to me but I will not have you ruin her self-confidence with your stupid remarks. Do you understand?'
'It was just a joke,' he replied.

'It's not a joke. It's stupid. She's 7 years old and is still developing her sense of self-worth. I grew up with put-downs and I know the damage it does. How funny do you find it when people can't understand your English? How funny do you find it when people ask you to repeat words or repeat what you said because they can't work out what you said?' She paused, 'It makes you furious, you swear at them, don't you?' 'When you are perfect, you can criticise a little girl who is doing her best in everything she is studying. Just butt out if you can't say something encouraging.' And she walked off to get herself another drink. Little did both parents know that Angelique could hear when they argued.

Unfortunately, Alexei couldn't help himself; he would still make demoralising remarks and say they were just in fun. Gilda had the usual response and, as always Angelique heard the quarrelling. 'I still need to find an out-of-school activity for Angelique,' thought Gilda. 'She is so artistic and has beautiful movements, so perhaps ballet or gymnastics. No, they're held in un-airconditioned rooms; crazy in this heat.' Angelique liked swimming and was part of the school team but she also had to take a sport during the off-swimming season.

'I know, ice skating! That is in the cold and she can incorporate athleticism with musical movements. I'll go check it out.' And so Gilda rang Ice World at Acacia Ridge. One afternoon after school she and Angelique went to an afternoon skating session for children to see what these classes offered. From the moment Angelique entered the ice rink and saw the children skating, it was 'love at first sight.'

'Would you like to learn ice skating?' Gilda asked her. 'Oh, yes, please,' replied Angelique without taking her eyes off an older girl who was doing a beautiful spin. 'Good, that's settled. You can do this sport instead of sports at school,' replied Gilda who was just as excited about it as her daughter. The rink had a children's program called Aussie Skate and an adult program. However, the next term would not start until December, a couple of months away.

In the meantime, Gilda decided to learn ice skating and joined the Coffee Club social get-together during the day. Sessions were held every Tuesday and Thursday morning. 'I need to get a head start because Angelique will catch on quickly.' Little did Gilda know that it wasn't a sport that came easily to an adult beginner? 'I'm going to need lessons, I think. That'll help. I'll join the adult Aussie Ice Skate program when Angelique starts.'

Suddenly, Gilda felt alive again and ice-skating was the beginning of years of pleasure. At the Coffee Club, Gilda met many wonderful people, women and men of all ages up to 75 years, some of whom had been ice skating for years. They mostly practiced ice dancing and only a few focused on free skating. Gilda loved it.

It didn't take Gilda long to make friends; she was gregarious and had always found it easy to get along with all types of people. Compassion for others developed from her own hard life which meant she always had a good word to say, or an ear to lend, when someone with problems wanted emotional support.

Finally, the big day came. Angelique was all decked out in her new ice skating leotard that Gilda had sewn. She also wore tights, gloves and knee-pads, as well as a tracksuit over her leotard until she warmed. Angelique looked so cute. It was December and both of them joined their respective sections of the Aussie Skate program. Angelique had worn her ice skates at home and felt comfortable in them on the carpet but when it came to being on the ice, her feet went all over the place and away from under her and she had to hold onto the barrier all the time.

'I don't like this,' complained the cautious Angelique. 'It's so slippery. I'm going to fall over if I don't hold onto the barrier. I don't know if I want to do this.'

'You'll get used to it, trust me,' said Gilda, 'Just lift your feet and 'march' on the ice, keep your hands stretched out in front of you, and bend your knees; don't try push sideways yet, just 'march,'' Gilda advised. Other children came up to Angelique asking her name, who was her Mum, was her Dad here, what school she went to, and so on. It didn't take long before she allowed herself to fall on her one of the cheeks of her bottom, if that was the best course of action; she even laughed as she fell. All the other children fell at one time or another and they also just laughed.

Soon, Gilda watched with pride as her daughter played with the other children as they 'taught' each other, and it seemed they had been friends for years. 'Now this is a better environment to do a sport in,' Gilda thought. They were then all called by the individual coaches to start the lessons. After her group lesson was over, Gilda went and sat in the stands and was soon talking with some of the mothers. This meeting blossomed into a weekly social event after each training session. 'My goodness, all these mothers know so much about the sport,' she thought as she watched them instruct their daughters and sons from the barriers. It seemed that everyone was an expert.

Instead of just going to group lessons on Saturday morning, mother and daughter also went on Thursday afternoons when another Aussie skate session was held. As usual, Gilda immersed herself in the skating world and soon became involved on a Committee of Aussie Skate Mothers. Gilda also joined the Queensland Ice Skating Association.

Added to this, she religiously went every Tuesday and Thursday morning to the Coffee Club. This time was sacred; nothing else could be scheduled for this time. It annoyed Alexei that she became so 'fanatical', as he put it, about going to these sessions. She tried, unsuccessfully, to explain to an uncomprehending Alexei that 'I just love this time; I love the people, they are so genuine, uncomplicated and warm. I love skating and the cold; it's so exhilarating skating to beautiful music. And, I love the speed I'm gaining skating forwards and backwards with the cold air blowing against my face.'

Each Easter and Christmas, the Figure Skating Club staged an Ice Show, and 1985 was no exception. Although Angelique was still quite new to the sport, she quickly became competent and whizzed around on the ice. She became a member of the 'chorus' of young people in the Ice Pantomime. Gilda was part of the adult 'chorus' dressed as a lollypop with a big, round, striped ring on her head and long white pants to resemble the sweet. 'I've never been in such a performance in my life, it's fantastic and so much fun. Everyone is supportive. I never knew such things existed.' Angelique had more exciting costumes and was even doing spins during the performance. The night of the public performance the atmosphere was electric. The "ice theatre" was professionally lit and the temporary set had double curtains for the performers to enter and exit the ice surface. Spectators filled the stands and everyone clapped enthusiastically at the end of each number. Gilda mused, 'I never thought that I'd be an ice-skating performer.' Alexei came to watch the show.

Mother and daughter went to the rink more often during the school holidays. It was an ideal place to be in during Brisbane's steamy, humid, hot summer vacation months. Most of the other children also went skating and many came to Coffee Club with their mothers. Gilda became close to mothers who had children around Angelique's age or a bit older and they would all then go to each other's places for lunch or just chat while the children continued playing or swam.

During Coffee Club sessions, there was always wonderful music playing, usually upbeat music with good rhythm. The ice dancers practiced their dance manoeuvres working with waltzes, foxtrot, rumba and other dance rhythms. Some danced with a partner while others rehearsed solo. Generally, the main lights would be dimmed and strobe lights used to add atmosphere.

One Saturday morning after Gilda and Angelique returned home from Aussie Skate classes Alexei said, 'How long is this nonsense going to go on for? You spend more time at the rink that you do at home.'
Because Angelique was present, Gilda decided to make light of it, 'Oh, I don't know. What do you think, Angelique, should we pitch a tent in the rink grounds?' The little girl laughed and went to her room to change.

Gilda glared at Alexei and went to make herself a drink. 'By the way, I've invited the parents of one of Angelique's friends from the rink over for a BBQ at 4.00 PM. The husband is a motor bike racing fanatic so we won't be talking ice-skating all afternoon. I'll make the salads and you can take care of BBQing the meat.'

This family, Eric and Caren Cuthbert and their daughter, Amy, were to become long-time friends.

And so started a means by which Gilda could have more people in the house and be less alone with Alexei. For her, it was also a way to subconsciously justify her increased intake of alcohol and a means of numbing the empty feeling within.

CHAPTER 28
1986-1987

It was now 1986, and during the seven years since Angelique's birth, Hanna had been either silent, distant or terminated any attempted conversation when Gilda tried to contact her. Hanna, never initiated a call. For Gilda, this was a mixed blessing. On one hand it was a relief that she did not have to deal with her a quarrelsome mother, but on the other hand it was painful because Gilda deeply desired that Hanna should be a doting grandmother to Angelique.

Just prior to the little girl's eighth birthday, Hanna rang. Without a polite salutation, she said to Gilda, 'I think it's time the child had serious German lessons with me. She needs to know the language of her heritage. I know you speak German to her but it's time for more structure. I am prepared to give her weekly lessons.'

'Hello, Mom, nice to hear from you,' Gilda replied. 'There is no need for that nonsense, just tell me when she will come.' 'Okay,' said Gilda to herself, 'down to business. Nothing changes.' Then speaking directly to Hanna she said, 'I'll ask Angelique what she wants to do.' 'Rubbish, she will do as she is told.'

Gilda thought, 'Good heavens, this is not such a good idea. She hasn't mellowed with age or with having a man,' Gilda thought. 'Mom, I will ask her,' repeated Gilda trying to stay calm and not say something she would regret. Hanna snapped, 'You will see that this relaxed way of upbringing will lead to no good. Ask her then, and ring me back.' Then the phone went dead.

'Schatzi, come here, please, that was your grandmother on the phone. She'd like to give you German lessons at her house once a week. I said I'd ask you first and get back to her or, you can ring her back.' 'That sounds wonderful,' the little girl enthused. 'Schatzi, darling,' her mother said, 'are you sure? She's not an easy person, you know that.'

'Don't worry, Mum, I'll be fine.' 'Do you want to ring her back or shall I?' 'I'll ring her. I'm a big girl.' 'Hello Oma, grandmother. It's me, Angelique.' 'Oh, my darling, how nice of you to ring.' 'Mum told me you want to give me German lessons.' 'Yes, my little darling. When can you come?' 'Is Wednesday straight after school okay?' 'Yes, of course, darling, whatever suits you.'

'She was really nice about it, Mum,' Angelique informed her mother after she hung up. 'I hope Wednesday afternoon suits you.' 'Yes, sure, I'll pick you up from school, drop you off and then pick you up. It's not far but just a bit too far to walk.' Angelique went back to the pool. Gilda thought, 'I'll bet the old hypocrite was nice to her. She'd better be nice to her when she's there.' thought Gilda.

The day came for the first German lesson and Hanna was ever so sweet when Gilda and Angelique arrived. 'Come inside, darling,' she said to her granddaughter and ignored Gilda. 'Look, darling, Oma has baked some biscuits and here is a glass of milk for you before we start. You must be hungry. Tell Mum to go so that we can get started,' Hanna droned in her sweetest voice.

Gilda just threw her mother a warning glance that said, 'Ultimately I'll make the final decision if you aren't nice to her'. Gilda gave her daughter a kiss and left.

An hour later, she returned to pick her up. 'Oh, what a delightful and intelligent girl,' Hanna gushed. 'We did so much work. Now don't forget to do your homework for next week, darling,' Hanna added for effect before they left.

When they were in the car, Gilda asked her daughter, 'How was it?' 'Good. Oma likes to talk so I let her. She doesn't want an answer.' 'Was she nice to you?' 'Oh, yes.' 'Good,' Gilda thought, 'That's the main thing.'

Gilda learned later that Angelique could daydream and still appear to be listening. 'It's something I learned to do in class when the lessons get boring,' she innocently told her mother. 'It stopped me from getting into trouble for day-dreaming.' Inwardly, Gilda laughed, 'Angelique's already smarter than I am!'

Ice skating had become all important and time consuming. The younger skaters were the future competitors and there were training sessions before and after school Monday to Friday. The morning sessions started at 5.00 AM and finished at 7.00 AM and consisted of figure and free skating. The children then showered and dressed for school. Gilda brought additional food for Angelique to supplement her very early pre-session breakfast.

Mother and daughter had a precise clock-work routine every morning. They left home at 4.45; Angelique would change from pajamas into skating attire in the car (she became quite adept at it), had her snack, put on her boots and was on the ice at 5.00. Afternoons were similar. Gilda collected Angelique from school at 3.15 PM, who changed in the car, had her snack and put her skating boots on. She then did some homework till the session started at 5.00 and they left at 7.00 PM. After a shower at home, there was dinner, followed by homework and piano practice. Bedtime was 9.00 PM. They operated like a well-oiled machine; like every skating mother or father. Mostly it was the mothers and the fathers would pitch in cooking or buying dinner. It was a fanatical group who loved the process and the result.

Each morning that Gilda and Angelique prepared for their early morning ice skating training session, Alexei simultaneously prepared to leave for his plastering business. And, every morning Alexei would ask, 'Are you going skating this morning?' And every evening when Gilda and Angelique returned home, he posed the same question, 'Have you been skating?' The answer never varied; an emphatic, 'Yes!'

One day, almost simultaneously, both girls said, 'Why do you ask the same question? You know the routine,' Angelique added, 'Dad, a lot of fathers come too.' Alexei ignored that.

Around mid-year there were a series of competitions, and Gilda and Angelique had entered their respective category. 'It would be nice if you came to see Angelique compete,' Gilda suggested. 'All the fathers you know will be there.' 'Yes, please, Dad, will you come? I'm quite good now,' the little girl pleaded.

'Okay, I'll meet you there. I have some quoting to complete.'
The atmosphere at the ice rink was electric. Music was playing. The competitors, females and males were in their finest costumes. Skating boots gleamed. The stands were filled with parents, relatives and friends. Angelique still looked small - she hadn't yet had a growth spurt - and was a little plump. Her name was called and she stepped onto the ice. Her father came up to her and said, 'Good luck, darling. I don't know how you can do your jumps though because you're so fat.'

Gilda heard Alexei's inept comment and stifled a gasp. Quickly she said to her daughter, 'Darling, you look beautiful, just remember that and skate like you always do. I'm so proud of you.' With that Angelique glided to the middle of the ice and positioned herself for the music to start. The music began and she executed a perfect technical program which combined technique and artistry. She was beaming when she came to the barrier and went to her mother and hugged her. 'I knew you'd be wonderful, 'Gilda said and then turned to glare at Alexei.

There was much clapping that afternoon. The children and adults were such a pleasure to watch. The competition was keen in all groups and each competitor did his and her best. Angelique won her division against six competitors and Gilda came third in her adult division. Both were ecstatic. When Gilda and Angelique arrived home Gilda ignored Alexei as they entered the house. 'Schatzi, would you go across the road to the shop and get some ice cream, please?' When she had left, Gilda was about to get stuck into her husband when he said, 'I'm sorry, I shouldn't have said that, should I?'

'Oh, so you do have a brain! What on earth possessed you to say that to her just as she was going on the ice to compete. You will NEVER come again. Do you hear, NEVER! I don't know what makes you so insensitive but you definitely have 'foot-in-mouth disease'. You wonder why your Jugoslav friends shut you out.

Maybe it's because you speak to them in the same way that you talk to your daughter. They're adults and they don't have to put up with your boorish talk and from now on, Alexei, neither will Angelique. I will make sure that you don't do it again, I will make it my business to defend Angelique from your constant barrage of stupidity.

A few months later, mother and daughter were dressed up to go to an evening symphony concert performance at the Queensland Performing Arts Centre. Alexei's parting comments to his daughter was, 'You'll become a little snob like your mother.'
Gilda snapped back, 'Thanks Alexei, you have a lovely evening, I know we will. Come on Schatzi!'

Three months into 1987, Alexei's mother came to visit. Gilda was pleased to see her mother-in-law because she enjoyed a good relationship with her. The visit kept Alexei occupied as he was the only one she could converse with. He invited some friends of his nationality to meet his mother but not many took up the invitation. Accordingly, Alexei's mother was largely on her own when Alexei was at work. Gilda tried to converse but her command of the language was small. Unbeknown to Gilda, her mother-in-law chided her son for not being a better husband. Gilda discovered this after her mother-in-law had returned home.

During the August school holidays, the family went to Fiji for two-weeks. Angelique always loved to travel; she had been introduced to it when she went with her mother to Europe at five years of age and multiple times afterwards. That love of travel stayed with her. Gilda also loved exploring new places; she researched the travel destination diligently which ensured a balance between leisure at the pool leaving time to mingle with the established culture at the selected destinations.

During the Fiji holiday, Gilda acknowledged for the first time since Vienna, that there was something seriously wrong with her life with Alexei. It became markedly apparent when they were speaking with a group of people on the outside deck of a cruise ship. One of the men said, 'I've left Canada and this is my farewell holiday. I was fed up with my life and thought it was time I was less selfish and helped out and did something useful. I'm off to work on some aid projects in Africa. My girlfriend didn't want to go, so we broke up.' Others were also involved in areas that needed help outside of where they lived. 'I've never heard that people do that,' Gilda thought. Then she heard others saying, 'You are responsible for your own reality. You have to decide what you want in life and create it. No one else can do it for you. Your thoughts create your world.'

'This is completely new to me and I'm liking it. Maybe that's what's wrong; we're just so focused on our own little world. When I get back, I'm going to get more involved with the skating club committee and see if I can get funding and sponsorship for the skaters by getting their photos in the newspapers and getting free advertising when there are events. It's a very expensive sport, and the parents need support.'

Gilda also had a shock while on the boat. She and the Canadian spoke a lot and she could sense that she was attracted to him and he to her, 'Oh heavens, that can't be, I'm married and have a daughter.' The experience unnerved Gilda, a loyal and faithful person.

When Gilda returned to Brisbane, she went all out to get publicity for the skaters and succeeded in something that had never been previously attempted. She contacted all local papers in Brisbane, Outer Brisbane and the Gold and Sunshine Coasts where competition skaters lived. Every week for several months, skaters were featured either on newspaper front or second pages with multiple stories about various ice skating groups, skating sessions at Ice World and upcoming competitions. She was also able to get a skater into Brisbane's main newspapers sports section, 'The Courier Mail.'

John, a former US Pairs Champion came to Brisbane to be a resident coach and this launched another publicity drive. Gilda went into promotion-mode as well as hiring him to coach Angelique. She organised a special welcome pool party for him inviting about 30 parents and their children. John was to become a life-long friend.

His fiancée arrived a few months later and Gilda was her family representative, when they married from Gilda's home.

Gilda's stomach had started to feel progressively worse and she had to take the tablets more than once daily. Her resilience and fight would get her through and then in the evening alcohol would unwind her. She found that she was able to avoid Alexei if they both drank. He would fall asleep in front of the TV and she would go to bed and sleep undisturbed.

One evening a group from skating went to Ye Old English Pub for an evening out on the town. There was clearly a mixture of English, Scottish, Welsh and Irish. After the entertainment and the meal were over, everyone mingled with other guests to look at the memorabilia in the various rooms. A 'buxom wench' came over to Gilda, pulled her aside and said, 'I'll sit ye down here with Rob.

Now there's a man who's got an eye for ye. He'll turn ye on. That man of yours has lukewarm water comin' out of his veins but Rob, he could scald ye. Have some fun. What harm can come sittin' at a dinner table and talkin. I'll take care of your husband and get him out of the way.' With a wink and a roar of laughter she said, 'Come on, Alexei, me boy, you and me got some talkin' to do and some beer to drink.' She grabbed his arm and before he knew what had hit him, she whisked him away. Alexei was ripe; he'd been drinking and a good flirt was just what he needed.

Rob, the owner, sat down at Gilda's table and with a wide grin said, 'Aye, lassie, you havin' a good time?' 'Yes,' replied Gilda, embarrassed and lost for words. 'It's quite merry here, isn't it?' Rob was looking at her intently. 'Come, I'll show you the trophy room,' and made to get up from the table.

'No..., thank you, I'd better go back to the others,' she said trying to sound in control but she felt that she stammered and was not remotely in control.

Rob put his hand on hers on the table and that made her sit down again. 'I meant it when I asked, 'Are you having fun?' I didn't mean just in here, I meant, are you having any fun at all?' 'Look, Rob, I'm married and a fling for an evening isn't for me.' He continued to hold her hand on the table.

'Now, it's not obvious but I've been looking at you all night and at your husband and, it wasn't hard to figure out. I didn't mean a fling for an evening. I…' Gilda quickly released her hand to move away and head for the bar to find Alexei.

At that moment, John came to the rescue. 'There she is,' he said to Angelique,' releasing her hand so that the little girl ran to her mother.

'Rob was just telling me about all the awards and trophies that his pub has received. Let's go to see them,' Gilda said, regaining her presence of mind.

'Oh, yes,' replied the little girl excitedly and looking at Rob she said earnestly, 'I'm going to get lots of trophies and medals when I compete.' They all burst out laughing and followed Rob while Gilda squeezed her daughter's hand and as she looked at her said, 'Yes, you will,' and then she added, throwing John a wink, 'but then, you've got such a great coach.' The fraught intensity of the situation had been broken.

Angelique then went with Rob to look at some of the costumes in a cabinet and John whispered to Gilda, 'Are you alright?' 'Yes, I'm fine, thanks.' 'You shouldn't be surprised. You won't believe me when I tell you, you are an extremely attractive woman. If I didn't have a fiancé….' he joked

'Stop, John, that's not funny.'

They all came back into the bar and Alexei was dancing provocatively with his 'abductor'. 'I think we'd better be going home. It's getting late for Angelique.' Gilda announced and everyone agreed. They all said their farewells.

Alexei was about to accuse Gilda of flirting with Rob when she said in a quiet yet strong voice, 'Stop! My conscience is clear but your lecherous look could have devoured that woman had she lead you away. Don't drink so much if you can't handle it.' Luckily, Angelique didn't hear that interchange because she was saying goodbye to her friend Amy. Alexei sulked all the way home and for the following week.

'Great, peace for a couple of weeks,' Gilda smiled.

News came that Alexei's mother was seriously ill and so they decided that it would be best for him to visit her just in case anything happened. Alexei left immediately for an initial two week period.

His absence was a blissful time for Gilda and Angelique. The little girl slept on Alexei's side of the bed. There was no one constantly asking where they were going and what they were doing.

Angelique completed her homework without interruption. Mother and daughter now played cards or a board game in bed before going to sleep. They were free to watch TV programs of their own choice. There were no arguments or discord. For Gilda, even taking Angelique to her German lessons seemed less of a chore and she was less irritated with Hanna's haughty behaviour towards her.

Life was running smoothly, peaceful and happy. Gilda didn't need her stomach tablets but she never made the connection between happiness and conflict.

After three weeks, Alexei returned.

CHAPTER 29
1988-1989

In 1988, with Hanna still giving Angelique German lessons, the door was open for greater communication between Gilda and her mother. Ivan proved to be an ally, as did his adult daughter, Danika. Ivan's marriage had ended some time ago and he had lived alone in a house one street away from Hanna. Hanna and Ivan had a lot in common. Both liked reading the literary classics in German and English, but Ivan had larger literary reading points of references than Hanna in that he read in his native tongue, Latvian, as well as in German and English. Ivan was self-employed; he operated an independent post office at St Lucia. They loved attending symphony concerts, opera performances and plays. Hanna was studying for her Master of Arts degree at the University of Queensland and had encouraged Ivan to begin a Bachelor of Arts Degree.

One afternoon when Gilda picked Angelique up from her German lesson she said to Hanna, 'Angelique and I are going to Alma Park Zoo on Saturday. Would you and Ivan like to join us?' Hanna looked suspiciously at Gilda and asked, 'Why?' 'Come on, Oma,' Angelique coaxed excitedly, 'it'll be fun. All the mother animals have recently had babies.' 'What time are you planning to go, Hanna asked. Gilda responded, 'On Saturday morning if we collect you and Ivan around 9.30 it will take about 45 minutes to get there; we should then beat the weekend lunch-hour rush. We can eat when we arrive and then wander through looking at all the animals and take some photos.' Predictably from Hanna came, 'I'm very busy, you know. I don't have time to spend a whole day there.' 'Oh, Oma, you can cuddle some of the baby animals,' coaxed Angelique.

'Well, Ivan can't come and I cannot stay long. I have much to do.' Angelique jumped off her chair and wrapped her arms around her grandmother's neck. Hanna stood still; she didn't know what to do. 'Angelique, please, control yourself, that is no way for a lady to behave,' said Hanna as she held the child away from her. 'Wonderful,' added Gilda. 'We'll pick you up on Saturday at 9.30.'

When Gilda and Angelique arrived home, the little girl excitedly told her father, 'Guess what! Guess what! Oma is coming with Mum and me to Alma Park Zoo on Saturday.' Alexei looked at Gilda. 'Is that wise,' he asked, 'You know what she's like. A volcano is more stable than she is.'

'It'll be fine,' Gilda replied, 'She always behaves better when Angelique is present. In any case, Angelique is excited about it.' Alexei was still dubious.

Saturday was a beautiful autumn day, sunny with a blue sky, just perfect for a trip to the zoo. 'Okay, my beautiful, ready? We have to leave in 5 minutes. You know how Oma hates when someone is late.' Gilda called from the kitchen. 'Ready,' replied Angelique and came to her. 'Oh, don't you look gorgeous in your pink overalls and pink T-shirt. And, of course, sand shoes with pink shoe laces.' Angelique beamed with pride, 'Bye, Dad,' she called. 'Good luck,' Alexei replied.

Angelique rang the doorbell and Ivan opened the door, 'Mmm, you look lovely, little one,' 'Come on in', he said. 'No, that won't be necessary,' Hanna called, 'I am ready. My goodness, Angelique you look like a 'Lausebub', a larrikin,' Hanna exclaimed when she saw what Angelique was wearing. 'I chose it myself and dressed myself,' said Angelique.

'Gilda, it is up to you to ensure that the child is decently dressed. She should wear a skirt and blouse, short socks and decent shoes. She's too young to understand these things; it's up to you to teach her. But, what can one expect when you dress the way you do. You've also put on too much weight.' And with that she marched out the front door to the car.

Ivan gave Gilda a flicker of a smile and she said, 'Nothing changes.' 'I can see I'm going to have to swallow a lot today but I will, said Gilda. I want Angelique to have fun, she's so looking forward to this outing,' she thought.
The trip to the zoo was a continuous German lesson. Hanna sat in the front seat of the car and insisted speaking only in German and

expected Angelique to reply in kind. Because her replies were full of mistakes, Hanna then proceeded to correct them. Gilda turned on the radio in an effort to interrupt the incessant lesson but Hanna demanded that it be turned off because it interrupted her 'lesson'.

After about 30 minutes, Gilda said, 'This is supposed to be a pleasurable day at the zoo not a German lesson. Enough is enough.' 'Very well,' Hanna replied haughtily, 'if you want your daughter to grow up uneducated like you, then don't blame me.' Hanna turned to her pupil and said, 'Angelique, my Schatzi, darling,' but she was interrupted by Angelique who said sweetly and innocently. 'Oma, no one calls me Schatzi, only Mum, that's just for her.' That brought all conversation to end and Gilda couldn't resist an internal smile while Hanna looked sternly and silently straight ahead. Gilda and Angelique sang to tunes they knew while Hanna sat expressionless in the front seat looking like a dowager empress.

When they arrived at the Alma Park Zoo it was quite early and there was plenty of parking. Just inside the gate were adult kangaroos and two Joeys. 'Oh, look, Mum, aren't they beautiful?' Angelique squealed with delight as she ran up to the Joeys lying in the dirt, sunning themselves and scratching at insects in their fur. 'Angelique, are you crazy,' Hanna shouted, 'they are filthy and full of germs. Come back here!' But Angelique didn't respond; she was enthralled with the cute Joeys. A caretaker, looking at Gilda, asked if the little girl would like a photo with them.

'Oh, yes,' replied Angelique.' Many photos later they went to other animals; emus, koala bears, more kangaroos, platypuses, rabbits, monkeys, and ponies. There was a donkey pulling a cart so Angelique went for a ride.

It was time for lunch and Hanna insisted on supervising Angelique's hand-washing after having touched so many, 'filthy animals,' as she called them.

The car was quiet on the way home. Angelique, exhausted by the sheer delight of inspecting the Zoo's animals rapidly fell asleep in the back seat. Gilda did not initiate a conversation and Hanna had nothing to say to her daughter and a relieved Gilda was relaxed behind the wheel. When they reached Hanna's house and the car stopped, Angelique awoke and rubbing her eyes said, 'Bye Oma.' 'Goodbye, Angelique, and don't forget to do your German homework. It's the only way you will improve.' With that she headed for the front stairs.

'Bye, Mom,' Gilda called to her mother. No response. Hanna opened the front door, went inside and swiftly closed it. Angelique came into the front seat of the car and said, 'It's so much nicer with just the two of us, isn't it?' 'Ja, Schatzi, it sure is,' replied Gilda giving her daughter's hand a squeeze.

'Well, how was it, 'Alexei asked when they came inside. 'Same as always but pleasant enough. I need a stiff drink.' added Gilda.

During Coffee Club meetings at the ice rink, Gilda met women and men whose occupations were in what she knew as the 'Healing Arts.' One was a medical intuitive and others practiced numerology, reiki, kinesiology, kahuna massage, esoteric surgery and other healing techniques. She became good friends with a medical intuitive who gave her a book on self-healing and self-care.

'Gilda,' I know it's none of my business, but I'm worried about you,' she said over coffee after a session.

'Why? I'm fine.'

'No, you're not.'

'Yes, I am, I'm as healthy as a horse,' Gilda replied laughing.

'Well, no you're not, are you? You have continuing issues with your stomach.'

'How do you know?'

'That's what I do. I'm a medical intuitive. I 'sense' things and then apply my medical training. I can 'sense' your unhappiness, and there are physical signs.'

Gilda was about to get up. 'Wait, stay, please, I want to help you. You can try to hide it from others and you can even try to hide it from yourself but it's not good for you. It can get very serious. Do you want to take that risk,' she said looking towards Angelique? 'I won't say anymore. I just want you to think about what I've said. You've got so much going for you but you need to make changes. Please let's stay friends. I won't bring it up again unless you want me to.'

Gilda stayed seated as though nailed to the bench. She stared at her friend and allowed a smile to break the intensity. No one had ever spoken to her like that. She could feel the authenticity of her friend, 'She's for real. She's not prying. I don't know how to handle this,' Gilda thought.

Her friend never brought it up again and their friendship strengthened.

The year rolled on with the usual routines of ice skating training and fun at the ice rink, piano and theory lessons for Angelique and lots of parties. Angelique enjoyed school. 'What a difference a good teacher makes,' Gilda thought, 'I really miss teaching but only a couple of years to go.' Gilda kept herself busy being in charge of publicity and public relations for the State Ice Skating Association and she expanded this by organising activities for some interstate athletes.

Christmas intensified the involvement with skating as there was once again a Christmas Show with its many rehearsals. Angelique had solos now and that entailed even more time spent at the rink. Proud fathers jokingly commiserated with each other in the ice rink carpark about the amount of time their wives and children spent at the rink.

When the Show was over, the social involvement continued. Some families went camping but most stayed at home socialising around the pool. Many of the families became very close as a result of the many hours spent together. They knew a lot about each other as they gossiped about their home life. However, no one knew what was going on in Gilda's life. She also worked hard to keep from Angelique her increasingly bitter and continual disagreements with Alexei. However, ever-fresh in Gilda's mind were the words that her medical intuitive friend said to her particularly when she experienced her on-going feelings of intense illness.

By the end of January 1989, the ice rink skating programs were back in full swing: this included public sessions and the private programs of the Aussie Skate Club, competitions, and the morning and afternoon training sessions. After one of the Coffee Club sessions, the Brisbane-based President of the National Ice Skating Association asked Gilda to come upstairs to his office.

'Gilda, thanks for coming up, I won't take too much of your time but I have something important to ask you,' Daniel began. 'As you know the figure skating office is at present amalgamated with the ice hockey office in Canberra. It's a part-time position with both sports administered together. The Australian Sports Commission has decided to separate the two ice sports and will make the administration of figure skating a separate, full time position. He paused for a moment and said, 'I have spoken to the other three executives and we are unanimous that we should offer you that position. The office would be set up wherever you want to live. It can move from Canberra to Brisbane if that suits you better. As you know, the other executives are dispersed between Sydney, Melbourne, and Perth and I'm here, in Brisbane. With communication these days, distance is not an issue. The head office for ice skating is in Davos, in Switzerland. You have done such an excellent job in promoting the sport Australia-wide. We feel you will do much for the sport in the future.'

Gilda looked at Daniel while she digested what he had said. To check, she repeated parts of what he said. When she had clarified everything, she said, 'Goodness, that's awfully kind of you to say those nice things about me. Do you mind if I think about it for a couple of days?'

'No, not at all. Take as long as you need to think about it and let me know your decision. What has also impressed us is that you stay out of the politics of each group. Ice skating can become very emotive as we're dealing with the competition results of people's children, the many hours and expense the sport demands, and the many volunteers who feel entitled to air their views in a not always constructive manner. You manage to be friends with everyone, even with the parents of the children your daughter competes against.' They then spoke of the salary and other aspects of the position such as the possibility of interstate travel to try to create better relations between the ice rink managements and the State Figure Skating Associations.

Gilda left his office thrilled. She couldn't understand why. Admittedly, she loved the sport, but she had thought of going back to teaching the following year, this offer, now, was completely unexpected. She had never thought that what she had done so far for the sport had been that great. Also, Gilda had never considered that she might run a national sporting office. There are 40 plus member countries of the International Skating Union. 'This is not small stuff,' she thought. Well, they think I can do it. I'll keep this to myself until I've thought it through.'

Gilda wasn't able to look at figure skating in the same way again. Her eyes had been opened to see the untapped possibilities for the three separate ice-skating disciplines; Free Skating, Ice Dancing and Pairs Skating. 'I think the next big thing is going to be Precision Skating. That's perfect for children and adults who may not be good enough on their own or with a partner in the other disciplines but are still very good, especially in a team.' Gilda had joined the new Adult Precision Team that John was currently training with the object of competing in this event at the next National Championships in Canberra. If this wasn't possible, they would skate in an existing age group competing against younger teams.

Her thoughts turned to the need for a newsletter so that everyone in the sport throughout Australia and overseas would know what is happening in the way of developments in the Australian ice-skating scene.

In this year, 1988, Gilda invited Hanna to the National Championships which were held in Brisbane so that she could fully appreciate Angelique's skating skills. Hanna declined. Also, the foot-in-the-mouth Alexei was under strict instructions from Gilda to stay in the stands with the other fathers, a suggestion that Angelique's coach reiterated.

Gilda was simultaneously arranging a Christmas trip to Austria and Macedonia. One of Alexei's brothers had already died of cancer and another from excessive drinking. Both these events had taken their toll on his mother's worsening health, so it seemed prudent to go given the rapidly declining state of her health.

A week after Daniel had offered Gilda the position of National Executive Director of Ice Skating Australia she went to his office to tell him that she accepted his kind offer to administer the National Office and would like to undertake the role in Brisbane. 'That is wonderful,' Daniel enthused jumping out of his chair and shaking her hand and saying, 'The other Executives will be just as pleased as I am.'

The meeting between the two was brief. An office was allocated to Gilda upstairs at the ice rink. Files currently in Canberra would be air-freighted to Brisbane. Office equipment for her new office was agreed on and her starting date was set for the following Monday. Salary negotiations were short, but for Gilda, very, very sweet. This all happened in 15 minutes.

'Oh, hell,' thought Gilda, 'I'm going to have to tell Alexei pretty quickly. I can tell Angelique on the way home, she'll be thrilled but, Alexei? Oh bugger, I'll tell him tonight too. It's really got nothing to do with him. I'll be at work when he's at work so the rest of the routine stays the same. He knew I wanted to go back teaching anyway.' she said trying to convince herself that it was no big deal that she hadn't mentioned it earlier.

Gilda and Angelique drove off and after the usual 'post mortem' of the session in the car, Gilda trying to sound as relaxed as possible aid. 'Angelique, Schatzi, I have some news to tell you. Actually, it's good news, at least for me, and I hope it's going to be for you too. Daniel and the other Executives have offered me the national administration position and I've accepted.' Gilda then told Angelique what had transpired and when Gilda finished, Angelique jumped out of her seat and put her arms around her mother's neck. 'Hey, easy does it, I'm driving,' Gilda laughed, 'I guess that means you are happy too?' 'Oh, Mum, this is wonderful. It means I'll be at the rink more often.' Gilda laughed as she knew that her daughter invariably did her homework both for school and for piano theory when she was at the rink.

Just before they arrived home, Gilda said, 'There's only one problem, I haven't told your father yet.' She looked over at Angelique and feigned mock-guilt. They entered the house and Angelique ran to her father calling excitedly, 'Dad, Mum's got some great news; she just told me.' 'Oh, hell, talk about going head first into the burning pit,' Gilda thought as she put on a forced smile, 'Well, Angelique, since you dying to tell your father, why don't you go ahead?' Angelique with childlike exuberance told her father all the details.

'So, you're taking a job at the ice rink. You'll be one of the 'rink rats,' Alexei said sarcastically to Gilda. In a friendly voice, Gilda replied, 'Not exactly. It is the top paid position in Australia. As you know I had intended to return to teaching next year. While this is a change of direction and the pay isn't as good as teaching, it'll be a challenge, and I'm up for that.'

All that came from Alexei was a sarcastic comment, 'You may as well both live at the rink for all the time you both spend there. I don't care what you do.' 'No more often than the other mothers and their children,' Gilda replied sweetly and then added, 'And some fathers too. Alexei, would you care for a drink?' Without replying, he went off in a huff to watch TV.

'Well, I'm going to have a celebratory drink! Angelique, would you like a glass of orange juice and celebrate with me?' 'Yes, Yes, Mum!' They toasted and then drank their respective drinks from crystal glasses.

CHAPTER 30
1990-1991

1990 didn't start too well for Hanna. She was irate when Gilda collected Angelique one afternoon after her German lesson, 'Don't think I can't see what your daughter is doing. She placates me and then does exactly as she pleases. She's a loafer and a day-dreamer.' 'Mum, Oma's not being fair. She asked me to do some work and I did it.' 'Yes, she did, but when I came back into the room I caught her day-dreaming.' 'But I had finished my work, Oma.' Angelique was almost in tears. 'Yes, but if you finish work I set, you then revise. Work is never completed. You don't just sit and do nothing.' Gilda called Angelique over to her. 'Mom, I'd be concerned if she hadn't done what you asked, but as she had, I don't see that you need to reprimand her for sitting waiting for you to come back. Where were you anyhow, that she had all that time alone? Angelique is supposed to be having a lesson with you. She's only 11 and will do what any normal 11 year old does, wait for further instruction once she has completed a task. In any case, she probably needed a breather.'

'She's just like you - insolent. She gets it from you. That might be what an average child from here would do but Angelique must learn to be ambitious to get on.'

'Perhaps you both need a break, just like there are school holidays, you both may need a break from these lessons,' Gilda proposed trying to defuse the growing tension.

'That will happen anyway. Ivan and I are going to Europe in a couple of months and we will be away eight weeks.' Both Gilda and Angelique had to control themselves hide their pleasure at hearing this news. 'That will be lovely for you both,' Gilda said refraining from showing any emotion.

'I can just imagine how backward the child will be when I return.' That was it for Gilda. 'That's it. I've had enough of you bad-mouthing Angelique. I will not have you putting her down and insulting her in the same way that you have done to me for most of

my life. In future, I will ask her what happened during a lesson, what your behaviour was like towards her and, if I think that you are destroying her confidence, she will not return.' Hanna started to walk away. Gilda's anger at her mother increased, 'Angelique loves you and is always pleased to see you but you have no idea how to be warm to her. I can understand that you and I clashed, but with her, you must be blind. She's sweet, obedient and a good-natured child. Ask Ivan, go on, and ask him. Ask anyone!'
'Have you finished,' Hanna asked icily.

'No. I want to warn you that if you try the tactics on Angelique that you did with me, she will not return to classes and you will only see her in the presence of others and me. Even that is conceding more than you deserve but, as I said, she sees you as her grandmother.'
'Come on, Schatzi, let's go,' said Gilda as she took Angelique's hand. When they were in the car, Angelique said, 'I'm sorry, Mum.' Gilda looked lovingly at her daughter. 'Never apologise for what is not your fault. You did nothing wrong. This was something that needed to be said long ago. I'm sure there have been times when she has behaved poorly to you but you are too nice to ever have told me. What I saw today, what she said about you was inexcusable. Believe in yourself, don't allow others to intimidate you, stand up for yourself, you will always do that nicely because that's who you are. Remember that. I am so proud of you and I thank God daily that I am blessed you and I are mother and daughter.

One day Alexei came in from collecting the mail and frowned as he read a letter. 'My mother is very ill,' he said, 'the doctors don't think she'll pull through this time so I need to see her.' He organised one of his employees to supervise the plastering work that his business had to complete over the coming three weeks and Gilda made all his travel arrangement for the flight to Skopje.

While Alexei was away Gilda and Angelique again had a wonderful time. They went to the beach for the day on both weekends, and took in a movie about Mozart. Angelique slept on Alexei's side of the bed and the days and evenings were peaceful and harmonious. Hanna and Ivan were also in Europe and met up with Alexei in Skopje for a few days. His mother had passed away but he stayed on a few extra days tidying up her personal affairs.

The day came when Alexei returned to Brisbane but Gilda was not looking forward to it. She parked the car at the airport, walked to 'Arrivals', went up the escalator and waited for the doors to open for passengers to enter the arrival lounge. Alexei come to her with open arms but she froze and stood motionless as he embraced her and wanted to kiss her. 'Alexei, let's go home.' she said, avoiding his kiss. In the car, he did all the talking. He told her what his mother had said, that he should be a better husband and father; he also mentioned that Hanna had agreed with his mother. He was so excited telling Gilda how he was going to change and be a better husband that he didn't notice her coldness.

They arrived home. He brought his suitcase into the living room and moved to embrace her. Gilda moved backwards and away from her husband. 'Alexei, I'm leaving you,' she said calmly looking directly at him. He looked at her stunned. 'What?' 'You heard, 'she repeated, 'I'm leaving you.' 'But', Alexei said, 'I will change, I'll make it up to you.' Gilda, struggled to keep her composure and said, 'It's too late. Things like that can't be made up. Life and marriage aren't like a shopping list where you can add and subtract things.' She couldn't believe how calm she was.

He now felt wounded, lit a cigarette and glared at her
.
Gilda continued, 'I'll ask Angelique who she wants to live with. Although I want her to live with me, I will abide by her decision. We'll split our assets in half. I will move out and you can stay here if you want.' 'Just like that,' Alexei said, 'As simple as that? How long have you been planning this?'

'I haven't been planning this at all. I'm as surprised as you are hearing me say this. I have no idea where it is coming from but I'm glad that it's being said. In a few days, I'll ring the removalist. You earn considerably more than I do, so I'll take all the furniture; it's not worth much anyway. 'Well, for someone who hasn't thought about it, you've certainly got everything planned,' said Alexei angrily.

'You can believe me or not but what you are hearing is totally unplanned.' Gilda didn't know at that time that she would have many such experiences which were unexplainable and yet occurred in her favour.

That afternoon Gilda picked Angelique up from school and they went to the rink. After the session, Angelique came up to Gilda's office. She asked her mother if she had watched her skating, if she saw her spins, if she saw her backstrokes and how they were improving and so on. When Angelique had finished, Gilda said, 'Schatzi, before we go home, I have something to tell you.'
'Every time you talk like that, I know it's serious,' the little girl replied. When they were seated, Gilda came straight to the point, 'Schatzi, I'm leaving your father.' She waited until it had sunk in. It took only a few seconds and Angelique looked at her mother and said, 'This means the fighting will stop. I won't have to block my ears when you two yell at each other. Does that mean we will move into another house? When are we leaving?'

Gilda looked at her daughter incredulously, 'Slow down. All those questions.'

'You didn't think I could hear when you two fought but I could. I would step into my closet and close the door and put my hands over my ears but I could still hear you.'

'I'm sorry, Angelique, I didn't realise.' 'It's okay, Mum, really. When do we move?' 'Angelique, I want you to carefully decide who you want to live with. It's important that you make a clear decision.' 'Mum, what a question! Of course, I want to live with you. Dad always puts me down and he's not interested in what I do.' The two embraced and Gilda breathed a sigh of relief. Angelique smiled; she felt very grown-up.

That evening, Alexei didn't come home.

'Didn't Dad come home last night?' Angelique asked the next morning. 'No, he must have stayed with a friend.'

Gilda deliberately divided their assets in half. 'I know I'm losing financially and I would get more if I went through a solicitor. Alexei wouldn't be where he is today with the business, and we wouldn't have the properties if it hadn't been for me. Also, I could get alimony but I don't want to risk the possibility that he gets regular custody of Angelique. It would ruin her.'

Alexei thought the division of assets was fair. Quickly, he took up took up with a woman, and seemingly, very quickly, didn't care about anything else.

The final hurdle had been to tell Hanna. To Gilda's surprise, Hanna had little to say about her leaving Alexei. Hanna also told Gilda what she had learned that his mother had said about him needing to improve as a husband and father.

Gilda bought an old house that needed work but they both liked it and the two settled there. A couple of weeks after Gilda had moved out, Alexei called and asked, 'Gilda, can we please see if we can't make up and get back together again? It's no fun without you. Can I come over and talk with you?'

'What about your girlfriend? Doesn't she satisfy all your needs,' Gilda asked. 'She means nothing. I want that we get back together again.' 'How do you propose we get back together again when she has moved in with you and you're sleeping with her?' He couldn't answer that but he repeatedly telephoned asking Gilda to return to him. Gilda, stood firm. She was steadfast in keeping her new-found freedom and peace of mind.

During summer Alexei asked if Angelique could come with him to visit his girlfriend's mother at the Gold Coast. Angelique didn't want to go. 'Look, Schatzi, what's between your father and me shouldn't affect your relationship with him. He is your father and although he has a funny way of showing it, he does love you.' 'Oh, alright then,' Angelique agreed She didn't like the girlfriend because she tried to act like a mother to her. So they left Friday night.

When Angelique returned on Sunday evening and Gilda asked about the weekend she was horrified to learn that while Alexei and the girlfriend were in their bedroom asleep, Angelique was in a room at the other end of the low-set house, sleeping by an open, unscreened window with no securities.'

Gilda confronted Alexei on the telephone, 'You must be out of your mind. You and your girlfriend were asleep at one end of the house while you left an 11 year old in a room with no security screens on the open window at the other end of the house?' He wanted to say something but she continued,' 'I was the one who suggested she stay with you because you are her father but, that is the first and last time. Until she is much older and can have more control over her surroundings and can ring me, she will never go away with you again. What if someone had climbed in the window attacked her? What then? Who would have suffered? - Not you. Angelique would have. You and I are finished, and your time with Angelique is limited from now on.'

Although Gilda had initiated the split, it was hard on her. They had been through a lot together and had worked hard for what they achieved and she often thought to herself, 'This is best for me and for Angelique. Why can't I just enjoy it? I'm free, I'm finally free.' This freedom took a long time to become a reality. It would take Gilda five years before she could adjust. For, apart from Angelique, Gilda was completely alone.

Although most of their friends were from her side, Alexei had alienated them by playing the maligned, misunderstood husband who was prepared to do anything to bring the family together again. Alexei portrayed himself as the victim and concealed the existence of his girlfriend.

Some of Gilda's friends from the ice rink shunned her also and kept out of her way except to talk skating. It took a couple of years for everyone to realise what had really happened but by that time it was too late. Gilda, view was that she didn't need them, 'I didn't expect them to take sides but to just cut me off completely – stuff them!'

Gilda loved her career move. Everyone had made her welcome, the Executive, members of the State Associations, the Coaching Association, skaters' parents and everyone who had anything to do with figure skating whether locally or interstate. Her office was set up just as she wanted it, frugally, but with everything she needed. There were already interstate trips including the annual AGM in Canberra. Although she enjoyed these trips she disliked leaving Angelique with Alexei.

The German lessons continued with Hanna but with Gilda monitoring them. Gilda and Angelique went to Hanna's for dinner when there was a celebration such as a birthday and Viennese festivities. Ivan's daughter, Danika, was also always present. She was an easy-going, pleasant woman and both Gilda and Angelique got on well with her.

There had also been quite a few road trips interstate for skating competitions with Amy and her mother as both Amy and Angelique competed in the same events and the four of them, two mothers and two children travelled by car together to Sydney, Canberra, Bendigo and Melbourne and then back to Brisbane. There they met others from Brisbane who had driven down separately or flown. These trips during Angelique's last year of primary school were always a grand adventure.

1991 started with great excitement for Angelique as it was her first year at secondary school. Gilda had enrolled her at the nearby Yeronga State High School. 'It will do her good to go to a State school and mix with students of both sexes and from different economic and social groups.'

With Gilda working fulltime, she stopped going to Coffee Club. The Executive gave her total freedom to do what she did during her day because she always worked till at least 7.30 PM most weekdays and worked each Saturday morning when Angelique skated. In the short time since Gilda took on the position, she had already proved the executive committee's faith in her. She had written a training manual, Figure Skating Book 1, A Practical Guide for the Beginner Skater and the Aussie Skater, which was endorsed as a Level 0

Coaching Council Manual. She introduced other innovations; off-ice training, such as gymnastics with organised classes each Saturday morning.

Gilda also wrote a quarterly print newsletter called, 'Ice Skating Down Under' that had international, national and local subscribers which informed and inspired skating within Australia and abroad. Rapport with the Australian Sports Commission and the Australian Olympic Committee was developed. She loved her work.

On the home front, the run-down elderly timber dwelling that Gilda bought when she separated from Alexei had been re-decorated and a covered deck added to the back of the house. Carpets were laid and the interior and exterior of the house painted. Gilda and Angelique were comfortable in the house which was now equipped with security screens.

Mother and daughter started a new tradition. For the next few years, each May they went to O'Reilly's Rainforest Retreat in the Lamington National Park south of Brisbane where they frequently took extended bush walks.

Without her realising it, Gilda was on a new path in her own personal development. She undertook much research to better qualify herself for her position and to improve skating standards. She came across concepts to do with mental strength, mental preparation, the power of the mind and the importance of the choices we make. She thought about that for a bit but it was too soon in her personal development journey, she didn't yet understand what she was reading. 'But most of the time I can't control what happens in my life so how can I have choice about how I react. I just have to react the way I see fit. I'm not just going to stand back and take things and have people walk all over me, not anymore!'

This was however, the beginning. As Ralph Waldo Emerson said, 'The mind, once stretched by a new idea, never returns to its original dimensions.'

And so it was with Gilda's mind.

CHAPTER 31
1992-1993

One Saturday morning in 1992, Angelique was practicing the piano when she suddenly stopped and said in a frustrated voice, 'This is hopeless. The keyboard can't cope with the pieces I'm now playing. I can't play as fast as the piece needs to because the piano action doesn't respond quickly enough.'

'Yes, I've noticed that,' said Gilda, 'Even when I play, it's as if the keys are stuck. We really need a better piano; I should talk to Karen.' Gilda's neighbour, Karen, was an accomplished pianist and piano teacher. Both mother and daughter had started taking lessons with her and Angelique, at this time was making great progress and at this stage of her life hoped to make a career in music. Her exam results were always at the level of distinction and high distinction and she was also taking violin lessons with one of Brisbane's well-known violin soloists, a member of the Queensland Symphony Orchestra.

'Okay, I have an idea, Gilda said to Angelique, 'Ellaways is now running its end-of-financial year sale of all its instruments. Why don't we go and have a look at what they have?' Angelique jumped off the stool, rapidly went to her bedroom, picked up her handbag and said, 'I'm ready!'

Gilda burst out laughing, 'Whoa, not so fast. Some of us have to work at looking good when we go out. I need to change and…' 'Yes, yes, and put my lipstick on,' Angelique teased. It was a standing joke. Gilda always had to apply her lipstick and dab perfume before she went out. With upstairs locked and their dog Perro under the house, they headed for the carport.

Before we go to the music store, a significant digression on the matter of a dog!

'Perro,' Spanish for 'dog' had started out as Hanna's dog. When she and Ivan came back from overseas, Hanna went on and on and on about how she missed having a dog and that she would really love to have one. Because she moaned about it every time they saw her, Gilda and Angelique gave her a fully vaccinated eight-week old puppy for her birthday. Hanna adored the little fellow and made a fuss over him. However, sometimes happiness is short-lived! The next morning Hanna rang Gilda and as soon as she heard the receiver lifted she shrieked, 'Come at once and take that dog back to the pet shop. I don't want him.'

'What do you mean, you don't want him,' said a totally unprepared Gilda. 'Exactly what I said, that dog has to go back. I don't want it. It howled all night and I didn't get a wink of sleep.' 'But it was his first night in a strange place and he's just a pup. Where did he sleep? "I shut him in the laundry downstairs but I could still hear him; he never stopped. My nerves, my nerves, my poor nerves are on edge. I didn't sleep a wink. He peed all over the floor of the laundry,' Hanna wailed hysterically.

'Did you put paper on the floor,' asked Gilda. 'Yes, of course I did. Do you think I am an idiot? He has to go.' Hanna, now completely out of control shouted, 'I don't want him. You and your stupid gifts! You did it deliberately to annoy me and if you don't come immediately and take that dog, I'll put it out on the footpath.' 'You can't do that,' Gilda said. 'Yes, I can, and I will, Hanna said,' 'If you're not here in 15 minutes, he goes out onto the footpath and it'll be your fault if he gets run over.'

'My mother is insane,' thought Gilda, 'How does Ivan put up with her? What can I do? I can't take him back to the pet shop. That poor pup,' she thought. 'I know; I'll ask Angelique if she wants a pup of her own.' She did! Angelique was happy, the pup was happy and so was Gilda. They quickly visited Hanna, collected Perro and successfully transferred him to Angelique.

Perro turned out to be a wonderful pet and he took his role as Angelique's guardian very seriously, never leaving her out of his sight when they were out together.
Back to visiting the music store.

'See you Perro, we won't be long,' Angelique told the dog as she patted him goodbye and latched the door. Gilda and Angelique headed off to Ellaways. When they arrived, they were overwhelmed. There was an enormous show room filled with shiny, new, magnificent instruments ranging from small pianos to concert grands.

They ambled through each aisle until Gilda suddenly stopped dead in her tracks, gasped and pointed, 'Oh my goodness, look at that one! Have you ever seen anything so beautiful in your life?' And she was off in full speed toward the grand pianos. 'Hey, hold on,' Angelique countered looking in the direction her mother was moving to, 'It's not going to run away.'

Gilda stopped in front of a Beale baby grand in a brown timber with its wing and keyboard open. Its finish was full-gloss and the stool beckoned to be sat upon. Gilda's mouth was partly ajar as she gazed adoringly at the vision. Angelique also stood in front of this jewel. Then they both looked at each other to check they weren't dreaming. Angelique spoke first, 'I bet it'll cost the Earth.' Gilda replied, 'I bet we're made for each other.'

Just at that moment an elderly salesman approached them and spoke softly to Gilda, 'Isn't she a beauty? I can never understand why people want black Grands.'

'No,' replied Gilda still in a daze as she sat down and gingerly touched the keys. One note, then another, a triad, a chord, the left hand and then the right hand. Gradually her right foot moved to the sustaining pedal, while simultaneously gently placing both hands on the piano's keyboard and gently started to play. She went into another world as she played her signature piece, 'La Paloma', The Dove' by the Spanish Basque composer, Sebastian Irádier.

The stick holding up the piano lid ensured the sound of the music penetrated throughout the showroom. Gilda ended the piece with the double pianissimo tonic chord with the right hand and accompanying octave chord of the left hand, so that barely a whisper of sound escaped before she released the pedal. 'You were made for each other,' the salesman said. Gilda smiled, 'Yes, what I did I just tell my daughter.'

'Angelique took over from her mother and played the serene adagio movement from Beethoven's Piano Concerto No. 5', 'the Emperor.' 'Oh that is so beautiful, Angelique really does deserve a better instrument.'

Then to the reality of the business of buying a new piano! What sort of a deal can you do for us?' Gilda asked the salesman. 'I think I can help you,' he said, 'It's the end of financial year stock-take, you have a keyboard to trade in and…let me go to my supervisor and I'll see what I can do.' He returned smiling. 'Madam, it's a showroom model and because it's the only one left, we can reduce the price even more. We will, of course, have it tuned before delivery.' 'Done, sold,' said Gilda once she heard the price. She tried to stay contained and mature, but didn't completely succeed. 'When can you deliver it to Corinda?' 'In three days,' came the answer. After they had walked a discreet distance out of the store, both women hugged each other and jumped for joy.

'I can't believe it was so easy,' Gilda said. 'I can't believe the price either. Somebody up there certainly likes us.' The baby grand took pride of place in the living room. It was rarely alone as it was in perpetual use and its sound generated a continuing stream of joy into the household.

Because of her work, Gilda now used the internet in the same way that she previously used a library. She still had no satisfaction from doctors regarding her stomach issues because they couldn't find anything physically wrong. She continued to rely on tablets when she went out locally and when she travelled interstate on business. Her medical intuitive friend from skating was still trying to help her but Gilda, without realising it, had built around herself an impenetrable emotional wall that was closed to all comers including Angelique. Gilda's self-sabotage was intense.
The wounds were deep.

At the beginning of 1993, Gilda had new carpets laid. When she moved into the house, she had the exterior timber walls painted pink as a mark of her independence. It certainly stood out, a high-set, timber house on a high corner of the street. When she gave directions, apart from the address, she added, 'The pink house on the corner.'

About two weeks after the house had been painted, mother and daughter came home one evening to discover they had been burgled. 'Perro, let's go down and see if Perro is OK.' Gilda was frantic as she hurried downstairs to find that Perro was unharmed and safely locked up in his enclosure. 'The stolen stuff's insured but Perro's irreplaceable,' she said as she kissed and hugged him. Most of Gilda's jewellery and a lot of her expensive clothes, particularly ski wear, had been stolen. The jewellery was mostly what she had inherited from Hanna's mother, as well as what she had bought herself. Angelique lost jewellery that had been gifted to her at her baptism.

It was obvious how the burglars had entered. Gilda kept a key in the inside lock and, although there were bars on the window that was kept open, one of the burglars managed to get the key. The police agreed and said they would investigate further. About two weeks later, the police rang to say they had no clues as there were no finger prints. A month later, when Gilda moved the beds to vacuum the carpet, she found a woman's pearl earring on the floor. Obviously a woman accomplice had tried on the ski-wear and clothes for size. The house, and its lack of security made Gilda uncertain about their safety and shortly after the robbery she sold the house and moved elsewhere.

Gilda's next major work project was the forthcoming Australia-wide Skating Tour to unify areas of the diverse ice-skating fraternity by getting them to communicate better with each other.
The Executive agreed with her plans to meet with office bearers of the State Associations, the State Coaching Association, and ice rink managers. Gilda also arranged to be present at skating sessions to introduce herself to the local communities and to meet Australian skaters who would represent Australian in coming international

competitions. The executive committee approved her two week travel itinerary starting in August; first south to Sydney, then Melbourne, west to Perth, followed by Adelaide and finally Hobart in the south. Gilda arranged for Angelique to travel with her.

'I wonder if I should contact Kenneth (her friend from the Australian Navy) before I get to Hobart or if I should just leave it as a surprise when I get there. It's been such a long time since we had contact, before I was married,' she pondered. 'I think I'll wait till I get there. Who knows, it may not be convenient or wise. He could be married by now.'

August came and Gilda and Angelique headed for the airport. 'Do you realise, Schatzi that, apart from the AGM, this is my first big business trip. I can't believe it's happening. This job has given me so many new opportunities. I love it. I love the people. If only the rest of Australia would know what goes into this sport, it would be valued more.'

When they landed in Sydney, they were picked up by the President of the NSW Figure Skating Association and on the way to the Macquarie Ice Rink the conversation was mainly about inaugurating an annual Boot Camp for top athletes in Sydney to supplement the one held by the Australian Sports Commission. Gilda met office bearers of the independent Australian Coaching Association, a significant group in charge of coaching standards in the sport across the country. This pattern was replicated in the other cities. Finally, it was time to fly to Hobart. 'I don't know why I feel so nervous,' she thought while still in the air. 'I guess there's been a lot of water under the bridge since Kenneth and I last saw each other.'

'Mum,' Angelique addressed her mother as they were about to land in Hobart. 'Are you going to get in touch with Kenneth?'

'Goodness,' replied Gilda, 'how did you remember him?' Angelique gave her mother an impish smile, 'I remember you telling me about him.' Gilda gave her daughter a make-believe smack on the arm, and replied, 'I don't know. It's been so long. I'll see.' 'Oh, go on. I want to see one of your ex-boyfriends.' Gilda knew that she could complete her obligations and still have time to meet with him.

The phone rang and then a man's voice said, 'Hello, Parker here.' Mustering her courage, Gilda said, 'Hello Kenneth, its Gilda. I'm in Hobart.' There was silence at the other end. She was about to hang up. 'Gilda? My Gilda from Brisbane?' 'Yes, I'm in Hobart for a couple of days and I was wondering if it's convenient to have a coffee together.' 'Yes, of course. Gilda…I can't believe it. 'I know,' said Gilda, 'It's been a long time. How are you?' 'Yes, it has been a long time, over 20 years. How are you?' 'I asked first", Gilda joked. 'You haven't changed. Still as cheeky as ever,' said Kenneth jovially, 'God! it's good to hear your voice. I'm fine, but could be better. What's wrong?' Gilda asked apprehensively. 'Oh, the old system has let me down. I'm in a wheel chair now.' 'But are you're okay otherwise?' 'Yeah, but I can't get around like I used to. When and where can we meet?'

'We could meet tomorrow afternoon,' said Gilda. 'I'm here on business and I can leave my daughter with parents at the ice rink for a couple of hours.' 'Your daughter? How old is she?' '14 and a half.' 'She must be beautiful if she's anything like you.' 'Flatterer. 20 years is a long time and people change.' 'No, you won't have changed, said Kenneth, 'What time do you want me to pick you up from the rink?' 'Does 2.00 PM suit you?' 'Yes, that's good.'
'Do you know where the rink is?' 'Hobart isn't that big and there's only one ice rink. I'll see you then, Gilda and … Thanks.' Then the phone was silent. Gilda stood next to the counter for a while looking at the phone as though seeing a phone for the first time.

Suddenly she heard her name from behind, 'Mum, Mum, I've been calling you for ages,' said Angelique. 'Sorry, Schatzi, my mind was miles away. What's up?' 'Mrs Hurst, the mother of one of the skaters I competed against when they came up to Brisbane, has asked me to go shopping with her after the session tomorrow afternoon. Can I go, please?'

'Yes, of course,' Gilda replied. 'That fits in well. I've just organised to meet Kenneth at that time.'

'Oh, no,' said Angelique, 'I don't want to go with them then. I want to go with you.' Now, hold on, Angelique. When Kenneth arrives, you can come and meet him and I'll introduce you to him. He already knows that you are here but, it would be nice if I could talk to him alone after all these years. If we meet up again, then you can be there too. Is that a deal?' 'Oh, okay, it's a deal.' Angelique feigned disappointment by bending her head. 'Oh, stop it, you villain.' Gilda laughed.

The following day, on the dot of two, a middle-aged man rolled into the rink in his wheel chair. He looked very sporty with his woollen cap. He had a blanket over his legs. Gilda approached him and gave him a peck on the cheek. Angelique walked shyly over to them.

'Schatzi, I'd like you to meet Kenneth, a dear friend from way back.'

'Hello,' said Angelique as they shook hands.
'Hello, Angelique, your mother told me you are beautiful and she's right.' Angelique blushed. 'Please call me Kenneth,' he continued. 'Okay, let's go,' said Gilda, 'Schatzi, here's some money in case you need it. Have fun shopping and I will see you here at 5.30,' She kissed her daughter who then went to put her skates on and join the practice session.

'See you here at 5.30,' Gilda called out. 'Okay, bye, Mum.'
Kenneth's car was set up to column-drive with switches for pedals because he couldn't use his legs. After he slid into the driver's seat, he pressed a knob and a crane lifted the wheel chair onto the roof of the car. Gilda watched this and couldn't believe how illness had changed Kenneth. In an instant 20 years flew past into her consciousness to the time that they walked briskly arm-in-arm near the Brisbane River on their way to the National Hotel for dinner. Gilda felt a surge of compassion for her once vibrant companion. 'Hey, I can feel that energy!" Kenneth said, 'It's okay, really. I do very well. I'm lucky. I can afford the trappings that get me around. Besides, I've got used to it. It's been a few years now.'

'But what happened?' Gilda had never encountered anything like that before in real life, not to someone as energetic and full of life as

Kenneth had been 20 years ago. 'I'll tell you all about it when we get to the restaurant,' he said.

They went to a restaurant on Hobart's waterfront. The owner and the waiters knew Kenneth and moved a chair at their table to accommodate his wheel chair. When they were settled, he asked Gilda, 'Do you mind if I hold your hand?' 'No, of course not. I'd like that.' It was like old times his large, strong hand covering hers on the table. 'Life's a puzzle, isn't it? We meet up again when I'm a cripple.' 'Oh, don't say that! Are you in pain?' 'No, my quack pumps me up with pills so I don't feel anything,' Kenneth said with the matter-of-fact smile she knew so well from 20 years ago. They laughed.

After they had eaten and left the restaurant, she pushed his chair along the boardwalk until they stopped at a bench where Gilda could sit and where he could have his chair next to her as they overlooked the harbour. Gilda wistfully said, 'It's as though that view goes on forever and then drops off the face of the Earth.' Kenneth leant over and gave her an extended peck on the cheek. She turned her face and lightly kissed his lips.

'You've no idea how often I dreamt of that,' he said. Her hand caressed his cheek as she smiled at him, 'It wouldn't have worked out, Kenneth.' and after a pause she continued, 'I don't know what love is but, I do know what love is not. Forgive me, Kenneth, I cared for you too much to put you through my insecurities. At least we can still be friends, very special friends.'

'Maybe you're right, maybe not... Mate,' he said grinning and giving her a gentle dig in the ribs. They both laughed as he had always called her 'mate'.

'Oh, look at the time! We'd better get back to the rink. They'll be back from shopping soon.' She jumped up in order to grab hold of the handles of his wheel chair. 'Wait,' he said holding her hands so that she sat down again, 'Let's keep in touch, Love, regularly in touch. I doubt I can come up to Brisbane but come down anytime you can. I'll pay the costs.' 'Yes, I promise.'

Kenneth then drove her back to the ice rink. She waved as he drove off. When he disappeared from sight, she made her way into the rink to meet Angelique.

'Hello, well how did the shoppers go,' Gilda asked as she saw the trio. 'Oh, the girls only had a bite to eat. They were too busy chatting to look at the shops,' Mrs Hurst said. 'Thank you so much, Mrs Hurst; it was very kind of you to take Angelique with you. 'No problem, please call me Jane. Angelique is a delight. We hope to see you both again on your next trip to Hobart. In the meantime, the girls can keep in touch.'

After they completed their farewells Gilda and Angelique made their way back to their hotel and almost as soon as they entered their room the phone rang. As she held the receiver, she addressed her daughter. 'Schatzi, Kenneth is on the phone and is asking us out to dinner tomorrow evening, is that okay with you?'

'Yes, of course, Mum.' 'Good, see you both tomorrow then at 7.00 PM at your hotel entrance.' Kenneth said before they hung up. 'He's a nice man, Mum.' 'Yes, he is Schatzi." Gilda then noticed that there her message light was on. After she accessed the message she said, 'Oh goodness,' she exclaimed, 'my mother is ill and is in hospital.' Gilda rang Ivan who confirmed that Hanna had been taken to a private hospital and that she should come back as soon as possible because it seemed serious. Gilda was able to change their flights to the next morning. She rang to tell Kenneth the situation, and that they were returning earlier to Brisbane. 'I'm so sorry, Kenneth, I really am,' she said.

'Does your mother know where you are?'

'Yes, I gave her a copy of our itinerary. She said she wanted to know where her granddaughter was.' 'I guessed as much,' Kenneth replied. 'You're not suggesting that my mother has faked being ill because she knows I'm in Hobart?' 'Never mind,' Kenneth said, you must go back just in case there is something wrong with her.' 'But, Kenneth, I can't believe that.'

'Sorry, Gilda, I'm sorry I mentioned that. I'll ring you end of next week. Okay?'

'Yes, of course.' Gilda was now suspicious. 'Surely, Hanna wouldn't do that? No, I can't believe it. Even she wouldn't be that conniving and stoop so low.'

When Gilda and Angelique returned to Brisbane, they immediately contacted Ivan to ascertain whether they ought to go directly to the hospital from the airport. He told her, 'I can't believe it. Hanna is on her way home in the ambulance. She had complained of heart pains and the doctors did tests, but nothing showed. They were going to hold her another day for observation but she perked up this morning and demanded to be sent home.'

'Ivan, did you tell her, we were coming home?' 'Yes, I did.' 'Okay, thanks, Ivan, we'll go home now. Mom will need to rest when she arrives home. Please tell her, I'll be in touch later today.'

'I can't believe it.' Gilda told Angelique, 'That dragon, that bloody dragon, she faked it so that my time in Hobart would be shortened. Is there nothing she won't manipulate? One day she'll cry wolf once too often.'

In the afternoon, Gilda rang her mother. 'Hello, Mom, I hear you're feeling better.' 'Yes, Darrrling,' Hanna replied, breathing heavily. 'Good, then I won't disturb you,' Gilda replied matter-of-factly. 'How was the trip,' Hanna asked in her sweetest voice.

'Good thanks. You'd better rest. Good bye.' And with that, Gilda hung up, 'That'll cheese her off. Serves her right.'

The following week, Gilda's answering machine recorded several messages from her mother. They remained unanswered.

CHAPTER 32
1994-1995

On a cloudless, hot Sunday morning in January 1994, Gilda and Angelique were sitting on the back deck eating Viennese pancakes dripping in different savoury and sweet toppings. 'Umm, I love these Palatchinken. I could have them for every breakfast,' Angelique gushed. 'Me too,' Gilda agreed, 'one of the best dishes to come out of Vienna.'

They sat eating and listening to the birds in the trees and the clucking of their two chickens in a downstairs pen. Perro sat on his rug at their feet and beautiful music played from the kitchen radio. 'Ah, isn't this idyllic,' Angelique asked. 'Yes,' her mother murmured as though in a trance. Suddenly she sat up like a bolt of lightning. 'Okay, I have an announcement to make.' 'Oh, heavens that sounds ominous,' her daughter joked and laughing added. 'Not sure I'm up to it this early in the day. Well come on, enough with the suspense,' Angelique coaxed as Gilda remained silent.

'Right…' Gilda began, 'It is my 50th birthday this year and, it's time for some major changes. First of all, I'll sell this house and buy a newer, larger one. The baby grand piano will then have a better placement so that you can teach piano as an income when you are ready for University in a couple of years. 'Okay, I approve so far,' her daughter said with mock solemnity. 'Secondly, I'll agree to the divorce your father is asking for – he'll pays all costs, of course, because it's his girl-friend who is pushing for the divorce so she can become socially respectable.' They both burst out laughing. 'Okay, so far? I'll telephone a couple of real estate agents and see who has time to come around today.

An agent came that afternoon who, based on Gilda's requirements, identified four possible houses on his books. He drove the women to three nearby properties in Corinda but they were unsuitable. 'Now that we have those three out of the way, I think you'll find the one we're going to inspect now will be just right,' the agent assured them. After five minutes, Gilda saw the direction he took as they headed towards Durack and asked, 'Isn't this a bit too far out?'

'Not at all,' the agent assured her, 'The Motorway into the city is just ahead of us and the house is then five minutes further. The city centre is 20 minutes away on the Ipswich Motorway.'

Gilda had always liked living high up, either on a hill or a high-set house. Once they turned off the main road, they went downhill. 'I'm not sure I would like living in a gully,' she said.

'It's actually not in a gully; it's half-way down the hill but there are other houses further down,' responded the real estate agent.

They turned into the street and pulled into a driveway. It was a low-set brick house on the hilly-side of the street, located on an elevated block of land which had a well-manicured garden. 'Come inside, you'll be surprised,' the agent said.

After they had looked at three bedrooms they walked through the L-shaped lounge-dining room which had an archway to the kitchen. From that part of the house, a sliding door lead to a patio which framed a lovely view of the terraced back garden and trees.
As they headed for the back door, the agent said, 'And now, ladies, the surprise!' He ushered them into a spacious, newer, one-bedroom fully self-contained unit made of the same brick as the main house. The unit also had an open-plan lounge dining room, and combined bathroom and laundry. Another sliding door led to the back patio and the terraces. The unit had its own front entrance at the side of the main house.

'This is perfect for the grand piano and as a casual eating area,' said Gilda, 'The present bedroom could be my study,' said Gilda.

'Angelique, you could have two of bedrooms in the house as your bedroom and study.'

Angelique went to both kitchens and tried the drawers. 'Good, the drawers don't stick they are pulled out and pushed shut,' she said. 'Oh, you and your drawers,' Gilda laughed. Angelique perpetually complained about the drawers in the kitchen of the old house they currently lived in. They then walked from the unit through the house again and around the garden, and then up to the top of the terraces. 'So, what do you think?" the salesman asked. 'It has possibilities,' Gilda replied. 'We will think about it and get back to you.'

When they arrived back at Corinda, the two women went to the deck to discuss the house. 'I just don't know that suburb, Durack, or the area,' Gilda said, 'I really like the house and the adjoining unit; it's perfect for what we need. If only the house was in another suburb.'

'Well, it's close to the ice rink and to school,' Angelique pointed out, 'much closer than from where we are now.' 'Yes, and the price is good because it's an unknown suburb. I guess I've always lived in the Western suburbs; this is South-West Brisbane. How about I put the house on the market and see what happens.'

Before committing to the new property Gilda drove there several times with Angelique and they both agreed that they would like to live there.

Gilda was able to quickly sell her house because it was on two blocks of land. The Brisbane City Council had recently changed the building block land regulations for private dwellings and two houses could now be built on the present block.

Within a month all formalities and payment had been settled and they moved in. Gilda had security bars installed before they took possession, just as she had done in the previous house.

By evening on the removal day mother and daughter were exhausted. Apart from the furniture and the grand piano, which was professionally moved, they did the rest by themselves. Gilda waited about a month till they had settled in before she rang Hanna. Hanna rarely now rang Gilda. 'Hello Mom,' she said when a female voice answered. 'Yes, what do you want?' 'How are you?' 'I'm busy. What do you want?' 'I wanted to invite you and Ivan over for lunch to our new house in Durack.' 'It's too far.' 'When you go to the continental butcher, you could come then. We're only five minutes from him.' 'No, we don't know the way.' 'I could meet you at the butcher's shop and you could follow me home.' 'Then we still have to get home. It's too far. In any case, I'm not interested. You've probably done something stupid again.'

Gilda couldn't believe what she just heard. 'What did you say?' 'No one moves house so often unless they made a mistake,' said Hanna. You have always done stupid things and now is no different. I'm busy now,' and hung up.

Gilda sat holding the phone. 'What's up Mum?' Angelique asked. 'Oh, nothing.' 'That was Oma, wasn't it?' 'Yes.' Then Gilda told her daughter what had transpired. When she had finished, she asked, 'Why does she hate me so much? She's always hated me. But why?' Angelique didn't know what to say. Gilda pulled herself together and said, 'Never mind. 'So ist es', that's the way it is. Let's not ruin our day.'

Gilda would see Alexei when he came to pick their daughter up. Sometimes he would bring the girlfriend, Anita, other times not. They had a volatile relationship and they were always fighting. Twice they had broken off the relationship but both times had re-started.

One afternoon Alexei said, 'Gilda, Anita is insisting that I divorce you. Do you mind?' "Why should I mind,' said Gilda, 'it's been five years. You're the one wanting the divorce so you pay for it.'
Up until now, Alexei hadn't paid any child support but Gilda had been able to receive the full Child Endowment payment from the federal government. Alexei would only pay if Angelique wanted an item such as a dress when they were out together. This didn't happen often because Gilda preferred to take care of such things herself so as not to be indebted to him.

'Anything interesting in the mail today, Mum?' Angelique asked one day.

'Bills, bills and more bills and one from the Child Endowment Department. Oh, and here's a juicy bit of mail, the divorce papers.'

Gilda opened the envelope and read. 'Oh, that bloody idiot, Alexei has told the solicitor that he pays for your clothes. Why the hell would he say that? It's simply not true.'

She then opened the Child Endowment letter. 'I knew it. As soon as they saw the false claim that I'm getting money from your father they've cut the endowment payments completely.'

'What do you mean?' Angelique asked.

'Because your father said that he buys all your clothes, the Department made a calculation and based on that and as a consequence, I'm not eligible for any payments at all. Never mind, Schatzi. How about you take Perro for a walk before it gets too late?'

After her daughter had left Gilda rang Alexei. Foregoing pleasantries she demanded, 'Why did you say you buy Angelique's clothes?' 'I didn't say that, I told the solicitor that I buy some. 'Tell me what you have bought? A scarf? A cheap skirt at a sale? What else? Tell me, tell me, because I don't know of anything else!' There was silence on the other end.

'Do you realise that because of your brilliant remark, the Child Endowment payment has been completely cancelled? What do you think you should do now?' She waited for an answer but none came. 'Well, Alexei what I could do is go to a solicitor and demand alimony for the time remaining till she is 16 but I'm not going to risk that you are entitled to any custody whatsoever. That was why I didn't insist on official payments all these years. I didn't want that you have any official claim on her, and have you ruin her life. But how do you think she feels when she sees that you, her own father, doesn't financially support her at all? What are you going to do about it?'

After a pause during which Gilda could hear him puffing at a cigarette. He said, 'What do you want me to do?'

'Ideally, get out and stay out of our lives. It's not up to me to tell you what you should be paying or doing for OUR daughter. You've always been good at avoiding making decisions. Don't think I haven't heard what you've been telling people about how I always made the decisions and never gave you a chance. Yes, that's true because nothing would have been decided if I didn't take charge. Well, you can stop crying 'poor me' because, although the friends you had turned against me want to be friends again, I'm not interested. They are all yours but they've seen right through the charade. As for paying, think about paying for her university fees!' It was months later that Angelique told Gilda that Alexei had asked her what he should pay for her. Gilda was horrified but decided to leave it as she didn't want her daughter to get into trouble from her father for having told her. As Gilda suggested, he paid Angelique's annual university fees.

Gradually, the two girls were comfortably settled in the new house plus unit. One evening over dinner, Gilda said, 'How would you like to have a house-warming party? You could invite kids you skate with and any other friends from school and their parents and I'll invite my Coffee Club friends from skating.' 'That sounds great,' said Angelique, 'When?' A date was decided.

Guests, including the immediate neighbours started to arrive at the appointed time on the evening of the party. 'Oh, my goodness,' said Gilda, 'everyone is bringing a plate as well as alcohol. We have so much food now.' The house was perfect for entertaining. It was all one level going out the two sliding doors to the patio, one from the house and the other from the unit. 'There are tables and chairs on the top terrace,' Gilda informed everyone, 'There's a beautiful view of the mountains from up there.'

Music played and people danced wherever there was room inside and outside. Others were involved in philosophical discussions, and others talked skating. As the evening wore on the children sat in front of the television set and watched, 'Mary Poppins.' The boys complained until the girls told them to be quiet.

All parties end and when everyone had left there wasn't much to clean up because all the guests helped with the party tidy-up. After the last pecks were deposited on cheeks, Gilda locked the front door. Angelique came to her mother and put her arms around her and said, 'That was the best party ever.'

'Yes, Schatzi, it was very special.'

Gilda was busy at work. She prepared to go to Budapest in November as the team leader for the Australian contingent to the World Junior Figure Skating Championships. Angelique was to go as the Assistant Team Leader. The Australian team consisted not only of the skaters but the full complement of Australian international judges. The competition was to be spread over seven days but there were training days in Budapest before the starting date of the Championships. After the event, Gilda and Angelique planned to visit Austria for four weeks.

The plane landed at Budapest's Ferihegy International Airport. Alighting from the plane, the air was cold and a sharp wind cut their faces. A car waited to take them to the Inter-Continental Hotel. When it stopped at the hotel, the two women looked at each other astounded. 'Have you seen anything so gorgeous,' Gilda asked looking at the hotel as she waited for the driver to open her door. The hotel was the epitome of old world glamour, glitz and elegance but modernised with the latest comforts. Multiple times daily until the small hours of the morning there were shuttle buses between the hotel and the ice rink.

'Look, Mum, there are the Canadian Pairs Champions, Barbara Underhill and Paul Martini, World Champions and Olympic reps.' Angelique could hardly contain her excitement. She had always been a fan of theirs. They were commentators for this event. 'Where?'

'Over there at the round marble pillar near the chandelier. 'And look, there are the Russian singles skaters, Ilia Kulik and Irina Slutskaya.'

'We'd better get to our room quickly before you jump out of your skin, Missy'. Oh, but it's so fabulous seeing these people in real life. I can't believe I'm here.' They went up to their room. It had a broad panoramic view over the Buda and Pest Rivers and as customary, the Budapest castle was lit up every evening.

Gilda had now slipped into her organising mode, 'We'd better get to bed early as we have to be at the rink at 5.00 AM. Meals are available 24 hours in the dining room so we'll go downstairs on the way to the bus and pick up some food for the first practices. We can have a hot breakfast when we return at 9.00 am. 'I won't mind going to bed early,' replied Angelique, 'I'm beat. I didn't realise how tired I was till I came back to the room.'

The next morning, they saw Australia's Single Ladies' skater, Joanne Carter; she was Australia's hope to do well and she did. Of the 45 entries from 45 countries, she not only made the cut off after the Short Program but she also skated the Long Program, coming 19th overall; a magnificent feat accompanied by ecstatic applause.

With the Championships completed, Gilda and Angelique caught the train for the 2.5 hour ride to Vienna. 'What a nuisance that there are no escalators or lifts. These damn suitcases weigh a ton when you have to carry them up and down stairs,' Gilda complained as they searched for their platform at the station. 'I'm so glad we're going first class,' Angelique commented, 'The seats are cushioned and not wooden benches. Two hours on those and you'd have a sore butt.'

The scenery leaving Budapest was typical of many cities, industrial warehouses and factories polluting the decrepit-looking workers' abodes. The train gained speed and Budapest's slums were left behind to be replaced by the Hungarian countryside. Animals were mostly in shelters protected from the winter cold. Fields were empty of vegetation and lay dormant before spring planting commenced. The odd farmer was out checking fences that had rotted under the weight of frost and snow. Smoke from chimneys billowed skywards connecting with stray clouds in the grey sky. The monotonous, rhythmic clatter of train wheels on steel rails lulled Angelique to sleep and Gilda was left with her thoughts. 'What an adventure this has been. Even the last five years since I left Alexei. I could never have dreamed all this would happen. I'm starting to understand what I've read, "Be clear on what you want and let the God, the Universe, Spirit, Source, the ethers, whatever it's called, take care of how it will come about".'

Gilda mused over that for a few moments before her thoughts took over again, 'I wanted to be free again, to give myself and Angelique the opportunity to create our lives the way we wanted them, together and independently. I still don't know where I got the courage to leave Alexei. I hadn't planned it. It just happened that fateful day. I'm going to call that "something" that orchestrates my life 'God'. I know that many books say that people object to that but for me God is NOT from any religion, God is the Higher Entity that takes care of "How" when I know my WHY and WHAT.' Gilda gave a chuckle as she caught herself. 'Oops, I'm starting to sound like I'm on a soapbox, heaven forbid! My way of seeing things is right for me, I won't inflict them on Angelique; she must find her path for herself. I'm not going to ram my beliefs down her throat.' It made her feel good having articulated and clarified what had been mystifying her about how her life was evolving. 'I'll call this trip from Budapest to Vienna the Revelation Journey.'

She tried to contain her laughing but was unsuccessful and it woke Angelique. 'What's so funny,' asked a sleepy Angelique. 'Oh, nothing.' Gilda smilingly replied. 'Don't tell me you've had another revelation?' That was it, Gilda really laughed out loud now, 'Ah, I knew you were psychic,' Gilda managed to get out between laughing fits.

The four weeks in Austria were perfect. After staying in Vienna a few days, they travelled south to Salzburg, staying there and seeing the surrounding sights including the lakes where 'The Sound of Music' was filmed. Snow even fell to add to the atmosphere and then further south over the Grossglockner Mountain, Austria's highest peak to Klagenfurt for a few days to Graz, before heading back to Vienna.

In 1995, Angelique started her final year of high school, Grade 12. She was voted one of six Prefects to assist the Head Girl with student affairs and liaising with academic administration. She was thrilled and had never expected that she would have such a position.

Despite Gilda's efforts to help her daughter develop her self-confidence, a lot of damage could not be undone from her early years. She was also exposed to those influences everytime she visited her father. Comments such as, 'You've put on weight', 'Your skin is blotchy,' 'What's the matter with you, are you getting moody like a typical teenager?' 'It was just a joke,' he would say when he insulted her.

Although Alexei could dish out insults he couldn't take any retaliatory criticism. Many a friend was 'excommunicated' for having said something that Alexei took as an insult, even when it wasn't. He tended to put people on a pedestal from which they would fall at the slightest remark. He also did that with Angelique. She never knew how he would be when she went to see him. Her position as a school prefect meant a great deal to her. Even Hanna came to the induction ceremony.

Gilda continued her education in the ice skating field. She obtained her Level 1, Sports Specific, Ice Skating Accreditation, and Level 1 and Level 2 Sports Administration. 'I think the next study I should undertake is a business training course. I need to know how I can better market the sport and make it more mainstream in Australia.'

One Sunday when she was home alone Gilda started to read one of her personal development books which dealt with healing retreats undertaken by a group of people on the northwest coast of the USA. 'Oh, my goodness, doesn't that sound heavenly? I would love to go on something like that.' Her reveries were interrupted by the phone. 'Wonder who that could be?' 'Hey Gilda, how are you,' a female voice said at the other end. 'Joan? I'm great. This is a surprise. How are you?' Joan was a friend of Gilda's who lived in Sydney. She had been married to John, the ice skating coach who had come to work in Brisbane. Joan and John had moved to Sydney because opportunities for both of them were better there. They had since gone their separate ways and Gilda remained friends with both.

'What are you up to?' Gilda asked. 'Not much, having a lazy Sunday and I thought of you.' 'Oh, I see. You only think of me when you have nothing better to do, eh,' Gilda joked feigning being hurt. 'You know better than that,' Joan replied as though she had taken the bait. 'Listen, honey, I'm going for a 3-day weekend retreat in August at Picton, just outside Sydney; that's a month away. I wondered if you can also come.'

'Seriously? You won't believe this. I'm just reading about a retreat and had said, that I'd love to go on one. Now you ring and tell me about a retreat that you're going on.' 'There you are honey,' said Joan, 'divine intervention. What do you say? Can you get time off work?' 'I'm sure I can. I work long hours and they are very good that way. I'll just have to see about Angelique.'

Angelique could come too but I'm not sure that she's in the headspace for this yet. It'll be quite an eye-opener for you also. Can she stay at home? She's old enough and she can have a girl-friend stay with her.' 'Yes, I suppose that's an option,' said Gilda.' She'd love it. I can have an adult call in and keep an eye on them. I'll also tell one of the neighbours.'

Gilda was tremendously excited, 'Count me in!' 'Fabulous! I'll send you the program,' Joan replied excitedly. 'This is just what you need, honey.'

Gilda could hardly wait for the Picton retreat in August. She flew to Sydney and Joan picked her up from the airport. 'Good that you took the first flight out of Brisbane. It's only 90 kilometres to Picton from Sydney, so we should get to the farm by 10.00 AM,' Joan informed Gilda after they had hugged.

'You have no idea how excited I am. I read what you sent but, as you said, most of it is new to me.' 'No worries,' said Joan, 'you'll be fine. They are a great bunch of people. There'll be women and men of all ages.'

After they left the city and drove along the highway for about 30 minutes, Gilda exclaimed, 'This is truly beautiful countryside. I read up on the area; sheep and cattle farming were important industries in the early days. Now there are a lot of 'alternative lifestyle' occupations there.

'Yes, it is so tranquil and beautiful with a better feel about it than city life.'

Finally, Joan turned off the highway into driveway where a large sign flapped in the wind announcing that they had arrived at the Earth to Ethereal Retreat. They drove under an extensive arbour that in spring and summer would have been loaded with flowers. Now in winter the arbour's dried branches still looked majestic and extended the full length of the driveway leading to a closed gate. 'Hello, there,' a cheerful voice called. Joan and Gilda looked around. 'Over here,' the voice invited. To the right, they saw a middle-aged woman approaching them riding a horse. 'You're just in time for a hot cuppa and freshly baked pumpkin scones with buckets of fresh cream and jam.'

Both friends laughed and Gilda said, 'I like this place already.'

'Eat as much as you like,' the voice called, 'You'll work it off on the horses before we go to lunch.'

'Do they think of everything in relation to the next meal?' Joan added beaming.

Joan parked the car and they walked to the bungalows where they found one with their names on the door. The interior was simple, a single bed for each with a night table in between. Gilda opened her drawer. 'Oh, my God look what I found in my draw,' she said holding up a metal figurine of an owl, 'I've always felt an affinity with owls.' Joan looked in her drawer; there was an eagle. She picked it up in amazement, 'I have an affinity with eagles. How would they know that about us?' Each sat silently on her bed, holding her gift, lost in thought.

'This is an uncanny start,' Gilda said breaking the silence. 'Hey, anyone home,' a voice asked. 'Yes, come on in,' Joan replied. 'Hello, I'm Athena, the organiser of this event. I do Psychic Drawings. I'll be doing one for each of you over the weekend.' 'Did you put the gifts in our drawers,' Gilda asked. 'What gifts? I haven't put any gifts anywhere,' said Athena.

Both Gilda and Joan showed her. 'Oh, how interesting,' Athena responded. 'Funny things go on here on retreats. Good things, but don't be surprised at anything that happens. It's all for the best. Good start!' And with that she hurried away adding, 'Meet you at the horse corral in an hour; we're all going horse riding.'

'Since we only have an hour, may as well unpack and get to know what the various buildings are,' Gilda suggested. 'Sounds good to me,' Joan replied.

Both women went about their unpacking in silence, engrossed in their thoughts about what had thus far eventuated. In sync and still in silence they finished getting organised and headed for the door to explore the compound before heading for the corral.

Kim from the property was to be their guide as they rode along a narrow trail. 'Anyone a bit apprehensive on a horse,' Kim asked. Hands went up. 'Okay, I'll give each of you a gentler horse,' said Kim. Gilda was amongst that group. Joan had ridden all her life and was comfortable with her allocated mount.

They rode one behind the other. Those more experienced in the front with Gilda's group at the rear. They came to an open paddock and the horses grazed while their riders rested. Suddenly, Gilda's horse decided to walk toward the path. She tried to turn his head back to the group but he gently nudged Gilda in his favoured direction.

'Gilda, tug Jimbo's rein to the left to come back,' Kim called. 'I'm trying to, but he wants to go to the path.' At that moment,

Jimbo started to trot and all Gilda could do was concentrate on holding on. Once the horse was on the path he cantered, gradually quickening his gait until he was galloping. 'Holy shit,' Gilda thought, 'What do I do now? Just hold on I suppose.'

The horse was in full flight. Gilda was strong so she was able to hold on and soon she got the gist of moving with the horse and allowed the horse to do its thing. 'Wow, this is amazing. What a feeling,' she thought when suddenly she saw a low-hanging branch over the path ahead. It wasn't going to be an issue for the horse but it would be an issue for Gilda if she stayed upright.

'Holy cow, I'm going to have to duck or be knocked off the horse.' Gilda ducked, her head beside the horse's neck just like riders in Western movies.

Jimbo slowed down when he approached a clearing and came to a halt. Only then did Gilda sit upright on the horse. When he stopped, Gilda dismounted and went to face the horse, 'What did you think you were doing? You're supposed to be a gentle fellow, tame for types like me.' The horse nuzzled her and snorted as though he was laughing. Gilda laughed too and patted him. She immediately felt an incredible bond and love for the horse. He had taught her so much about herself in that short encounter, that she could think quickly in times of urgency and keep calm, and that she did have a high degree of confidence, something that she sometimes doubted. Gilda held her head next to the horse's cheek and he didn't move. 'Jimbo, thank you,' she said with tears of joy pouring down her cheeks and wetting his.

The others arrived and all called, 'Are you okay, Gilda? Are you alright?'

Gilda put her arms around Jimbo's neck and said, 'Yes, I've just had the best ride of my life and I thoroughly enjoyed it. I felt so safe on him that I let the bridle loose and let him take control. Kim, I was meant to experience that, please don't go mad at him or hold it against him. He did me an enormous favour. If I can only let life take its course like I did during that ride, nothing can go wrong.'

Turning back to Jimbo she said, 'You taught me that, you magnificent creature. I'm going to miss you. I'll never forget you.'

By the time the riders returned and took care of the horses, the sun was sinking and twilight started. Everyone then went to get ready for dinner and for the post-dinner program. There were a variety activities ranging from aura-soma, psychic drawing, numerology, psychic reading and healing modalities. Two-and-a-half hours were set aside each evening for everyone to attend demonstrations on topics of interest. There was an introductory talk on the first night and when all sessions were over they all met in the spacious lounge, warmed by a large open wood fire, and talked about the day and their impressions. Cask wine accompanied the discussions which went for hours.

'I'm going to have a psychic drawing done tomorrow,' Gilda told Joan, 'I have no idea what to expect.' 'I think I'd like to go for a ride again,' Joan responded, 'Interested?' 'Cheeky,' Gilda replied giving her friend a mock-punch on the arm.

The next day, Gilda went to Athena who did the psychic drawings. She sat and waited for her art work to be completed. When Athena had finished, she turned it around and showed Gilda. 'I don't know what to say,' Gilda exclaimed, 'Athena, how did you come to that?' 'I just painted what came to me when I looked at you and within you, I saw there was someone else in your life who was equally if not more important to you than you are to yourself. Is that right?' 'Yes,' Gilda agreed, 'My daughter. What you cannot know is that my daughter has an affinity with mermaids and I have an affinity with owls. You painted a mermaid for the main picture, my daughter, and a smaller owl on a perch at the bottom of the picture, me. That is so us.' 'I only paint what I see in you,' replied Athena. 'I'm glad you like it and that it resonates with you.'

Gilda was speechless and couldn't take her eyes off the painting. It was a simple painting in two colours, but it was filled with meaning. This artist would not have known that Angelique loved representations of mermaids and Gilda, of owls. Gilda and Angelique each had quite a few ornaments in their respective symbol.

On the last night after the evening session when all were gathered in the lounge, Gilda spoke to the group, 'I have a request. I have recently been divorced and want a new last name. I've had a few last names in my life but now I want a permanent one for the new me.'

They all laughed and so she explained what she meant by having a few surnames.

'After doing the Numerology workshop, I was inspired to create a last name that would have all the attributes for a beautiful, balanced life. I want to keep my first name and I also want to keep the first letter of the name I was born with 'H'. Therefore, friends we have work to do! Oh, and by the way, I also want a name that no language can mutilate AND it must be a neutral name that is not associated with any nationality. As of tonight, I am a Citizen of the Universe.'

'I'll drink to that,' said one fellow. Another fellow said with a big smile, 'You don't want much do you?' Gilda pointed and wagged her finger at him in mock reprimand. 'To work, Mister! she commanded.

An hour or so later, after much hilarity, partly due to the heat, partly to the wine and partly because of the crazy names the group came up with, success was achieved.

'From tonight on, I will be known as GILDA HOLLTEN.' Gilda triumphantly announced, 'I'll change my name by deed poll when I get back home to make it official.'

And so a new signature energy field was activated for Gilda.

CHAPTER 33
1996-1997

By 1996, Gilda's life was almost consumed by her work at the ice rink, dealing with maintenance needs of her house and exchanging her car. She didn't travel as much for work because all the groundwork had been done. Outwardly, it was a peaceful time. She had less and less contact with her mother who had made it clear that their worlds were much apart, Hanna being an academic while Gilda lowered her station from teaching to working in an office. Angelique was now in her first year at Griffith University and making new friends.

While all seemed peaceful on the surface, Gilda still had her inner demons. She couldn't put her finger on what was going on inside but she would over-eat and over-drink when alone. 'I don't know what's wrong with me,' she reprimanded herself. 'I have a great job and a house I love, and Angelique is healthy and happy. I have nothing to complain about and yet I feel something is missing. It's not a man, heaven forbid, been there, done that. It's just…It's just that I'm not developing and I don't know what to do or how to change that.'

'I want to find out more about these strange happenings I've experienced, such as when I got off the boat on Lake Geneva, some years later in Paris when 'something' or 'someone' held me back from crossing the street. If that hadn't held me back, I would be dead, hit by a bus going full pelt through a red light. It was on my left side and I didn't see him coming. Another time driving down the hill of the Toowong cemetery when my car went into a time warp otherwise a car on the wrong side of the road would have hit me and again I'd be dead, Angelique possibly too as she was in the car with me.'

'What about when I died giving birth to Angelique. Oh, yes, when I was on a Healing retreat at Warwick and I felt the difference in the temperature when I entered the tree-lined path and then when I went out of it. That wasn't the weather. There was something special there. Or when I stood on the grate and felt the exorcism of negative energies as I had a shaking fit; I even had a witness there.' 'When I rode Jimbo at Picton, that wasn't just me, that was something else within me in control, and other instances I can't remember at the moment. All of these things were real, perhaps more real than I feel that my daily world is. But how do I find out about that dimension? There's more to life than this! I KNOW it, I FEEL it.'

Towards the end of the first quarter of the year, Gilda went to Daniel, the President of Ice Skating Australia, 'Is this a convenient time to talk to you, Daniel? It'll take about 10 minutes.'

'Yes, of course, Gilda, What's on your mind?'

'I want to promote ice skating so that it becomes better known by the broader public, so that it becomes more mainstream. It's the ideal sport for hot climates and is an all-round activity for fitness, fun, artistry, creativity, camaraderie and longevity. The cold is also good for the skin.'

'It would be more popular if more people were as passionate about the sport as you are, 'he joked, 'What do you have in mind?'
'I've been researching courses that can educate me in improving my business savvy. The Australian Institute of Management (AIM) has a great six months' course that includes all aspects of business management and marketing. It's an immersion program of a full-time week each month with assessment, and the other three weeks I'd be at the office. My office work contributes to the practical assessment. Here are four copies of the program so that you and the other three Executive can peruse it and decide for yourselves if you think it's worthwhile for me to attend.'

'Just like you to be so thorough, Gilda,' Daniel responded with a smile and said, 'Thank you, I'd be delighted to look at the prospectus, as will the others. Will it be okay to let you know in a week?'

'Yes that would be fine. The course doesn't start till June. I'm just asking for the time off and I'll pay for the course,' Gilda said. Gilda left elated, she had a good feeling about it and she desperately wanted to pursue that study.

A week later, Daniel called her into his office. 'Gilda, the other Executive and I have discussed your proposal in great detail and we support your request. We have decided that we will allow you to have the time off on full pay and the Association will also pay for the course and other expenses you might incur such as parking.' Gilda was speechless. The course cost was over $10,000. 'I don't know what to say, thank you. I'll come back evenings when I don't have work to complete for the following day and check correspondence and anything else that needs immediate attention.'

Gilda could hardly wait till June.

Her first subjects were 'Introduction to Personal Computers', 'Accounting for Non-Accountants and 'Planning, Budgeting and Cost Control.' 'The computer subject will be fine but the other two, yikes.' After looking at the total course content, she said, 'Yep, I knew it would be all that Profit and Loss Balance Sheet, Assets, Liabilities, Income Statement Accounts, and Depreciation and so on. I'm glad we have a Treasurer. I will get the hang of it but it's not my greatest area of interest.' 'Ah, this is more my stuff, Effective Communication, Principles of Management, Writing Effective Managerial Reports.' There were nine other subjects and Gilda found them very interesting and clearly saw how the course content would help her in managing and marketing ice-skating as a sport. On 29 November, 1996, Gilda graduated. 'Gosh, this was an exhilarating experience. I've learned so much. I couldn't have ever believed that there was so much to running a business. Basically what I'm doing is running a business.'

To further her education, in November, Gilda enrolled in and successfully completed the Queensland Justice of the Peace (JP) accreditation course. She thought, 'I would have liked to study law but I wouldn't have had the maturity or the staying power when I was younger. Mom always said that I had no patience, that I couldn't stick at anything, didn't focus on details and that I was immature for my age. Oh, well. I'm happy where I am.'

Shortly after, when mother and daughter were sitting watching a travel show on TV, Gilda asked Angelique, 'What'll we do for Christmas this year?' 'I don't know, Mum. Did you have something in mind?' 'Not really,' said Gilda, 'but it's been such a full-on year, we need to treat ourselves. What do you reckon?'

'Sounds good to me.'

'How about we go somewhere for about 10 - 12 days? Somewhere not too far that we don't travel for days on end.' 'How about some island,' Angelique offered. 'Yep, that sounds good. We've been to New Caledonia, Fiji and Vanuatu. Tahiti is expensive, I've heard. Where else?'

'What about the other direction? How about Bali? We just saw something about it on TV.'

'Brilliant idea. You're a genius! Yes, that's it. Is that okay with you?'

'It's my idea, isn't it?' Angelique replied cheekily. Gilda jumped up, grabbed her daughter and gave her a squeeze, and asked, 'Do you want to do some research on the internet and I'll get some brochures from the travel agent?'

And so the two weeks before Christmas, Gilda and Angelique went to Bali. After they arrived and settle into their hotel in Sanur, it was time to plan their stay.

'You know what, Mum, I like what the man at reception said about hiring a private car for the day and having a local take us around. What do you think?' 'Yes, I do too.' The following day they waited at the hotel foyer for their private transport. A man jumped out of a four-wheel drive car and approached them. Mother and daughter could see a couple in one of the back seats and a young girl in the front seat.

'Hello, and welcome to Bali,' the man said enthusiastically with a big smile, 'I am your driver today. My name is Ben. Follow me to the car and I'll introduce you to the other people on the tour.' They followed him and when they approached the car, they saw a 13 year old girl holding a little monkey.

'OMG,' exclaimed Angelique,' 'It's a monkey and it's alive.' 'Yes, it belongs to my daughter Laila. He is called Monk.' They learned that it was short for 'monkey' and that Ben and Laila were their tourist companions for the day. Colin, a young Australian, was the Assistant Manager at the hotel and his girlfriend Gisele, a ballet dancer with the Western Australian Ballet company, was visiting from Perth. All six were soon chatting like old friends. Monk sat on Laila's shoulder the whole time.

Halfway through the day, the couple and Gilda and Angelique were discussing further travel around the area and they all agreed to hire Ben the following day to further explore Bali's hinterland and along Bali's northern coastline.

Before the end of the second day, Ben took them to his house to meet the whole family. The Aussies were amazed how big the family was; it seemed to have as many inhabitants as a Balinese village. Everyone was very friendly and welcomed the tourists into their world. They showed them the new temple they were building for their clan's religious ceremonies. They gave the visitors exquisite mementos of their visit - everyone was touched by this generosity. We all thanked Ben for welcoming us into his home and meeting his family. We all thought it an unforgettable and incredible experience. This was really the highlight of their Bali visit. After Ben and Laila left, Angelique and Gilda went up to their hotel room. 'That was amazing. Pity Ben was booked up tomorrow; we could have gone with him again,' Gilda said.

'Yes,' Angelique agreed, 'what really struck me was how little these people have compared to us and yet how happy and hospitable they are, and without exception it's not for the tips or any ulterior motive; they just are genuinely happy. I'm not sure I can say that of many people back home.'

'Nope,' Gilda replied, 'makes you wonder, doesn't it?'

Gilda and Angelique always sent Hanna postcards from wherever they went although Hanna never acknowledged that she received them. They would always ask if she received them, and then, a curt 'Yes' was the reply.

The 1997 work year started and, although Gilda tried to implement strategies and ideas she had learned at the AIM, each of the figure skating arms were independent of each other and fiercely intent on keeping things that way. Each guarded their autonomous status and largely had a 'them and us' attitude.

Gilda could also see that the international results did not improve and she was concerned that the Australian Sports Commission could reduce or withdraw the funding that provided her salary.

She sat in her office pondering her next move when the phone range. 'Hello, Gilda, here is a voice from the past. It's Mary from Ipswich Girls Private College.' It took Gilda a second to register, 'Well, hello, this is a surprise. How are you?' 'I'm great. I've rung to ask you a favour.' 'Sure, fire away, you know I can't refuse you anything,' Gilda joked.

'Well, we'll see,' Mary replied. 'I'm taking four weeks long service leave in October and I was wondering if you would be available to replace me for that time. You know I'm Head of the German Department so you'd have those duties as well. I can't think of any one as good as you to replace me or who I'd entrust my department to.'

Gilda was floored. She had to digest what she had just heard but then she said determinedly, 'Yes, I'd love to.' Inwardly she said, 'This is another one of those instances. I ask for something and it comes to me, heavens!'

'Fabulous, you're an Angel. Mrs Trundle, the Principal, will also be pleased.'

'But she doesn't know me.'

'No, but she knows all about you and I've already filled her in.' When they hung up, Gilda had a massive smile on her face, Now, don't tell me that there isn't someone 'up there' looking after me', she said out loud this time. Angelique was out so she had to contain her excitement till she returned.

Gilda had leave owing to her and she was able to take the four weeks off without a problem. There were no competitions and no imminent ones; it was a quiet period for figure skating.

Unexpectedly, Hanna rang end of September. 'Gilda, this is just a short call. I'm organising Krampus. I want to know if you and your daughter are coming this year. 'Well, that's getting straight to the point,' Gilda thought. 'Hi, Mom, how are you?' she asked. 'Enough with that nonsense. Are you two coming or not?' 'We always come when you invite us for Krampus. I thought it was a tradition.' 'Very well, then we'll see you on Saturday, 6 December at 6.30 PM.' Hanna hung up.

'Who was that?' Angelique asked. 'Who gets to the point and never has a conversation on the phone?'

'Oma?' 'Jackpot' 'What did she want?' 'To invite us over for Krampus.' 'Already? It's only October tomorrow.' 'Yep. Who knows why? I said yes, Saturday, 6 December at 6.30 PM.'

Krampus is an Austrian celebration during which a devil-dressed man with a bag and whip accompanied by a papal-dressed man in white visits houses identifying children who have been good or naughty throughout the year. Good children receive nuts, nougat and chocolates in new shoes and naughty children are put into the devilish fellow's bag to be dealt with unless that child promises to be good the following year. All room and table decorations are in red. There is a lot of fun and hilarity. Both characters are usually played by uncles or male friends.

At the beginning of October, Gilda started at the Ipswich College. She went upstairs as directed to the foreign languages staff room.

'Hello, I'm Gilda,' she said as she entered the room. 'Hello and welcome,' came a cheery reply, 'I'm Helen, and I teach French. This is Marcel. He's Head of French.' Marcel waved because he was on the phone. 'The other two people will be here shortly. Sanae who teaches Japanese sits over there and Ina, who has multiple hats, sits there.'

Gilda laughed as Helen pointed to various desks and went directly to Mary's desk. Mary had left everything Gilda needed with multiple written instructions on how things worked for Form time, exam procedures, where the classroom was, and so on.

'What a gorgeous veranda,' Gilda exclaimed as she walked out of the small staff room with the windows. 'Yes,' commented Helen, 'The toilet is there and the long table is where we have lunch or escape from each other,' she added. 'There's also another toilet and two showers around the corner as you go to your classroom. It's great up here. We can escape from the 'madding crowd' that lives downstairs.'

'I know, I am going to be happy here,' thought Gilda, 'No wonder Mary has stayed here all these years.'

After meeting each class once, Gilda and the students got on well. She was back in her element. 'I have so much more to share with the students now than just the subject matter, I can casually include life experiences and integrate reading that I've done to help them develop to adulthood.' The girls also liked hearing about these experiences and had lots of questions. When Gilda did grounds duty, girls would come to her and ask more about various topics that had been to cut short in class because of lack of time.

One day she was called to the Principal's office. 'Come in Gilda, please sit down, invited the Head Mistress. 'I felt it time I welcomed you and that we met each other. Mary was right, you do fit in well with us and the girls are really enjoying your teaching. If a position became available for next year, would you be interested in teaching at the College?'

Gilda was surprised. She hadn't expected that. Yes, Mrs Trundle, I would certainly be interested. I would love to teach here.'

'Good, I was hoping you would say that. I don't have anything at the moment but things can change at short notice. It all depends on enrollments as to what extra subjects we can offer the girls.' With that the meeting ended.

Gilda walked off as though she were floating. 'I've obviously made a good impression; that's amazing. I love it here. The school has such an old-worldly elegance with modern amenities. Academically and technically, the school has the latest facilities. The girls are really nice as are the staff. The grounds are beautiful with ancient trees, rose bushes and gardens. I would love to work here,' she thought as she went back to the staff room. Gilda had some spare time before her final class and was able to digest, with some pleasure, the positive events of the day.

October came to an end and Gilda was sad to leave the college, 'Oh, well, moving on. Life goes on,' she said as she bounced back to her job, 'I like this work too and it's been good to me.'
Before long it was December and Christmas show rehearsals at the ice rink were in full force. Krampus at Hanna's was also upon them. 'Come, Schatzi, it's time to go to Oma's. Can't be late otherwise she'll bring it up the whole evening.' 'Yep, ready in a flash,' said Angelique, 'See you Perro, won't be long.'

Exactly at 6.30 PM they rang Hanna's front doorbell, 'Yes,' came the imperious greeting from inside. 'It's us,' Angelique called. 'Oh, yes, just on time.' Hanna replied opening the door and standing back. 'Hello, Mom, Hi, Ivan,' Gilda greeted. 'Hello, Oma, hello Opa,' Angelique said. 'Hello Darlings,' Ivan said jovially as he too came to the door, 'Come into the lounge. What you would you like to drink? Ivan asked. 'No, no, not in the lounge, we'll sit immediately at the table,' Hanna directed, 'The food is ready to serve. I've cooked long hours and I want it eaten when it's fresh and hot.' 'Nothing ever changes,' Gilda thought.

'Hello Danika,' Gilda greeted when she saw Ivan's daughter, 'Nice to see you again.' 'Nice to see you too.' Danika replied. Further pleasantries between Gilda and Danika were sharply terminated as Hanna took command of social proceedings, 'Ivan, you cut the meat and bring the salads in from the kitchen,' she ordered, 'everybody to the table'. She was in top commanding form. 'Angelique dear, take your elbows off the table. This meat was especially cut for me the way we have it in Vienna. Don't gobble it down, eat it slowly.' Gilda and Angelique, sitting side by side, kicked each other under the table. They then looked at Danika and each raised an eyebrow. 'Fine form, we're in for some evening,' was what that look implied.

Ivan brought the meat to the table and went back for the salads. 'What is that man doing?' Hanna complained and called, 'Ivan, the meat is getting cold, hurry up! What are you doing?' Hanna, annoyed and impatient, rose from her chair and went into the kitchen. All the others could hear was some of Hanna's muffled complaints. Then they both came out carrying serving dishes. When they had settled at the table, Ivan offered wine to Gilda. 'Yes, please, Ivan.' 'Not for me Daddy,' Danika got in first. Hanna then started dictating the finer points of eating, Viennese style, 'Gilda, you don't eat the herrings with the salad. You eat it with Kren, the horseradish, Hanna instructed as she saw her daughter commit a table faux-pas. 'I like it this way,' Gilda replied. 'You'll never learn how to eat properly. You are such a peasant. I don't know who you take after, certainly no one in my family. Gilda didn't reply and continued eating in the way that she preferred.

Hanna then turned her attention to Angelique, 'Oh my heavens, Angelique! That is no way to eat the herrings. You don't put tomato sauce on them. Who brought the tomato sauce? Take it away, Ivan, it's disgusting food,' 'I brought it,' said her granddaughter, 'I knew you didn't have any so I brought my own, just in case. I don't like herrings much and so I thought I'd drown them in sauce to make them edible.'

Everyone burst out laughing, except Hanna, who continued with, 'Gilda, your daughter is growing up to be a peasant just like you. You're getting fat too, however, you're not as fat as Danika, but still too fat, and you don't have the height to carry it. Danika is built like a house but she's at least taller.'

Everyone was aghast at Hanna's comments. 'Oma, that wasn't nice,' Angelique admonished her grandmother. Hanna responded, 'You'll understand when you are older that I am saying it for the best to improve your mother and Danika.'

And so the evening went on. Suddenly, Hanna said, 'You've all been here long enough, 1.5 hours. It's time for you to go. Ivan, you can start washing the dishes.'

Ivan didn't move. He had Dutch courage from the champagne and wine but he knew he would pay for it later. 'I'll turn my hearing-aid off and she can carry on all she likes. I won't hear a thing,' he said to himself, chuckling inwardly. Ivan cared deeply for Hanna but he had learned that when she was on this tangent, silence was the best course of action. She had long denied him her bed but he accepted that. Truth be told, he felt inferior to her. Despite strong and unbiased evidence of his talents and skills, his self-worth was low in her presence. Quite likely, Ivan believed Hanna's self-created story of her background; most people did.

Almost immediately after Hanna had issued her dictate, everyone rose and said their goodbyes. Hanna, as imperious as a dowager empress stood erect at the front door dissuading any closeness or affection. The door then slammed shut.

'Danika, I will see you at the next gala event - Christmas Eve - I guess,' Gilda said with a laugh. Danika just shook her head and replied resignedly and devoid of any enthusiasm said, 'I suppose so.' 'Well, Angelique, another Krampus bites the dust, let's go home.'

The two left for their peaceful love-filled sanctuary.

CHAPTER 34
1998-1999

Just after the holiday break beginning in January, 1998 as Gilda opened her office door, she saw a note on the floor. 'Who can this be from?' she thought. 'Gilda when you can, please ring me. Great news. Daniel.' 'Wow, I wonder if…. Oh, I hope so, that would be fabulous.' She put her things away and dialed.

'Daniel speaking,' a voice replied, 'It's Gilda, Daniel. How are you? What's the good news?' 'The Bid you submitted has been successful! Brisbane has been awarded the 2000 World Figure Skating Championships.' 'Really?' Gilda almost jumped out of her chair, 'That is amazing. Fabulous!' 'Yes, congratulations, you did a wonderful presentation. We now need to promote the event to get as many people to come from overseas as we can. How would you like to go to Minneapolis in March?'

'March, this year, to the USA?'

'Yes. The 1998 Championships are being held there and we can use the opportunity to promote our World Championships in advance'. 'Sure. I'd love to. I can get onto producing promo material right away. The badge templates are ready; they just need to be manufactured and it won't take long to design stickers and other souvenirs and have them produced.'

'Good,' Daniel said, 'I'll leave you to book your flight and accommodation. The State Association is sending two representatives to help you with logistics so that you will be free to mingle with officials from other countries and with office bearers from the International Skating Union to promote the event.'
After she hung up, Gilda had to digest what had just happened. 'How incredible is that the Bid I produced in addition to the costings the Treasurer calculated ensured that we won the Bid over other countries that wanted the 2000 Worlds. That is marvellous,' Gilda thought, 'I spent weeks on it and I have to agree that it is good, very comprehensive and beautifully laid out. It even included suggested travel options for various lengths of time before and after

the Championships. I'm so excited. In a few months I head for the USA, two weeks all expenses paid. I'll see if Barbara from the State Association wants to stay a week longer, we can go together to Los Angeles, Disneyland and maybe go south and do a Tijuana tour.' She paused and thought for a few minutes. 'Okay, to work, lots to do, globetrotter,' she joked to herself.

The weeks leading up to her departure were full on. Not only was it necessary to manufacture and produce various memorabilia but they also had to be air-freighted to the ice rink in Minneapolis. Departure day finally arrived. Gilda said her goodbyes to Angelique who couldn't accompany her, she was in her third year at Griffith University, her graduation year for her first degree. Barbara was on the same flight as was the other person from the State Association although they sat apart.

The trip from Brisbane to Minneapolis was long with a plane change in LA. 'It's freezing,' Gilda said when they left the terminal in Minneapolis and went out onto the street to hail a taxi. 'This must be what Antarctica feels like. What an icy wind.' Fortunately, they didn't have to wait long for a cab. The hotel was 5 Star and Gilda had her own room, while the other two shared.

Over dinner that evening, Gilda briefed her colleagues, 'I'll head to the rink at 5.00 AM tomorrow morning. I want to catch some of the officials who'll be watching the practices. It'll also give me a chance to see where all the parcels are that I sent over. What time are you guys coming?' 'We'll get there about 9.00 AM. Is that okay, replied Barbara. 'Sure, that's fine, I should have everything sorted by then.' The next morning, it was dark as Gilda headed for the ice rink. 'Good thing I found out about these connecting above-ground walkways that link all the buildings right through to the ice rink. The weather is glacial this morning, let alone creepy. It's still so dark outside. What an ingenious setup. These walkways mean that you don't have to go outdoors for almost a circle of a few kilometres. Gilda was well-prepared with warm clothing to brave the weather for the long walk to the ice rink, if necessary.

When Gilda arrived at the building which house the ice rink the inside temperature wasn't much different to the outside weather. This changed when she got to the offices and where people and skating associations had trade booths. She warmed up considerably after climbing numerous flights of stairs to get to her ultimate destination, the Australian booth, as yet unmanned.

'Bummer, that's no good. We're too high up. No one will find us unless they come especially up here because they know we're here. I'll see if I can have us shifted closer to the action. Doubt it but no harm in trying.' As Gilda expected, it wasn't possible because all spots had been allocated. 'Never mind, it'll just mean that one person will man the booth and the rest of us will circulate to tell people that we're up here. I might even be able to call on the parents of our competitors to help out a bit.'

Gilda's day was largely spent independently of her other two companions because she worked to a different agenda. Her job was public relations; wooing people from other countries to come to Brisbane when the Worlds were held in 2000.

Eleven hours later at 7.00 PM, Gilda left the rink. There was hardly any one left. 'I'll go down to the nice Chinese place I saw in the food hall to get some takeaway to take back to the hotel.' She went there and started chatting with the lady while the husband filled her dish. It was a family business but now just the husband and wife manned it because the children were at college in Michigan. 'It must be long hours for you both,' Gilda said. 'Yes', the owner replied, 'but, once a month, our cousin and his wife come for a day so we can have a break.

Almost every evening for the two weeks Gilda went to her Chinese friends. Each time she came they gave her more and more food till one time she said, 'Thank you so much that you always give me more, but I can't eat it. It's too much. Please just give me the normal amount.' So, instead, they would pack a sweet or give her a drink in her parcel without her knowing it until she arrived back at the hotel.

Midway through World Figure Skating Championships, Gilda was able to take time away from the rink and to go to the large mall called Mall of America. She stepped onto the bus and had only a $20 note to give to the driver. 'Sorry lady, you have to have the correct money and put it here,' the driver said pointing to a coin slot. 'Oh, sorry, I didn't know. I've just come from Australia and I don't have any coins.' 'Nothin' I can do. I don't handle money,' the driver drawled. Suddenly from behind, a man put coins into the slot and said, 'That's for your fare, lady. Enjoy your stay.' 'Oh, thank you but how can I repay you?' 'It's a welcome to America gift,' said the dark-skinned man who had inserted the coins.

The man was about to put money in the slot for himself, but the bus driver covered the slot and waved the man to go inside the bus. 'These people are amazing, so kind and generous,' thought Gilda. When the two weeks were over Gilda went to her Chinese takeaway for the last time. Only the husband was there. 'Where's your wife?' Gilda asked. 'She's not feeling well, so I told her to stay home. Sunday is not so busy; I can manage on my own. Tomorrow my cousins come.'

'I came to get my last dinner and to say goodbye,' Gilda said, 'Tomorrow, I leave Minneapolis and fly to LA for a week before I leave for Australia. I have some small gifts for you both, a T-shirt each with a painting of Uluru, the big rock in the centre of Australian and a Koala bear for your shop – as a mascot, if you like.'

'Oh, my wife will be so sad to miss saying goodbye. Thank you for your gifts. Safe trip home.'

'They have been so nice to me, I'll miss them. I love this city and the capital and sister-city, St Paul. Everyone has been so friendly and obliging.'

Gilda and Barbara flew to LA and then took a bus to their accommodation at Anaheim. It was abuzz with noise, excitement and bright lights. Gilda said wide-eyed when they arrived, 'Let's check out the rooftop pool while we wait for our luggage to come up to the room.' They climbed to the top of the building and were struck dumb by what they saw. 'OMG, look at this view' Barbara said.

'Everything is lit up and you can see the Santa Monica Mountains in the distance. Pity it's too cold to swim but a glass of wine up here later seems in order. What do you reckon, Barbara?' There was a firm nod of the head signaling agreement. The two friends had five days in LA. One day was spent at Disney World. 'It was nice to see,' Gilda remarked, 'but it's not my scene really.' 'Mine either,' replied Barbara.

Another day they took a bus tour around the city which included Universal Studios, Rodeo Drive, houses of famous people, the Hollywood Hills and shopping malls.

The drive to Tijuana was on the next day's agenda and they arrived at the bus depot well ahead of their departure time. 'Can you believe that there are so many buses leaving from one place? There has to be about 30,' Gilda remarked as they waited to be directed to their bus, 'I've never seen so many buses, not even for school sports days.'

'Hola! Who's going to Mexico today? To Tijuana? I am José, your driver for the adventure,' a happy fellow called out on his lapel microphone and laughed mischievously as though he held a secret. 'Vamos, let's go. Vamos a Tijuana, señores y señoras.' José waved his passengers onto the bus. He was about 5 feet, 152.4 centimetres, and stepped into a massive bus capable of holding about 60 passengers. As everyone soon discovered, José's driving skills were extraordinary. He maneuvered the mammoth bus as if it were a mini-minor: no corner was too tight, no road too narrow.

After crossing the US/Mexican border, José announced, 'I come from here, Tijuana, and I have a big family here. I will take you to see all the tourist areas on your itinerary AND, if you are interested, instead of taking the highway back to LA, which is not interesting, I can take you to see my family and how we live here. We'll be taking narrow roads, some will be dirt, but you will see more interesting things than if we go on the freeway. There is nothing to buy and you will be safe.' With that he burst out laughing as though reading some people's minds. 'It will mean that we will get back to LA a little later and it will be dark. Is there anyone who will be inconvenienced by this or is not interested? If even one person cannot go, we cannot do this.'

No one put their hand up and the atmosphere in the bus was as though everyone was holding their breath for it to stay that way. 'Bravo,' José announced. 'We go the back way and hope we don't meet up with any terrorists.' He burst out laughing at his own joke. 'No need to worry. Everyone will know you are with José and even at the market place, you will not be bothered because you are with me.'

And indeed that was so. Other tourists complained about being constantly badgered by sales people but not one person on José's bus was targeted.

'This is an extraordinary experience,' Gilda commented to Barbara near the end of the day. 'I could never have imagined such a day. I'm all shopped out. I bought myself a black leather jacket as well as handbags of different coloured leathers and suedes. There are handbags for Angelique and other bits and pieces. It's all so cheap here and you'd never see that variety back home.'

Everyone climbed into the bus with an air of excitement. When everyone was seated, José announced, 'Now, my friends, you will see something special.' Then for effect, he revved the engine so that it sounded like it was about to be air-born. All those at window seats were glued to the outside scenery so as not to miss anything. Those in aisle seats craned their necks over seats or in the passageway. This went on for about 15 minutes and then the bus turned off the main highway onto a dirt road.

Suddenly, just like when the curtain opens for the beginning of a musical, dozens upon dozens of children ran from every direction toward the bus. Barefooted girls in colourful skirts and blouses, and boys in shorts with sleeveless colourful shirts and ran beside the bus, calling, singing, yelling, laughing, and waving their hands. José honked his horn as accompaniment. It was a true fiesta. Some boys had tambourines; others had sticks that they clapped in rhythm.

Finally, the bus came to a stop. José jumped out, held his hands up in the air and all the children knew that that was a sign for silence. José had something to say. 'Okay, niños y niñas, these people are my friends and I have brought them so that they see how we live here in Tijuana so mind your manners, okay?' 'Si, Si!" the children chorused. 'Si, Si, José!

We all alighted from the bus and started to wander around. There were tables loaded with home-baked cakes and biscuits, and other delicacies. After a short while, one of male tourists borrowed José's microphone and asked if everyone could be quiet for a moment. All the passengers had met up when they were at the markets and organised that as a group, they would buy sweets, chocolates, biscuits and different fruits for the children. Everyone also contributed US$5 cash. José had no idea. When he saw the tourists bring out the gifts, he couldn't believe his eyes. The cash was placed in an envelope and given to him for whatever the family needed. When he received the envelope, he became emotional.

'Gracias, mi amigos, this has never happened before. On behalf of my family, thank you and God bless you. Vaya con Dios, go with God.' Everyone cheered, music started and there was dancing till it was time to drive back to LA.

'This has been extraordinary.' Gilda said turning to Barbara and then realised that she was asleep. 'Don't blame her, I'm exhausted too,' and Gilda nodded off instantly. Both friends woke a couple of hours later when the bus stopped at their final destination, the Los Angeles bus terminus. Australia beckoned.

At the end of May, two months after the trip, notification arrived from the International Skating Union that the approval for the World Championships in Brisbane had been withdrawn due to the lack of interest from the television stations in Australia to broadcast the event. Everyone involved was devastated. 'This is unbelievable,' a disgusted Gilda said and waved the piece of paper that announced the cancellation. 'What's the matter with our TV stations? Only one small one, SBS, showed any interest in broadcasting the event. That's absurd. Nothing will ever change here. It's impossible to change the culture from the larger mainstream sports. Things don't look good then for the future of my position here either.'

In July, Gilda received a phone call, 'Hello, is that Gilda Hollten?'

'Yes, I'm Gilda Hollten.'

'This is Trudi Wilson of Ipswich Girls Private College. I am Mrs Trundle's Secretary. Mrs Trundle would like to speak with you and was wondering if this is a good time.'
'Yes, now is fine,' Gilda replied holding her breath. 'Good, I'll put you through.'

'Ah, Gilda, hello. Judith Trundle here. I have a full-time position available starting next year for French and German. I wonder if you are available.' Gilda was stunned and hesitated for a moment. Mrs Trundle continued, 'If this isn't a good time I can ring back when you've had time to consider my offer.'

'No, no, I mean, yes, yes, this is a good time. I am just so surprised. Yes, yes, I would love to take the position.'

Gilda was in such a hurry to get the words out that she stumbled over them. 'Good, I am pleased,' replied Mrs Trundle, 'My secretary will have all the paperwork ready for you in the next couple of weeks. Can you come in three weeks to complete the formalities for the appointment?' 'Yes, yes, of course,' said Gilda making every effort to contain her excitement.

'Good, I'll put you back to Trudi and you can both go from there. Thank you, Gilda, I am delighted.'

When Gilda and Trudi ended their conversation, she said to herself, 'Holy Molly. That certainly came out of the blue. The Executive won't to be too pleased with that. I'll wait until I have a signed contract from the College before I resign from here. Oh, well, that's life. Now, back to work, enough excitement for one day.' But she couldn't stop smiling; it was all she could do to concentrate, 'I wish I could tell someone but there is no one, only Angelique. I'll have to be patient until tonight.'

'Oh, Mum, that is fantastic,' Angelique exclaimed when her mother told her the news. She flew into her arms and gave her a big hug. 'This is going to be so much better for you. Ice skating was fun while you were building it up but now it's a dead-end job. Too many 'chiefs' with their own agendas. You need more stimulation. Anyway, skating's not going to go anywhere. Everyone thinks they know it all and won't work with others in case they lose their power. You're such a good teacher.' Gilda was always amazed at the wisdom that came from her daughter.

Three weeks later Gilda signed the employment contract with the College. 'No excuse now not to resign,' she thought, 'but something just doesn't feel right to tell them yet. I'll tell Sue-Ellen from Coffee Club and ask her what she thinks. I trust her and she knows all these people for a long time.'

When Gilda told her friend, Sue-Ellen she asked, 'What does your contract say about giving notice?' 'I have to give a month's notice.' 'Then, that's all I'd give them. They'll take it personally.' 'Oh, really, no, they've always been nice to me.' 'Yes, because you've been of use to them. I've seen how they, not all four but some of them, treat people they get a grudge about.' 'Okay, well, how about two months. They have been very good to me.' 'NO,' her friend said emphatically, 'One month, that's what you legally need to do. How long have you worked there?'

'Three months short of ten years.'

'That means morally they should pay you pro rata long service leave. I bet you won't see a cent. They would have had to pay you long service leave if you had stayed 10 years, but it's not currently a legal obligation for employers like these to pay pro rata. It's coming but that won't help you. You'll see, they won't pay you.'

At October's end Gilda submitted her resignation for mid-December. 'I can't just give them four weeks. 'It doesn't feel right,' she thought. 'When I resign now that will give them six weeks to find a replacement. In December I'll go to the College, pick up the texts I'll need and any other material for next year. I can then also pack for our two weeks' trip to Paris in January before the school year starts.

Gilda thought going to Paris for two weeks would be a good way to brush up on her French and hear up-to-date colloquialisms. Her French was still very good and some things she thought of first in French rather than in her native German or English. Angelique was, of course, all for that idea. 'Hey, Mom, you definitely need to go to Paris and I need to carry your suitcase,' Angelique teased.

Sue-Ellen was right about how some of the Executive took Gilda's resignation. On the Monday morning before she handed in her resignation, Gilda handed went to see Daniel at his ice rink office. 'Hello Daniel, do you have a minute?' Gilda couldn't understand why she was so nervous. Her body was shaking, her skull was tense as though something was constricting it, and she couldn't keep still the hand that held her resignation letter. 'Yes, of course,' he answered jovially. 'What can I do for you, Gilda,' as he motioned her to sit down.

'Thanks, Daniel, this will only take a minute,' she replied declining the chair. 'I've come to hand in my resignation.' He stood rigid for a moment, turned around, glared at her and said, 'I see.'

'Here it is.' she managed to say, her mouth dry as a parched leaf in the desert. 'I want to say though....' she started.

Daniel didn't take the letter but turned his back to her and began reading correspondence on his desk. She opened her mouth to continue but decided against it, put the letter on his desk and left the room.

The news soon went around the rink and people came up to her office to find out more and to wish her well. Interstate members of the skating community also rang her to tell her that they would miss her because they recognised how much she had done for the sport. Even two of the ice rink managers from interstate rang to say how sorry they were to see her go.

On her last day just before she was about to leave her office, she said to herself, 'I'm sorry to go too. I've loved this work but it's not going anywhere. I can't believe how I've clearly meant nothing to the Executive, not me, not my work. They haven't even given me a card, not said goodbye, nothing. Only David, the Treasurer, in my final payment letter said nice things and wished me well. Sue-Ellen was right. They didn't pay me pro rata long service leave.'

Gilda was briefly sad but then thought, 'Oh well, life goes on. Lots of wonderful things ahead.' She reached the door of her office and turned around, 'Thanks darling office and job. I've loved you very much. She glanced around solemnly and then walked down the long flight of stairs for the last time.

December was filled with visits to the College, packing and doing as she pleased. Gilda over decades had cultivated an inner survival mechanism that switched itself on immediately when needed. It was so effective that she could mentally diminish occurrences so that they wouldn't continue to hurt her. Unfortunately, it also happened to events that were pleasurable and she would often need to ask Angelique about things that had happened in the past or when they took place.

The trip to Paris in January 1999 was perfect. On the way over Gilda sat next to a French lady. They started chatting and as soon as this lady heard that Gilda was going to brush up her French, from that moment on, she spoke French to her at every possible opportunity, only stopping to sleep.

After a few days in Paris, Gilda said to her daughter, 'You never cease to amaze me. We've only been here a few days and you already understand so much of daily usage. You're such a bright bunny. A month here and you'd be a local.'

'I can cope with that. Can I stay?' Angelique joked. 'Uni can wait. Maybe I should stay a year and really learn the language,' she suggested with a smile.

Two weeks were over and Gilda said, 'These two weeks have flown. I can't believe it. When I'm here, I feel like when I was a little girl and lived here. I was very, very happy in Paris. I think that sentiment has stayed with me. It was during my formative, imprint years - that has stayed in my subconscious.'

'I've just had a brilliant idea,' enthused her daughter, 'Why don't we plan to do a road trip for three weeks sometime in the near future?' 'YES! Absolutely! You can plan it; you're good at that. You know how much I love to travel.'

At the end of January, the school year started with a pupil-free week of in-service training programs, department meetings, exam times planning, computer bookings and staff meetings. 'Isn't that just like Mary, everything I need is neatly on my desk. What a gem. Even Marcel has put together all the French information and texts that I need. Okay, time to go to my first class, Grade 9 French.' 'Bonjour, tout le monde. Asseyez-vous, s'il vous plaît! Good morning, everyone, please be seated.' After roll-call, Gilda did what was customary with a class that she had for the first time. 'Okay, girls, before we start with the actual French lesson, I'd like that we set the ground rules for this particular class.' The students murmured. 'Yes, you heard correctly. As you know, there are school rules and these are, by default, included in the class rules. However, I've found that every class group has its own dynamics, so it's not a 'one-size-fits-all situation.' The class looked surprised and listened eagerly.

'I would like each of you to write down five things that you find are important when you are in class; five things that make the class a learning pleasure to be in. I'll give you about 10 minutes, and then we'll see if you need more. Please do your own work and don't look at your neighbour's list.'

You could have heard a pin drop on the carpeted floor. Concentration was evident.

'Anything that will ensure that you get the most out of your lesson in this class,' Gilda added. After 10 minutes, she asked, 'Does anyone need more time?' Half the class raised their hands.

'Another five minutes then.' When the five minutes were up, Gilda again asked, 'Does anyone still want more time?' No hands went up.

'Good, I'd like a volunteer scribe to come out and write the responses on the white board.' Hands waved in the air. The girls loved writing on the board. Gilda chose a girl, 'Okay Sonja, come on out, please.' Gilda gave the girl a blue marker.

'Hands up, what have you written? No calling out please. Everyone is entitled to a turn. Sonja will write what is called out.' 'Hey, slow down, you lot,' Sonja called, 'I'm not a machine.'

Suggestions came flying, 'To understand what's being taught.' 'To hear what's being taught.' 'To be respected.' 'That homework is done for every lesson.' 'That assignments are handed in on time.' 'No talking when the teacher is explaining something.' 'Ask if you don't understand something when it's being taught, don't just sit there.' And more.

Finally, there were 20 different items on the board. 'Please jot down all 20 in your book,' Gilda requested. 'Now girls, I'd like you to write down 10 of the 20 that are of greatest importance to you – five minutes.' After the five minutes, she added, 'Girls, we'll repeat that process with the top five that you identify as being important – three minutes.'

'Pens down. Please and looking to the front.' Sonja again crossed out items until five were left on the board.

Now, I'd like you to pay attention to this next part of the process. Go over the original list of 20, and if there are any items there that you feel passionately should be on the list, write them now separately with your reason why. That is, you have to have a reason why you feel a particular item should be reconsidered.'

From the whole class of 29 students, there were three items. 'Does anyone have anything to say?' No one raised their hand, then suddenly, one of the girls in the back row raised her hand, 'Yes, Elsbeth.' 'I'd just like to say, I like what we just did. I know I'm one of the talkers in the class but, I've never felt before that what I have to say matters.' There were nods, and mutterings of approval. 'Well, thank you, that's the idea because what you feel DOES matter. It matters a lot. You are the important ones here and we are here to help you achieve what you want,' Gilda paused,' then continued, 'Now without putting a damper on the mood, I'd like to mention that, this also places quite a lot of responsibility on each of you individually and on you as a group. Without ALL of your cooperation, what we have just achieved won't work.' She paused again to let her words sink in, then said, 'It also applies to me because, I also agree to the Terms Agreement and to the repercussions if the principles are violated.'

Late one afternoon when Gilda was alone at home, the phone rang. She lifted the receiver and heard heavy breathing. 'Is that you, Mom?' Silence. 'Hello!' 'Yes', Hanna gasped as though on her last breath, 'Yes, it's me.' 'What's the matter,' an alarmed Gilda asked. 'I'm sick, I'm so sick.' 'Is Ivan there?' 'Yes', Hanna replied, 'But he is useless.'

'Well, what does he say? Put him on the phone.' 'No, I need to talk to you privately. He's useless.' 'Do you want me to come over?' 'No, no, I'm so sick. I'm so sick,' and she hung up. Just then Angelique opened the front door and saw her mother sitting astounded by the phone.

'What's the matter?' Gilda told her what had just happened. 'Ring back,' suggested Angelique.

Gilda rang back but the line was engaged. 'I've got to go over and see what's going on,' Gilda said looking concerned, 'I'll ring you if

I'll be long.' It was all Gilda could do to stay on the speed limit. When she arrived at her mother's and rang the doorbell, Ivan answered and said, 'Ah, darling, what a lovely surprise, come in.' Without answering, Gilda entered the house and asked frantically, 'How's Mom, where is she?' Ivan looked surprised, 'She's fine, why? She's in her study,' 'She just rang me to tell me she's very sick.'

Ivan looked surprised and called to Hanna, 'Schatzi, did you just ring Gilda?' Laughing charmingly, Hanna said, 'Oh, yes, hello dear. Why did you come?' 'What do mean, 'hello, dear why did you come?' 'You said you were sick, very, very sick, you gasped it, and then you hung up.'

'Oh, but no, you are exaggerating,' Hanna laughed, 'Come in and have a drink. So nice to see you.' Hanna was now in entertainment mode; the perfect hostess.

Gilda was relieved but also furious. 'No, thank you. I'm glad to see that there is nothing wrong with you. You're just being your usual self,' She glanced at Ivan who had a knowing and apologetic look, she said, 'It's okay, Ivan, sorry to have disturbed you.' Gilda then left.

'Calm down, girl, deep breath. Take it easy,' she kept repeating to herself as she drove home making sure that she stayed below the speed limit. When she arrived home, Angelique said, 'That didn't take long.' 'Because, there's nothing wrong with her. She was just having some fun,' Gilda said sarcastically. 'She even offered me a drink, which she seldom does'.

'Are you kidding?' Gilda filled her daughter in on the details and said, 'From now on, we leave the answering machine on. If it's her, I'll ring in the morning and see if anything is wrong. Ivan never goes out at night without her, so he'll be home. That's the last time she plays that prank.'

It wasn't the last time Hanna tried that but it was the last time either Gilda or Angelique lifted the receiver, and didn't ring her back when they heard her voice on the answering machine. The next morning when Gilda rang, Hanna said frivolously that all was well, and asked why she was ringing when she, Hanna, was busy. 'She'll do that once too often and no one will believe her,' thought Gilda.

CHAPTER 35
2000-2001

Gilda had never told her mother that she had a position at the Ipswich College. 'I don't want her to ruin things for me. The less she knows about what I do the better. In any case, she's not interested, so why bother telling her?' But, as ill-luck would have it, Hanna found out. One of Hanna's previous colleagues rang her because the school was so thrilled to have Gilda, another member of the family, teaching at the College. Hanna's previous colleague added fuel to the fires of jealousy by saying, 'And you know Hanna, Gilda is such an excellent teacher, just like you were. She's so popular with the girls,' her former colleague enthused.

'That is very nice,' Hanna said coolly. 'I was just on my way out,' and hung up on her caller. Hanna immediately telephoned her daughter, 'Gilda, come over this instant,' she demanded. That was all she said before returning the phone to its cradle.

'Who was that,' Angelique asked. 'Mom,' replied Gilda, All she said was that she wanted to see me immediately.' 'Is this another one of her hoaxes?' 'I've no idea. Absolutely no idea, but I need to go just in case Ivan isn't there and something really is wrong.' 'But we were going shopping,' her daughter complained. 'Yes, and we'll still go shopping but first we'll see what's up.'

'Good,' replied Angelique in a firm voice, 'I can be there for moral support in case she is nasty to you.'

Gilda, however, was disturbed and realised that she had started to shake. 'Bugger, my stomach is playing up again. I'll take a tablet before I go. I won't let Angelique see me taking it.' Shortly after, they left for the 15 minute car ride to Hanna's home.

'I don't have a good feeling about this,' Gilda said as she stopped the car in the driveway. 'Me either, but then I never do when we go to visit Oma,' Angelique said as she bounced up the front stairs and enthusiastically pressed the front door bell.
Hanna opened the door and said abruptly to Gilda, 'Come into my

study. Ivan has gone on foot to get milk and bread. 'Hello, Oma,' Angelique greeted cheerily. No reply.

Gilda knew by Hanna's behaviour that she was in trouble. 'So, you are still a sneak,' Hanna sneered, 'You haven't changed. You didn't tell me that you are teaching at the College. You thought that I would not find out. Well I did.' She waved her finger threateningly as she raised her voice, 'YOU will ruin the reputation I have built up at the school. My excellent reputation will be ruined because you are useless, USELESS! Do you hear? USELESS,' Hanna shouted.

'What are you talking about?' Gilda said tentatively realising how nervous she felt - her heart pounded and her throat was dry. The more her mother yelled at her, the more she had to make a fist till her nails cut into her skin to stop herself from shaking. 'Okay, so I didn't tell you. Would you have been interested? No! You would have ridiculed me, like you do now. So, why should I tell you?'
'I must know because I am so respected at the College and I will not have you ruin my reputation. You are a nothing. You never have been anything and you never will be anything. None of you would be anything if it wasn't for me.' Hanna then lunged at Gilda as she continued to scream at her. Angelique came to her mother's aid and when Gilda successfully avoided her mother's attempt to hit her, Hanna lost her balance. Gilda and Angelique caught her and put her back in her chair. 'YOU GOOD FOR NOTHING TRAMP,' Hanna screamed as she shook off her daughter and grand-daughter and then proceeded to shout at Gilda, 'I'll tell them what you are really like. They don't know you like I do. GET OUT. GET OUT BOTH OF YOU.'

Just then they heard the front door. Ivan had returned. 'Hello, Darlings,' he said cheerfully as he saw them, 'This is a nice surprise.'

'Hello, Ivan,' Gilda and Angelique chorused, both relieved at Ivan's return, which had silenced Hanna. Angelique took over as a soloist saying, 'Mum, yummy, Opa, that fresh bread smells delicious.'
'Would you like to join us for breakfast, 'asked Ivan. Hanna

immediately looked lovingly at her daughter and grand-daughter and said, 'No Ivan, I've already asked them but they have other arrangements.' 'Yes, Ivan,' Gilda affirmed, 'that's right, we do have other arrangements.' Maybe another time, thanks. We're off now. Bye, bye.' 'Bye,' Angelique cheerfully mimicked and gave Ivan a hug before she headed for the front door with her mother.
'Don't I get a hug as well,' Hanna asked in mock hurt. Angelique glared at her and gave her grandmother an air-hug. Hanna moved toward Ivan and affectionately put her arm through his.
When they got to the car, Angelique asked her mother, 'Are you okay? I can't believe what I just experienced. Is this what you had to put up with when you were a child?'

'Yes.'

'Oh, my goodness. If I hadn't seen it with my own eyes, I wouldn't have believed it. It's a wonder you turned out normal.' Gilda burst out laughing. 'That's the first time I've ever been called 'normal'. You are so adorable. You know what? Some serious retail-therapy is what we need. We're not going to let her ruin the beautiful day we have planned. She'll do what she'll do as regards the College. I can't control that but what I can control is that we will have a super day together, as always.' Gilda drove a short distance and just out of sight of Hanna's home stopped the car and burst into tears. 'Sorry, Schatzi, I can't help it. It just came out of left field. Normally I can prepare myself before seeing her but, this was so unexpected. I'll be okay in a moment.'

'Mum, it's okay to cry. She was beastly to you; she was about to hit you. You have to let it out.' Looking her daughter tenderly in the eyes, Gilda said, 'Thank you, Schatzi, I love you very, very much and God blessed me when he allowed me to be your mother. You're so special. You don't realise what a special person you are. I'm going to call you 'my Angel on Earth' because that's what you are. You are so beautiful with everyone – you're special. With that she squeezed her daughter's hands gently before driving off.

They drove in silence in a mutual world that no one could invade. They didn't need to speak. They had a special bond that transcended the need to communicate. Yes, they would, as usual, have a wonderful time together.

College life went on as usual. 'I don't think Mom will ring the school. She's all bluff and hot air, explosive, eruptive hot air but that's the way she is. What else is there to be said?'

Gilda had plenty to keep herself occupied and Hanna out of her consciousness. She was enjoying her Master's studies and was achieving good results in her subjects.

Krampus celebration around the 5 December was spent with Hanna, Ivan and Danika with the usual snide remarks from Hanna. Everyone had come to expect the evening to run its invariable course. Ivan would drink a little more than usual and turn his hearing aid off unless someone other than Hanna spoke. It was a standard joke. Now that Angelique could drive, Gilda also drank more. The champagne and wine helped the evening pass merrily. Customarily, Gilda and Angelique spent Christmas Eve together in the traditional Viennese manner. On Christmas Day Angelique drove to the Gold Coast to celebrate Christmas with her father and his new wife, Alana, and on New Year's Eve she met with friends but was, as usual, home soon after midnight.

Gilda had narrowed her circle of friends since leaving ice skating and preferred to spend time alone. The friends she did retain were like her, predominantly 'hermits'. Her usual companion was Bubbles, a stray white cat that had adopted them and had totally fitted in with their life.

This development to prefer being alone had occurred gradually. Gilda focused on self-development literature. The more she read on these topics and explored via the internet on modalities to rid herself of past environmental conditioning, the more she realised that she did actually like her own company. She philosophised, 'I enjoy Angelique's company when she is home and when she's out, I like being alone. Well, I'm not actually alone, I have you, don't I, Bubbles?'

On 1 January, 2001, Gilda rang her mother. 'Happy New Year,' she said to Ivan when a voice answered the phone. 'Happy New Year to you too.' Ivan replied, 'What are you up to?' In the background Gilda heard Hanna saying to Ivan, 'If that is Gilda, I'm too busy to come to the phone.' 'I suppose you heard that,' Ivan said in an embarrassed tone.

'Yes, I did. It's okay, Ivan. Just pass on the message,' Gilda said. Just as she was about to hang up, Hanna came to the phone and asked, 'Have they sacked you yet?' 'Hello, Mom, Happy New Year.' 'Enough of that rubbish. Are you still working at the College?' 'Yes, I am.' 'Not for long, you won't be. You'll see.' The line went dead. Gilda contemplated this last message from her mother. 'Why do I bother, seriously, I need my head read. I know now what she's doing. She's playing mind games with me. She has been all along only I've just never realised it. What I can't understand is, why does she keep doing it?' Gilda switched the answering machine on and moved to a shady umbrella on the patio.

Being intelligent and able to 'pick' questions that could be on exam papers, Gilda was able to fly through her two previous degrees with ease. Her Master of Education was proving not to be so easy. There were no exams; assessment was achieved by completing assignments of varying lengths in each course subject, which also had a major final written assignment.

Now, Gilda was on the home stretch of her final year. One day, when Angelique came home from tutoring, she caught her mother in an angry and rebellious mood sitting on the sofa with a piece of paper in her hand. Angelique was now a tutor in two courses at Griffith University.

'Hello, there, happy, what's the matter with you,' she asked her mother. 'This comment on my final Psychology of Education assignment. I'm furious, it's bloody insulting. The guy says that I've waffled and not answered the question.'

Her daughter burst out laughing, 'Has someone finally caught you out?' 'That's not funny.' Angelique saw how upset her mother was and thought better of continuing with the jokes. 'Do you want me to look at the topic and what you've written?' I don't know what good that will do as it's not in your fields.' 'Nevertheless, let me have a look. Perhaps I can give you another perspective?' Angelique sat down to review her mother's work.

'I'm going to get some vodka,' Gilda said defiantly and left the house.

When Gilda returned, her daughter asked, 'Feeling better?' 'No not really, I'll make a drink, that'll help but, I still have to redo that stupid assignment.' 'Yes, you do,' said Angelique, 'but did you read what he said?'

'Yes.'

'Read it out to me and get it off your chest.'

Gilda read aloud the lecturer's comment, 'Gilda, this assignment does not do you justice. I know you are capable of better work. Based on what you have submitted I would need to fail this work. You would still pass the subject. However, I'm prepared to give you the weekend to work over it and resubmit it on Monday. The choice is yours. Kind regards, Tom.'

'See,' Angelique said jubilantly, 'He knows you can do better if you address the topic and I agree with him. You've waffled to meet the word count and you haven't directly responded to much that was asked. You just rushed through it at the last minute to get it done. Does that make you feel good? I bet it doesn't and I'm glad he sent it back. You've suffered from enough lack of self-worth over the years. It wasn't your fault, it was Oma's doing, but you don't need to perpetuate it now that you can control it. Redo this and it'll be a huge step towards you liking yourself and feeling you're worthy. You are anyway, but....you know what I mean, don't you?'
'Yes, I do,' Gilda replied in a slow, contrite voice, 'Yes, you're right. It's really up to me now, isn't it? Blaming my mother now for everything is self-destructive. As a result of my reading, I know that I'm in control of how I respond to situations and that I'm in control

of how my life pans out. If I don't redo the assignment, I'd be living a lie. That's not me. Thanks, Schatzi. I'll have it completed by Monday.'

She got up and the two hugged. 'Thanks again,' Gilda said.

'Hey, least I could do. How often have you helped me?'

Two weeks later, Gilda came home from collecting the mail and triumphantly waved a piece of paper in the air. 'Guess what?' she teased Angelique, 'Bet you can't guess.'

'Bet I can, but I'll let you have your 'Triumphal March,' Angelique joked.

"I got a Distinction for my Psychology assignment and one overall for that subject. My first Distinction ever,' Gilda said excitedly still waving the assignment in the air. 'I'm so proud of you, Mum, really proud. Congratulations.'

The College was going through tough times with low enrolments for all year levels especially Grade 8, the entry level for admission to secondary school. There was talk that some subjects would need to be dropped. Every teacher in elective subjects was concerned. 'I don't like the sound of this, Mary, the head of the German Department, said one day, 'I've heard rumours that this school is going to cut out French and join up with the Boys' College until the current students finish Year 12, and then cease teaching it altogether.'

'That would be terrible' Gilda commented, 'That would mean that there wouldn't be a need for a second French teacher.' 'Correct,' Mary replied, 'Marcel has already applied for Head of French positions at other schools; this would just leave Helen and you to relocate.'

By October it became evident that there would not be a full complement of new students for Grade 8. In addition, new enrollees had declined in the College's Primary School which meant that the following years would also be lean.

A few days later, Mrs Trundle, the Principal, called Gilda to her office. 'Gilda, I'm sure you know we are having problems with student numbers. The administration, with the Trustees approval, has decided not to offer French as a subject in the future. The decrease in numbers means that we also need to let go one of the Mathematics and one of the Science teachers. Sadly, I can only offer you a part-time position for next year and possibly the year after. We are hoping that the year after that will stabilise again and I can again offer you full-time teaching. Helen is in the same position. I'm hoping that you will stay with us. You and Helen will be given relief work which is paid extra when you are part-time.'

Although Gilda had anticipated this, it was a blow when it became a reality. On the way home from school, it really hit her and she wept. 'I shouldn't be taking it like this,' she admonished herself, 'I knew it was a probability. It's more the financial insecurity that has hit me.' Gilda couldn't help herself, 'I've never been in this position before, it's awful.' Her tears flowed.

As soon as she arrived home, the phone rang; it was her friend from Sydney, Joan. 'Hi gorgeous, how are you,' she asked when Gilda answered the phone.

'Oh, Hi, Joan, so nice to hear your voice, I've been better. I just got told that the school can only give me part-time work for at least the next two years.'

'Gilda, I hate to say this, but I'm very glad,' replied Joan. 'What do you mean?' 'Well, I have a full-time job for you here.'

'What! You're kidding.'

'No, seriously, listen. Patrick wants to start a College of Hospitality and Tourism here in Sydney. He's been bankrupt and so can't be a Director. In any case, he's a great chef but knows zero about business and administration. That's where you come in. You built up the ice-skating office from nothing to the internationally-respected office that you left. I also know zilch about education, and again that's where you come in. You and I would be registered as directors with the Australian Securities and Investment Commission, ASIC, and Patrick will do his thing in the background with food. How is this sounding so far?'

Gilda was excited, she liked nothing more than a challenge but she contained herself. 'Keep talking.'

'I can feel you saying yes.'

'Keep talking, cheeky.'

'I know it's not ideal but, you could live with us at the beginning for the duration of the College set up. Being close will be convenient during the set-up. Also rental accommodation is bloody expensive in Sydney and, we also have two spare rooms, one could be your office and the other your bedroom. Still sounding okay?'

'Keep going.'

'As regards salary, the College couldn't initially pay you what you are worth but would pay you what you are currently getting teaching and you could live here rent free. You'd just need to buy your own food. Electricity would be paid by the business because you'd be mostly using it for work. The bedroom is furnished; you'd only need to bring your personal stuff. I think that's about it. What do you say – interested?

'Yes, I am interested, sounds fun. You are aware that I know absolutely nothing about hospitality and tourism?' 'Minor technicality. How much did you know about the ice-skating business when you started?'

'You've got a point – nothing. Yes, I can walk the pavements and go to similar colleges, get their brochures and prospectuses, make out I'm going to be a client and get pricings.'

'Yep, you already know what to do. Oh, by the way, we have a contact in hospitality at the University of New South Wales and we can rent their facilities to conduct our courses.'

'Joan, let me think about it for a couple of days. You know that I have a cat, and I would bring him with me.

'No problem, my dog is so fat and docile. He hardly moves anywhere. They'll get on fine.'

'When would you like me to start?'

'ASAP – tomorrow,' the friend laughed.

'The earliest I could come would be beginning of December when school finishes.'

'That's fine, whenever you can.' They hung up.

'I can't believe this happened, again.' Gilda said.

When Angelique arrived home, Gilda told her of the day's events.

'Good heavens, things sure don't happen to you by halves,' Angelique said when she heard her mother's story.

'No and, you'll be going away for three months, middle of November so that would work out perfectly.'

'What do you think about it? How do you feel about it?'

'You know me; I love a challenge. I also like Sydney. I'd have my car so I could get out of the house when I need to. I think I need to give this a go. I'd get bored with part-time teaching. You don't really belong in the school when you're part-time. Also, I can't rely on relief work with regards to extra income.'

'I think you've already made up your mind, haven't you?'

'Angelique, I want you're okay too though. If you don't agree, I won't go and I'll never hold it against you. You have to tell me truthfully what you think.'

'Okay, you know what Joan's like. She's very self-centered. If it doesn't suit her, if she doesn't get her own way, she'll dig her heels in and nothing will budge her. She won't even communicate; it'll be a wall of silence. I also don't like Patrick. He's a loud, foul-mouth-swearing hot-head but I guess as he can't have an active role, it shouldn't be a problem.'

'So, what does that mean?'

'Mum, you know I'll support you no matter what. If you want to go, go, you can always come back. Just don't sign a contract. If you have to, give yourself a probationary loophole. Make sure that everything Joan has promised is down on paper and that you must sign each cheque.'

The house was empty when Angelique left for her extended holiday and Gilda was sad. 'Luckily, I have this new adventure to plan otherwise, I would go crazy.'

The College was sad to see Gilda go. On her last day, Mrs Trundle came to her at the languages staff room and said, 'You are welcome back at any time, Gilda. Should you return to Brisbane, please contact me.'

Joan flew from Sydney to Brisbane so that Gilda didn't have the long 14 hours plus drive on her own.

On 1 December, 2000, with the car filled up with petrol for the 1100 kilometre drive so Sydney, and with her personal belongings, and Bubbles on a lead in his cat carrier with his rug, Gilda left her home in Brisbane to embark on her biggest solo adventure yet. Her car's CD player blasted out the magnificent Italian music from the motion picture, 'Big Night'. As she and Joan drove along the highway the two friends sang gaily along with the melody, improvising some of the words…

"Buona sera, signorina, buona sera, it is time to say goodbye to old Brisbane…."

CHAPTER 36
2002-2003

'Well, my beautiful boy, you never thought you'd be an interstate resident, 1100 kilometres from home, when you decided to adopt me, did you?' Gilda said to her cat, Bubbles after they settled at Enfield where they would initially live in Sydney. The trip from Brisbane went smoothly, with Joan and Gilda taking turns driving. The only stops were to fill up the petrol tank, get food and allow Bubbles to go to the toilet. He was on a soft collar and lead and, as though he knew, he would relieve himself each time given the opportunity. 'You're my clever boy. You're going to be such a buddy helping me settle in.'

It was evening when they arrived but Patrick wasn't home yet. Joan showed Gilda the two rooms. 'This is the office. It faces the street and might be a bit noisy as your bedroom. Come with me and I'll show you your bedroom. It is away from our bedroom so we'll all have privacy.'

'Looks great,' Gilda replied, 'It really does. I'll just take Bubbles for a little reconnaissance-walk in the garden now, if that's okay? He's such a smart little fellow, it won't take him long to know that this is home.'

'Yes, sure. I'll make us something light to eat. It's a bit late for a heavy meal, isn't it?'

Gilda had settled in by the time Patrick returned in the New Year from a trip. 'Hello there, my girl,' he greeted her as he entered, 'So, this is the cat. Careful the dog doesn't get ya and has ya for dinner,' he said and roared laughing.

Gilda was silent. 'That's not funny,' she thought, 'I'm glad I won't have much to do with him. Then to her hosts she said, 'I'm beat, I'll head for bed. Thanks for a great trip down, Joan. Night all.'

The following evening, the three of them ate dinner together. 'You won't have to put up with us every evening,' Patrick said. 'You're free to do as you please and so are we.' 'Patrick,' Joan said to change the conversation, 'Why don't you take Gilda with you tomorrow when you visit the providores so that they meet in case she needs to work with them.'

'Sure, do'er good to get to know the industry. Not that she'll have much to do with 'em; they're my problem, the bastards.'
'I don't need to come with you, Patrick, if you have things to do. I might be in the way,' Gilda suggested, hoping for a reprieve. 'Na, you won't be no problem, ma Dearie. I'll tell ya if ya get on me nerves.' He then grabbed Joan and gave her a passionate kiss.
'If you don't mind, I need to take Bubbles out. Thank you for the lovely dinner, Joan,' she said as she left the table. To herself Gilda thought, 'I'd better leave before I vomit. When she left the room, she whispered to Bubbles, 'This is going to be interesting.'

After four days, she no longer had to train Bubbles that this was home. He could go outside without her, minus collar and the lead. At night so that Bubbles could come in and go out as he pleased, she left her window open. An owl chime hung at the window of the low-set house in case more than her little four-legged friend wanted to climb in. One evening, she noticed that he didn't go out. 'Hey, my little darling, don't you want to go out during the night?' The cat smooched up against her and hopped on her lap. 'You know what? I think you're staying in to protect me. Aren't you amazing! Such a super smart boy. Okay, I'll close the window and then we can both get a good night's sleep,' she said as she gave him an enormous cuddle and a kiss on the forehead.

The next morning Gilda was ready to go with Patrick but the house was silent. She waited till 10.00 AM. 'Maybe, he's already left without me. Joan catches the train to work at 7.00. Tentatively, she called softly, Are you still here, Patrick?'

Suddenly she heard from his bedroom, 'Oh, fuck, what's the time. Fuck, 10.' She waited. Five minutes later he came out. Patrick had dressed and said. 'Cumon, we're off. I've gotta call on someone first. He's not far from here.' As they approached the shop, it was clear that it was shut.

'What the fuckin' hell! He's shut! What the fuck! He shoulda rung me. Fuck, fuck, fuck!' Patrick slammed his foot on the accelerator, reversed rapidly, slammed on the brakes, swerved as he did a U-turn and, without looking for oncoming traffic, entered the stream of cars. A car had to brake and honked his horn at Patrick. 'What's ya fuckin' problem, arsehole. Ya lookin for a fuckin' fight?' He then accelerated and gave the driver the finger.

Gilda was on the verge of saying she wanted to get out of the car. 'I'd better stay,' she thought, with that temper, who knows what he'll do.' They completed what Patrick had to do and he drove her home before leaving again. 'What on earth does she see in him? He's a brute. I've NEVER met anyone like that, every second word is swearing. I'm going to have to watch what I say. She's obviously besotted by him. How could she go with someone like that after John who is such a gentleman?'

Gilda was able to avoid having much personal contact with Patrick, especially not being alone with him again. She bought the necessary office equipment and whenever she needed to talk about the business she made sure Joan was present.

Shortly after Gilda arrived the three of them had a meeting and Joan clarified what the long-term plan was for the College. She started, 'What we envisage for the College is that it will have not only Government accredited Barista and other hospitality training courses but that for the tourism side, there'll be a three to five-year program training indigenous people as waiters.'

'That sounds excellent,' Gilda said, 'Tell me more.'

'Well, that's about it,' said Joan, 'developing it and making it work and making money is up to you. You'll submit the plan so that we can get Government funding.'

'Oh, okay, no problem. Let me think about it and I'll check in with you if what I come up with is what you have in mind and we can go from there.' 'Holy Molly,' Gilda thought, 'this is throwing me in the deep end. I love the idea though. Actually, it's really exciting. Right, girl, it's time to start walking the pavements of the inner city. I need to see what similar colleges are doing and what they are charging.'

Four weeks later, on a Friday, Gilda asked when the Joan and Patrick could meet to discuss the business development plan she had produced. By Monday, Gilda still didn't have a reply. 'Hey, guys, can you make time next weekend for us to meet; it'll take a maximum of an hour.' During that week, she spoke to Joan when Patrick wasn't home. 'Joan, is something wrong?'

'No, nothing's wrong. What do you mean?'

'You both seem to be avoiding making a time for the three of us to meet. I'd like to show you the plan I have to get funding and also give you a rundown on how the courses are going for accreditation.'

'Just go ahead with what you're planning. It'll be fine.'

'But why don't you want that we meet?'

'Just leave it, will you? I don't want you on my back as well.'

'What do you mean, as well? Is Patrick giving you trouble?'

'No! For God's sake just shut up and get on with it,' and with that Joan stormed out of the house, got into her car and drove off at an absurd speed.

'Well, that went well,' Gilda told Bubbles who just purred at her and rubbed his head on her legs. 'Something is wrong but I can't work out what it is. It has something to do with Patrick, but what...? I don't know.'

Gilda continued working on the proposal in conjunction with her other work of developing the initial Barista courses. She had made good contacts with other colleges who, when they saw that she wouldn't be competition, helped her with more than she had hoped for. They even gave her more contacts, including trainers capable of facilitating the courses. She had also developed a good relationship with the people in charge at the University of New South Wales' hospitality department. Several meetings with the NSW State Government's indigenous liaison representative and others with indigenous elders and leaders to see if they approved of her ideas were also fruitful and positive.

She was convinced that the courses were valuable and that she was working on an amazing project. Late at night as she lay in bed she thought, 'Everyone is so helpful and supportive. It's such a pity that Joan and Patrick aren't interested in it. I don't understand what's going on. Oh, well. Doing the final artwork for the official document is going to be such fun. I know exactly how I want to do the final presentation. They'll love it.'

The afternoon before the official meeting to submit the proposal upon which depended whether the College would get Government funding for the next three to five years, Gilda asked her friend. 'Joan, are you sure you don't want to come with me tomorrow? You're one of the Directors; you're very much a part of this.'

'No, I can't.' Patrick then came home and the discussion ended.

However, Gilda wasn't going to let it ride, so she started, 'As you know tomorrow is the official meeting with Tony Wilson, the government's indigenous representative that I've been working with. Would you like to see the submission I've prepared?'

Neither spoke.
'Come on guys, this is for you too. It's your business as well. Patrick, you mightn't be able to be a Director but you're part of the team.'

'Oh, for heaven's sake. Can't you just shut up about it,' Patrick roared. 'Let's go have a look, or she'll never shut up. She's like a kid with a new toy. They gave a cursory glance, not opening the 30-page document. Patrick said sulkily, 'I hate it.' Joan said, 'It's awful. It's not what I had in mind'

Gilda controlled herself and calmly said, 'You've both had plenty of opportunities to have input. I've asked you over and over again but you've shown no interest. Tony is very happy with it as are the indigenous elders and other members of the communities. Stiff bikkies, if you don't like it. You're not the most important people in this, they are. It's a good thing you haven't had any input or it would never have been completed.' She took all the copies with her and thought to herself, 'I don't trust them not to rip them up before tomorrow.'

The next morning Gilda dressed in her best. 'A girl's got to look the part when she's going to an extra-important business meeting. This is the big league now,' she laughed to herself.

'Good morning, Tony,' Gilda said when she met the Government representative. 'Good morning, Gilda. Your colleagues aren't with you?' He was clearly astonished.

'No, unfortunately, they aren't able to be here but they asked me to thank you on their behalf for all the help you have given me and to apologise for being unable to attend this morning. 'I see,' he said in such a way that Gilda could see, he was not happy. He raised an eyebrow and then addressed the topic at hand.

'Gilda, I won't keep you long. As you know, I've had lengthy discussions with our Elders and parents of potential candidates. They like very much that your plan involves them with every step of their children's training. They are also very pleased that you have incorporated cultural aspects of the different communities. We will all work well together which is excellent and I congratulate you. The Government has seen fit to allocate a grant of $35,000,000 for five years with the option of reviewing it for a further allocation.'

Gilda wanted to jump through the roof but she held herself in check. 'Thank you Tony, I'm thrilled and that's putting it mildly, and I want to thank you most sincerely for the generous help with time and resources you've given me. I could not have done it without you.'

'One last thing,' Tony said suddenly becoming very serious, 'The grant is provisional on you being always in charge of this project. Should that not be the case, the money will be immediately withdrawn.'

Tony and Gilda shook hands and she left. 'Oh, my God, that's what we've all wanted from the start. This is amazing.'

Gilda could barely wait till she could meet Joan and Patrick together. Excitedly, in the evening when Joan and Patrick arrived home, she told them the good news.

'I suppose, we'll have to have a bit of a party next Saturday and invite the NSW crowd and some others who'll be useful in the future,' Patrick said to Joan, ignoring Gilda. Both then went about their usual night-time routine.

That was it. Gilda stood stunned. 'Something is going to have to change. I'm not putting up with this much longer. I seriously don't get it.' However, she said, 'Incidentally, Monday week I'm interviewing potential trainers for three positions that are available. Sometime over the next week could you please look over the criteria they need to meet to make sure I haven't omitted important points. Patrick, this is your area of expertise so I'd love your feedback.'

Very little was spoken the following week. In actual fact, Patrick and Joan were hardly home; it almost seemed as though they were avoiding Gilda. The following Saturday, they held the party in the backyard. Patrick hired a marquee, a barbecue facility, and bought drinks and food. The party went well but neither Joan nor Patrick spoke to Gilda. Everyone congratulated her and said how they were looking forward to working with her. On Sunday, Gilda reminded them about the trainer criteria for the coming Monday but received no response. They were watching TV, which is all they did when they were home.

At 8.00 PM, Gilda made a decision, 'Okay, this is it.' Bubbles, who was usually out at this time, suddenly appeared in her bedroom. 'Great that you've come back early, Sweetheart, because we're driving home. I've just started packing things and putting them in the car. Come with me and hop on your seat.' He followed her and immediately jumped on his blanket and stayed there.

After 30 minutes, Joan went to Gilda and asked surprised, 'What are you doing?'

'What do you think it looks like?'

'Where are you going?'

'Back to Brisbane. My resignation is on my desk. Maybe you'll find the time to read it, if not, no loss. I forgot to tell you that the funding grant is only available if I lead the project. As I won't be, you two, equally, are responsible for losing the grant and the demise of the College.'

'But why are you going?'

'Joan, you know for some time, I've been wondering why you've changed towards me and I couldn't work it out. But it was at the party on Saturday that I realised what was going on. Patrick is jealous of me and even more so now because of the kudos and attention I'm getting as a result of getting the grant. He always has to be in the limelight and now, because of his bankruptcy, he can't be Mr King Pin. He's not a team player. Patrick doesn't give a crap about the College; it's all about him and his wounded pride. In all my talks with people, I've always included my 'two colleagues' but, neither of you could give a shit about the College. All you two have are oversized egos. He is so full of himself that he can't be civil to anyone he interacts with, and you are so enamoured of him, that you will put up with his crap. Well, I don't have to. Good luck for the future and I'm sorry our friendship is ending this way. If you don't mind, I need to finish packing.'

Joan stood still for a moment and then said, 'Let me help you carry things.'

Gilda looked at her without emotion, 'No thank you, you've done enough.'

By now, it was 10.30 PM. Gilda drove off and said to Bubbles, 'This is going to be fun. I have absolutely no idea where I am in relation to the highway back to Brisbane. I'll go to a service station and ask.'

The same convoy of cars followed each other from Sydney to Brisbane, each seeming to need petrol at the same service stations. 'It's comforting to see the same cars and that we wave to each other.'

By 9.00 AM the following morning, Gilda caught herself several times falling asleep at the wheel after swerving and suddenly waking up. She had stopped previously to stay the night at a motel but there were no outside lights to break the darkness where the cabins were situated generating an uncomfortable feeling, so she drove on. She decided to park at a service station until dawn to get some much needed sleep. Bubbles made no move to want to go out, so the two friends fell asleep together.

It was the middle of March 2002 and not a good time to look for teaching positions. The new school year had already started and all teaching positions taken. She registered with the Catholic Schools Association for relief teaching, and notified the Ipswich College that she was back in Brisbane and available for any work. Soon she received relief teaching in Ipswich and then in Brisbane.

At St. Claire's, in Brisbane, she received relief work and then a part-time appointment to teach German. The Principal, a nun, took an immediate liking to her and gave her extra work so that she was earning more than if she were employed full-time. Gilda's choreographic skills from the ice skating days came in handy for school musicals and she staged a roller blading item for Speech Night. In May, she received full-time teaching at St Claire's.

Angelique had returned from her 'rites-of-passage' holiday and was amazed when she heard her mother's Sydney story. 'Joan's behaviour doesn't surprise me at all. Seriously Mum, you've got guts. Not many people would have decided to quit like you did, when you did, nor do the long drive home at that hour. You really are an inspiration.'

'Hey, I didn't do it alone. I had my little white fluffy bundle supporting me. We certainly had an adventure. Have I told you how smart you are?' She picked up Bubbles and gave him a mammoth squeeze.

'Mum, can you please take credit where it's due? You still can't see how incredible you are. Oma sure did a job on your self-worth, or lack thereof. How is the old girl? Have you heard from her?' 'No, there were no messages on the answering machine. I had forgotten to turn it off. She doesn't know I was away, luckily, otherwise she'd have more ammunition to shoot at me. At this point, I'm just so grateful that I got part-time and then full-time so quickly.'

Gilda abruptly changed the subject and said to her daughter, 'You know, I feel like going back to Vienna so how you would like to visit Vienna over Christmas? We can stay with Eva and Gregor again. They were fun. 'You know me, when it comes to travel, I'm in.'

When Gilda and Angelique arrived at the Vienna airport, their friends were there to meet them. However, from the beginning, Gilda sensed that something was different. They were saying the right words but Gilda couldn't put her finger on it. Angelique noticed it too, 'Mum, were these two always like this,' Angelique asked her mother after a couple of days.

'What do you mean?'

'I don't know, it's as though they look down on us, especially you. The snide remarks they make when you say something, especially about life in Brisbane or Australia. The haughty way they reply as though we live in a colony, a backward place compared to Vienna and Europe. They also make very racist, judgmental remarks about people who are "below them", chimney sweeps, street workers. It's all about class distinction with them. They won't go on the tram because they don't know who last sat on the seat – comments like that – it's awful.'

'You've noticed it too,' Gilda said, 'I thought I was being picky. They never were that way; or at least I hadn't noticed it. Your father used to make racist remarks and they laughed with him, but I thought they were just being polite. I'd really like to go and live somewhere else but Mom would have a fit if she found out. Eva's mother is Mom's best friend and it's all about appearances. Whenever I bring things up from the last visit, it's as though they never existed, as though I'm making them up. How about we book going earlier to Venice?'

'Yes, let's go into the city centre and go to a travel agent.'

'Venice, here we come,' Angelique said with some exuberance after they had successfully arranged an Italian itinerary with a travel agent.

Venice was freezing cold in January, 2003 but both mother and daughter had the clothes for these conditions. Clothes they could only wear in Tasmania when sightseeing in Australia, padded coats that Gilda humorously called their 'Michelin coats', fake-fur hats that covered their ears, thick gloves, soft woollen scarves and fur-lined boots past the ankles. 'Even blizzards won't penetrate this garb,' she joked.

'You know what, Angel,' Gilda addressed her daughter as they were riding on a Vaporetto skimming over the waters of the Lagoon from the Piazza San Marco heading for Burano, 'All this reading is finally paying off. I can listen to Eva and Gregor without the need to respond to what they say if I choose not to.'

'Mum, I can sense a philosophical discussion coming on. Mind you, I love it when you're in this mood and it's the perfect spot. Here we are in Venice, what a surreal place, filled with history of beauty and brutality.'

'Exactly, and what do you choose to focus on?' 'The beauty, of course!' 'Yes, but what did we, as a family, previously always focus on?' 'Oh, I see what you're getting at.

'Yep, our tradition, even back to Mom's influence and then with your father has always been to be picky, to focus on what could go wrong, to focus on the negative, on what's annoying.'

The past is over. It's only purpose is as a gauge for how we've moved on, to learn from what is good and what not to hang onto. It's not a life-boat; it can be a block of concrete around your neck to drag you and hold you down, to drown you from a future that can be magnificent. I don't want to end up like Eva and Gregor who live in the past, and who are miserable and complaining all the time'. 'And,' interjected Angelique, 'One of the reasons you're such a good mother is because you don't want to be what you experienced. Now, don't argue with that. You ARE a great mother.'

'Here's our stop. We've arrived at Burano,' Gilda advised.

'You can't get out of it that easily. Agree with me that you are a great mother.'

'I won't admit to being "great" but I'll concede to being 'okay'. Angelique playfully made out as though she was going to push her mother off the gang-plank. Both burst out laughing and explored the delightful island with its famous coloured front doors, and buying jewellery and glassware the island is noted for.
It was a pensive trip back to San Marco Piazza, both deep in their thoughts.

'Reading in that book that we only have 'now' was such a revelation, bloody obvious when you think of it. The past is a 'has-been' and the future is a 'not-yet', which may never come. All that we can enjoy is this very moment, just now – that's it. AND my present moment is PERFECT. Apart from the fact that Venice is unforgettable, I'll never forget it for me finally 'getting' that. I guess that's what they call an 'aha' moment.'

After their Vienna and Venetian holiday, Gilda went back to teaching and Angelique started a new position in the taxation section for one of the Big Five accounting firms in Brisbane.
By the end of the year, Gilda could see that there was something wrong with her daughter. 'Schatzi, you don't seem your cheery self these days. Is anything wrong?'

'I know I shouldn't complain but I feel suffocated at work. I should be grateful to have got the job from so many applicants but…,' she hesitated.

'But what', her mother asked. 'I can see you're unhappy.'
'The work is repetitive and boring. I like working with figures and that's why I did a Master of Professional Accounting but this is beyond repetitive. I also know I have to do 'my time' before advancement but, I've seen people who've been there three and four years still doing the same stuff. I'd die if I have to do it that long.'

'Hey. It's okay, you don't have to die. There is an alternative.'

'What,' Angelique said putting her lower lip out as she did when she was younger.

Gilda burst out laughing.

'It's not a laughing matter,' her daughter complained.

'I'm laughing at your lip.' They both laughed.

'Okay, then, what's the alternative?'

'Leave, quit, resign, look for another job.'

'I can't do that. I haven't even been there a year.'

'I didn't say, quit immediately. I just said it was an option, just so that you move way from things being bleak'

After thinking a moment, Angelique said, 'Um, well, I can also ask my immediate boss if she can give me more interesting work as well as what I have to do.'

'Now you're thinking. When will you do that?'

'Tomorrow,' Angelique exclaimed filled with renewed enthusiasm.

'That's my clever girl. What would you like for lunch? Or, how about we go to Cleveland and eat by the water?'

'Fabulous. I'll go and change'.
When Angelique had left to go to her room, Gilda thought, 'There is nothing more important in life than to be happy, nothing and, from my readings I now know, that only I can make myself happy. As I now say, 'Happiness is an inside job.' Whatever my circumstances I can change them through how I think. Sometimes, it's bloody difficult but…that's it.'

'Come on slow poke,' she teased her daughter. 'It'll be dark before we get there.'

CHAPTER 37
2004-2005

Hanna was now 84 years old, Gilda was 60 and Angelique, 25.

Hanna had stopped telling Gilda that the way she was bringing up her daughter would lead to her being spoilt and useless.

Nevertheless, Hanna persisted in trying to educate Gilda to become the model daughter she wanted. Fortunately, from Gilda's perspective, they didn't see much of each other and when they did meet, Gilda braced herself for the inevitable. Sometimes, Hanna merely made snide remarks, but at other times it was full-out yelling of insults. No visit was ever pleasant.

Despite Gilda and Angelique's resolve not to answer the phone, they would forget. 'I'm coming' Gilda shouted as she came puffing into the house, to be told by Angelique, 'It's Oma' as she handed her mother the phone. 'Oh, hello, Mom. What's up?' Gilda asked as she took the phone.

'Gilda, what have you been doing? You are puffed. You are not as fit as you should be. You eat too much, that's why you are fat.' 'Listen, Mom, if you rang to insult me, I'm hanging up'.

'No, no wait, I must speak to you. Ivan has gone out and we can talk alone,' Hanna said.' 'Well, fire away. We're talking now.' 'No, you must come here. I can't tell you over the telephone,' countered Hanna. 'Why, said Gilda? Because someone will hear what you have to say? Come on, you're in Australia, you've been here over 50 years, people don't eavesdrop on phone calls. In any case, I'm sure what you want to tell me isn't top secret espionage information.' 'You can never be too careful, my mother always said,' whispered Hanna.

'Look, tell me now,' said Gilda. 'No, come over,' and history repeated itself. Hanna hung up and left Gilda dangling. 'Damn, she always does that. In all conscience, I can't not go.
Gilda had been gardening when her mother phoned so she

showered and then drove to her house. She rang the front door bell and heard her mother's thump, thump, thump footsteps approaching. Hanna opened the door with a morose look on her face and slumping shoulders. Alarmed, Gilda asked, 'What's the matter?' 'Come in so that I can close the door,' was the reply. 'Would you like some tea?' 'No, thanks. Can you please just get on with it? "Ivan isn't…."' and Hanna stopped. 'Ivan isn't what?' Hanna chewed her lips and then continued, 'Ivan isn't really well.' 'What do you mean, Ivan isn't really well? If he is unwell it means he's sick.'

'Well, in a way, yes.'

Gilda was starting to lose patience. 'Which one, is he, well or sick? You always do that, talk in riddles.'

'You'll be sorry when I'm gone.'

'Let's keep you out of this,' snapped Gilda, 'we're talking about Ivan. If you don't tell me what's going on, I'm leaving. I mean it. And, it'll be another bloody wasted trip.'

'I am telling you, but you're not listening.' Hanna was starting to get agitated.

'There's no need to get upset. I'm asking you to clarify what you mean about Ivan because at this point, I have no idea what you're talking about.'

Hanna put her head between her hands. She'd been doing that for years every time she wanted sympathy.

Gilda silently thought, 'If I say anything, she'll start to scream at me. I'll just wait.'

Finally, Hanna spoke. 'Ivan isn't well.'

'What's wrong?' Hanna just shook her head and shrugged her shoulders. 'How long has he been unwell?' Gilda prodded.

Hanna again shrugged her shoulders.

'Has he seen a doctor?'

Suddenly, without any warning, Hanna leapt from her chair and waving her arms at her daughter screamed, 'You always make life difficult for me. You never listen. I've told you everything but you don't listen. You're still the insolent, rude, rotten child you have always been.'

Hanna didn't come any closer, so Gilda remained seated. But Hanna was relentless, 'GET OUT, GET OUT YOU PIECE OF NOTHING. Get out before I throw something at you.' As she made a move for her, Gilda rose and left the house. Just as she was about to drive off, she saw Ivan walking along the street.

Gilda backed up, got out of her car, and went over to him. 'Hello, Darling,' Ivan said smiling. 'Hello Ivan. How are you?' 'Good, beautiful day, isn't it?'

'Ivan, I need to speak to you quickly,' and as briefly as she could, Gilda told him what transpired.

'Oh, no need to worry,' said Ivan, 'you know what your mother's like. Always tries to dramatise things. No need to worry".

'But what about her outbursts? They are getting worse.'

'That's just who she is,' Ivan said, patting Gilda on the shoulder, 'Would you like to come in for a coffee?' "No, thanks. I'll be off then. Bye, bye.'

'Bye, bye, Gilda.'

As she drove off, Gilda asked herself, 'Are they both nuts. What sort of a world do they live in? Two weeks later, Hanna rang again. The answering machine replied. Hanna had left a message, 'Gilda, it's your mother. I want to tell you about Ivan, please call back. Darling I must to talk to you."

Gilda listened and when the message was complete, she said out loud, 'Well, DARLING, doesn't want to talk to you.'

Every ten minutes after that for the next hour or so, Hanna rang and left the same message for Gilda. Then the messages stopped. 'Hell, I hate this. On the one hand, I'm sure she's playing games but on the other hand, what if she isn't?' She waited for about 15 minutes. 'I can't stand this any longer. I'll have to go over.'

When Gilda arrived at her mother's house, Ivan was in the garden clipping rose bushes.

'Hello Ivan. Can you come inside, please? Ivan sensed that something was amiss. He washed his hands under the front tap and then went inside. Hanna was seated. Gilda saw that her mother was nervous and was fidgeting with her hands.

'Right, you two,' said Gilda, 'I'd like some answers. No beating around the bush, straight answers.' Looking at Ivan she asked, 'Ivan, are you ill?'

'Now, Gilda, where are your manners,' interjected Hanna.

Ignoring her mother, Gilda continued, 'Ivan, I asked you a question.' Ivan looked pained, embarrassed. Hanna interjected, 'Gilda we don't talk about such things in this house.'

'Talk about what things? What makes us so different from other families that we don't talk openly to each other? Why is unmannerly to talk about illness? It shows that people care, which would be a bit of a novelty in this house.'

Ivan held his hand up to quieten Hanna. 'It's alright Schatzilein, I'll answer Gilda's question. Gilda, I have bone cancer.'

'What? How long have you known?'

'About 10 years. The diagnosis was difficult because at first the doctors thought it was the gunshot wound in my leg from the war that made things a bit difficult. But for sure, I have known for seven years.'

'Ivan, I'm truly sorry,' said Gilda.

'See what you've now done, you, insensitive piece of shit,' Hanna spat venomously at her daughter. 'Hanna, please,' Ivan implored, 'There is no need to talk to Gilda like that. She only wants to help.' 'Gilda help? How can she help? She can't help herself let alone someone else. She can only ruin things. She's ruined my life.' Gilda glared at her mother and then looked back at Ivan, 'Is there anything I can do to help?'

'You can get out,' screamed Hanna, 'There is nothing you can do. Now everyone will know the shame that is in our house, another shame,' yelled Hanna.

'What do you mean 'shame'? And what do you mean by 'another shame?' It's no shame to have cancer. It's sad, yes, but nothing to be ashamed of. Ivan, is that why you kept it a secret?'

Ivan didn't reply. Dejected, he looked down at the floor. His six feet frame had suddenly shrunk. 'Do you really feel ashamed because you have cancer?' Gilda waited but no answer came. Gilda continued, 'This is crazy. Where do you get such idiotic notions from? It's a stupid way of thinking from the old country that, if someone isn't perfect outwardly, it's shameful for the family. Instead of supporting Ivan, Mom, you condemn him like a leper. That is just plain cruel.'

Gilda paused and then said slowly and fixed her eyes on her mother. 'Now I get what you meant when you said 'another shame' – it's me, it's my left eye; it's MY SMALLER, BLIND EYE. I've been an embarrassment to you.' She paused again for effect, 'Let me make you aware of something. I was a baby, six months old in YOUR care when it happened but it has never occurred to me to hold it against you because things happen in war-time. We both survived and live a very good life despite our differences. Think about that.'

Turning back to Ivan, Gilda asked, "What does the doctor say? Tell me the truth.'

'They aren't sure, maybe I have two or three years left.'

Gilda was horrified, she was speechless.

With all the determination she could muster she said, 'Okay, then, a question Ivan, what do you want to do with the rest of your life? You've said you may have two or three years, what do you want to do in those years? You don't have to answer now, but it's something you need to think about. You need to think about yourself and the simple fact that we are here to help you.' She waited for a moment for it to sink in and then continued, 'Look, there's no need to talk about this everytime we meet but, if there is a development, we need to discuss it. Is that understood? And, if there is anything we can do, you need to tell us. Does your daughter know?'

'No, Danika doesn't. Please, don't tell her. I'll tell her when I'm ready.'

'Ivan, she loves you, she would want to know.'

Hanna wanted to rejoin the conversation and interjected, 'Why? So that her mother and her husband can gloat about the situation?' 'Hanna, that is despicable, it's too disgusting to comment on,' Gilda replied. Continuing, she sought confirmation, 'Ivan, will you let me know what's going on…please…we're family for heaven's sake. Angelique and I care about you. You and Mom are not alone in this.'

Tears came to his eyes. It was as though the tension and strain of having to keep his condition a secret for so long had released itself. His eyes said it all, they looked softly at Gilda. Nothing more needed to be said.

No one was paying attention to Hanna and she was clearly unhappy, 'Enough of this sentimental schmooze. Don't you have to go home, Gilda? Leave us to sort out this mess you have put us in.'

That evening Ivan rang Gilda to say that an ambulance had taken Hanna to the nearby private hospital again. The ambulance paramedic was concerned about her heart. 'Thanks, Ivan, I'll contact the hospital. How are you? Do you want me to come over?'

'No, Darling, I'm alright. I'll have a whiskey or two,' he chuckled. 'That's my boy, good idea. I'll join you in spirit with a vodka,' she said and they hung up.

Later, Gilda rang the hospital and was told that Hanna was undergoing tests and would then be lightly sedated to sleep. She was to ring in the morning when the test results would be known.

Gilda rang the following morning and was asked to come to the hospital. Gilda was assured that the doctor simply wanted to speak to her. He saw Gilda immediately upon arrival. 'We've done thorough tests on your mother as we did the last time and, just as the last time, the tests found nothing. In future, unless a doctor has seen her and admits her, we do not have the resources for repeated self-admissions that seem unwarranted.'

'I understand, doctor. I'm sorry she's causing problems. I'll take her home now, thank you.'
Gilda waited for Hanna and drove her home. As she got into the car, Hanna moaned, 'Diese Idioten wissen nichts', 'these idiots don't know a thing.' 'Es ist wirklich etwas los mit meinem Herz; 'There's really something wrong with my heart.'

'Mom, please give it up. It's me you're talking to, so cut the crap.' When they arrived at Hanna's, Gilda walked her to the front door and when Ivan opened it Hanna went inside. Gilda said matter-of-factly to him, 'They won't take her again, she bullshitted the whole thing for the second time. She'll have to find another hospital in future.'

Hanna fired up at Gilda, 'You'll all be sorry when I turn out to be right. I'm putting a curse on you and your daughter that you both die and both go hell.' The front door then closed.

One Saturday morning, Angelique reminded her mother of a conversation they had after returning from their last European trip.

'Remember you said that we could go puppy-hunting when we returned?'

'Goodness, I thought you'd forgotten. What a shame you haven't.'

'I've just been so busy.'

'Um, yes, new boyfriend, eh,' Gilda teased.

'Oh, Mum, he's just a friend,' Angelique replied blushing.

'Oh, I thought you two had got married and forgot to tell me.'

Angelique gave her a friendly punch on the arm.

'Okay, let's go to the puppy place.' Her mother acquiesced while rubbing her arm as though it were hurting.

The Pets Paradise Animal Barn was owned by the father of one of Gilda's teaching colleagues He had a strict policy about buying animals from him. No pets were sold at Easter or Christmas and before you could buy a dog from him, you had to spend time with it in a room especially designed for bonding. Gilda and Angelique saw three puppies that interested them which were brought to the Bonding Room – two Maltese terriers and a miniature Poodle. The Maltese Terriers played with Gilda and Angelique while the apricot Poodle stayed and observed what was going on. After an hour, a young couple came and the two Terriers were taken to them in another room. Instantly, the Poodle came to them and played. She was adorable. It was clear that all three got on. After about two hours, Gilda said, 'I think we've 'bonded' enough. I'll tell the sales assistant that we'll let her know our decision tomorrow morning.'
'What, you don't want to take her home now.'

'Angelique, please don't pressure me. I still remember how I had to do everything with Perro and pay all the expenses.'

'Well, I was younger then and I also didn't earn much,' her daughter replied indignantly.

'As I said, we can give our answer tomorrow. This is a long-term commitment and I don't really want another dog even though she's gorgeous.'

During the evening, Angelique kept subtly bringing up about the puppy. Gilda firmly avoided any discussion.

'I just can't go through the anguish of when I had to have Perro put down. It was excruciating. I still also remember when I had to do the same with Benno. I don't want to go through that torture again,' she said to herself.

The next morning, Gilda rang Pets Paradise Animal Barn intending to decline to take the poodle. Angelique already had a woeful look on her face. 'Good morning, you're holding the apricot Poodle for us. I'm just ringing to tell you that we'll be at your place in an hour to collect the pup.'
'What did you say?' Angelique asked astounded.

Momentary silence.

'I can't believe I just said that… I had no intention of saying that… Who the hell, said that through me, said Gilda. She stood in amazement holding the phone in her hand and repeated, 'I had no intention of saying that. I don't want another responsibility.'

'You can phone back and cancel,' her daughter suggested dejectedly.

'No, it's okay. We're obviously meant to have her. Come on. Let's get ready and pick her up.'

'You'll love her, Mum, and I'll help out with the work and financially.'

Gilda smiled kindly at her daughter and said, 'I know I'll love her.'
'What'll we call her?' Angelique asked.

'How about Mirabell after the Palace in Salzburg,' Gilda replied.
'Perfect. She is our Prinzessin Poodle'

At the end of the year, Angelique was asked by a major Australian airline to work in their Corporate Tax division and she accepted the position. This meant that she and Gilda were now able to fly with this airline on stand-by and only needed to pay airport taxes but no actual fares.

For several years, Gilda had attended free information evenings on personal development and Angelique mostly came with her. From these courses they acquired some knowledge but none of the courses strongly resonated with them. Gilda thought to herself, 'I feel like I'm on the cusp of something, a major change, but I can't imagine what.'

Towards the end of the year, they went to a Christopher Howard evening on Neuro-Linguistic Programming (NLP). Gilda had never heard such empowering concepts before. 'This is exactly what I'm looking for but it's such a lot of money.' After the talk, Gilda spoke with a crew member and learned about the payment options. It took her forty-five minutes before she signed up for the whole program using the payment option.

In 2005, Gilda attended the NLP training sessions during school holidays and fortunately, the week-long courses were held at those times. Three-day courses included a weekend so, in no time, she was able to get through a substantial amount of material and apply it in her daily life and her teaching.

'I just love the idea that life is a game,' she mused. 'What are the goals of playing a game, having fun and succeeding? I can bring that into the classroom as well as into my own life. For example, it'll now be the Game of Learning German. Why do we play that game? To Have fun and succeed through learning. Each child learns differently. Nevertheless, each student can still enjoy what they are learning; that's the emphasis I'll now place on teaching the subject. It's no longer to pass an exam, it's to enjoy it. It'll just be the success that'll be different depending on the desire and reason why the student is learning the language - if they just want to learn it in Year 8, there'll be a different motivation than if a child wants to go on to Year 10 or year 12. No child will then feel that they have to have the same approach to the subject, nor be evaluated against another student – stuff that stupid Bell curve. This puts real meaning into the buzz concept that, 'We are all unique.'

Something she learned which made a big difference in her own life was that, beliefs are not necessarily true. A belief can be a lie, often beliefs can't be proved and no one knows how they eventuated in the first place. They often just came down from generation to generation or societal norms that may no longer be applicable.
For Gilda, the concepts were new and challenging. 'That means that the point is not, whether the belief is true or false BUT whether it empowers me or not? Is it good for me, for others and for the environment if I act as though that belief is true? That is huge. It basically turns my view of the world as I've learned it on its head unless it empowers me. That is going to take some getting used to,' As 2005 wore on, Ivan's cancer was speedily progressing in his body. it was obvious that Ivan was being badly affected by the condition of his body. To ease the discomfort, he was drinking more whisky.

'You shouldn't drink so much,' Hanna reproached him.

'Why? Do you think I'll live longer if I don't,' he replied. 'Nothing can slow the decline and drinking whisky helps at the moment. Maybe in the future I may not even be able to enjoy that. So, leave me alone with your opinions and wisdom.'

Hanna was shocked. He had never spoken to her like that. 'You will see that I am right,' was all she could say. What Hanna said made no sense but she had to have the last say.

'I'll ring Gilda and tell her how obnoxious he has become and because I am so weak it's affecting my health. It's all her fault anyway for having brought it out into the open.' She dialed Gilda. 'Damned answering machine again. It's always on. Gilda, it's your mother here. Ring me when you come back, Ivan is becoming impossible. I can't handle him. You know how ill I am, my heart…' Gilda heard the message and smiled, 'I bet he's taken his hearing aid out, is drinking whisky and she's furious because she can't get through to him. Good for you Ivan!'

CHAPTER 38
2006-2007

Whenever possible, Gilda crewed at Neuro-Linguistic Programming (NLP) events to hone her skills whether these were in Brisbane or in Sydney. In addition, she enrolled in Stocks and Share Trading courses. 'I've always been fascinated with that area. It's not something that is familiar to me as no one in our European circle did that sort of thing. It was looked on as gambling.' To study this new area, Gilda had found a husband and wife team from the Sunshine Coast just north of Brisbane who conducted these courses and she and Angelique often attended weekend workshops there. 'Teaching is really changing,' Gilda said to her daughter one Saturday morning as they sat on the patio eating plain and chocolate croissants with butter.

'What do you mean?'

'Even though we're a private school, we're starting to be inundated with government forms to complete if the school wants to keep receiving funding. There's one checklist after another and, in addition, they are starting to tell us how to implement the curriculum that they have set.'

'Um, bureaucracy justifying the way they spend the taxpayers' money.'

'Yes, that's true.' 'These croissants are delicious. I especially love the chocolate ones, her daughter gushed.

'I prefer the plain ones,' Gilda replied, and so ended the depressing conversation about education. It was a glorious summer's day. They ate in silence for some time listening to the birds, watching butterflies land on flowers and looking at the beautiful shrubs on the upper terraces.

'I have an idea,' Gilda said breaking the reverie. 'Why am I not surprised?' Angelique joked.

'I'll apply to teach German to adults at TAFE evening classes. That'll be an interesting diversion from only teaching school children. I'll also write a six week course on using NLP in daily life. The evening sessions are two hours, that'll be just the right amount of hours to make it beneficial because some of its principles have helped me enormously. This is getting really exciting.' 'Sounds good to me,' Angelique said dreamily gazing into the blue sky and munching on a chocolate croissant. She knew better than to try to dissuade her mother when she had one of her 'brilliant ideas'. 'And then I can apply to do corporate training courses at the University of Queensland's Adult Education division's two day programs. And that is what Gilda did, enjoying the experience immensely. 'I love teaching these evening classes. Teaching adults is quite a different dynamic and I'm in total control of the curriculum and how I implement it. I like that. As for UQ courses, they are really stretching me but I thrive on that.'

Soon UQ was also asking Gilda to submit tailored proposals for in-house training requests from specific organizations. These needed to be scheduled at weekends because she still taught full-time.
In March, 2006, the family got together for Ivan's birthday. 'Come on Sweetie. Ready?' Gilda asked her daughter. 'Yep, in a couple of minutes. I wonder what sort of mood Oma's going to be in tonight. She'll be in her usual pontificating mood but otherwise…it's anyone's guess. I'm bracing myself for anything. She's worse than a volcano,' Gilda replied.

'Darlings,' Hanna greeted them at the door, 'Right on time as always, so nice to see you. Oh, my goodness, what a pretty dress you have on, Angelique! Oh, and Gilda, you too! Look Ivan, don't the girls look lovely,' she gushed. Ivan agreed as he walked up to them with a bottle oil in one hand. He was obviously in charge of making a salad.

The doorbell rang again. 'Ah, Danika. The other two have just arrived. Come on in, don't you look nice too,' she schmoozed looking Danika up and down. Gilda and Angelique glanced across at each other. Danika caught their glance and raised an eyebrow. Hanna followed Ivan into the kitchen. Gilda spoke first, 'I don't know why, but I feel it's like the calm before the storm.' The other two nodded. Danika said, 'We'd better be on our best behaviour, I'd say.'

They sat in their usual places at the table. 'Oh, but no, my Darlings,' Hanna said waltzing into the dining room with arms fluttering and waving them into the lounge. 'Come first into the lounge and let's have a glass of champagne. Ivan is just finishing off the salads. Then we'll have a birthday toast first.' She then called out, 'Ivan, will you please stop what you are doing, we want to toast your birthday, Darling.'

Silence from the kitchen. Ivan didn't appear.

'Ivan, Darling, did you hear?' Hanna raised herself elegantly on her tip toes showing her long dress to full effect and held her hand to her lips as she called again. Still nothing. Hanna was about to investigate when Ivan called, 'Yes, there in a moment.'

'But, Ivan, please… that is no way to behave. You're holding us up, Darling,' Hanna said grandly yet sweetly. 'Oh, boy,' thought Gilda, 'this is going to be an interesting evening. How long can she keep this up?'

Hanna then went into the kitchen. Those in the lounge could hear muffled German being spoken. The voices were kept low but they kept hearing Ivan's name with Hanna being the only voice that could be heard.

Then, they both appeared. Hanna was charmingly gliding along, a big smile on her face. Ivan followed carrying a bottle of champagne. He had a dead-pan look on his face and didn't say anything as he started to pour the champagne. When everyone had their glass filled, Hanna ceremoniously continued with a childlike giggle, 'He's such a workaholic. I had to drag him away from the kitchen.' Happy birthday, Darling, she said with a coquettish laugh.
'Happy birthday, Daddy,' Danika said. 'Happy birthday, Opa,' added Angelique. 'Happy birthday, Ivan,' contributed Gilda.
They all took a sip, Ivan emptied his glass and as he had the bottle

in his hand, he refilled his glass. Again he emptied it. Again he refilled it and winked. Gilda, Danika and Angelique stifled a laugh. Hanna had turned to look at the dining room table and hadn't seen Ivan's antics. She looked at the other three as they giggled and asked what was funny.

'Oh, nothing, Mom, it's just a happy occasion, isn't it?'
Hanna eyed Ivan but he had a poker face and said, 'Beautiful weather today, wasn't it?' This was all too much and everyone couldn't hold a straight face and burst out laughing. 'What is funny? What is going on?' Hanna demanded.

'Oh, it's nothing, Oma,' Angelique said as she put her arm through her grandmother's trying to avert a scene. 'I demand to know what is going on,' Hanna said drawing her arm away. She was now starting to go over the edge.

'Mom, it really isn't anything,' Gilda said calmly. 'Ivan was just being a bit cheeky. He drank the first glass in one swig and then filled it again making out as though he had only taken a small sip. That's all. Just some tomfoolery. It's his birthday.'

'I see,' Hanna said venomously, 'You are making a fool of me behind my back'.

'No, Schatzi,' Ivan said trying to placate her, 'it was just a bit of nonsense.'

'So, you think it is just a bit of nonsense to ridicule me behind my back? To make fun of me; to make me look like an idiot?'

'Hanna, I wasn't making fun of you,' Ivan tried but Hanna glared at him with such ferocity that everyone was stunned by her reaction. 'Oh, hell, we're in for it now,' Gilda murmured under her breath and then looked over at Ivan who had a grin on his face. I wonder how much he's already had to drink. Now, he's playing with fire.'
'Shall we all sit down to eat,' Ivan suggested going to the table to hold Hanna's chair for her. Silently she sat down but it was obvious she was stewing. Everyone sat in their places – Hanna and Ivan at

the head of the table, Gilda to her mother's left, opposite her was Angelique and next to her sat Danika.

Ivan went around the table pouring the remainder of the champagne. Danika stopped drinking. She had to drive home. She didn't drink as a rule, not even finishing her first glass. Gilda however, had no trouble keeping Ivan company.

Gilda spoke first holding a dish of Wiener schnitzel toward her mother, 'Here Mom, would you like some?'

Hanna took a piece of Schnitzel without saying a word. 'Ivan, a piece?' He took one, 'Thanks, Darling.' Gilda offered a filet to the others before taking one herself. In the meantime, the salads were doing the rounds. There was an ominous silence as they ate. 'Delicious, isn't it,' Gilda said hoping to liven things up. 'Indeed,' replied Danika. Ivan went to get the white wine from the kitchen and helped himself to more food when he returned. 'More wine, Gilda?' 'I'd hate to see the birthday boy drink on his own,' Gilda jested.

Hanna spoke for the first time. Her first words were ominous. 'Yes, Ivan, just keep eating and drinking, you're already so fat, why not get fatter,' Hanna said offensively. Ivan didn't look up from his plate and just kept eating. It didn't take long for his daughter, Gilda and Angelique to work out that Ivan had turned his hearing aid off and couldn't hear Hanna.

Gilda had to get up and move to the toilet or she would have burst out laughing. When she got into the bathroom, she turned the taps on and flushed the toilet so that no one could hear her stifling her laughter with the hand towel.

From the lounge room she could hear Angelique's unmistakable loud laughter. 'Oh, no, now the shit's going to hit the fan. And it did. When Gilda returned to the table, Hanna was standing behind her chair. Gilda slid into hers and sat down.

'You think you are all so clever. You think you are all so smart.

Ivan, you are drunk. You are disgusting. As for you Gilda, your daughter has no manners. You have brought her up to be an imbecile, a stupid idiot. But what can one expect from someone like you. I tried to give you the breeding that is part of our family heritage but first, you married beneath our class, then he divorced you and took another woman because you were not good enough for him in bed. As for you, Danika, your mother is a whore. She ran off with your father's best friend and your husband ran off with other women. I'm not surprised. How could he live with someone as fat as you? How could he look at someone like you every day? You are repulsive.'

'Hey, hold on Mom,' said Gilda, 'that's uncalled for. What's got into you? What's the matter with you?'

'You shut up, shut up before I thrash you. You are still my daughter and I can do whatever I like to you and say whatever I like.' Gilda rose from her chair and defiantly stood in front of her mother. 'You lay a hand on me and I can assure you, you'll be sorry.'

Hanna took her glass and threw the contents at Gilda and laughed in her face. 'You're a mess anyway, clean that up off yourself.' With that Hanna sat down triumphantly giving her head a jubilant shake to one side, 'I am always the smart one; remember that.'

'Well,' Danika began, 'On that note I think I'll go home. Bye, Gilda, bye, Angelique, goodbye Daddy.' She then gave him a peck on the cheek and said 'Happy birthday.'

After Danika had left, Gilda said to Ivan, 'We can't go and leave you alone with her when she's in this state.' 'It's alright, he replied, 'She'll just yell for a bit and then go into her room and close the door. She'll give me the cold shoulder treatment. You both should go home.'

'I'm not happy about leaving you.'

'Really, I'll be fine. Go. Thanks for the lovely present. I'll enjoy it.'

'Keep the mobile close to you and if you need me, just ring and I'll come over.'

He smiled as he guided them to the front door.

'Bye, Mom.' 'Bye Oma.'

Hanna had left the table and gone to her desk in the adjoining room and turned her computer on.

Ivan shut the door behind them and started cleaning up from dinner. 'That's another birthday out of the way,' he thought. Gilda learned from Ivan that he and Hanna didn't speak again that night nor the following morning.

Not long after the disastrous birthday party, Angelique met a young man with whom, it would eventuate, she would have a serious relationship.

In December, Gilda and Angelique did a tour of Spain, Portugal and Morocco. 'God' thought Gilda, 'I love going away. You leave all the crap behind. No one can get in touch as you're on the move so much.' It was a lovely holiday. There was another single mother and her son. He was bit older than Angelique and they became good friends.

Two weeks after Gilda returned home from the tour, in 2007, the pupil-free week started with preparations for the new academic year that would start after the Australia Day long weekend. The following weekend, Ivan rang to say that Hanna had admitted herself to a private hospital in the city. 'Okay, Ivan, I'll look after it. How are you?'

'Oh, you know, some days are better than others but I'm alright. Don't worry.'

'I wonder if he's told Danika yet. I don't want to bring it up,' Gilda thought.

After school, Gilda picked Angelique up from work and they went to the hospital. The nurse showed them to Hanna's room. 'Oh Darlings, how nice of you to come,' she oozed sweetly as the nurse tucked her sheet in.

Another nurse came into the room and said, 'The doctor would like to see you, Mrs Hollten.' 'Coming. Won't be long Mom,' Gilda said as she and Angelique left Hanna's room.

'I see you did manage to make time in your busy schedule for your sick mother,' the doctor said as he saw Gilda. Gilda was taken aback by his attitude and tone of voice.

It took her so off guard that she replied defensively, 'I teach during the day and came as soon as classes were over.'

The doctor continued his verbal attack, 'Your mother has told me all about you and how you don't care for her and don't visit her when she's in hospital. That she often has to stay longer in hospital because you don't have time to pick her up.'

'Excuse me!' Gilda said. 'I don't like your tone and you have no right to talk to me like that. You are accusing me of neglecting my mother. You know nothing about the situation and yet you judge the situation. I wish to speak to your senior.'

'There is no one else here,' the doctor said smugly.

'Very well, then I will speak to the sister or another medical person in charge and make a formal complaint against your attitude towards me and with regard to your accusations.'

Angelique was furious and stepped forward saying, 'How dare you speak to my mother like that! You are taking the words of a woman who makes a habit of admitting herself into hospital so much so that the last hospital will no longer admit her without a doctor's referral. That is why she admitted herself here.'

'Never mind him, Angelique, I'll deal with him later. I'm going back to Mom.'

'I'll be there in a minute, Mum, I will talk to the doctor.'

Not long after, her daughter came back and said to Gilda that the doctor wanted to speak to her.

'I have nothing to say to him, nor am I interested in anything he has to say to me.'

'Mum, I think you should hear him out.'

'No,' said Gilda as she turned to her mother, 'I've had about enough of this. What did you tell that doctor? He accused me of neglecting you.'

'Oh, no, darling, he would have made that all up. I told him that you would be here as soon as school finished, that you always looked after me. I never complained about you. He's such a nice man, a bit young and that's why he would have misunderstood. Charming fellow though, isn't he?' Hanna then stretched out her hand to hold Gilda's hand. Gilda moved away to avoid contact. 'You've been flirting with this one too! I don't believe it. You're the limit,' Gilda said as she moved further away from her mother's reach. At that moment, the doctor looked into the room. He had heard everything Hanna said. He waited until Gilda came out to have her mother discharged.

'I'm terribly sorry, I believed what she said. What can I say?' Gilda looked at him coldly and said, 'It's not your business to jump to conclusions nor to judge the family of any patient entrusted to you. You are here to go by the medical facts not by what an emotional, manipulating old woman tells you. Did any of the tests show anything wrong?' He shook his head. 'Then there are no MEDICAL FACTS, are there?' He shook his head. She looked at him sternly, 'I have nothing more to say to you except that I hope our paths never cross again and, that you've learned from this experience. Move please to let me pass.'

Hanna and Angelique were waiting for Gilda as she returned from getting car. 'Darling…' Hanna started.

'Just get in the car and don't say a word, NOT A WORD. Do you hear? I've had enough of you. Ivan is the one who is really dying and you continue with these antics. You don't give a shit about him. You don't give a shit about anyone. You are so full of yourself. How you ever became so rotten, I don't know. I guess it's because no one ever stood up to you from the beginning.

Hanna started to speak. 'Shut up,' Gilda said, 'just shut up.'
They arrived at Hanna's. Immediately, Ivan was at the front door with a concerned look on his face. Calmly, Gilda said to him, 'Again, there's nothing wrong with her.' Hanna looked imploringly at him but you could see that he no longer had the energy to play her games. He walked off to his study and sat at his desk looking over stamps with his magnifying glass.

A month later, on a Thursday evening, Gilda received a call, 'This is the General Hospital, and we've just admitted Ivan Martin. He was brought here by ambulance. Your name is here as a contact.'
'Yes, thank you. I'm leaving home now. I'll be there soon.' 'What's up Mum,' Angelique asked. Gilda gave her daughter the bare facts,

'Opa's been admitted to hospital. I'm going there now.'

'I'll drive you and stay with you.'

When they arrived at the hospital, admittance personnel took them to Ivan. Gilda greeted cheerfully, 'Hey Ivan, what's up, buddy?'

'Your mother panicked. I just tripped. Look, it's nothing.'

'Oh, okay, then. I'll just go and see the doctor. See what he has to say. Angelique will stay with you.'

'You bet, Opa. I won't let you go jogging tonight,' Angelique joked.

Ivan laughed. The very thought of him going jogging was ludicrous. He and exercise never travelled together.

'Hello, doctor, I'm Gilda Hollten. Ivan is my mother's partner.' 'Oh, yes, interesting case, Mrs. Hollten.' 'What do you mean,' Gilda asked.

The reason the ambulance was called was because he had a fall. But the fall was so minor that there is hardly an injury. However, maybe you know, but there is more that is wrong with him.' Gilda related the conversation she had with Hanna and then with Ivan and said, 'So, as you see, I have no authoritative information, just what my mother and Ivan have told me.'

'Umm, I see. It's necessary that we do more tests but they can't be done till tomorrow. We'll make him comfortable tonight and he can have a good night's rest.'

'What do you think it is, doctor?' 'It's just suspicions on my part at the moment. I would rather wait till I see the test results.' 'Of course, I understand,' said Gilda.

Gilda retuned to Ivan to tell him that he needed to stay the night because tests had to be done in the morning. 'I was just about to make myself a whisky at home,' Ivan said with a sad face.

'Well, you can have two, tomorrow,' Gilda comforted him as she gave him a farewell peck on the cheek.

'What did the doctor say,' Angelique asked. Gilda told her.

'Oh, dear, that doesn't sound too good.' 'No,' Gilda replied frowning.

They went back to Hanna's house. 'How is he? How is my Darling? I've been worried sick. I feel so ill. I've been so worried. I'm so ill,' Hanna said in her best Academy Award performance style as she placed her hand over her heart.

'Let's go into the lounge,' Gilda said avoiding her Hanna's embrace. 'Mom, sit down. The truth now, why did you call the ambulance?' Hanna tensed, defensively, 'What do you mean?'

'You know exactly what I mean. Ivan's fall wasn't the reason you called the ambulance. The doctor said that it must have been minor as there is no evidence that he fell, no bruising, nothing. Why did you call the ambulance?'

Hanna could see that she had been caught out. She held her head in both hands and feigned sobbing.

'Stop it! Just stop it,' Gilda said firmly, 'You wanted him out of the way because you didn't want to deal with him anymore. Tell the truth'.

"No, no, he fell,' Hanna yelled.

'Tell me the truth or you'll never see us again. We'll pick Ivan up from hospital and he can stay with us. Tell the truth for once in your life. And cut the crying nonsense. It's not going to work this time.'

'I am scared. I didn't know what to do,' Hanna pleaded.

'Don't lie. Why did you call the ambulance? We know he didn't fall. He may have tripped but you then saw your chance.'

There was silence for a brief moment and then in a belligerent manner, Hanna replied.' 'Oh, shut up. What do you know,' she spat at her daughter, 'I would now have to look after him. I am the one who needs looking after. I've looked after everyone all my life. All my life! I've given everyone everything. No one has ever given me a thing. I've worked for everything I have. I gave your father everything and then the war came and he left me. Then I had to look after you.'

Hanna continued her rant until she had exhausted her mental list about who she had helped finally returning to the especially 'ungrateful' Ivan.

Gilda and Angelique looked at each other horrified, lost as to what to say or do next.

Suddenly like a viper, Hanna turned and looked at them both and said with increased hostility in her voice, 'Get out of here. Get out the two of you. You are filth. You are rubbish. I've never needed anyone. Everyone has always needed me. Yes, I did want him out of the house. Why should I now look after him? He's dying. So what? So what? Everyone dies. But I need to look after myself because I'm alive. I'm alive. He's had it anyway. Get out.'

Gilda ignored her mother's outburst, and turned to Angelique and quietly said, 'She's crazy. I can't leave her alone. Who knows what she'll do.' Gilda turned to her mother saying, 'Look Mom, I'll stay the night and tomorrow. We'll work out what to do. I'll ring the College and tell them I won't be in and we can sort everything out. There are aged-care groups that send people to help out.'

'I'm not having strangers in my house who will rob me. Get out, I said. Get out both of you. I don't need anyone. GET OUT.' Hanna then went to the kitchen and came back threatening them with the broom repeating, 'GET OUT.'

'What the hell do we do,' Gilda asked Angelique as they returned to the car. She'll be okay tonight and I don't think she'll play one of her tricks because she won't want the neighbours to know what's gone on. Tomorrow I'll ring that Eureka place that advertises aged-care help.'

The next day at the hospital, Gilda's worst fears became a reality. The doctor said, 'Ivan does have bone cancer. It's hard to say how long he has to live, perhaps a few weeks, but not long. It would be best if we kept him here and then we can transfer him to palliative care as soon as necessary. I'm sorry.'

Gilda stared at the doctor. 'Are you alright, Mrs Hollten?' the doctor asked putting a hand out in case she needed support. 'Yes, thanks, doctor. I was expecting it but it's still a shock to actually hear it. You're sure? Only a few weeks?'

'A few weeks at the most,' was the reply.

Silence, then Gilda asked, 'What should I do now? I've no experience in this. I've never seen anyone die before nor known anyone who was dying.'

'Come, sit down. Nurse, would you please bring Mrs Hollten some tea? The doctor then went through what would happen during the palliative care treatment and then after that. I suggest that you and other loved ones come as often as you can. His discomfort will escalate and he'll be mostly comforted with increasing amounts of morphine."

Gilda wept.

The doctor waited before he continued, 'Coming to see him is not only good for him but it'll also be good for your closure when he passes on.'

Gilda nodded with a hint of a smile. Gilda informed Danika, Angelique and Hanna.

Danika visited her father daily on her own, and Gilda and Angelique picked up Hanna and they visited him at other times.

A week later, the hospital rang to say that Ivan had been moved to palliative care. For over a week, Gilda, Hanna, Danika and Angelique took turns to sit at Ivan's bedside.

Ivan spoke normally and everyone contributed to keeping the mood calm but interactive. Suddenly, Ivan took a deep breath, gave a big sigh and the next instant he was gone.

It was over. Ivan was 81, Hanna was 87, Gilda 63, and Angelique 28.

Danika took care of the funeral arrangements but she said, 'Gilda, would you please take charge of everything on the day of the funeral and read the eulogy. I don't think I'd be able to hold it together if I had to do anything at the funeral.'

'Yes, of course. Just tell me what you want me to say and do.'

'I leave up to you. You'll know what to say. You'll be better at it than I would be.'

'Angelique has offered to organise the music for the ceremony. Is that okay with you?'

'Oh, yes, indeed, thank you.'

A week after the funeral, they met at Hanna's house to discuss Ivan's Will. Danika already had a copy so it was a short, amicable meeting. After Danika left, Hanna said, 'I wish to say something before you also go. I am now the Matriarch of this family. There are just the three of us and, from this moment on, what I say goes,' she said to her daughter and granddaughter.

Both Gilda and Angelique looked at her and then at each other. Gilda turned to her mother and said, 'Mom, are you serious?'
'Of course, I'm very serious and I suggest you take what I say seriously as well.'

'Listen, Mom, you've always had delusions of grandeur. Honestly, how long have you known me? 63 years? I've never done what you've said just because you said it. What makes you think I'm about to start now? And as for Angelique, she is a young woman and makes her choices as she sees fit. I don't expect her to do 'as I say', nor can you.

'Angelique, you will do as I say,' said Hanna.

'Mom, stop trying to intimidate her. Angelique, if you want to leave, you can.'

'No, it's okay, Mom, I'll stay here and support you.'

'Very well, Hanna said, 'I'll disinherit both of you.'

'Aha, so that's the game you're going to play now.' Gilda said.

'Forget it. It's not going to work. You can disinherit us if you want. Neither of us cares. Any form of blackmail like that will just drive us away. Think about it. You are on your own now, so I suggest we all get on and help each other. I don't want to see you suffer but, equally, I won't let you bully us, especially not Angelique. Do you understand?'

No reply.
'Okay then, time for us to go,' Gilda said, 'Bye Mom, I'll ring you later. By the way, can I have a key to the house? Now that you are alone, it would be wiser that I can have access.'

'I don't have a spare key,' Hanna replied sullenly.

'Okay, then I'll take the set of keys that were amongst Ivan's personal effects that I brought from the hospital. I know where I put them in his study.'

A couple of days later, Angelique approached her mother, 'Mum, got a second? I need to talk to you.'

'Sure, Schatzi, what's up?'

'I'm planning on moving in with Errol. I hope that's okay.'

Gilda was stunned but she pulled herself together, 'Yes, of course, Sweetie. If you're serious about each other, it's important you live together. What's the old saying, 'try before you buy?'
'Thanks, Mum, you're the best. Gotta fly now, he'll be here any minute. We're going to the beach. I'll move out over the weekend. Okay?'

'Okay, no problem. Have fun. It's a beautiful day.'

After they left Gilda sat on the patio and Mirabell jumped on her lap. 'Well. My girl, it's just you and me now.' 'I've been blessed, really lucky to have Angelique live with me for so long. I hope this is the right guy. I hope he'll treat her well, she deserves it, my Angel on Earth. Tears started to gently cloud her eyes, trickle down her cheeks and land on her hands as she was patting Mirabell. She gave her pet a big hug.

Once again she felt numb but this numbness was different from the usual when she needed to cope. This dull pain constricted her heart and almost left her breathless.
By the end of the weekend, Angelique had moved out. Gilda would walk into her room and lean at the door just gazing into the now characterless room.

The following Wednesday, Gilda went to her mother's house to take her shopping. This was now a weekly occurrence so that Gilda could monitor that her mother ate properly. Although 'Meals on Wheels' came twice a week, Hanna also liked fresh fruit. The two would sit at Hanna's favourite coffee shop at the Centre and have coffee and cake before Gilda drove her mother home. She ensured that the foodstuffs were put into either the fridge or the cupboard. On one occasion she smelled something was off and saw rotting fresh smoked salmon in the cupboard.

Over coffee Hanna said, 'You're living alone now and so am I. It would make sense if you moved in into the unit downstairs. You'd have a completely separate residence. It would be such a comfort for me to know you were there. We wouldn't get in each other's way. You have your career and you know how independent I am. I'll soon be 88 and who knows what could happen.'

'I'll think about it,' Gilda replied.

On the way home, she thought, 'Actually, it does make sense. I'll set the boundaries before I move in and keep her to them. I'm at the College during the day anyway.'

That weekend she and Mirabell moved into the unit under Hanna's house. It was comfortable - a large bedroom with room for a desk, sideboard, wardrobes and lounge chairs. The sliding door opened onto a patio. The room next to it contained a small but adequate kitchen and space for a small dining suite. That also led out to the same patio. Gilda's car was parked under the house with a locked garage door and entrance directly into her lockable unit. The patio accessed a beautiful garden with flowers and trees to which Ivan had loved to escape. He also had a fern house. All the large trees had massive ferns growing on them. Since his death, a gardener was employed to cut the lawn and keep the undergrowth from becoming a jungle.

On Sunday afternoon when Gilda moved in, mother and daughter enjoyed pleasant coffee and cake on the patio and in the evening after Hanna had gone back upstairs, Gilda and Mirabell stayed outside looking at the stars.

'I think I can make my home anywhere, as long as you're with me of course, little girl.' Gilda squeezed Mirabell who constantly tried to lick her face. 'Oh, no you don't, cheeky. You know I don't like that. I can make a home out of anywhere. Maybe it's because I've moved around so much when I was young and I can create my world in my imagination as well as adding some personal, important possessions such as CDs of music I love, pot plants, and books. Whatever it is, this abode is okay, eh, gorgeous? Damn, time to go inside, the mosquitoes are starting to bite. I'll need to buy some repellent. Oh, well, time to get ready for tomorrow.'

During the Easter break Hanna started to come downstairs more often. One day Gilda said, 'Mom, I'm trying to work. How about we organise that before 11.00 AM that you don't come here. I have some serious teaching commitments and I have courses to prepare to deliver at the University.

Hanna was about to say something but she stopped herself and went back upstairs. Shortly after, Gilda again heard the thump, thump, thump of Hanna's footsteps coming down the internal staircase. Gilda closed her entrance door to give her mother the message. Hanna came to the door and knocked. Gilda called, 'I'm busy and it's not 11.' Silence, then a few seconds later more knocking. 'I won't answer this time.' The knocking continued. 'This is my house,' Hanna called out, 'You'll open the door.'

Gilda went to the door, opened it and said, 'Don't try that approach, Mom. I can leave at any moment. I've asked you to be considerate and I mean it.'

'I'm bored,' Hanna moaned.

'There are a lot of places you could go where older folk gather.'
'Not with those peasants. They are not of my social class.'

'Then read or listen to music. You have plenty that can keep you occupied. Watch TV.'

'I don't feel like any of that.'

'Suit yourself, but I have work to do,' and with that she returned to her laptop. Hanna hovered around but Gilda ignored her and she finally left. 'I don't like the way this is going,' Gilda thought, 'I'm going to have to make sure I don't lose my patience otherwise we'll have a run in.'

The first month passed without major dramas.

One Saturday, Gilda and Hanna were at the shopping centre and a woman stopped them. She and Hanna greeted each other. Hanna introduced Gilda, 'This is my daughter, Gilda.'

The woman looked surprised and repeated, 'Your daughter?' Immediately Gilda knew what was going on. 'Yes,' Gilda cheerily replied, 'I'm her daughter. We've been going shopping together ever since her partner died and I now live with my mother so that she isn't alone and to help her out.'

The woman looked between Hanna and Gilda and it suddenly occurred to her that what Hanna had previously told her were lies. 'I see,' she responded. 'It's been very nice to have met you, Gilda.' Turning to Hanna she said, 'Looks like you've not been all alone after all,' and with that she left them. Hanna made out as though nothing had happened. Gilda inwardly smiled and silently thought, 'I wonder how many more such encounters we're going to have.'

Towards the end of the third month since Gilda had moved in, at 10.00 AM, Gilda heard Hanna thump, thump, thumping down the stairs louder than usual. 'Oops, that doesn't sound too good.' The entrance door was shut. 'Open this blasted door. I'm sick of it being shut. It's my house and I want to come and go as I please.'

Gilda came to the door and said, 'Sorry to contradict you but, I'm a tenant here. I pay my way and with that I have rights to privacy if you want to get official. 'You insolent, bitch,' Hanna replied and lifted her walking stick to strike Gilda.

'Don't you try it,' Gilda warned.

Hanna started her usual rant, 'I'm sick of this life. I'm sick of not having any friends. I'm sick of this country. Why did I ever leave Austria?'

'Listen, Mom, you've chosen this life. With your haughtiness, and your bad temper, you've chased away people who were kind to you.'

'Who?'

'The lady in the wheel chair across the road, for one. She's such a lovely lady.'

'Oh, her, she's stupid.'

'See, listen to yourself. Who do you think you are to speak of her like that and then complain you have no friends?'

'You always stick up for other people and never for me.'

I don't 'stick up' for anyone but fair is fair. You put up with that nosy busybody who helps you with the computer. Heaven only knows what you tell her about me. She's always rude to me whenever she comes when we happen to see each other. She's even sent me emails accusing me of being a dreadful daughter. I wish you wouldn't give people my contact details."

'I don't,' Hanna objected. 'How did she get my email address?'

'From the phone book.' Her mother replied.

'Mom, don't lie, phone books don't have email addresses unless you specifically put them in.'

'See, you did, that's why it's there.'

'Okay, let's go look at the phone book.'

'Stop, will you. Just stop. There you go again. Always against me. I wish you had never come to live here.'

'That's easy fixed. I can move out today.'

Hanna wasn't prepared for that and stormed off upstairs making an even bigger noise than on the way down.

'Honestly, if it weren't pathetic, it would be funny,' Gilda silently thought.'

However, the situation was starting to have its effect on Gilda. She drank more in the evenings and the confidence that had taken years to build up diminished. She felt like the helpless, useless child that Hanna always said she was. The only things which counteracted this were her College, TAFE and University teaching. Each time she arrived home, a dark cloud dragged her down.

At the beginning of her fourth month with Hanna, Angelique moved back into the house. Her relationship had turned sour. Gilda's thoughts were now more on how she could support her heartbroken daughter. 'What the hell am I doing here with this woman who is getting progressively worse when my beautiful child is aching?'

One evening, towards the beginning of the fifth month, Gilda came home from a course at 9.30 PM to find Hanna in her unit.

'What are you doing here,' Gilda asked.

'Let me remind you, it's my house.'

'We're not going to go through that again, are we?'

Gilda went inside and saw that all her drawers were open and her clothes strewn all over the place. 'What have you been doing here?'

'I wanted to see what you have said about me'

'In my drawers?'

'People hide letters in drawers. I know you talk about me behind my back, you always have.'

'Have you gone crazy?'

'If I'm going crazy, it's because of you. You drive me crazy. No wonder I have to tell people how awful you are to me otherwise they wouldn't know.'

'You know what? I don't care what you tell people. I don't care what you think of me. I've tried my hardest to accommodate your whims all these months, took you places, everything you've asked for. I've put my life on hold but it's never enough, is it? Well, you know what, no more. I'm leaving tonight; now to be exact. You can stay and watch me pack or you can go upstairs but, I'm leaving now. If you plan to get ill, you know the phone number of the hospital in the city. They haven't yet put sanctions on you.

'I'll disinherit you.'

'Do what you want. You will anyway.'

With her car loaded and Mirabell on her front seat Gilda started to

drive out. 'Give me back my keys, you bitch.' 'No, I'm keeping them in case I need to get in and help you one day.'
'I don't want your help, I'd rather get help from the devil than from you, you bitch.'

Gilda drove off and called Angelique, 'Schatzi, just letting you know, I'm on my way home, for good.'
'Oh, Mum, thank God, thank you.'

Gilda patted Mirabell's head. 'We're going back to where we belong, gorgeous. You'll soon see your darling Angelique again. And so will I.'

That night, the two best friends talked for hours – tears were mixed with laughter. Each had stories to tell but Gilda largely did the listening as the most important person in the world for her needed to be heard, to release the heartbreak from her first big love. As 2.00 AM approached Gilda asked, 'What is the best medicine? What cures all?'

'Travel,' her daughter suggested.

'Funny that, that's the answer I was looking for.' They embraced. 'Let's continue after some sleep. What do you say?'

'Yep, good night, Mum. I love you so much.'

'Good night my darling, sweet dreams. I love you lots and lots too.'

'Where's Mirabell?'

'I think she's already gone to bed. She's had enough of human dramas.'

They both laughed tears of joy.

CHAPTER 39
2008-2009

In December, 2008, Gilda and Angelique headed for Spain, Portugal and Morocco. Spain had changed since they were last there. It had lost its "funness" and had become frenetic. The only places that still had the same feel were Starbucks, the little bars off the beaten track from which you could often hear local music, and The Prado art gallery. Gilda and Angelique often went to Starbucks, not because of the coffee, neither drank it, but for the WIFI. Gilda drank tea and her daughter, water, always carrying around her health bottle with an internal filter.

Portugal was a wonderful surprise. The country had modernised itself without sacrificing its identity and culture.

'I just love Lisbon,' Angelique commented, 'What amazing energy the city has and the locals are so happy and friendly. They hurry but it's not chaotic and the place is so clean.'

'Don't tell me you love Lisbon more than Cacais,' Gilda teased.

'Well, it's not my fault that Cacais seems to be the only shoe store in the world to stock double A-and triple A-fitting shoes,' Angelique replied. She had bought nine pairs of shoes at the tiny shop in that coastal town.

'I'm only teasing you,' her mother reassured her, 'they are all exquisite and I would have done the same were it not for the possible damage to my limited supply of Euro currency. That shoe store didn't have my C fittings, so I was saved. It's the usual problem, if a shop has clothes or shoes for you, it won't have them for me and vice versa.'

Morocco made a deep impact on both of them.

'I can't get over the poverty of many people, and the simple lifestyle of people like the Berber cave dwellers that are the polar opposite of the super-rich,' she remarked one day, 'and although they see us with a $ sign over our heads, our experience has been that they never rip you off.'

'I know what you mean, yes, they've been so nice to us. Remember when we wanted to cross the street to go to the toilet (Gilda's stomach, although a lot better was still unreliable) and the nearest traffic lights were about a kilometre apart. A group of ladies dressed in their Niqabs helped us cross the busy boulevard. One took your arm and another took mine and guided us through the traffic of flying cars on six lanes of traffic. When we got to the other side, we turned to thank them and they just disappeared. We were still in a daze about what had happened, especially when we saw the traffic?'

'Yes, that was extraordinary. It was as if Angels whisked us from one side of the road to the other. I had no feeling that we were actually on the ground, and I didn't feel as though I was flying. It was indescribable.'

Back in Brisbane after such experiences and the anticipation of a new academic year with all the unexpected unknowns that kept materialising in education, Gilda was unsettled. 'I love the children, and I love teaching,' she said to her daughter over breakfast, 'But I've always disliked institutions and bureaucracies. They thwart out-of-the box thinking and create conformists. This is the wrong time to try such tactics. It's like going back to the Medieval times. People are becoming more and more open to the Consciousness movement and New Age ideas. With the Internet being such an increasing part of children's lives, virtually from the day they are born, trying to create clones just won't work. Sure, some people will feel safe and comfortable that way but that's not a secure way to control your life. What's the saying, 'The only permanence now is change?''

'Mom, you're off on an early philosophical start this morning. Heaven help the school,' Angelique commented.

'Oh, well, off the ladder to Utopia and back to the land of the humdrum. It'll be nice to see some of my colleagues again and hear what gossip has brewed over the holidays,' Gilda laughed.

During the Easter break, Gilda completed her second-last three-day Neuro-Linguistic Programming workshop before her accreditation. I can't say that everything I've learned gels with me but there are aspects such as the importance of your thoughts, the language you consistently use, beliefs, attitudes, values, what you focus on, and how you react to circumstances and other areas that really enhance how one creates life. I can see the benefit of this approach in daily life with my students. Even so-called 'weaker' students blossom and are not difficult when they feel empowered.'

After the August break, Gilda applied to have 10 days' unpaid leave to go to Sydney to complete the last NLP subject and she was called to a meeting with the College's Principal and Deputy Principal. 'Sit down, please, Gilda. I'd like to discuss this Neuro-Linguistic Programming study that you're doing.'

'Yes, of course,' Gilda replied cheerfully.

'What is it all about? I've never heard of it and nor has my Deputy.'

Gilda replied as briefly as possible while still identifying the benefits for the students as she saw them.

'I'm not sure that it's a good thing that you bring this type of material into the classroom,' the Principal said.

'Has there been a complaint?'

'No, on the contrary. Parents are happy. Even problem students are doing their homework, according to feedback from parents.'

'So, what's the issue?'

'Other staff are not happy.'

'Why? Because students work in my classes and not in theirs?'

There was an uncomfortable pause and then the Principal continued, 'Gilda I have to refuse your application for the 10 days' study leave you requested in October.'

'But why? There are no exams, nor have the preparations begun for the end-of-year exams. I would set work that I would correct on my return. I'm asking for unpaid leave and that means the relief teacher would be no extra cost.'

'Gilda I have made up my mind. You either don't go or resign.'

'So, let see if I have this right. You and the Deputy know nothing about what I use of NLP. The staff who object also don't know anything about it. The parents are happy as their children are happy and are doing well, and yet you say, I'm not to use any of the methodology and that is why you won't give me permission for the leave.'

'There's no need to be insolent,' the Deputy interjected.

'I'm not being insolent. I'm stating the facts as they are. Okay, I resign.'

Both Principal and Deputy were shocked; they hadn't expected this turn of events. 'Gilda, I'll give you a week to think about it. Don't be hasty,' the Principal appealed.

'No, its fine, Sister. I don't need time to think. I'll go back to my desk and write out my resignation. Thanks all the same.' With that Gilda left the room smiling at both ladies.

By the next day, the news had spread like a wildfire. 'How do people know? I haven't told anyone,' Gilda said to her friend in the staffroom.

'Incestuous place schools! People know about you before you know yourself.' Her friend laughed. 'Are you sure you're making the right decision? The kids need you. We all need someone like you.'

'Yes, I'm sure. I'll just stagnate here the way it's going. Everyone is too scared of parental litigation and parental expectations. Many parents want the school to take responsibility for bringing up their kids. Even if the girls do something against the rules, remember that incident?'

'Oh, yes. Do I ever! One of the girls disobeyed a school rule and posted a picture of herself in school uniform on Facebook. The school told her she would be suspended for three days. Her father, who is a lawyer, came to the Principal and threatened that he would make a public example of the school if his daughter was suspended.'

'Yep, and so she wasn't. The interesting thing is that the girl, I taught her and she's a lovely girl, said that she should have been suspended but with an overbearing chap like her father, who took the 'shame' personally, it was simpler to just do what he wanted. Yes, it's a good time for me to leave. I'll start my own business. I've still got my University and TAFE contracts till I build up my own life coaching business. I'll miss you though. I've loved working with you and with most of the others in this staffroom, not all.' They both laughed.

'Hi, guess what?' Gilda asked Angelique when she came home.

'You've resigned,' was the reply.

'How did you know?'

'I didn't but you seemed so pleased with yourself. It was a good guess.'

'Yes, I did and you know what? It's such a relief.'
'I'm glad you have too, Mum. You'd have gone nuts. You were already restless. In actual fact, I reckon that mentally you had already left the school; you've moved on. I know you, when something is over, it's over, there's no going back, there's no second chance.'

'Yes, that's right and that's how I've survived to get to where I am. I always had to make categorical decisions and stand fast or I'd have been bowled over by my mother. As it was, she still managed to sabotage a lot of what I did or planned.'

In October Gilda went to Sydney for the final NLP training. Every evening, no matter how late the day ended, there was homework for the next day. On one particular night, she was sitting at the table in her unit and had just eaten a late dinner, 'Right, let's get into it, 'Homeplay' time. If it wasn't so bloody interesting, I'd rather go to bed. I'm beat.' The answers wouldn't come; she simply couldn't understand how to do the set work.

'Listen you lot and, yes, I'm talking to you Conscious Mind and Subconscious Mind, I've had enough of the pair of you. If you two don't get your act together and cooperate with each other and work together, I'm going to trade the pair of you in for a newer models.' Gilda then burst out laughing, 'Anyone listening to me would think I was a fruit loop. Well, maybe I am.' The bottle of wine was still on the table and she poured herself a glass and toasted to all the fruit loops in the world. Gilda took another sip and laughed even more. 'I think hysteria is setting in. Good maybe these two dead beats I've got as minds might wake up.' And indeed, as though the magic lamp had been rubbed, Gilda was inspired and within the hour she had done the work for the following day.

When she returned to Brisbane, at 64 years of age, Gilda started her first business, "Maya Training Academy". She had already completed and delivered some University trainings and now was developing the eight weeks' NLP course that she would submit to TAFE to be considered for the beginning of the following year. Because of her advancing years, Gilda had taken an interest in the functioning of the brain and read avidly on anything to do with that topic. One of the first books was "The Age Heresy" by Buzan and Keene, followed by several books written by Dr Richard Restak and Dr Daniel G Amen, and Dr Joseph Murphy on The Power of the Subconscious Mind, and the classic, "Man's Search for Meaning" by Viktor E Frankl.

Gilda also attended workshops on the different domains of spirituality, Eastern and Western. New modalities such as Thought Field Therapy also known as Tapping, and Scientific Hand Analysis were added to her repertoire to help herself and those she taught to live their best life.

She became very interested in Attention Deficit Hyperactivity Disorder, ADHD, and Attention Deficit disorder, ADD. 'Had I or Angelique been students today, I would have been diagnosed with ADHD and she would have been labeled ADD, which would have been a lot of rubbish, on both our accounts.' Gilda researched intensively and the two of them co-wrote and published two books on the topic, "Fast and Furious Against ADHD: The Natural Way" and "ADHD and Super Simple Meals, 5-Day Meal Plan and Shopping List".

One of Gilda's contracts for her University teaching was a half-day workshop at Caloundra on Queensland's Sunshine Coast, entitled, "Time Management and a New Perspective."

She left the busy city traffic behind and turned onto the main highway leading north. 'Caloundra's not that far,' she thought, 'I should get there in about an hour. I'll be early which is good. I prefer being early.'

It was a week day and there wasn't much traffic going north at 10.30 AM. She was cruising at 100 kph in the left lane. There was a truck ahead and she planned to overtake it. Looking in every necessary direction she overtook the truck in the right-hand lane. Up ahead in the same lane was an SUV 4-wheel drive vehicle travelling slowly and hogging the right lane.

'What the hell is that driver doing staying in the fast lane?' Gilda asked herself. 'There's no car for miles in either lane. I'll just keep a safe distance behind it and it'll see that I want to pass.'

The other vehicle didn't move; it stubbornly stayed in the fast lane. 'Okay, I'll just have to go back into the left lane and overtake it from there.'

Gilda then went into the left lane, at the very same moment the other car shifted into the left lane. 'Oh, bloody hell,' she exclaimed. She took her foot off the accelerator to slow down. 'We're going too fast for me to brake.' She then sharply turned the steering wheel to get back into the right lane to avoid the SUV hitting her. Instead of speeding up, the SUV braked. Gilda also had to engage the brake but at that speed it caused her car to get out of control and then everything went blank.

Just as her car landed in a ditch between the northbound and the southbound highway, she came back to consciousness. Her car landed on one side before swaying to the other side and then stopping on all four tyres.

'I've got to get out in case it explodes,' she thought. 'Damn, the doors are stuck; I'll have to get out through a window.' She broke the glass of one, scrambled out, tearing her skirt and cutting herself on remaining glass fragments. Quickly she crawled on all fours up the incline to get to the road and away from the car.

'Geez, you were lucky,' said the truck driver amiably.

'Quick, get away from here, the car might explode,' Gilda called to him.

'I don't think that'll happen,' he said laconically pointing to how far away the car battery had been flung from her car.

'Oh, I see.' She burst out laughing, 'Where's the other car?'
'He drove off. I saw one person looking out the window and then it sped off, but I got the number plate. I'm staying here till the cops come and I can be an eyewitness for you. Bastards. Bloody cowards. It was all their fault.'

Suddenly, Gilda could hear her mobile ringing.

'It's over there, lady,' the truckie said pointing to a grassy patch beside the car.

Gilda answered. It was Angelique, 'Mum, Are you okay? I just felt something was wrong. Are you okay?' Angelique asked frantically.

It was only then that Gilda noticed she was bleeding from her hands and her legs. 'Gosh, how did you know,' she asked her daughter. 'I got an inner message. I felt something was wrong. Are you okay? What happened?'

'I'm fine, Schatzi, I had a bit of a car accident and I've just got some surface bleeding. I'll probably be a bit bruised tomorrow, but I tell you what, the safety bars for this brand of car are fantastic. The front and back are smashed up but the driving area is still relatively intact. Apparently, the car spun in the opposite direction of travel, and turned on its roof before landing back on all fours. I was unconscious throughout the whole thing so I have no idea what happened, but a truck driver saw the whole thing and is waiting with me to tell the police.'

It had not been the first time Gilda had been rendered unconscious to save her from a trauma that could otherwise have plagued her on a conscious level. It would also not be the last. She always seemed guided by a source higher than herself.

'I'm coming to get you.'

'No. not yet. I'm still going to do the workshop. After that, you can.'

Angelique knew her mother too well to try to dissuade her from doing the workshop.

'How will you get there?'

'I'll get the tow truck to take me there. It'll surely be from Caloundra as I am only about 15 minutes from there.'

'Apart from the truck driver, is there anyone else there?'

'No, what do you mean?'

'There's no woman there?' Just at that moment a female voice spoke from behind Gilda.

'Hello, is everything alright here?' she asked in the sweetest, soft voice. She was slim, dressed in a flowing skirt and loose shirt-blouse and sandals. On her head, she had a straw sunhat. No handbag.

'Yes, thank you, but where did you come from? There's nothing for miles around.'

She smiled sweetly and ignoring the question replied, 'If you're sure I can't help then I'll be on my way. I may be needed elsewhere.'

The truck driver called, 'Hey lady, the paramedics and police are here.'

Gilda turned to the woman to thank her but she had disappeared.

'Where on Earth did she go? Angelique are you still there?'

'Yes, who were you talking to?'

'I was talking to a strange woman who appeared out of nowhere and disappeared into nowhere.'

'I thought so. This is going to sound really strange, Mum, but that was an Angel.'

'You know Schatzi, that's not the only thing strange about all this. The truck driver called out to say the paramedics and police are here. He spoke to the police for a couple of minutes and he's disappeared and he didn't drive away. He just vanished.

'Got to go Sweetie, a paramedic wants to talk to me. Thanks Gorgeous. See you about 4 or 4.30, if that's okay? Oh, before you go, can you please ring Cynthia from the Uni and tell her what's happened and that I'll be about 15 minutes late but I'm on my way.

Thanks.'

'I'll be there earlier. Look after yourself, Mum, do you hear? I love you.'

'I love you too darling. Sorry to put you through this.'

Gilda turned around to the man who was waiting to speak to her.

'Hello, could I have some water please?' She saw a box filled with bottled water and suddenly realised how thirsty she was.

'Yes, of course. We'll drive you to the hospital now.'

'Why? I'm perfectly okay.'

'You'll have concussion. The truck driver told us what happened.'

'I don't have concussion. As you can hear, I'm lucid and I have a workshop to go to when the tow truck comes.'

'You should go to hospital,' the paramedic insisted.

'Look, I know you mean well but I'm not going to a hospital. I've just done enough damage to my body. I'm not going to a hospital to get sick. Everyone who goes to hospital is either sick or gets sick. They are infested places. I'll find my own forms of healing when I get back to Brisbane. Thanks, all the same.'

He was about to say something. 'Look, are you going to force me to go?'

'No, we can't force you to go.'

'Good, then give it up. I'm not going and in any case if you had tried to force me, I'd have rung my solicitor. Really, I'm fine. Thank you.' Later, a Kineseologist friend of Gilda's assessed that she had internal bruising and treated it accordingly.

In the meantime, the tow truck had arrived. 'Wow, lady, you sure did some damage. She's a write off.'

'I figured as much. I like that car, oh, well. Listen, are you going to Caloundra?'

'Yes, I'll turn the car in there.'

'Can you do me a favour, please? I have to give a workshop at the Caloundra Hotel. Do you mind dropping me off there?'

'No, that's fine, it's not out of the way. You sure you're okay?'

'Yes, I'm fine. I look worse than it is. Bit of blood, torn skirt, torn pantyhose, easy to clean all that up. I checked my laptop which was on the back seat and it's fine, as is my briefcase. All good to go.'

'Okay, then, climb in. You were lucky, lady.'

'Yes, I guess my Angels were looking after me. Oh, but I suppose you'll think I'm nuts talking about Angels.'

'No, not at all, my Missus is into all that stuff. I'm used to it. We've got a lot of friends like that too. The Sunshine Coast is full of those types. Don't go for it much meself, but that's what she does for a living. She has workshops at home too for that Chakra and intuition stuff. She's a Healer. Pretty busy too.'

'Well, I'll be!' Gilda said inwardly. 'Thanks God, thanks Angels, thanks to all my spirit buddies. You sure had your work cut out with me today. Lesson learnt too about my driving, I may need to be more patient.'

When Gilda arrived at the Hotel, one of the seminar organisers was waiting for her in the foyer to carry her belongings. When she entered the Conference Room everyone stood up, and clapped and cheered her.

'Oh, my goodness, what a welcome. I've never had this before,' she exclaimed.

The workshop was a success. 'I can tell that I have challenged a few of the teachers and administrators, which is good. Everyone did well with the activities and group sessions. Wonderful, what a great group.'

Hanna was not handling living alone at all well. There was no one she could boss. There was no one over whom she could impose her brilliance. Gilda often received more than 10 emails a day from her mother, all along the same lines. 'I hate this life.' 'I don't want to live any longer,' 'You have to help me die,' and 'Life is so boring.' Many a time Gilda when she answered Hanna's telephone calls, because he felt sorry for her, although she knew how the conversation would go. One Saturday when Gilda was cleaning the house, she answered the phone. 'Gilda, it's your mother. I must speak to you. Can you come over?'

'No, Mom, I'm cleaning the house. What's up? And don't say, I have to come over because I won't. Talk now or hang up.' There was a pause.

'You make my life so difficult,' Hanna complained. 'Very well. I want you to go to the doctor and get a prescription of sleeping pills for yourself.' Gilda froze; she knew where this conversation was leading.

'Why don't you go to your doctor to do that and get them for yourself?'

'She only gives me a single script and only for a night's supply.'

'Then she doesn't think you need them.'

'You can be such an idiot. I don't need them to sleep. I want to kill myself,' Hanna exploded.

'Come on, Mom. You don't need to euthanise yourself; you're not painfully, terminally ill.' Quickly Gilda added, 'Don't concoct something now to make out you are.'

Hanna changed her tone, 'I am ill, none of you believe me, not even the doctors at the hospitals, nor at the surgery. But I know I'm ill.'

'Look, Mom, you're bored at home and that's understandable. You need to get out. There's a community bus that can pick you up twice a week and take you to activities for people in your situation where you can have fun. You can spend the day there. They provide all the meals for a small sum, and then bring you home. I'm happy to take you to places during the day if I'm not working.'

'NO, but for heaven's sake will you stop with these places. I've told you, people who go there are not of my social class and they are stupid.'

'Okay, well how about we organise for a person to come to you and they can play cards with you or read to you. Have someone come once a week for guitar lessons.'

'Oh, you are too stupid to talk to,' Hanna said and hung up.

'Well, that's at least one way to end the call,' Gilda thought.

Almost immediately, the phone rang again. It was Hanna. 'I'm serious, if you don't get me those sleeping tablets, I'll cut my wrists and it'll be messy when you find me dead.'

'Mom, do you realise that what you are asking me to do is to assist you to kill yourself?'

'I don't care. I'm your mother. You have to help me. You'll be able to talk your way out of it.'

'She's impossible,' Gilda thought.

'Well, say something, you piece of rubbish. For once, do what I tell you. I've done everything for you and the least you can do is give me this wish. Ivan was younger than me, how dare he die before me. He was to look after me as I got older.' And so Hanna continued her rant.

'Mom!' Hanna didn't stop, 'Mom! Mom,' Gilda yelled into the phone. 'Will you stop or I'll hang up!'

Silence. 'That's better. Now listen. No more talk about killing yourself.'

'Why? So that you can sleep better?' Then Hanna went into her best theatrical voice. 'I will kill myself with or without your help. One day you'll arrive at the front door because you won't have heard from me for a few days, you'll ring the doorbell and there'll be no answer. You'll wait but no one will come. You'll ring but no one will answer the phone. So, you will unlock the front door. You will see blood stains on the pale carpet in the lounge and there you will find me dead on the floor. The bloody knife will be beside me. I'll have died all alone and it will be completely your fault, completely.'

It was all Gilda could do not to laugh and clap such a performance. 'You know, Mom that was a brilliant performance. Have you finished?'

'You are too stupid to talk to.' The line went dead.

Gilda started to receive teaching contracts from State Schools. When she was teaching at St Claire's, she was nominated to represent the school at a Queensland Education Department initiative to pilot online marking. Usage of the Internet for research and online methods of learning had made a major leap in teaching within all subject areas. She was interested in these new methods. Although she had retired from full-time teaching, she was still registered with the State system and so it contacted her. Over time, these contracts became numerous.

'Um, I've never taught in a public school before. I've only taught in private schools. This'll be a bit of a learning curve!' After her first week, Gilda said to her daughter, 'You know, I have a new respect for kids who go to State Schools and for teachers who teach there. Some of the classes are hellish. During this first week, I've had to teach over kids yelling to each other from one end of the room to the other, and others who threw chairs around the room. I sent at least six children to the punishment room per day, but not sent some who should have gone because the punishment room was overflowing. One child, suspended from school, came to class and 'mooned' me – I never knew what 'mooning' was till today. I'm being educated,' she laughed. 'The Deputy Principal goes around the school during the day and collects students whose behavior is really bad. The focus isn't on teaching, it's on crowd control.'

Angelique asked, 'Do you think you'll survive?'

'I'll give it a go, that's for sure. There are some really sweet kids who also try despite their home environment. Twice a week, two different charity groups come and cook breakfast for the students and that's the only meal some of these kids get. Some kids stay away from home because their mother or father has a new boyfriend or girlfriend every week and they make such a racket when they are drunk that the child sleeps elsewhere. What sort of a chance do these children have? I want to stay and make a difference. I see them at lunch time, just be someone they can talk to, if they want to, that is. When I do grounds duty, kids come up and talk to me. I know it helps them.'

'Yikes, that sounds awful. Those poor kids'

'Yes, it's another world and I'm so glad I'm experiencing it.'

Chapter 40
2010-2011

By 2010, Gilda's Life Coaching business had transformed itself rapidly including a number of name changes. She added aspects of the different modalities and schools of thought she studied. The latest had been Scientific Hand Analysis. To examine the usefulness of this technique, she and Angelique went to a four-day workshop in Phoenix, Arizona. This was the start of frequent visits to America over the next two years. At these events Gilda met people who were in line with the direction her thinking had been taking after her many years of involvement in personal development. These people, mostly women, were to become long-standing friends. They were gentle but strong people many of whom had survived incredible sicknesses or personal dramas but maintained their faith in the miracle of life.

After the Phoenix event, mother and daughter holidayed in Las Vegas and the environs of the Grand Canyon and then flew to San Francisco, stayed a week there, then hired a car and visited the nearby Napa Valley vineyards. On the drive down to Los Angeles where they planned a 4-day stay, they stopped at towns leisurely visiting famous places en route such as Hearst Castle and the Getty Vila.

'This has been an extraordinary two weeks,' Gilda said to her daughter. 'Your driving has been incredible; such long distances and driving on the opposite side of the road. I know you did it in Hawaii but this was monumental.'

'Thanks, Mum, it was such fun. Yes, what an amazing experience. I still can't get over the wonderful people we met in Phoenix. I'm so glad we signed up for further courses and we'll see them again next year.'

'Yes, next year is going to be very interesting. No news from Brisbane about Mom is good news,' she added.
Before they left for the States, Gilda had organised with Eureka Aged Care to ring at Gilda's cost if there was a problem. She and

Angelique decided not to tell Hanna that they wouldn't be in the country otherwise she would have panicked. They said they were interstate for a short while and that satisfied her. Daily Meals-on-Wheels had also been arranged.

'It's only two weeks,' Gilda had said, 'It's only once we wouldn't have gone to see her because we'll be back for the second week.'

When they returned, there was a message on the answering machine from Eureka to give them a call. 'Gilda, you're back. Thanks for calling. I didn't contact you while you were away but I wanted you to know that your mother has been very difficult,' 'Oh, I'm sorry to hear that,' Gilda replied.

'Oh, we're used to it. Some of these old people can be quite a handful and very self-willed. Your mother wouldn't let our lady in during the first week. Our staff-member would come every day but your mother wouldn't open the door. In the second week, she let her in only once. I didn't contact you because we could tell that she was alright the next day and kept monitoring her that way.'

'Oh, my goodness, thank you so much. I'm so sorry for the inconvenience.' 'Don't worry about it; it happens all the time. Not to the same degree as with your mother; she's a special case, but it does happen. Your mother yells out, 'Get out, I didn't call you,' and then slams shut the inside door.'

'Even though I'm back, do you mind still sending the lady every day? Most of the time I know my mother is okay because she sends me multiple daily emails but it's still reassuring that there are others keeping an eye on her.'

'Yes, of course, we can. I also had a call from Meals on Wheels; your mother currently isn't letting them in every time they call. So unfortunately, you will still have to pay for the meal because it wasn't cancelled in advance.

When Angelique came home from work, Gilda relayed what she had been told. 'Do you think she's losing it a bit?' Angelique asked.

'I really don't know. She only allows me to stay about an hour and then tells us to go. In that hour, she seems to hold it together okay. I mean, she's her normal unpleasant self. Otherwise when we go shopping, she seems all there.'

Often on a Saturday morning Gilda would take Hanna to the supermarket and after shopping, as part of their routine, coffee and cake. On one such morning, Angelique came with them.

When Angelique and her mother arrived at Hanna's, it took a short time for her to open the door. When Hanna finally came she was in her dressing gown. The shower was still running
'Aren't you well?' Gilda asked.

'Wouldn't you like that! That I die? Hanna bellowed at her. Gilda was stunned and looked surprised, 'What brought that on?'
'You know exactly what I mean. You want me to die because you think you'll get all my money,' Hanna hissed, 'But you're getting nothing. Do you hear? Nothing,' she then stormed off into her study.

'Mum, the shower's still on. Do you want me to turn it off? Angelique asked.

'Yes, thanks.' Gilda answered and followed her mother. She saw her sitting at her computer. She had just turned it on.

'Are we going to the shopping centre? We don't have to if you're not well. Give Angelique your shopping list and I'll stay here with you.'

'I'd rather stay with the devil than with you. You big piece of shit!' At that moment, Angelique entered the room and moved towards her mother. Gilda was sitting in a chair near the computer. Hanna was sitting in front of the computer but, suddenly swung around on her swivel chair and looked straight at Gilda.

'You think I don't know what your plan has been? You've wanted to drive me crazy all these years so that I go to a mental house. It might run in the family, my mother…' and then she stopped herself. Gilda and her daughter looked at each other. Angelique motioned to be quiet and then pulled up a chair to sit beside her mother, but in front of her grandmother.

'Yes, have your daughter sit next to you. She can't protect you from my words. You've been the bain of my life since you were born. If I didn't have you, I could have had any man after your father left me but I was stuck with a baby. I was stuck with you. I often thought, I often thought I'd be better off without you but, I couldn't do it. Oh, yes, don't think for a moment that I hadn't thought of it. You whore, you tramp, you piece of nothing.' Hanna's well-spring of venom had been tapped and all her anger and corrosive vengeance flooded out.

What Hanna had failed to notice was that Angelique was recording it on her iPhone. That was why she went to sit next to her mother and had motioned her to say nothing.

'Get out, the pair of you, get out, you're both whores!'

'Mom, you're not well, we can take you…'

In the meantime, Angelique had gone back to the bathroom. 'Oma,' she began when she returned to the study, 'I found these in the shower recess. Hanna looked belligerently at her granddaughter, 'You're just as stupid as your mother. I always wash my underpants in the shower.'

'But, had we not been here, the water would have overflowed.'

'Yes, and it would have been your fault and your mother's because you stopped me from finishing my shower. You harassed me to go here into my study. You are the ones who stopped me from going shopping and now you are trying to say it was my doing and that there is something wrong with me. You are both as evil as the other.'

'Mom,' Gilda tried to placate her mother and tried to take her by the arm.

Hanna pulled away and screamed, 'There is nothing wrong with me! You drive me mad. You make me so angry. That's why I'm upset now. GO!'

Gilda and Angelique hesitated but then left. 'I'm going to ring the doctor. I can't let this go,' Gilda said. The receptionist answered the phone. Gilda told her what happened and asked what she should do.

'Are you the daughter?' 'Yes.' 'The doctor will speak with you although he is with a patient.'

'It's Doctor Farouk here. My receptionist has informed me of what you have said. I see your mother once a week and I can assure you there is nothing wrong with her. She has told me about you and about your negligent treatment toward her and I can see that you now want me to believe that she is not of sound mind.'

Gilda interrupted him. 'I'm not trying to get you to believe anything. I just wanted your advice on what to do given her outburst today.'

'As I just said, there is nothing wrong with your mother. You must have aggravated her. I suggest you may like to alter your behaviour towards her. I've found her to be a charming lady and very obliging. Now, I must get back to my patient.'

'Well, that was another sucker who fell for one of Hanna's Academy Award Winning performances,' Gilda said to Angelique, 'I'm going to send an email to cover my back just in case something comes up in the future. I've no idea what could happen but they are all so taken in by her that I'd rather be over-cautious. Good thing you thought of the video, thanks.'

Several days after Gilda had faxed the doctor a copy of her reason for calling, she received a call back from the receptionist to advise that the fax had been put on file.

'Thank you, and would you mind sending me a signed copy that you have received it so that I can file it also.' 'You never know. Documents can conveniently disappear. I'd rather have proof that they saw it,' Gilda thought. The receptionist agreed to send her a signed copy.

In January, 2001, the first of the three USA trips started at Los Angeles. This time Gilda and Angelique stayed only a week as they didn't want to be away from Hanna for too long. They had paid a substantial amount of money for this program and couldn't get a refund even under compassionate circumstances. It was wonderful seeing those friends again they had met in Phoenix the previous year. They had all stayed in touch on Facebook so it was as though time had stood still when they were physically reunited.

In March they all met up again in Las Vegas at the luxurious Wynn Hotel for a week's stay. The hotel was only affordable because of conference rates. The weather was superb and although it was March, it was hot enough to swim.

Las Vegas was followed by a 10 day June stopover in New York. Angelique had been to New York on her solo trip many years ago and she knew her mother would also love the city. She was right. It was also at this workshop that Gilda redefined her business. It was quite a pivotal point in her development. She had now done three presentations on stages in the US and felt very comfortable speaking in front of a large crowd. In fact, she loved the feel of being of service to a larger group at one time rather than the one-on-one consultations she had been doing in Brisbane. Gilda's topic always centered around personal leadership, that we are in control of our life and no one is responsible for our success or otherwise. In short, "How to be Your Own Personal Leader."

One July evening at around 10.00 PM, not long after Gilda and Angelique had returned from the USA, Gilda received a telephone call, 'Are you Gilda Hollten,' a woman asked

'Yes,' Gilda replied cautiously.

'This is Emergency Admittance at the General Hospital. Ambulance services received a call about a woman wandering the street around 9.00 PM. When they arrived one of Hanna Dobinski's neighbours was sitting with her on her back patio. Mrs Dobinski seemed confused and so the ambulance personnel brought her here. The neighbour gave us your details.'

'Yes, that's my mother. Is she okay?'

'Yes, there seems to be nothing physically wrong. We've given her a sedative and there is no cause for alarm, nor any reason for you to come to the hospital tonight.
However, can you come by at 10.00 AM tomorrow morning?'

'Yes, of course.'

'Who was that?'

'The General.'

'Oh, Oma up to her old tricks again?'

'Doesn't seem so.' Gilda told her daughter what she knew.

The following morning Gilda went to the hospital. She was taken to Hanna who greeted her with, 'I demand to go home. These people say they have to do tests; the usual rubbish from these hospitals. Get my things, I'm going home.'

A nurse approached Gilda but first spoke to Hanna. 'No, Mrs Dobinski, I'm afraid you still need to stay here for a bit longer. Dr. Chang wants more tests done.'

'You can't keep me here. I want to see the doctor.'

'He won't be long. He's just with another patient and he'll come right over to you, Dearie,' the nurse replied.

Hanna hated being called 'Dearie' and also hated not getting her way. 'Quick, Gilda, get my things from the drawer and let's sneak out,' she said.

'Mum, you can't do that, the doors are secured. You're here now and you'll have to wait till all the tests are done.'

'I 'have to' do nothing. I can do as I please.'

'Look Mum, you got yourself admitted; you'll just have to see the whole thing through.'

'You, idiot, I didn't admit myself, some fool rang for an ambulance.'

A doctor approached but this was not enough to temporarily silence Hanna. 'Listen, young man,' said Hanna, 'my husband was a doctor, an excellent doctor, a specialist. I know there is nothing wrong with me and I demand to go home; now don't play silly games with me.'

'Mrs Dobinski,' Dr Chang replied in the nicest way ignoring what Hanna had said, 'You're here because we're not sure that you're well enough yet to go home. So, be a good girl and get back into bed.' Hanna had thrown the covers off and was putting her shoes on. Two nurses appeared to dissuade her from leaving. The doctor called Gilda aside as they wheeled Hanna's bed away.

'Mrs Hollten,' Dr Chang said, 'Let's go to this room so we can talk in private. Once inside the consulting room and with its door shut Dr Chang said, 'Mrs. Hollten, I'm sorry but it is necessary to transfer your mother to a secure area because she continues to make attempts to go home. I can't allow that until we have made further tests. It appears that she has early signs of Dementia and it is for her safety that she needs to stays until we know what her health condition really is. I believe she lives alone. Is that right?'

'Yes, that's right. She has Eureka Aged Care people and Meals-on-Wheels attend daily but she often refuses them entry.'

'Would you describe her house?' Gilda explained that it was a high-set house with long steps downstairs into the under part of the house, and steps from the outdoor patio to the garden. There was a gas stove.

'Not really a house that is secure for someone who has Dementia,' commented Dr Chang.

Gilda had no clear idea what Dementia was but, she said, 'No, I suppose not. I tried living in the unit below her once but life was a nightmare.'

'I can imagine it wasn't easy,' Dr Chang said diplomatically. 'She should be settled now; I'll take you to her. After the doctor and nurses had left Hanna said to her daughter, 'You need to get me out of here.'

'Look, Mom, stop talking like that. I can't get you out of here and you are here for your own good.'

Hanna immediately started to verbally attack Gilda, 'You want me out of the way. You're happy now. You can go through my things at home to your heart's content now that I'm imprisoned here.'

'Mom, before I leave, I want to say one thing. Stop talking to me like that. I will try to get you home but in the proper way. Until tests are done and until the hospital gives you a clearance, I can't do a thing. Do you understand?' Hanna was silent and just glared at her daughter. Gilda left.

The following day, Gilda returned to the hospital. She had to press a button to be allowed into the secure wing. 'Hello, Mrs Hollten,' said one of the nurses, 'Your mother's just having her breakfast. She's a bit of a naughty one, and wouldn't have it when it came around and now she has demanded it and yelled she was hungry.'

The visit with Hanna proceeded in the usual way with Hanna demanding to go home. When Gilda was leaving, Hanna tried to sneak out with her by holding onto her arm. 'Mum, let go, you can't come with me.'

'Now, now, Mrs Dobinski, what's going on?' asked a nurse.

'Oh, nothing,' Hanna replied sweetly, 'I was just going out into the garden with my daughter. I was coming straight back.'

The nurse took her gently by the arm and led her back to bed, 'Not today, maybe another day,' she said. Another nurse who appeared to be in charge approached Gilda and asked, 'Will you be able to be here tomorrow morning at 10.30? Dr Chang would like to call a meeting of those who have done tests with your mother and observed her and, discuss the results with you.'

'Yes, of course, I'll be here,' Gilda said feeling drained. 'I've got to get out of here,' she thought. She went downstairs, and had a cup of tea in the atrium to refresh herself before going home. She sat dazed as she sipped her tea. She felt as though she was in a vacuum with the world going on around her but she wasn't a part of it. Eventually, she rose but still felt mentally exhausted.

When she arrived home, Angelique had already returned. 'Boy, you look like you've been through the wringer,' she said.
'You could say that. I'll pour myself a vodka and tell you about it. Do you mind if we go onto the patio? I need to be out in nature.'

Angelique knew her mother's fondness for going outdoors when she needed a recharge. 'How about we order pizza for dinner?'

Gilda nodded as she took a mouthful of her drink. 'Seafood?' Another nod.

'Holy cow!' Angelique exclaimed when she heard Gilda's story of the day's events. 'Would you like me to go with you tomorrow?'

'No, it's okay, Schatzi, thanks.'

The next morning, Gilda paid attention as to how she dressed, 'I don't know what they've been told about me by Mom. I'd better look presentable.' When Gilda arrived, she was ushered into a room where people were already assembled around a table. Present were a psychologist, sociologist, and another man who had done tests with Hanna in a virtual house similar to the house she lived in. Also present were two nurses, including the ward sister. Dr Chang arrived and shortly after Hanna arrived accompanied by another nurse.

Gilda looked at her mother but she looked straight ahead and ignored her.

'Thank you for coming, Mrs Hollten.'

Hanna immediately said, 'That's not her real name; she made it up after her husband divorced her.'

Doctor Chang ignored her and introduced everyone of the hospital's professional staff who then recounted what he or she had observed through tests or interacting with Hanna.

Hanna sat in silence and listened with a clenched jaw.
When the nurse recounted that she had seen Hanna washing her underpants in the toilet bowl, Hanna jumped up, lunged across the table and shrieked, 'You whore, you, liar, that is not true. You filthy bum cleaner. You are not good enough to clean my backside.'

'Mum,' Gilda said trying to hold her mother back. Hanna almost knocked Gilda to the floor to release herself from her daughter's grip. One of the men who was at the end of the table, leapt to rescue her and pacified Hanna.

The sister then spoke, 'Mrs Dobinski it is true. The nurse called me over and I also saw what has just been described.'

Hanna was about to say something but decided against it; she knew she had better behave to get them onside. So, she sweetly said, 'Oh, I'm so very sorry, Doctor, I was just shocked that I could have done such a thing. I mustn't have been thinking. It won't happen again.' With that she gave the most charming smile and fluttered her eyelids flirtatiously.

Dr Chang waited until Hanna had finished and continued, 'I think we've heard enough. Nurse please take Mrs Dobinski back to her bed. I can hear lunch is being served.' With that the nurse gently helped Hanna from her chair and they both left the room.

'Mrs Hollten,' the doctor said looking at Gilda, 'There is no doubt that your mother is currently in the early stages of Dementia, but from what we have seen over the last few days, the process is accelerating rather rapidly. It would be foolish to allow her to go home. She is a strong-willed woman and will refuse to cooperate with any help that is obtained for her.'

'What are you saying,' Gilda asked him, 'that I should put her into a home?'

'Yes,' was the simple and straightforward answer.

'But, we don't do that. Our older family members stay with us till they die. We don't dump them into care.'
'I understand how you feel' Dr Chang replied gently, 'It is the same in my culture. However, there comes a point at which it is kinder to have them in professional care where they will be comfortable and are not at risk to hurt themselves.'

Gilda had a real struggle with that. She had vowed, she would always look after her mother, no matter what. 'She's been horrible to me all my life but I can't abandon her. She has no one else.' As though he read her mind, the doctor said, 'It's not abandoning her, it's putting her in the best care for her own good. You can visit her as often as you like.'

'What are the options?' Gilda asked.

'Regrettably, because of your mother's mental condition and attitude, there is no other option. She cannot be trusted to comply with home care so we cannot recommend it for her safety. She can't stay here indefinitely; this is a public hospital and we need the beds for incoming patients. We will transfer her to another section where patients stay until relatives can find alternative residence for family members but this can only be for two months or so. We are then authorised to have patients placed in the first available room at a Dementia facility anywhere it is available.'

Gilda knew it was the best thing to do but it was a fight within herself to agree to it. 'Very well,' she said, 'What do I have to do?' Her strong self took over.

The doctor explained the procedure. 'I would also recommend that you do not go to see your mother now. She may still be in an aggressive state but tomorrow she could have forgotten today's events. This is the way Dementia works.'

Gilda nodded, shook hands with the doctor, looked at everyone and said, 'Thank you' before leaving the room and the hospital.

At home, Gilda detailed the main points of the meeting to Angelique. 'Thank heavens for vodka and organic Cranberry Juice,' she joked. There's still pizza left from yesterday,' Angelique said. 'How about I make us a nice salad to go with it?'

Shortly afterwards while sitting on the couch as her daughter prepared dinner, Gilda continued, 'It's almost a relief that this has happened. Now, at least, we know where we stand but we need to find a facility for Mom. After a short silence Gilda continued, 'Liliana's mother had Dementia and Liliana was happy with where her mother lived. We can check it out.'

'Dinner is served al fresco. Time for another, more uplifting conversation. How about Placido Domingo and Latin love songs,' Angelique suggested. They walked out to the patio to the sounds of 'From my Latin Soul.'

Mother and daughter visited the aged-care facility, Alexandra Lodge, where Liliana's mother had resided and, as luck would have it, a bed had become vacant that day. Although there was a waiting list, the room was given to Hanna. It was a case of being in the right place at the right time or, was this positive intervention from another source as had often happened in Gilda's life? It would still take several years for Gilda to recognise that all her life she had been helped by 'other sources.'

The Alexandra Lodge supervisor showed Gilda and Angelique the area where Hanna would be cared for. The weekly menu was placed on a notice board for loved ones and friends to view, as was the daily entertainment and activity program. Weekly excursions were available to residents who were permitted to leave the premises. Hanna would not be one of those because from Hanna's behaviour in hospital, it was clear that she would always be looking for ways to escape. On Saturday nights different volunteer entertainers came and there was a sing-along or other ways to ensure a happy night.

Led by the Alexandra Lodge supervisor, Gilda went to inspect Hanna's new living quarters. 'This will be your mother's private, self-contained room. It's quite large and has a lovely garden view.' He then took them to a large open area room. 'Over here is the dining section and there is the recreation room with large-screen TV.' There were many comfortable chairs looking out onto a grassed, garden area.

'It's very nice,' Gilda remarked. 'My mother will be much better off here than alone at home.'

'Yes, all the meals are served keeping health requirements in mind. A doctor and other medical professionals visit once a week, more often if required. We also have permanent hairdressers and manicurists who come regularly. Residents can have a radio in their room and anything else from home of a personal nature. You just need to ask and we can arrange for them to have most of the comforts of home.'

Alexandra Lodge took over the responsibility of transferring Hanna, now aged 91, from the hospital to her new home. The facility supervisor suggested waiting three to four days before Gilda and Angelique came to visit to allow Hanna time to settle in.

The first visit was a shock. Neither had seen people with Dementia before. When they had come initially, most of the residents were resting in their individual rooms. Now, all of the residents were in the dining area or lounge. There were about 15 men and women in differing stages of the illness. Some were making noises, some were attempting to speak making animalistic sounds, another was vomiting, yet another yelled abuse into the air, and another banged the security door with her walking frame.

'Come in Gilda. I'll take you to Hanna; she's still in her room.'

'Thank you, this is my daughter, Angelique'

'Hello Dearie. Hanna is still getting used to her new area. She'll be fine though; it just takes some people a bit longer to get adjusted. Please follow me.'

'Ah, you've come,' Hanna greeted them happily. Gilda returned the greeting, 'Hi, Mom, you look well.'

'Yes, of course, I'm very well. I want to talk to you about that.' She put her finger to her lips cautioning Gilda not to say anything.

'Come on Hanna,' her Carer said, 'Dearie, it's time to finish dressing. Morning tea will be here any minute.' Looking at Gilda, she continued, 'Hanna loves her sweets, don't you Hanna? Here is your walker.'

When the three of them were seated and the attendant had left, Hanna whispered to Gilda, 'You have to get me out of here. I'll tell them you're taking me to the chemist and then we can drive home. They think I'm crazy, but they are the ones who are crazy,' she said, pointing to the other residents, 'Except for him,' pointing to a man in his late sixties sitting in a wheelchair, who had clearly been completely overtaken by Dementia, 'He flirts with me all the time.' Both Gilda and Angelique looked over to the man and then looked at each other.

Gilda had brought chocolates and fruit but Hanna said she didn't want them but to leave them and she would give them to the others, which never happened because she always ate them. Morning tea was served but Hanna refused it. 'But you always eat your share and more,' the attendant said.

Hanna, as ever was outspoken, 'She's an idiot. I never eat the food here. Never, not even the pigs in Austria would eat that stuff.' It was clear, however, that Hanna was eating because she had put on weight during the short time since her admission.

An hour went by with Hanna unsuccessfully trying to manipulate Gilda into helping her escape and bad-mouthing the staff and the other residents. Eventually, Gilda said, 'Mom, we need to go,' and saw the relief on Angelique's face. 'Take good care of yourself and do what they ask you to. If you do, it may mean that you can leave and go home.' Hanna wasn't listening; she was focused on her latest 'conquest', the sixties-something old, wheelchair-bound man.
The attendant in the office saw that Gilda and Angelique wanted to leave and pressed the button to open the front door. Entry and exit was only achieved with that buzzer or with a special swipe key-card.

'Angelique, this will take some getting used to,' Gilda said when they were in the carpark. 'I've never seen anything like it. It's so depressing. The really sad part is that, on some level, all these people know what they have become. They have to suffer their indignity and have no say in whether they want to continue that way or want to end it, nor do their loved ones.'

'It really is sad.' her daughter added.

'It's pathetically sad. If I get that way, take me to a country that allows me the choice to end it.'

'Mum, don't talk like that.'

'I'm serious. It's pitiful. On some level, every one of them knows what has become of them. Who suffers? Everyone who is emotionally involved, the person with Dementia and those who love them who see them suffering. 'Ugh,' she exclaimed and simultaneously shuddered.

With each visit, although Hanna fought to be in control when in public, Hanna's deterioration became noticeable. The willpower that had seen Hanna though her life ebbed slowly from her. She still tried to turn on her charm but she couldn't sustain it.

Gilda visited her mother once a week. Whenever Angelique came, Hanna ignored her. It was obvious she still recognised Angelique and knew enough to continue hurting Gilda by ignoring her daughter.

But as time went by, Angelique said, 'Mum, I don't think Oma recognises me anymore.'

'You're right. I don't think she does either. There doesn't seem to be any point in you coming. What do you think?'

'No, I guess not and I really find this place awfully depressing.'

'No need to come after this visit.'

Gilda planted that idea in her daughter's head because she didn't want Angelique hurt when one day she realised the twisted game her grandmother was playing.

For some time, Hanna had been allowed the responsibility of looking after her laundry basket and showering herself until it became obvious that she wasn't able to. Clean items were amongst soiled items. Other behaviours also indicated that she could no longer take care of herself.

On one visit, towards the end of 2011, Hanna and Gilda were going as usual to the dining area. 'Wait, I want to bring my handbag,' Hanna said. When she returned, she led them to a corner table, opened her handbag and pointed to a knife concealed in it. 'When you are leaving, I'll walk with you to the front door and when they press the buzzer to let you out. I'll take the knife out of my bag so that they can't stop me from leaving with you.'

Gilda was horrified and thought of ways to avoid a crisis. However, Hanna was completely focused on the getaway. 'Enough of this talking, we can talk when I'm home.'

'Okay, Gilda said, 'Why don't you go to your room and put your shoes on. You can't wear your slippers to go home.'

As Hanna slowly pushed her walker towards her room, Gilda went to the office and told the attendant what Hanna was planning. The attendant called one of the men and all three went to Hanna's room. Her back was to the door as she put on her shoes and her handbag was at her feet. The attendant went to grab the bag but Hanna was faster and clutched it to her but lost her grip on it. With an almighty leap of strength, Hanna flew past the male attendant and hurled herself at Gilda who was standing at the door.

'You bitch, I'll get you for this,' she screamed and hit Gilda in the face. Gilda's spectacles went flying and she would have been knocked to the ground had not the male attendant caught her. In the meantime, the female attendant grabbed hold of Hanna. Other staff members came running to help control the situation.

Gilda was taken into the office. A bruise was already forming under her eye. 'My glasses, where are my glasses?'

'Here, I've got them,' someone said, 'They are okay. They're not broken.' 'Here, have some have some water,' another attendant offered.

After Gilda composed herself she said, 'I'm never going into her room alone again and, in future when I come, I'll make sure that she and I are never physically close again. Maybe she should also have plastic cutlery. I'll just go and say goodbye to her.'

Hanna was sitting on her bed facing the garden outside her window. 'I'm going now, Mom.'

'Get out. I've never been able to trust anyone in my life. I can't trust you either. I gave birth to you. I should have let you die when your eyes became infected. Instead. I saved you, a traitor. I never want to see you again.'

'Mom, that sort of talk used to affect me, but not anymore. I'll still care for you because you are my mother, you have no one else, and you are a human being but, that's it. You can say all you want. It won't do you any good.'

Still shocked, Gilda returned to her car and for a while she sat motionless staring out through the windscreen. Mechanically she started the engine and drained of emotion and exhausted she drove off into the stillness that surrounded her.

'The worst is over,' she said out loud. 'The worst is over. It's not going to be easy; it'll be a long road to my healing and there'll be rough patches but, I know that I'm not alone. One of the first things I'll do is give up the vodka. I don't need it anymore. At 67, I've got my life back again, I'm luckier than many. How many people get a second chance like this? Thank you, God.'

Gilda's new life began.

Chapter 41
2012-2013

'I feel like I'm buried alive living here. I've been in Durack for 18 years, the longest I've ever been anywhere. That's long enough,' Gilda said one morning as she sat at her desk writing the weekly newsletter for her clients. These newsletters always contained a Message from her related to what she observed about life today, or books she was reading or had read that she thought would be of interest to her subscribers. She always included her interpretations of the books and how they helped her and how they could help them to live their best life in today's complex environments. There was another section on helping readers develop their writing skills and another called, 'On Self-Creation' that gave them personal development techniques for the many areas of life. The latter two sections always contained activities for the week to help cement the skills by incorporating them into their daily life schedule. In the meantime, she had also written a self-help book called, "Wake Up And Live: 5 Steps to Revolutionise Your Life And Live Your Purpose".

Gilda had been living alone for about six years. Although Angelique's romance hadn't worked out she experienced what it was like to live away from home and enjoyed the freedom of coming and going as she pleased. Although Gilda had never kept tabs on her activities, it was time for both mother and daughter to live apart. They still rang daily and emailed multiple times each day, even seeing each other at least twice a week. They also still travelled together.

'None of my friends are so much fun or so easy to get along with when I travel as you are, Mum,' her daughter told her. There was no change in the mutual closeness they had for each other, but both enjoyed their independence.

'When I sell the house, I'll move closer into the city. I started off near the city when Mom and Pop moved into our first house, now I'll be going back to that vicinity.' As usual, once Gilda made a decision, it was full steam ahead. With her usual good fortune, she found an excellent real estate agent. Property prices had gone down in Brisbane and Durack was not an easy suburb to sell.

'Within reason, I don't care what I sell for. I just want to leave. It's been a wonderful house, exactly what I needed throughout those turmoil-filled years and I've loved the area but it's time to move forward with the new life that I've been offered.'

'I'm going to have to sell or give away a lot of furniture because I want to downsize. I'll be sad to let the 7-seater Florentine lounge suite go but it's never going to fit into a unit or smaller house. The single beds, the second lounge suite in the unit, the two black chests of drawers, the old fridge, the large washing machine, outdoor furniture and, oh my goodness, lots of crockery and cutlery, baking dishes and other kitchen utensils. I'll give it all to the flood relief centre in Ipswich. Some smaller items like paintings and computer tables I can put on the footpath and people can help themselves.'

There wasn't a lot of interest in her house but her agent was diligent and an ace at following up potential clients. Within two months, the house was sold on a 30-day contract. Packing was an onerous job. Gilda had hundreds of books, material from the many courses she had attended or taught as well as hard copies of the multiple courses she had written. All of these items were added to the contents of two kitchens and also three wardrobes filled with clothing, shoe boxes, and so on.

'Angelique, have you seen the prices of houses in the areas I'm looking at? They are insane.'

'Yes, I know, 18 years is a long time since you last looked at real estate in Brisbane. The inner suburbs have come back into vogue.'

'Well,' said Gilda, 'maybe I should rent first to see whether I even like living in those suburbs; everything has changed so much. I'm not sure I want to face city living again.'

'Now, come on Mum, where's that adventurous spirit of yours? You'll get used to it. You can live with me while you look. I've got the double garage where you can park your car and store boxes.'

Gilda soon learned that renting proved extremely difficult. Because of high demand, Real Estate agents no longer cared whether you rented a place. On average there were 20 to 30 interested parties for any property and it was the agent who, with the owner's approval, could pick and choose a future occupant. To make matters worse, Gilda had her dog, Mirabell. Even a five kilogram, house trained poodle was regarded as a liability.

'This is pathetic,' Gilda complained one day after inspecting four units and two houses. 'Both houses are disgustingly old, neglected, dirty and smelly. In the olden days, landlords would never have dared give such a property to an agent, nor would an agent have taken such a property. It's not as though the rent is cheap either. I'll need to move out of town at this rate. Even the rental arm of the agency that sold my house is the same. Being a client from a sale made no difference. I don't get any preference.' 'Just keep looking,' advised Angelique.

Living with Angelique was easy. They each had their own bedrooms with their own private facilities. The lounge and dining room that separated their rooms was large and led out to a big balcony. The unit was on the top floor which meant the balcony overlooked the beautiful park below. Its location made it easy to attend ballets, concerts and other productions in the city, and travelling to the airport.

Conversations inevitably turned to Hanna, now permanently hospitalised in the Dementia facility. As Gilda prepared to visit Hanna, she said to Angelique, 'After the last episode with Mom, I'm not looking forward to going there. I'll need to keep away from her as much as possible just in case she has hidden another knife.'
On arrival, Gilda pressed the buzzer to be allowed into Hanna's area. She was greeted by one of the attendants. 'Ah, Gilda, come on in. We've had to move your mother as she needed more individual care and a place became vacant this morning. We were planning to ring you but here you are, I'll take you to her; it's just the building across the path from here.'

As Gilda entered with the nurse, she was stunned at the condition of this group of people. Most of them sat in comfortable chairs, with blankets over their knees and a glazed look of non-awareness. Some women cradled cloth dolls, lullabying them as though they were babies. Attendants were going around cleaning away dribble from residents who no longer had muscle-control. Others sat shaking or nodding, again with little control of their limbs. One woman came over to Gilda and wanted to pat Mirabell who was always a favourite. Mirabell was quite oblivious to the condition of the residents and allowed it for a short while then, she suddenly became restless.

'Oh, I wouldn't let her pat your dog for too long. This patient is sometimes violent.'

'Oh my God, she might try to strangle Mirabell,' Gilda thought and in a flash she whisked her dog away and walked off.

Two other people, men, were laying strapped to a bed that inclined and faced the garden. They no longer could walk and this was one way to give them a change of scenery.

All of a sudden, she became aware of an incredible thumping noise coming from the lounge as though someone was trying to break the glass or trash a door. Gilda looked over and indeed, there was Hanna incessantly thrusting her walker with all her might at the security screen doors. Crash, crash, crash! She screamed, 'Let me out, you crooks! Let me out. I'm calling the police.' With each outburst Hanna bashed the doors with ever-increasing force. Three attendants ran to her. One attempted to get her hands off the walking frame and Hanna struck out at her with full force. The nurse ducked and Hanna only got her mildly on the shoulder. A male Carer came to the aid of the other and grabbed Hanna's hands from the back but she was so strong that he had difficulty holding her. Finally, the four of them managed to get her into a chair and strapped her into it. She saw Gilda. 'You piece of shit; this is all your fault. You wanted me out of the way, now you've succeeded. Call the police, I order you to call the police, you useless lot.'

Gilda was horrified not only because of what she had witnessed but because of the public accusations her mother had just made. She looked helplessly around trying to say something but nothing would come out.

'It's alright, Gilda, come into my office and sit down,' the nurse in charge said as she put her arms around Gilda's shoulders.

'None of that is true,' Gilda managed to say. 'It's not true. I didn't want her to come here but the hospital staff pointed out that it would be best for her.'

'It's okay. It's okay. Don't worry. We don't believe her. We know what she's like. The section that she came from warned us about her lies. They said they believed her when she first came because she was so charming but then they started to see another side of her and warned us about it. Gilda, your mother is too far gone. It's not her nice side that is dominant now, as you saw.'

Gilda continued to shake. She had never seen anything like that, let alone experienced it.

'I'll ask one of the staff to get you a cup of tea.'

After Gilda had drunk her tea, the woman in charge said, 'Your mother seems to have settled. Would you like to see her?'

'I don't know. I suppose so. Yes, please.'

'Your mother is still strapped to the chair so she'll be physically harmless.'

'Does she often try to hit the staff?'

'Yes, we're waiting for the doctor to come tomorrow and depending upon what he says, we may need to ask your permission to have a restraining order for her,'

'What does that mean?'

'It would mean giving us permission to mildly sedate her when we see that she's about to get aggressive.'

'And what does that entail?'

'It would vary on the circumstances,' said the nurse. 'It may be in the form of a mild tablet in a drink or again, a mild sedative via an injection. The doctor will prescribe the dosage and check it when he does his weekly visits.'

'Okay, I'll be advised by what he and you say. I certainly don't want to be responsible for any of your wonderful staff getting hurt.'

Gilda went over to her mother. 'Does she need to stay completely restrained?' she asked the Carer who stayed with her. 'We can take two straps off but I would suggest that the middle strap stays. She is very strong but the middle one would keep her contained if she should suddenly try to get off the chair.'

'Have you been a bit of a cheeky girl,' Gilda said to her mother hoping to keep the conversation light.

Hanna growled at her like a wild animal and said threateningly. 'You wait till I get back home. Then you'll see what I'll do to you.'

Just the very thought of it terrified Gilda and she clutched tightly onto Mirabell. 'I'm going now, Mom,' Gilda said rising from her chair but she made no move to give her mother a peck on the cheek as had been previously customary.

As she walked back to her car she thought about the role of Hanna's Carers. 'How do these people do it? They are seriously Angels, putting up with that every day not just from one but from many. Every day would be so unpredictable and dangerous.'

In September, Gilda and Angelique went to Phoenix again. Gilda had been invited to be a guest speaker at a three-day event, her topic was "How to Tap into Your Purpose and Leadership Values".

Arrangements had been made so that someone from Hanna's care facility could phone Gilda at her expense if there was a need. The head nurse said she didn't think there would be a problem because Hanna was 'as strong as an ox,' as she put it. It was her mental state that was deteriorating.

After the three-day event mother and daughter were invited to attend with a select few for a five-day Mastermind retreat at Canyon Ranch in Tucson. Before they left, Angelique had started a serious relationship with a young man and throughout the trip Gilda noticed that Angelique's mobile phone and iPad were in constant texting and email use. Her daughter and her new friend were conversing as much as possible within the difficulties of multiple time zones. As a result of those five days at Canyon Ranch, Gilda's life took an unexpected turn. Conversations about various people moving from where they lived in the US to Los Angeles were rife. 'Hey, Gilda, why don't you move here too, then the team would be in one spot,' one of the participants said.

'Oh, you never know, I just might,' Gilda teased.

'Why don't you?' Angelique said seriously but with a smile. Gilda looked at her. 'I guess, there's nothing stopping me, except you and Mirabell, and Mom, of course.' She paused before continuing, 'I think, Angelique, you are pretty well taken care of,' she said smiling at her daughter. 'That just leaves Mirabell. I could try it out for a couple of months and, if I like it, have her flown over. I'd just need to find out about her re-entry into Australia if I want to return.'

'I'll keep an eye on Oma,' Angelique said.

October became a month of organising the November move to Los Angeles. Gilda and one of the women who was also moving to Los Angeles decided to set up an LA residence, rent a house and buy the necessary house appliances. These arrangements ran unbelievably smoothly.

As November approached, it was obvious that both Gilda and Angelique were becoming increasingly brave in their attempt to hide how they felt. Neither actually said anything but, it was 'in the air'.

'I'll be fine,' Gilda would repeatedly say to herself and to Angelique. 'I've got to do this. I feel at such a loss. I'm lacking in interest about my Life Coaching business here; I don't want to continue it. Finding a place to live with Mirabell is proving impossible. I'm in limbo; I've never felt like this before.'

The day before Gilda left, she visited her mother. Hanna had stopped speaking English some time ago and had reverted to her mother tongue, German, which Gilda was told was a common symptom of advanced Dementia. But as Gilda quickly discovered, even in German, her mother's sentences were incoherent. She no longer spoke full sentences. Because of her excessive aggressiveness, most times Hanna was mildly sedated.

The LA departure day arrived. Mother and daughter took photos at the unit with each other and with Mirabell. It was clear that they were being stoic. At the airport the bustle of checking in was a welcome diversion. Soon it came time for Gilda to go down the escalator to the Customs area.

'Take good care of yourself, Schatzi, you know I love you very much,' Gilda said as she embraced her daughter. I'm pleased there is someone you can turn to while I'm away.'

'I'll be fine, Mum. You look after yourself. I love you too.'

It's funny, at times like that all words stay blocked inside and only inane comments come out. What you really want to say just won't come out, possibly because they would cause an avalanche of tears.

Gilda stepped onto the downward escalator and looked back upwards till Angelique's head disappeared. Then, she had to concentrate on travelling overseas on her own for the first time in the past 25 years.

It was finally time to board. She sat in her seat, the doors shut and the plane moved to the runway. It was only then that Gilda could release her long suppressed tears.

Nineteen hours later her friend, Judy, collected Gilda from Los Angeles airport and the excitement of settling in started immediately.

Gilda originally planned to stay three months before making a longer commitment. She and Angelique skyped every day and everyday her daughter held Mirabell to the screen. Gilda's stay was filled with wonderful adventures but, after two months she thought, 'I love it here. I love the friendliness of the people and there is so much to see and do but I think I'm ready to go home. I now know why I came. I would never have seen the other side of some people had I not experienced it personally. It's very sad but, that's their choice. It was wonderful to see others and reconnect with them. However, those that I might have worked with, well no, we're not on the same wavelength.'

At the end of January, 2013, Gilda returned to Brisbane to a joyous welcome from Angelique and Mirabell. House-hunting became a priority. Two days after her return, Gilda visited her mother.

'Hello Mom, how are you?' Hanna was sitting in the lounge and Gilda took a chair to sit in front of her. Hanna grabbed Gilda's hands and tried to speak. She managed a few unintelligible words and then her eyes and Gilda's locked. Gilda saw the fear in her mother's eyes. Those steel blue eyes that could previously cut you down with a glare were terrified and pleading.

'Mom, it's okay. You'll be okay,' Gilda said in German, holding her mother's hands and holding her look. 'There's nothing to fear. You'll be alright. Mom, I know you're holding on because you're afraid to die. You're afraid what God will do to you.' Hanna nodded. 'But, there's nothing to be afraid of. There's nothing to hold against you.' Gilda continued, 'Mom, I forgive you. I forgive everything you did to me. That wasn't the true you. There is nothing for God to forgive. He only sees the true you. He has always only ever seen the beautiful you that he created. I would like that you forgive me too for not being the kind of daughter you would have wanted… please.'

Although Hanna used religion whenever she needed to, a remnant of her Catholic upbringing, she had a genuine fear of going to hell.

Gilda continued, 'Mom, there is no hell; your hell has been here on Earth. Everyone's heaven or hell is in the life they create for themselves on Earth. God is not to be feared. The god/Goddess is love. You have nothing to fear. You've suffered here. It's peaceful once you die. I've told you that; I've experienced it.'

There was a pause. Hanna's hands relaxed their grip. A tear fell down her cheek and she gently raised one hand to stroke Gilda's face. She gave a slight nod and sighed.

'Mom, let go when you want. We've made peace with each other, and with God you've always had peace.'

They sat a little while longer looking into each other's eyes and then a nurse came to say the doctor was here to see Hanna.

Gilda waited until the doctor approached her after consulting with her mother. 'She's as well as can be expected,' he said. 'She's also a fighter so it's hard to say what will happen.'

'I'll be back in a couple of days.'

Two days later Gilda arrived at the Facility.

'Hello, Gilda, your mother is in her room in bed. She's been there the last couple of days and she hasn't moved. We're feeding her with a drip because she won't eat.'

Gilda went to her mother's room. She saw her half-sitting on her bed with her eyes closed. 'She looks like a corpse,' Gilda thought, 'her features are pointy, her cheeks are hollow, and everything is motionless. Her skin is so tight over her face. The only movement is breathing from her open mouth. I doubt she's aware that I'm here, although, I think on some level she does know.' Gilda waited a while to see if Hanna would move but she didn't.

'Mom, let go. I love you and I know you love me. There is no more pain, there is only peace and love and forgiveness,' Gilda whispered before she left.

The next morning, there was a message on Gilda's mobile to contact the Facility. 'Gilda Hollten here, could you please connect me to Ruby block.'

'Oh, yes, Gilda, your mother passed away during the night. She was very peaceful.'

'Thank you. When do you want me to come? Good, I'll be there.'

Gilda hung up. Angelique came into the room. 'Oma passed away last night.' Gilda whispered.

'Are you okay?'

'Yes, I'll be fine, thanks.' Gilda felt numb again as she took a sip of tea. 'It's over; her torment is over.'

'Now she's at peace.'

'Bye Mom, au revoir, auf Wiedersehen.'

Part 4

Gilda's Afterword

Hanna's Legacy

CHAPTER 42
GILDA'S AFTERWORD

Gilda learned many years later that Hanna's behavioural symptoms were those of a condition recognised as Narcissism; in fact, she was only aware of this a few years before her mother's death. Even those who recognised that something was wrong with Hanna, had no idea what was going on, nor would they have known what to do or with whom to consult. It was a 'closet condition', publicly avoided at all costs.

Without realising it, Gilda had always been able to hover within the eye of the many hurricanes that swirled around her as she grew up and later on. Since she could remember, her intention had always been to have peace in her life. Nevertheless, her temperament was such that she would not be walked over. Her motto had been, "I'll stand up for my life". Only later on, through the awareness she gained from reading and studying other ways of looking at life, and from observing how her daughter behaved, did she learn as she often says, "It is better to be kind than to be right."

In Gilda's words...

'Everyone dances to the tune of her or his self, through the way they see the world in which they live, through their filters. I was the same and, I am still the same although my filters have changed. Filters, or the way you see the world and your role in it, are developed through life experiences and as they are remembered when growing up. They aren't necessarily anyone else's reality, but they are your reality. They are so real that they often blind us. If you only apply your humanness to the interpretation of these experiences, you tend to react rather than proact, which means to not think of the consequences before you act, the result being, you aren't often kind. However, if you were to apply your non-humanness, if you come from Source, that is, your Higher Self, you are always kind.

Your divinity, your Higher Self, whatever you choose to call it, doesn't need to fight to prove it is right, it knows it is right, there is a knowing, the ego cannot interfere. That doesn't mean, we can't have opinions, but not act them out at the expense of another, not by belittling, embarrassing, or humiliating another, and making them feel that you don't care, that they feel bad.

Each of us has a magnificent uniqueness that doesn't need to fear being in competition with another person. We are a part of a divine plan and our contribution on Earth is necessary. Once I started to respect who I was, I changed what I ate and what I drank because I realised that in the long run, I wasn't doing myself any good. I had heard Dr. Greg Emerson speak several times on the impact of certain foods and I decided to put his 30-Day Challenge, about what one eats and drinks, into practice. It changed my life and Angelique's life. I've stayed eating along those lines ever since; that's at least 15 years ago.

For many years I drank spirits and other strong alcohol in the evening; I used these as a crutch to numb me. My desire to give up this form of addiction was so strong that I had 'outside forces', non-human forces helping me, and, when it did happen, it happened almost overnight. I've never drunk spirits since. Cutting down on wine was much harder, there was a tradition involved as well as a habit. If I didn't have wine in the house, I didn't miss it but, once I had the first glass, my subconscious recognised the familiar feeling and I wouldn't stop until I had finished the bottle. The result was that the next day I was disgusted and annoyed with myself. However, I've overcome that as well.

The emotional wounds were deep. There are still times when I am fearful that I did something wrong and that I will get into trouble, even as a septuagenarian. My heart palpitates, my head aches and my hands shake when I write. I'll wake up fearful in the early hours of the morning. I then need to talk myself out of this fear, tell myself that it's over, that I'm not in trouble and no one is going to verbally, emotionally or physically hurt me.

I've found that by setting a daily personal intention to be kind to myself and to others, or something similar, my day becomes more pleasant. Having now done this for years now, my life is wonderful and I can say that, I am truly happy, free and filled with joy and gratitude. Each evening, I give gratitude for everything that has happened that day, and every morning, I give gratitude for this new day and what it will bring.

Why do we humans feel we have to know everything, have an answer to everything? When I am vulnerable and I'm not a know-it-all, I feel stronger, I actually feel less vulnerable and, I can also sense that others are not threatened by me. In those situations, not only do I feel more powerful but so does the other person. As Dr. David Hawkins says in his book of the same title, "It's Power without Force."

It's getting rid of the old clichéd paradigm of win/win and evolving it to the consciousness of **Gain/Gain**. We already are all Winners in our non-human form, but it's in our human form that we need to "gain" a clearer perception of the evolution towards living through love, respect and compassion

Ever since I have been open to receiving love from Angelique, I've been able to give it. Because I didn't know what love was not having received it as a child, I also didn't recognise that there was no love in my marriage, not from my side and not from Alexei's. It also took years for me to trust that Angelique really loved me, loved me unconditionally. When she was an adult, she told me that she knew that I didn't believe in her love and it had hurt her. I didn't know that. She says that she now knows that I do trust that her love is unconditional, just as I love her unconditionally.

Unconditional love doesn't mean that you are blind to any aspect of the person; it means that you don't hold anything against them and won't bring it up in a quarrel or when on a power trip. Not one of us has the right to belittle another. Not one of us is human-perfect. We can intend and aim to be our most-perfect-self at any given time, and be that role model. It's a choice.

Children learn by example. If we scream at them, that's what they learn. I learned screaming in my childhood. If we are disrespectful to our partner or anyone else, that's what they learn.

If we are kind and loving, that's what they learn. If we say "I'm sorry", apologise and mean it, that's what they learn. I'll repeat a quantum poem I love…

THE INDIVIDUAL

We are each given our own
Universe to design as we choose.
And we create everything that occurs within it.
Our outer world is nothing more
than a reflection of our inner world,
because the Universe changes
based upon who or what
is observing it.

Anonymous

For years I understood the words but, equally for years, I didn't know how to apply them to daily life. There is a time-lapse for consolidation, to integrate such words as they are a quantum leap from what we learn and experience through our upbringing, our education system and society's norms.

The poem makes it sound so simple, doesn't it? In actual fact, it is simple, it's just not always easy to apply. It's highly dependent upon how much responsibility we want to take for creating our life – the good, the bad and the ugly.

I'll explain how I see it.

When we have issues with another person, it pays to look at when we exhibit those same characteristics. We usually dislike on another some part of our shadow self. The more vehemently we dislike something on someone, the more important it is to see that parallel in ourselves in order to keep a rational rather than an emotive perspective.

As an example:

Hanna didn't trust people because she herself wasn't trustworthy. I don't mean in material dealings, I mean she was emotionally dysfunctional and therefore, on an emotional level, she didn't trust anyone, not even the child she gave birth to. She had to belittle her because that's how she felt she had the upper hand. She saw being hurt by others as validation of her view that people weren't to be trusted. Hanna manipulated her first husband as she saw in him a way out of her perceived lower socio-economic class to a better future. She used her friend, Fritz, knowing he was in love with her. When her first husband left her, she abdicated any responsibility. She always saw herself as blameless and the victim.

How often do we see this in life? We may not always be in control of events but, we are in control of how we react to them and learn from them. Therefore, we are ALL responsible for our life because we control our mind. Everything we do started out as a thought. That thought became an act, either verbal or physical.

Hanna saw vulnerability as a weakness, not as the strength that it is. She thought that force showed strength. Power, not force makes permanent positive changes. I had to learn that too but, my destiny was different from my mother's and that's why I made my life the way I did with the help of learning from reading, courses and seminars and Angelique's influence; from having an open mind.

Could Hanna have done it differently? Yes, she could have. But she chose this path and this was the path she had to take. Was it her behaviour towards me that I needed to accelerate my spiritual development? More than likely it was. We cannot fulfill our evolution in any lifetime alone. We're always dependent on others but we always have choices; nothing is set in stone.

That is THE foundational premise, CHOICE. How we think leads to how we behave, and how we behave is the catalyst to our happiness or misery. How we behave is also the catalyst of our influence on other people's lives, especially those closest to us, positive or negative.

Hanna and I could have had a more harmonious life together. I wouldn't have needed till I was 67 years of age to have found the freedom I yearned for all my life. On the other hand, my life experiences helped Angelique to arrive at her happiness by 35 years.

When all our lives are enriched, we spread a different energy to Mother Earth and all who live on her. Without, not just survival, but growth on Mother Earth, we humans have the place to enact the story of our life.

Hanna's treatment of me, her daughter, and to a lesser degree Angelique, her granddaughter, with disdain, arrogance and cruelty, is a metaphor for how we citizens of beautiful Earth treat the Planet. We treat Gaia as though we own her, as though we can hit her, insult her, manipulate her, physically tortured her and then expect her to fulfill our every need and desire.

That won't happen and can't happen. We need to look at ourselves. Is a depleted, abused Earth the legacy we want to leave our children?

This remarkable Planet gives us constant opportunities to witness how wonderful we, her citizens, are in times of national disasters. In times of earthquakes, landslides, tsunamis, floods, and bush fires, we rally as a global community and send people, food, money and other resources to help those stricken with possible death and territorial annihilation. Why can't we do that in everyday life? Why do we need calamities to show our good side? Why not bring that side of us to the fore in our daily lives?

Fighting and yelling at each other is destructive, it humiliates. There is never a winner in such situations; whoever feels that they have won is pandering to their weak, negative ego. They will also find that, at the first opportunity, the person they humiliated will seek revenge. This is what goes on with politics, vendettas, and the like. Fighting only feeds the ego that doesn't have our best interests at heart.

Bliss or heaven is not some unknown state or some far-off place. Bliss and heaven is what we make of our life here on Earth. It's no coincidence that she is called Mother Earth. Her role is to nurture us and she does, despite the mauraudering we put her through.

Why don't we attack Father Sun? Because he would burn us before we had a chance to destroy him. Daily, he works tirelessly to produce the heat that is necessary for Earth to give us the food we need to eat and the water we need to drink. Without the sun, Earth would die, without Earth, we and our children will die.

Humans are not indispensable; we continually see evidence of a Higher Power helping us to overcome the massive mistakes of some people.

Any hate and disrespect we feel towards people is inherited as most of us have not personally experienced it.

In this story, there is no laying blame on anyone; I've witnessed and experienced the blaming game within my home life and then in my marriage. It's all about everyone taking responsibility. This may sound logical but logic doesn't stand a chance when emotions are involved, strong emotions. Sadly, "common sense" is not "common practice".

With love and blessings.
Gilda Hollten

CHAPTER 43
HANNA'S LEGACY

What are the characteristics of extreme Narcissistic behaviour?

With regard to Hanna's behaviour, no one knew that such a condition existed, and even those who recognised that something was wrong, would have had no idea what was going on, nor would they have known what to do or with whom to consult.

In a nutshell, it seems that a person who exhibits these behaviours has two selves, but it's not schizophrenia, the natural-self which is weak and lacks self-worth and a created-self which has an inflated ego, and has an arrogant, opinionated persona. The created-self generates a godlike image of itself in order to deal with the world as it wants the world to treat her or him, that is, in an elevated manner.

Here are the extreme characteristics of such Narcissistic behaviour that Hanna had:

a. felt superior to others believing that she was above the ordinary folk

b. felt she was more intelligent and she was therefore entitled to greater recognition from peers and others. If she didn't get that, her world collapsed around her and she would go into a rage

c. was so beautiful that she was irresistible, especially to men. She was an outrageous flirt

d. would look for a person's weakness, take advantage of it and keep playing on it

e. lacked empathy; she was always right

f. she was envious of others and created a story to be better than them and then, felt that others were envious of her brilliance and success

g. very defensive and very aggressive when criticised, becoming insulting and threatening

h. very self-righteous and wouldn't accept behaviour from others that she found unbecoming

i. felt alone and was often anxious and frightened

j. she was confused as to when the created-self was active or when she was her natural-self

Possible causes of this type of Narcissism are inconclusive however, genetic factors and childhood home environment are strong candidates. In certain moments, Hanna would start to say that her mother's mental health was in question. Her mother was also a despot, a dictator in her upbringing. Hanna, who was a sensitive person, would have suffered under such upbringing from a single mother who had to see through World War I alone.

Hanna, born in 1920, would have been deprived of basic necessities let alone having any luxuries and, as she liked the finer things of life, she developed coping skills that later moved towards excessive Narcissistic thinking and consequent behaviour. With each deceptive web she spun, she had to spin more to validate previous ones and to keep up appearances. This is also where the trust issue incubated. She didn't trust herself and the more she "proved" to herself that she was untrustworthy, the more she distrusted others.

The above would suggest alarming mental issues if you lived with such a person. The intention is not to blame anyone but equally Hanna should not be damned. The question that comes to mind is how people who interacted with her closely did not pick up that there could be something wrong in her behaviour. To damn her would be grossly unfair. She did the best she could; she had no help from those she lived with and she didn't have the mental capacity to deal with it herself.

It seems odd that Vladimir, who was a doctor, couldn't see that she wasn't all there. But then, that's easy to say from someone standing outside now looking in. Even as an adult, Gilda didn't really see it. When she did see that something had to be wrong, she didn't understand it.

Narcissism was and still largely still is a 'closet illness'. Someone who has it can't cure themselves; they don't even know what's going on; they are confused. If one can believe Hanna, she had often said to husband, Vladimir, that something was not right in her head; she often mentioned "my nerves". That was around 1970 and also to Ivan about 20 years later. If it is true, then no one took her seriously. Hanna couldn't stay 'sane' for long before something triggered her insecurity and the Created-self took over. Ivan saw it but chose to ignore it possibly because he was very ill by that stage.

This mental problem needs to be talked about openly, and recognised for what it is. Unfortunately, people with Narcissistic behaviour aren't easy people to get close to, or to try and help. What would have helped would have been people she saw in the medical profession, or the community care givers to be better trained in this sort of thing.

In retrospect it's very disappointing the lack of real insight and diagnostics people in the medical industry did when she was in their care. It appears that they are trained to see the "expected" (for example, 'this behaviour is normal for someone of this cultural background', or, 'at this age'). When Hanna repeatedly admitted herself into the local private hospital and then had rage outbursts, was that not a clue that something was not in order? Perhaps a mental health professional could have been called in. Would it have been too late?

Admittedly, research in mental health issues has progressed significantly in the last 20 years. It's an area that should not be a shame in the family. What is the Biblical saying? "There but for the grace of God, go I." We are responsible not only for ourselves but for others especially in our family.

Final words…

In the end, LOVE was supreme; true love is indestructible. As Hanna's human façade, her created-self weakened, when she allowed her masks to drop, she enabled her vulnerability to express itself through the fear in her eyes. The innocent child of the Creator emerged. The ultimate expression of the bond between mother and daughter was the trust that Hanna now felt for Gilda, the tear, the hand-clasping, the stroke on the cheek, the acknowledgment that she loved Gilda when Gilda said she loved her mother.

Compassion and forgiveness heal all wounds.

What's the point of it all?

The point is to learn from the complex lives of these two women.

From the Preface…

Let there be no judgment. No one is right. No one is wrong. We choose our path and it is our right to do so.

Perhaps we can learn something that will create for us a better world. These women honour us by sharing their life.

AUTHOR BIO

Gloria Hamilten is a writer and literary reviewer, a dreamer, storyteller, adventurer and lifelong learner. As far back as she can remember, she has been writing, from the time of her first poem at age 8, about her tabby, mangy, scarred cat, and about being kind to animals.

She loves to discover how other people see life, and how they really want to experience their lives, and then share stories about how we each envisage and get to where we want to go.

During high school, because she was born in Vienna, Austria, she was more focused on learning English rather than on creative writing and so her main creative outlet was drawing, again animals.

However, she always kept a diary which was multilingual. As she says, 'My writing was either in French, my main language at the time, German, which I had heard all my life and now spoke at home since we left France, or English, which I was still learning. Whichever language first popped into my head, I wrote that down. Gradually, English took over and became my dominant language.'

Once she left school, she sporadically continued the diaries but wrote more contemplative pieces about coping with life within a challenging family, being a migrant and the philosophising of a teenager finding her place in a diverse world. She lived in the moment as she could not envisage a future within the confines set by a Narcissistic mother and the emotional and physical abuse that resulted from her mother's condition.

When she started secondary school teaching, she thrust her writing creativity in ensuring that what she produced for her students was fun and engaging so that they first of all wanted to read it and then, learn from the material.

Her motivation was the same when she developed personal development and business development courses for adults, when she started her first offline business and then, went online in 2007.

Apart from secondary teaching, her careers include creating and facilitating courses for the University of Queensland's Corporate division, teaching German and NLP (Neuro-Linguistic Programming) adult evening classes for Queensland's Technical and Further Education (TAFE), Director of a College of Hospitality and Tourism in Sydney, National Executive Director of Ice Skating Australia, when she liaised with the Australian Olympic Committee and the Australian Sports Commission, and CEO of her own life coaching business.

She always circumvented the status quo. At school, she was able to do this because her students enjoyed her classes and therefore, did their homework and obtained good results which pleased the parents. As an adult, it was easier to write what she wanted to better the life of her clients and readers.

Humour, enjoyment, openness and learning have always been her modus operandi in her writing. Even her fiction works, such as short stories, have messages that gift wisdom to better the life of the reader.

To date, apart from thousands of articles and many short stories, she has written and published 5 books which are listed at the front of this, her first full-length fiction, novel.

She has a BA, B.Ed. St. and a M. Ed (Management), accreditation in Neuro-Linguistic Programming, and has studied and practiced Scientific Hand Analysis, Thought Field Therapy and many Esoteric philosophies.

www.GloriaHamilten.com
MaverickDaughter@gmail.com

www.ingramcontent.com/pod-product-compliance
Lightning Source LLC
Chambersburg PA
CBHW070547100426
42744CB00006B/240